Swing:
A Beginner's Guide

Swing:
A Beginner's Guide

Herbert Schildt

New York   Chicago   San Francisco
Lisbon   London   Madrid   Mexico City
Milan   New Delhi   San Juan
Seoul   Singapore   Sydney   Toronto

Swing: A Beginner's Guide

1234567890 CUS CUS 019876

IISBN-13: 978-0-07-226314-5

ISBN-10:   0-07-226314-8

Sponsoring Editor   Wendy Rinaldi
Editorial Supervisor   Janet Walden
Project Editor   LeeAnn Pickrell
Acquisitions Coordinator   Alex McDonald
Technical Editor   Hale Pringle
Copy Editor   LeeAnn Pickrell
Proofreader   Paul Tyler
Indexer   Sherry Schildt
Production Supervisor   Jean Bodeaux
Composition   Lucie Ericksen
Illustration   Lyssa Wald
Art Director, Cover   Jeff Weeks
Cover Designer   Jeff Weeks

About the Author

Herbert Schildt is a leading authority on the C, C++, Java, and C# languages, and is a master Windows programmer. His programming books have sold more than 3.5 million copies worldwide and have been translated into all major foreign languages. He is the author of numerous bestsellers, including *Java: A Beginner's Guide, Java: The Complete Reference, C++: A Beginner's Guide, C++: The Complete Reference, C: The Complete Reference*, and *C#: The Complete Reference*, and the co-author of *The Art of Java*. Schildt holds both graduate and undergraduate degrees from the University of Illinois. He can be reached at his consulting office at (217) 586-4683. His web site is **www.HerbSchildt.com**.

Special Thanks

Special thanks to Hale Pringle for his excellent technical edit, insight, and suggestions. Hale is a bona fide Swing expert and his input was of great value.

Thanks also to James Holmes for looking over several of the chapters and giving me the benefit of his expertise. James is an extraordinary programmer, the author of *Struts: The Complete Reference,* and my co-author on *The Art of Java*.

Finally, many thanks to Wendy Rinaldi, my long-time editor at McGraw-Hill. Wendy's advice, guidance, and steadfast support over the years are truly appreciated.

Contents at a Glance

Contents

Preface

Like many things in life, first impressions matter, and programming is no exception. The way that a program looks on the screen and the feel of its controls are the basis on which the user initially judges your work. Because first impressions often become lasting impressions, it is important that a program's user interface be both visually pleasing and easy to use. Fortunately, both goals can be achieved by using Swing.

Swing is the toolkit that defines the look and feel of the modern Java graphical user interface (GUI). Offering a comprehensive set of carefully crafted components, such as buttons, tables, trees, text fields, and scroll panes, Swing gives you the ability to create appealing interfaces that can be tailored specifically for your application and its environment. With its support for pluggable look and feels, its use of a modified Model-View-Controller architecture, and its ease of customization, Swing streamlines the design and implementation of world-class user interfaces. In today's highly competitive computing environment, Swing is something that no programmer can afford to ignore.

The purpose of this book is to teach the basics of Swing and to get you programming with Swing as soon as possible. It uses a "hands-on" approach that will have you writing real Swing programs by the end of Module 1. The book begins by describing Swing's architecture and design philosophy. It then focuses on the core aspects of Swing, including its component set and the basic techniques needed to use it. By the end, you will be able to begin creating your own professional-looking Swing-based applications.

It is important to state at the outset that this book is just a starting point. Swing is a large, sophisticated framework. It is supported by a wide array of classes, interfaces, and specialized techniques. Although this makes Swing very powerful, it can also make Swing seem overwhelming when you are just starting out. It is not the purpose of this beginner's guide to describe every aspect and nuance of Swing. There are other books that do this. Instead, this book is designed to open the door to the world of Swing programming by carefully explaining Swing's core features and basic techniques. These are the parts of Swing that you will use in your normal, day-to-day programming. After completing this book, you will have the skills needed to take on Swing's more advanced features.

One last point: Swing is not the easiest GUI toolkit to learn. It is, however, the most important. For today's Java programmer, Swing is worth the time and effort necessary to master it.

How This Book Is Organized

This book presents an evenly paced tutorial in which each section builds upon the previous one. It contains ten modules, each discussing an aspect of Swing. This book is unique because it includes several special elements that reinforce what you are learning.

Critical Skills

Each module begins with a set of critical skills that you will be learning. The location of each skill within the module is indicated.

Mastery Check

Each module concludes with a Mastery Check, a self-test that lets you test your knowledge. The answers are in the Appendix.

Progress Checks

At the end of each major section, Progress Checks are presented that test your understanding of the key points of the preceding section. The answers to these questions are at the bottom of the page.

Ask the Expert

Sprinkled throughout the book are special "Ask the Expert" boxes. These contain additional information or interesting commentary about a topic, using a Question/Answer format.

Projects

Each Module contains one or more projects that show you how to apply what you are learning. These are real-world examples that you can use as starting points for your own Swing programs.

Java Programming Experience Required

This book assumes that you have a working knowledge of Java. You need not be a Java expert, but you should be comfortable with the fundamentals of the language. If you need to improve your Java skills, I recommend the most recent editions of my books *Java: A Beginner's Guide* and *Java: The Complete Reference*. Both are published by McGraw-Hill.

Required Software

To compile and run the programs in this book, you will need a Java Developers Kit (JDK) from Sun. At the time of this writing, the currently released version is JDK 5 (J2SE 5), and this is the JDK against which the code in this book was tested. However, most of the code in this book will work with version 1.4, and even versions 1.3 and 1.2. Of course, it's best to have the latest JDK.

Don't Forget: Code on the Web

Remember, the source code for all of the examples and projects in this book is available free of charge on the Web at **www.osborne.com**.

For Further Study

Swing: A Beginner's Guide is just one of Herb Schildt's many programming books. Here are some others that you will find of interest.

To learn more about Java, we recommend

- *Java: The Complete Reference*
- *Java: A Beginner's Guide*
- *The Art of Java*

To learn about C++, you will find these books especially helpful:

- *C++: The Complete Reference*
- *Teach Yourself C++*
- *C++ From the Ground Up*
- *STL Programming From the Ground Up*
- *The Art of C++*

To learn about C#, we suggest the following Schildt books:

- *C#: A Beginner's Guide*
- *C#: The Complete Reference*

If you want to learn about the C language, then the following titles will be of interest:

- *C: The Complete Reference*
- *Teach Yourself C*

**When you need solid answers, fast, turn to Herbert Schildt,
the recognized authority on programming.**

Module 1

Swing Fundamentals

From a conceptual point of view, it is possible to divide most applications into two parts. First is the code that performs the actions supported by the program, such as downloading a file, querying a database, taking an order, or computing a financial result. Second is the user interface, which controls how the user interacts with the program. Although what a program does is, of course, fundamentally important, it is the user's interaction with the program (in other words, the program's "look and feel") that often determines the success or failure of an application in the marketplace. Therefore, the creation of appealing, consistent, and efficient user interfaces has become an important part of programming for the enterprise environment. For Java programmers, the way to create such interfaces is through the use of *Swing*.

Swing is a collection of classes and interfaces that define the modern Java graphical user interface (GUI) demanded by today's high-powered Web applications. Swing offers a rich set of visual components, such as buttons, text fields, scroll bars, check boxes, trees, and tables, that can be tailored to fit any application. By using Swing, you can give your applications the kind of up-to-date interface that users have come to expect. Moreover, to be a professional Java programmer implies mastery of Swing. It is an integral part of most Java-based applications.

The purpose of this module is to introduce Swing, including its history, basic concepts, design philosophy, and core features. As you will see, Swing is comprised of many interrelated elements that work together. This interrelatedness makes Swing a powerful, yet streamlined framework. It also makes it difficult for newcomers because the description of one aspect of Swing often implies knowledge of another. Thus, it is helpful to know something about many of Swing's features before any specific one is examined in depth. Toward this end, this module presents a general overview of Swing, including several of its key concepts. It also introduces a few common components and shows how to use them in some simple Swing programs. Subsequent modules will build on the foundation given here. Thus, a careful reading is advised. Also, many of the topics introduced here are examined in greater detail later in this book.

1.1 The Origins of Swing

Swing did not exist in the early days of Java. Rather, it was a response to deficiencies present in Java's original GUI subsystem: the Abstract Window Toolkit (AWT). The AWT defines a basic set of controls, windows, and dialog boxes that support a usable, but limited graphical interface. One reason for the limited nature of the AWT is that it translates its various visual components into their corresponding, platform-specific equivalents, or *peers*. This means that the look and feel of a component is defined by the platform, not by Java. Because the AWT components use native code resources, they are referred to as *heavyweight*.

The use of native peers led to several problems. First, because of variations between operating systems, a component might look, or even act, differently on different platforms. This potential variability threatened the overarching philosophy of Java: write once, run

Ask the Expert

Q: You say that Swing is part of the Java Foundation Classes. What are these?

A: The JFC is a set of classes that provide core support for GUI-based enterprise applications. Other parts of JFC include the AWT (Abstract Window Toolkit), Java 2D, Drag and Drop, and the Accessibility API.

anywhere. Second, the look and feel of each component was fixed (because it is defined by the platform) and could not be (easily) changed. Third, the use of heavyweight components caused some frustrating restrictions. For example, a heavyweight component is always rectangular and opaque.

Not long after Java's original release, it became apparent that the limitations and restrictions present in the AWT were sufficiently serious that a better approach was needed. The solution was Swing. Introduced in 1997, Swing was included as part of the Java Foundation Classes (JFC). Swing was initially available for use with Java 1.1 as a separate library. However, beginning with Java 1.2, Swing (and the rest of JFC) was fully integrated into the Java. Today, Swing is an integral and inseparable part of Java programming.

CRITICAL SKILL
1.2 Two Key Swing Features

As just explained, Swing was created to address the limitations present in the AWT. It does this through two key features: lightweight components and a pluggable look and feel. Together they provide an elegant, yet easy-to-use solution to the problems of the AWT. More than anything else, it is these two features that define the essence of Swing. Each is examined here.

Swing Components Are Lightweight

With very few exceptions, Swing components are *lightweight*. This means that they are written entirely in Java and do not rely on platform-specific peers. Because lightweight components are rendered using graphics primitives, they can be transparent, which enables nonrectangular shapes. Thus, lightweight components are more efficient and more flexible. Furthermore, because lightweight components do not translate into native peers, the look and feel of each component is determined by Swing, not by the underlying operating system. This means that each component will work in a consistent manner across all platforms.

Swing Supports a Pluggable Look and Feel

Swing supports a *Pluggable Look and Feel* (PLAF). Because each Swing component is rendered by Java code rather than by native peers, the look and feel of a component is under the control of Swing. This fact means that it is possible to separate the look and feel of a component from the logic of the component, and this is what Swing does. Separating out the look and feel provides a significant advantage: it becomes possible to change the way that a component is rendered without affecting any of its other aspects. In other words, it is possible to "plug in" a new look and feel for any given component without creating any side effects in the code that uses that component. Moreover, it becomes possible to define entire sets of look-and-feels that represent different GUI styles. To use a specific style, its look and feel is simply "plugged in." Once this is done, all components are automatically rendered using that style.

Pluggable look-and-feels offer several important advantages. It is possible to define a look and feel that is consistent across all platforms. Conversely, it is possible to create a look and feel that acts like a specific platform. For example, if you know that an application will be running only in a Windows environment, it is possible to specify the Windows look and feel. It is also possible to design a custom look and feel. Finally, the look and feel can be changed dynamically at runtime.

There are three look-and-feels that are available to all Swing users: metal, Windows, and Motif. The metal look and feel is also called the *Java look and feel*. It is a platform-independent look and feel that is available in all Java execution environments. It is also the default look and feel. A Mac look and feel is available for Mac users and a GTK+ look is available for Mac and Solaris. This book uses the default Java look and feel because it is platform independent. However, after completing this book, you might want to experiment with the other look-and-feels on your own.

Swing Is Built on the AWT

Before moving on, it is necessary to make one important point: although Swing eliminates a number of the limitations inherent in the AWT, Swing does not replace it. Instead, Swing is built upon the foundation of the AWT. It also uses the same event handling mechanism as the AWT. Although knowledge of the AWT is not required by this book, a general understanding of its structure and features is useful—especially for more advanced applications of Swing.

NOTE

For in-depth coverage of the AWT, see my book *Java: The Complete Reference, J2SE 5 Edition*, McGraw-Hill/Osborne (2005).

CRITICAL SKILL
1.3 The MVC Connection

In general, a visual component is a composite of three distinct aspects:

● The way that the component looks when rendered on the screen

● The way that the component reacts to the user

● The state information associated with the component

No matter what architecture is used to implement a component, it must implicitly contain these three parts. Over the years, one component architecture has proven itself to be exceptionally effective: *Model-View-Controller*, or MVC for short.

The MVC architecture is successful because each piece of the design corresponds to an aspect of a component. In MVC terminology, the *model* corresponds to the state information associated with the component. For example, in the case of a check box, the model contains a field that indicates if the box is checked or unchecked. The *view* determines how the component is displayed on the screen, including any aspects of the view that are affected by the current state of the model. The *controller* determines how the component reacts to the user. For example, when the user clicks on a check box, the controller reacts by changing the model to reflect the user's choice (checked or unchecked). This then results in the view being updated. By separating a component into a model, a view, and a controller, the specific implementation of each can be changed without affecting the other two. For instance, different view implementations can render the same component in different ways without affecting the model or the controller.

Although the MVC architecture and the principles behind it are conceptually sound, the high level of separation between the view and the controller was not beneficial for Swing components. Instead, Swing uses a modified version of MVC that combines the view and the controller into a single logical entity called the *UI delegate*. For this reason, Swing's approach is called either the *Model-Delegate* architecture or the *Separable Model* architecture. Therefore, although Swing's component architecture is based on MVC, it does not use a classical implementation of it.

Swing's pluggable look and feel is made possible by its Model-Delegate architecture. Because the view (look) and controller (feel) are separate from the model, the look and feel can be changed without affecting how the component is used within a program. Conversely, it is possible to customize the model without affecting the way that the component appears on the screen or responds to user input.

To support the Model-Delegate architecture, most Swing components contain two objects. The first represents the model. The second represents the UI delegate. Models are defined by interfaces. For example, the model for a button is defined by the **ButtonModel** interface. UI delegates are classes that inherit **ComponentUI**. For example, the UI delegate for a button is **ButtonUI**. Normally, your programs will not directly interact with the UI delegate.

Progress Check

1. What are the two key features of Swing?

2. Does Swing replace the AWT?

3. What does MVC stand for? What is Swing's adaptation of MVC called?

CRITICAL SKILL
1.4 # Components and Containers

A Swing GUI consists of two key items: *components* and *containers*. However, this distinction is mostly conceptual because all containers are also components. The difference between the two is found in their intended purpose: As the term is commonly used, a *component* is an independent visual control, such as a push button or slider. A container holds a group of components. Thus, a container is a special type of component that is designed to hold other components. Furthermore, in order for a component to be displayed, it must be held within a container. Thus, all Swing GUIs will have at least one container. Because containers are components, a container can also hold other containers. This enables Swing to define what is called a *containment hierarchy*, at the top of which must be a *top-level container*.

Let's look a bit more closely at components and containers.

Components

In general, Swing components are derived from the **JComponent** class. (The only exceptions to this are the four top-level containers, described in the next section.) **JComponent** provides the functionality that is common to all components. For example, **JComponent** supports the pluggable look and feel. **JComponent** inherits the AWT classes **Container** and **Component**. Thus, a Swing component is built on and compatible with an AWT component.

All of Swing's components are represented by classes defined within the package **javax.swing**. The following table shows the class names for Swing components (including those used as containers).

---

1. The two key features of Swing are lightweight components and a pluggable look and feel.
2. No, Swing is built on top of the AWT.
3. MVC stands for Model-View-Controller. Swing uses a modified approach called Model-Delegate or Separable Model.

JApplet	JButton	JCheckBox	JCheckBoxMenuItem
JColorChooser	JComboBox	JComponent	JDesktopPane
JDialog	JEditorPane	JFileChooser	JFormattedTextField
JFrame	JInternalFrame	JLabel	JLayeredPane
JList	JMenu	JMenuBar	JMenuItem
JOptionPane	JPanel	JPasswordField	JPopupMenu
JProgressBar	JRadioButton	JRadioButtonMenuItem	JRootPane
JScrollBar	JScrollPane	JSeparator	JSlider
JSpinner	JSplitPane	JTabbedPane	JTable
JTextArea	JTextField	JTextPane	JTogglebutton
JToolBar	JToolTip	JTree	JViewport
JWindow			

Notice that all component classes begin with the letter **J**. For example, the class for a label is **JLabel**; the class for a push button is **JButton**; and the class for a scroll bar is **JScrollBar**. The use of these components forms the subject matter for most of this book.

Containers

Swing defines two types of containers. The first are top-level containers: **JFrame**, **JApplet**, **JWindow**, and **JDialog**. These containers do not inherit **JComponent**. They do, however, inherit the AWT classes **Component** and **Container**. Unlike Swing's other components, which are lightweight, the top-level containers are heavyweight. This makes the top-level containers a special case in the Swing component library.

As the name implies, a top-level container must be at the top of a containment hierarchy. A top-level container cannot be contained within any other container. Furthermore, every containment hierarchy must begin with a top-level container. The one most commonly used for applications is **JFrame**. The one used for applets is **JApplet**.

The second type of containers supported by Swing are lightweight containers. Lightweight containers *do* inherit **JComponent**. Examples of lightweight containers are **JPanel** and **JRootPane**. Lightweight containers are often used to organize and manage groups of related components collectively because a lightweight container can be contained within another container. Thus, you can use lightweight containers to create subgroups of related controls that are contained within an outer container.

The Top-Level Container Panes

Each top-level container defines a set of *panes*. At the top of the hierarchy is an instance of **JRootPane**. **JRootPane** is a lightweight container whose purpose is to manage the other panes, plus an optional menu bar. The panes that comprise the root pane are called the *glass pane*, the *content pane*, and the *layered pane*.

The glass pane is the top-level pane. It sits above and completely covers all other panes. By default, it is a transparent instance of **JPanel**. The glass pane enables you to manage mouse events that affect the entire container (rather than an individual control) or to paint over any other component, for example. In most cases, you won't need to use the glass pane directly, but it is there if you need it.

The layered pane is an instance of **JLayeredPane**. The layered pane allows components to be given a depth value. This value determines which component overlays another. (Thus, the layered pane lets you specify a Z-order for a component, although this is not something that you will usually need to do.) The layered pane holds the content pane and the (optional) menu bar.

Although the glass pane and the layered panes are integral to the operation of a top-level container and serve important purposes, much of what they provide occurs behind the scene. The pane with which your application will interact the most is the content pane, because this is the pane to which you will add visual components. In other words, when you add a component, such as a button, to a top-level container, you will add it to the content pane. By default, the content pane is an opaque instance of **JPanel**.

NOTE

The three panes, glass, content, and layered, are sometimes referred to by their variable names within **JRootPane**. These names are **glassPane**, **contentPane**, and **layeredPane**.

Progress Check

1. All Swing components must be stored in a _____.

2. With only a few exceptions, Swing components are derived from **JComponent**. True or false?

3. In addition to the root pane, what other panes do all top-level containers have?

4. The top-level containers are a special case because they are heavyweight rather than lightweight components. True or false?

---

1. Container
2. True
3. The glass pane, the content pane, and the layered pane
4. True

CRITICAL SKILL
1.5 # A First Simple Swing Program

Before we look at any more theory, it will be helpful to examine a simple Swing program. Although quite short, the program demonstrates several key features of Swing and introduces the **JFrame** container and the **JLabel** component. As explained, **JFrame** is the top-level container that is commonly used for Swing applications. **JLabel** is the Swing component that creates a label, which is a component that displays information. The label is Swing's simplest component because it is passive. That is, a label does not respond to user input. It just displays output. The program creates a **JFrame** container and puts into that container an instance of a **JLabel** component, which displays a text message.

```java
// A simple Swing program.

import javax.swing.*;          ◀─────── javax.swing contains the
                                        main Swing classes.
class SwingDemo {

  SwingDemo() {
                                                    Create a top-level container.
    // Create a new JFrame container.
    JFrame jfrm = new JFrame("A Simple Swing Program"); ◀─┘

    // Give the frame an initial size.
    jfrm.setSize(275, 100);    ◀─────────────── Set the container's size.

    // Terminate the program when the user closes the application.
    jfrm.setDefaultCloseOperation(JFrame.EXIT_ON_CLOSE); ◀──┐
                                           Stop the program when the
                                           user clicks the close box.
    // Create a text-based label.
    JLabel jlab = new JLabel(" Swing powers the modern Java GUI."); ◀─┐
                                                        Create a JLabel.
    // Add the label to the content pane.
    jfrm.getContentPane().add(jlab); ◀─────── Add the label to the content
                                              pane of the JFrame container.
    // Display the frame.
    jfrm.setVisible(true);    ◀─────── Show the container and its contents.
  }

  public static void main(String args[]) {

    // Create the frame on the event dispatching thread.
    SwingUtilities.invokeLater(new Runnable() { ◀──────── Create the GUI on the
      public void run() {                                 event-dispatching thread.
        new SwingDemo();
```

```
        }
    });

  }
}
```

Swing programs are compiled and run in the same way as other Java applications. Thus, to compile this program, you can use this command line:

```
javac SwingDemo.java
```

To run the program, use this command line:

```
java SwingDemo
```

When the program is run, it will produce the window shown in Figure 1-1.

The First Swing Example Line by Line

Because the **SwingDemo** program illustrates several key Swing concepts, we will examine it carefully, line by line. The program begins by importing the following package:

```
import javax.swing.*;
```

This **javax.swing** package contains the components and models defined by Swing. For example, it defines classes that implement labels, buttons, edit controls, and menus. This package will be included in all programs that use Swing.

Next, the program declares the **SwingDemo** class and a constructor for that class. The constructor is where most of the action of the program occurs. It begins by creating a **JFrame**, using this line of code:

```
JFrame jfrm = new JFrame("A Simple Swing Program.");
```

This creates a container called **jfrm** that defines a rectangular window complete with a title bar; close, minimize, maximize, and restore buttons; and a system menu. Thus, it creates a standard, top-level window. The title of the window is passed to the constructor.

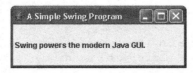

Figure 1-1 The window produced by the first sample Swing program

Next, the window is sized using this statement:

```
jfrm.setSize(275, 100);
```

The **setSize( )** method (which is inherited by **JFrame** from the AWT class **Component**) sets the dimensions of the window, which are specified in pixels. Its general form is shown here:

void setSize(int *width*, int *height*)

In this example, the width of the window is set to 275 and the height is set to 100.

By default, when a top-level window is closed (such as when the user clicks the close box), the window is removed from the screen, but the application is not terminated. While this default behavior is useful in some situations, it is not what is needed for most applications. Instead, you will usually want the entire application to terminate when its top-level window is closed. There are a couple of ways to achieve this. The easiest way is to call **setDefaultCloseOperation( )**, as the program does:

```
jfrm.setDefaultCloseOperation(JFrame.EXIT_ON_CLOSE);
```

After this call executes, closing the window causes the entire application to terminate. The general form of **setDefaultCloseOperation( )** is shown here.

void setDefaultCloseOperation(int *what*)

The value passed in *what* determines what happens when the window is closed. There are several other options in addition to **JFrame.EXIT_ON_CLOSE**. They are shown here:

JFrame.DISPOSE_ON_CLOSE

JFrame.HIDE_ON_CLOSE

JFrame.DO_NOTHING_ON_CLOSE

Their names reflect their actions. These constants are declared in **WindowConstants**, which is an interface declared in **javax.swing** that is implemented by **JFrame**.

The next line of code creates a Swing **JLabel** component:

```
JLabel jlab = new JLabel(" Swing powers the modern Java GUI.");
```

JLabel is the simplest and easiest-to-use Swing component because it does not accept user input. It simply displays information, which can consist of text, an icon, or a combination of the two. The label created by the program contains only text, which is passed to its constructor.

The next line of code adds the label to the content pane of the frame:

```
jfrm.getContentPane().add(jlab);
```

As explained earlier, all top-level containers have a content pane in which components are stored. Thus, to add a component to a frame, you must add it to the frame's content pane. A reference to the content pane is obtained by calling **getContentPane( )**. Using this reference, you add a component by calling **add( )**. The general forms of **getContentPane( )** and **add( )** are shown here.

Container getContentPane( )

Component add(Component *comp*)

The **add( )** method is inherited by **JFrame** from the AWT class **Container**.

    With the release of JDK 5 (Java version 1.5), it is no longer necessary to call **getContentPane( )** when adding a component to a **JFrame**. Instead, you can simply call **add( )** directly on the **JFrame** object, itself. The component will automatically be added to the content pane. Thus, in the **SwingDemo** program, the line

```
jfrm.getContentPane().add(jlab);
```

can be written more compactly like this when compiling with JDK 5 (or later):

```
jfrm.add(jlab);
```

Because earlier versions of Java are still in widespread use, this book will obtain a reference to the content pane explicitly, so that the code will work for all readers. Also, calling **getContentPane( )** makes it very clear which pane is being affected. However, if you will be working in a JDK 5 or later environment, then you can use the more streamlined approach.

    The last statement in the **SwingDemo** constructor causes the window to become visible.

```
jfrm.setVisible(true);
```

The **setVisible( )** method is inherited from the AWT **Component** class. It has this general form:

void setVisible(boolean *flag*)

If *flag* is **true**, the window will be displayed. Otherwise, it will be hidden. By default, a **JFrame** is invisible, so **setVisible(true)** must be called to show it.

Inside **main( )**, a **SwingDemo** object is created, which causes the window and the label to be displayed. Notice that the **SwingDemo** constructor is invoked using these lines of code:

```
SwingUtilities.invokeLater(new Runnable() {
  public void run() {
    new SwingDemo();
  }
});
```

This sequence causes a **SwingDemo** object to be created on the *event-dispatching thread* rather than on the main thread of the application. Here's why. In general, Swing programs are event-driven. For example, when a user interacts with a component, an event is generated. An event is passed to the application by calling an event handler defined by the application. However, the handler is executed on the event-dispatching thread provided by Swing and not on the main thread of the application. Thus, although event handlers are defined by your program, they are called on a thread that was not created by your program. To avoid problems (such as two different threads trying to update the same component at the same time), all Swing GUI components must be created and updated from the event-dispatching thread, not the main thread of the application. However, **main( )** is executed on the main thread. Thus, **main( )** cannot directly instantiate a **SwingDemo** object. Instead, it must create a **Runnable** object that executes on the event-dispatching thread and have this object create the GUI.

To enable the GUI code to be created on the event-dispatching thread, you must use one of two methods that are defined by the **SwingUtilities** class. These methods are **invokeLater( )** and **invokeAndWait( )**. They are shown here:

static void invokeLater(Runnable *obj*)

static void invokeAndWait(Runnable *obj*)
    throws InterruptedException, InvocationTargetException

Here, *obj* is a **Runnable** object that will have its **run( )** method called by the event-dispatching thread. The difference between the two methods is that **invokeLater( )** returns immediately, but **invokeAndWait( )** waits until **obj.run( )** returns. You can use these methods to call a method that constructs the GUI for your Swing application, or whenever you need to modify the state of the GUI from code not executed by the event-dispatching thread. You will normally want to use **invokeLater( )**, as the preceding program does. However, when constructing the initial GUI for an applet, you will want to use **invokeAndWait( )**. (Creating Swing applets is described in Module 10.)

One more point: The preceding program does not respond to any events because **JLabel** is a passive component. In other words, a **JLabel** does not generate any events. Therefore, the preceding program does not include any event handlers. However, all other components generate events to which your program must respond. You will see examples of this shortly.

Progress Check

1. What Swing class creates a label?

2. What package must be included in all Swing programs?

3. All code that creates or modifies the GUI must be executed on the _____ thread.

4. When using JDK 5 or later, are you required to call **getContentPane( )** when adding a component to a **JFrame**?

Ask the Expert

Q: I have seen Swing code that does not use the invokeLater( ) or the invokeAndWait( ) methods. Are they really needed?

A: In the early days of Swing, it was considered safe to initially display the GUI from within the main application thread. Thus, in the past, Swing applications did not usually call **invokeLater( )** or **invokeAndWait( )** to display the GUI at program start-up. However, Sun changed this assessment. Today, Sun states that it is no longer proper to initialize the GUI from within the main thread because it might lead to problems in a small number of cases. Frankly, there are many Swing applications in widespread use that initialize the GUI from within the main thread and operate without problems. (For example, because of its extreme simplicity, the GUI for the first example program could probably be created on the main thread without causing any harm.) However, for new code, the GUI should be created on the event-dispatching thread. Because creating the GUI on the event-dispatching thread is now considered to be best practice, it is the approach followed by all the examples in this book.

1. **JLabel**
2. **javax.swing**
3. Event-dispatching
4. No

CRITICAL SKILL
1.6 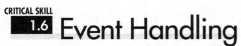 Event Handling

The preceding example showed the basic form of a Swing program, but it left out one important part: event handling. Because **JLabel** does not take input from the user, it does not generate events, so no event handling was needed. However, the other Swing controls *do* respond to user input and the events generated by those interactions need to be handled. For example, an event is generated when the user clicks a button, types a key on the keyboard, or selects an item from a list. Events are also generated in ways not directly related to user input. For example, an event is generated when a timer goes off. Whatever the case, event handling is a large part of any Swing-based application.

The event handling mechanism used by Swing is the same as that used by the AWT. This approach is called the *delegation event model*. Its concept is quite simple. A *source* generates an event and sends it to one or more *listeners*. In this scheme, the listener simply waits until it receives an event. Once an event arrives, the listener processes the event and then returns. The advantage of this design is that the application logic that processes events is cleanly separated from the user interface logic that generates the events. A user interface element is able to "delegate" the processing of an event to a separate piece of code. In the delegation event model, a listener must register with a source in order to receive an event notification.

Let's look at events, sources, and listeners a bit closer.

Events

In the delegation model, an event is an object that describes a state change in a source. It can be generated as a consequence of a person interacting with an element in a graphical user interface or generated under program control. The superclass for all events is **java.util.EventObject**. Many events are declared in **java.awt.event**. Others are found in **javax.swing.event**.

Event Sources

An event source is an object that generates an event. When a source generates an event, it must send that event to all registered listeners. Therefore, in order for a listener to receive an event, it must register with the source of that event. Listeners register with a source by calling an **add***Type***Listener( )** method on the event source object. Each type of event has its own registration method. Here is the general form:

public void add*Type*Listener(*Type*Listener *el*)

Here, *Type* is the name of the event and *el* is a reference to the event listener. For example, the method that registers a keyboard event listener is called **addKeyListener( )**. The method that registers a mouse motion listener is called **addMouseMotionListener( )**. When an event occurs, all registered listeners are notified.

A source must also provide a method that allows a listener to unregister an interest in a specific type of event. The general form of such a method is this:

public void remove*Type*Listener(*Type*Listener *el*)

Here, *Type* is the name of the event and *el* is a reference to the event listener. For example, to remove a keyboard listener, you would call **removeKeyListener( )**.

The methods that add or remove listeners are provided by the source that generates events. For example, the **JButton** class provides a method to add and remove an *action listener,* which is notified when the button is pressed.

Event Listeners

A listener is an object that is notified when an event occurs. It has two major requirements. First, it must have registered with one or more sources to receive notifications about a specific type of event. Second, it must implement a method to receive and process that event.

The methods that receive and process events are defined in a set of interfaces found in **java.awt.event**, **javax.swing.event**, or **java.beans**. For example, the **ActionListener** interface defines a method that receives a notification when an action, such as clicking a button, takes place. Any object may receive and process this event if it provides an implementation of the **ActionListener** interface.

There is an important general principle that must be stated now. An event handler should do its job quickly and then return. In most cases, it should not engage in a long operation because doing so will slow down the entire application. If a time-consuming operation is required, then a separate thread will usually be created for this purpose.

Event Classes and Listener Interfaces

The classes that represent events are at the core of Java's event handling mechanism. At the root of the Java event class hierarchy is **EventObject**, which is in **java.util**. It is the superclass for all events. The class **AWTEvent**, declared in the **java.awt** package, is a subclass of **EventObject**. It is the superclass (either directly or indirectly) of all AWT-based events used by the delegation event model. Swing uses the AWT events. It also adds several of its own. As mentioned, these are in **javax.swing.event**.

Table 1-1 shows a sampling of the event classes and listener interfaces defined in **java.awt.event**. Table 1-2 shows a sampling of the event classes and listener interfaces

Event Class	Description	Corresponding Event Listener
ActionEvent	Generated when an action occurs within a control, such as when a button is pressed.	ActionListener
AdjustmentEvent	Generated when a scroll bar is manipulated.	AdjustmentListener
FocusEvent	Generated when a component gains or loses focus.	FocusListener
ItemEvent	Generated when an item is selected, such as when a check box is clicked.	ItemListener
KeyEvent	Generated when input is received from the keyboard.	KeyListener
MouseEvent	Generated when the mouse is dragged or moved, clicked, pressed, or released; also generated when the mouse enters or exits a component.	MouseListener and MouseMotionListener
MouseWheelEvent	Generated when the mouse wheel is moved.	MouseWheelListener
WindowEvent	Generated when a window is activated, closed, deactivated, deiconified, iconified, opened, or quit.	WindowListener

Table 1-1 A Sampling of Event Classes in **java.awt.event**

Event Class	Description	Corresponding Event Listener
AncestorEvent	Generated when an ancestor of a component has been added, moved, or removed.	AncestorListener
CaretEvent	Generated when the position of the caret in a text component changes.	CaretListener
ChangeEvent	Generated when a component changes its state.	ChangeListener
HyperlinkEvent	Generated when a hyperlink is accessed.	HyperlinkListener
ListDataEvent	Generated when the contents of a list changes.	ListDataListener
ListSelectionEvent	Generated when a list selection changes.	ListSelectionListener
MenuEvent	Generated when a menu selection occurs.	MenuListener
TableModelEvent	Generated when the table model changes.	TableModelListener
TreeExpansionEvent	Generated when a tree is expanded or collapsed.	TreeExpansionListener
TreeModelEvent	Generated when a tree model changes.	TreeModelListener
TreeSelectionEvent	Generated when a node on a tree is selected.	TreeSelectionListener

Table 1-2 A Sampling of Event Classes in **javax.swing.event**

defined in **javax.swing.event**. Throughout the course of this book, the event classes and interfaces used by the various components are described as needed.

Adapter Classes

Although it isn't difficult to implement most of the event listener interfaces, Java offers a set of *adapter classes* that provide an empty implementation of event listener interface methods. Adapter classes are useful when you want to receive and process only some of the events that are associated with a particular event. You can define a new class to act as an event listener by extending one of the adapter classes and implement only those events in which you are interested. Not having to implement all of the methods defined by an event listener interface saves you a considerable amount of effort and prevents your code from becoming cluttered with empty methods. Also, it is common to implement an adapter through the use of an anonymous inner class, which can further simplify your code.

Not all listener interfaces have corresponding adapters. For example, there is no adapter for **ActionEvent** because it defines only one method. In general, there are adapters for listeners that define two or more methods. For example, the **MouseMotionListener** class has two methods, **mouseDragged( )** and **mouseMoved( )**. Empty implementations of these methods are provided by **MouseMotionAdapter**. If you were interested in only mouse drag events, then you could simply extend **MouseMotionAdapter** and implement **mouseDragged( )**. The empty implementation of **mouseMoved( )** would handle the mouse motion events for you.

Here is a sampling of the adapter classes. Most are defined in **java.awt.event**, but **MouseInputAdapter** is defined in **javax.swing.event**.

Adapter Class	Implements
FocusAdapter	FocusListener
KeyAdapter	KeyListener
MouseAdapter	MouseListener
MouseMotionAdapter	MouseMotionListener
MouseInputAdapter	MouseListener and MouseMotionListener
WindowAdapter	WindowListener

Although we won't be using an adapter class in this module, you will see several in action later in this book.

Progress Check

1. The delegation event model is based on event sources and _____ _____.

2. What is the name of the event listener interface for action events?

3. What do adapter classes do?

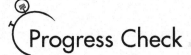

CRITICAL SKILL
1.7 ## Using a Push Button

One of the simplest Swing controls is the push button. It is also one of the most commonly used. A push button is an instance of **JButton**. **JButton** inherits the abstract class **AbstractButton**, which defines the functionality common to all buttons. Swing push buttons can contain text, an image, or both. In this module, only text-based push buttons are used, but other types of buttons are discussed in detail in Module 2.

JButton supplies three constructors. The one used here is

JButton(String *msg*)

The *msg* parameter specifies the string that will be displayed inside the button.

When a push button is pressed, it generates an **ActionEvent**. Thus, **JButton** provides the following methods (inherited from **AbstractButton**), which are used to add or remove an action listener:

void addActionListener(ActionListener *al*)

void removeActionListener(ActionListener *al*)

Here, *al* specifies an object that will receive event notifications. This object must be an instance of a class that implements the **ActionListener** interface.

---

1. Event listeners

2. **ActionListener**

3. Adapter classes simplify the implementation of event listeners by providing empty implementations of all methods in the interface. Thus, you need only implement those methods in which you are interested.

The **ActionListener** interface defines only one method: **actionPerformed( )**. It is shown here:

void actionPerformed(ActionEvent *ae*)

This method is called when a button is pressed. In other words, it is the event handler that is called when a button press event has occurred. Your implementation of **actionPerformed( )** must quickly respond to that event and return. As mentioned earlier, as a general rule, event handlers must not engage in long operations because doing so will slow down the entire application. If a time-consuming procedure must be performed, then a separate thread should be created for that purpose.

Using the **ActionEvent** object passed to **actionPerformed( )**, you can obtain several useful pieces of information relating to the button-press event. The one used by this module is the *action command* string associated with the button. By default, this is the string displayed inside the button. The action command is obtained by calling **getActionCommand( )** on the event object. It is declared like this:

String getActionCommand( )

The action command identifies the button. Thus, when using two or more buttons within the same application, the action command gives you an easy way to determine which button was pressed.

The following program demonstrates how to create a push button and respond to button-press events. Figure 1-2 shows how the example appears on the screen.

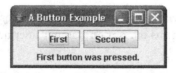

Figure 1-2 Output from the **JButton** demonstration program

```
// Demonstrate a button.

import java.awt.*;
import java.awt.event.*;
import javax.swing.*;

class ButtonDemo implements ActionListener {

  JLabel jlab;

  ButtonDemo() {

    // Create a new JFrame container.
    JFrame jfrm = new JFrame("A Button Example");

    // Specify FlowLayout for the layout manager.
    jfrm.getContentPane().setLayout(new FlowLayout());

    // Give the frame an initial size.
    jfrm.setSize(220, 90);

    // Terminate the program when the user closes the application.
    jfrm.setDefaultCloseOperation(JFrame.EXIT_ON_CLOSE);

    // Make two buttons.
    JButton jbtnFirst = new JButton("First");
    JButton jbtnSecond = new JButton("Second");

    // Add action listeners.
    jbtnFirst.addActionListener(this);
    jbtnSecond.addActionListener(this);

    // Add the buttons to the content pane.
    jfrm.getContentPane().add(jbtnFirst);
    jfrm.getContentPane().add(jbtnSecond);

    // Create a text-based label.
    jlab = new JLabel("Press a button.");
```

◄——— Note use of **FlowLayout**.

◄——— Create two push buttons.

◄——— Set the action listeners for the buttons.

```
      // Add the label to the frame.
      jfrm.getContentPane().add(jlab);

      // Display the frame.
      jfrm.setVisible(true);
    }

    // Handle button events.
    public void actionPerformed(ActionEvent ae) {

      if(ae.getActionCommand().equals("First"))
        jlab.setText("First button was pressed.");
      else
        jlab.setText("Second button was pressed. ");
    }

    public static void main(String args[]) {

      // Create the frame on the event dispatching thread.
      SwingUtilities.invokeLater(new Runnable() {
        public void run() {
          new ButtonDemo();
        }
      });

    }
  }
```

This is the **ActionEvent** handler for the push buttons.

Use the action command string to determine which button was pressed.

Let's take a close look at the new things in this program. First, notice that the program now imports both the **java.awt** and **java.awt.event** packages. The **java.awt** package is needed because it contains the **FlowLayout** class, which supports the standard flow layout manager used to lay out components in a frame. (More on layouts in a moment.) The **java.awt.event** package is needed because it defines the **ActionListener** interface and the **ActionEvent** class.

Next, the class **ButtonDemo** is declared. Notice that it implements **ActionListener**. This means that **ButtonDemo** objects can be used to receive action events. Next, a **JLabel** reference is declared. This reference will be used within the **actionPerformed( )** method to display which button has been pressed.

The **ButtonDemo** constructor begins by creating a **JFrame** called **jfrm**. It then sets the layout manager for the content pane of **jfrm** to **FlowLayout**. By default, the content pane uses **BorderLayout** as its layout manager. In a border layout, a component can be displayed in one of five locations; one is the center (which is the default location) and the other four are the borders. (Therefore, in the first example in this module, the label was added to the center of the default border layout.) However, for many of the examples in the first part of this book, **FlowLayout** is more convenient. A flow layout lays out components one "line" at a time, top to bottom. When one "line" is full, layout advances to the next "line." Although this scheme gives you little control over the placement of components, it is quite simple to use. However, be aware that if you resize the frame, the position of the components will change.

Notice that **FlowLayout** is assigned using this statement:

```
jfrm.getContentPane().setLayout(new FlowLayout());
```

Beginning with JDK 5, it is no longer necessary to explicitly call **getContentPane( )**. Instead, you can call **setLayout( )** directly on the **JFrame** reference. Thus, beginning with JDK 5, it is perfectly valid to write

```
jfrm.setLayout(new FlowLayout());
```

to set the layout manager for the content pane. For the same reasons as mentioned earlier when discussing adding components to the content pane, this book will continue to explicitly call **getContentPane( )**, but if you are using JDK 5 or later, you can remove this call.

After setting the size and default close operation, **ButtonDemo( )** creates two buttons, as shown here:

```
JButton jbtnFirst = new JButton("First");
JButton jbtnSecond = new JButton("Second");
```

The first button will contain the text "First" and the second will contain "Second."

Next, the instance of **ButtonDemo** referred to via **this** is added as an action listener for the buttons by these two lines:

```
jbtnFirst.addActionListener(this);
jbtnSecond.addActionListener(this);
```

This approach means that the object that creates the buttons will also receive notifications when a button is pressed.

Next, the buttons are added to the content pane of **jfrm**:

```
jfrm.getContentPane().add(jbtnFirst);
jfrm.getContentPane().add(jbtnSecond);
```

Remember, the call to **getContentPane( )** is needed only when using versions of Java prior to 1.5 (JDK 5), although its use makes it clear what is happening.

Each time a button is pressed, it generates an action event and all registered listeners are notified by calling the **actionPerformed( )** method. The **ActionEvent** object representing the button event is passed as a parameter. In the case of **ButtonDemo**, this event is passed to this implementation of **actionPerformed( )**.

```
public void actionPerformed(ActionEvent ae) {

  if(ae.getActionCommand().equals("First"))
    jlab.setText("First button was pressed.");
  else
    jlab.setText("Second button was pressed. ");
}
```

The event that occurred is passed via **ae**. Inside the method, the action command associated with the button that generated the event is obtained by calling **getActionCommand( )**. (Recall that, by default, the action command is the same as the text displayed by the button.) Based on the contents of that string, the text in the label is set appropriately.

One last point: Remember that **actionPerformed( )** is called on the event-dispatching thread as explained earlier. It must return quickly in order to avoid slowing down the application.

Progress Check

1. What class creates a Swing push button?

2. By default, the action command string associated with a button is the same as the text displayed within the button. True or false?

Project 1-1   A Simple Stopwatch

StopWatch.java

Although only two Swing controls have been introduced, **JLabel** and **JButton**, you can use these controls to create a fully functional and useful application: a stopwatch. The stopwatch contains two push buttons and one label. The push buttons are called Start and Stop and are used to start and stop the stopwatch. The label displays the elapsed time. Although quite simple, this project shows the ease with which GUI interfaces can be created using Swing.

---

1. **JButton**
2. True

Step by Step

1. Begin by creating a file called **StopWatch.java** and then enter the following comment and **import** statements:

```
// Project 1-1: A Simple stopwatch.

import java.awt.*;
import java.awt.event.*;
import javax.swing.*;
import java.util.*;
```

Notice that **java.util** is imported. This package is needed because it contains the **Calendar** class, which is used to obtain the current system time.

2. Begin the **StopWatch** class as shown here:

```
class StopWatch implements ActionListener {

  JLabel jlab;
  long start; // holds the start time in milliseconds
```

As the comment indicates, the **start** field is used to hold the start time in milliseconds. This value will be subtracted from the end time to obtain the elapsed time.

3. Begin the **StopWatch** constructor with the following lines:

```
StopWatch() {

  // Create a new JFrame container.
  JFrame jfrm = new JFrame("A Simple Stopwatch");

  // Specify FlowLayout for the layout manager.
  jfrm.getContentPane().setLayout(new FlowLayout());

  // Give the frame an initial size.
  jfrm.setSize(230, 90);

  // Terminate the program when the user closes the application.
  jfrm.setDefaultCloseOperation(JFrame.EXIT_ON_CLOSE);
```

These statements are similar to that used by the preceding examples and should be familiar to you.

(continued)

4. Enter the following code, which creates the Start and Stop buttons, adds action listeners for the buttons, and then adds the buttons to the content pane.

```
// Make two buttons.
JButton jbtnStart = new JButton("Start");
JButton jbtnStop = new JButton("Stop");

// Add action listeners.
jbtnStart.addActionListener(this);
jbtnStop.addActionListener(this);

// Add the buttons to the content pane.
jfrm.getContentPane().add(jbtnStart);
jfrm.getContentPane().add(jbtnStop);
```

5. Create and add a label using the following statements:

```
// Create a text-based label.
jlab = new JLabel("Press Start to begin timing.");

// Add the label to the frame.
jfrm.getContentPane().add(jlab);
```

The label is used to indicate the status of the stopwatch and to display the elapsed time.

6. Conclude the **StopWatch** constructor by making the frame visible:

```
  // Display the frame.
  jfrm.setVisible(true);
}
```

7. Add the **actionPerformed( )** method shown here:

```
// Handle button events.
public void actionPerformed(ActionEvent ae) {
  Calendar cal = Calendar.getInstance(); // get the current system time

  if(ae.getActionCommand().equals("Start")) {
    // Store start time.
    start = cal.getTimeInMillis();
    jlab.setText("Stopwatch is Running...");
  }
  else
    // Compute the elapsed time.
    jlab.setText("Elapsed time is "
        + (double) (cal.getTimeInMillis() - start)/1000);
}
```

Notice that a **Calendar** object called **cal** is created and initialized to the current system time by calling the static **Calendar** method **getInstance( )**. Thus, each time **actionPerformed( )** is called, **cal** will be initialized to the current system time.

Recall that, by default, the action command for a button is the text displayed by the button. Thus, the action command for the Start button is "Start." When the Start button is pressed, the current time (in milliseconds) is obtained (by calling **getTimeInMillis( )** on **cal**) and stored in the **start** field. When the Stop button is pressed, the current time is obtained and the start time is subtracted from it, yielding the elapsed time. This value is cast to **double** and divided by 1000. This converts the elapsed time into seconds.

8. Conclude by adding this **main( )** method:

```
public static void main(String args[]) {

  // Create the frame on the event dispatching thread.
  SwingUtilities.invokeLater(new Runnable() {
    public void run() {
      new StopWatch();
    }
  });

}
```

9. Here is all the code assembled into a complete program. Sample output is shown here:

```
// Project 1-1: A Simple stopwatch.

import java.awt.*;
import java.awt.event.*;
import javax.swing.*;
import java.util.*;

class StopWatch implements ActionListener {

  JLabel jlab;
  long start; // holds the start time in milliseconds
```

(continued)

```
StopWatch() {

  // Create a new JFrame container.
  JFrame jfrm = new JFrame("A Simple Stopwatch");

  // Specify FlowLayout for the layout manager.
  jfrm.getContentPane().setLayout(new FlowLayout());

  // Give the frame an initial size.
  jfrm.setSize(230, 90);

  // Terminate the program when the user closes the application.
  jfrm.setDefaultCloseOperation(JFrame.EXIT_ON_CLOSE);

  // Make two buttons.
  JButton jbtnStart = new JButton("Start");
  JButton jbtnStop = new JButton("Stop");

  // Add action listeners.
  jbtnStart.addActionListener(this);
  jbtnStop.addActionListener(this);

  // Add the buttons to the content pane.
  jfrm.getContentPane().add(jbtnStart);
  jfrm.getContentPane().add(jbtnStop);

  // Create a text-based label.
  jlab = new JLabel("Press Start to begin timing.");

  // Add the label to the frame.
  jfrm.getContentPane().add(jlab);

  // Display the frame.
  jfrm.setVisible(true);
}

// Handle button events.
public void actionPerformed(ActionEvent ae) {
  Calendar cal = Calendar.getInstance(); // get the current system time

  if(ae.getActionCommand().equals("Start")) {
    // Store start time.
    start = cal.getTimeInMillis();
    jlab.setText("Stopwatch is Running...");
```

```
      }
      else
        // Compute the elapsed time.
        jlab.setText("Elapsed time is "
              + (double) (cal.getTimeInMillis() - start)/1000);
      }

    public static void main(String args[]) {

      // Create the frame on the event dispatching thread.
      SwingUtilities.invokeLater(new Runnable() {
        public void run() {
          new StopWatch();
        }
      });
    }


}
```

Ask the Expert

Q: Can you review when a call to getContentPane( ) is not needed when using JDK 5 and later?

A: As you know, to add a component to a top-level container, such as a **JFrame**, that component must actually be added to the content pane. Prior to JDK 5, you had to call **getContentPane( )** to obtain a reference to the content pane and then call **add( )** on that reference to add the component. Beginning with JDK 5, the explicit call to **getContentPane( )** is not necessary because a call to **add( )** is automatically routed to the content pane when **add( )** is called on a top-level container, such as a **JFrame**.

Two other methods are affected by this change: **remove( )**, which removes a component from a container, and **setLayout( )**, which sets the layout manager. Prior to JDK 5, these methods also had to be called through **getContentPane( )** when operating on a top-level container reference. Now, they can be called directly on the top-level container reference and the calls are automatically transferred to the content pane.

As explained, this book will continue to use explicit calls to **getContentPane( )** for two reasons. First, it ensures that the code works for all readers. Second, it makes it very clear which pane is being affected. However, if you are using JDK 5 or later, feel free to remove the explicit calls to **getContentPane( )**.

CRITICAL SKILL

1.8 # Introducing JTextField

Another commonly used control is **JTextField**. It enables the user to enter a line of text. **JTextField** inherits the abstract class **JTextComponent**, which is the superclass of all text components. Although we will look at Swing's text controls in detail in Module 7, **JTextField** is introduced here because it provides a convenient way to obtain text-based user input.

JTextField defines several constructors. The one we will use is shown here:

JTextField(int *cols*)

Here, *cols* specifies the width of the text field in columns. It is important to understand that you can enter a string that is longer than the number of columns. It's just that the physical size of the text field on the screen will be *cols* columns wide.

When a user presses ENTER when inputting into a text field, an **ActionEvent** is generated. Therefore, **JTextField** provides the **addActionListener( )** and **removeActionListener( )** methods. To handle action events, you must implement the **actionPerformed( )** method defined by the **ActionListener** interface. The process is similar to handling action events generated by a button, as described earlier.

To obtain the string that is currently displayed in the text field, call **getText( )** on the **JTextField** instance. It is declared as shown here:

String getText( )

You can set the text in a **JTextField** by calling **setText( )**, shown next:

void setText(String *text*)

Here, *text* is the string that will be put into the text field.

The following program demonstrates **JTextField**. It creates a text field that is ten-columns wide. Whenever you press ENTER while in the text field, the current contents are displayed via a **JLabel**. Its operation should be clear. Sample output is shown in Figure 1-3.

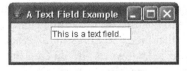

Figure 1-3 Sample output from the **JTextField** program

```
// Demonstrate a text field.

import java.awt.*;
import java.awt.event.*;
import javax.swing.*;

class JTextFieldDemo implements ActionListener {

  JTextField jtf;
  JLabel jlab;

  JTextFieldDemo() {

    // Create a new JFrame container.
    JFrame jfrm = new JFrame("A Text Field Example");

    // Specify FlowLayout for the layout manager.
    jfrm.getContentPane().setLayout(new FlowLayout());

    // Give the frame an initial size.
    jfrm.setSize(240, 90);

    // Terminate the program when the user closes the application.
    jfrm.setDefaultCloseOperation(JFrame.EXIT_ON_CLOSE);

    // Create a text field instance.
    jtf = new JTextField(10);  // ◄──────── Create a ten-column text field.

    // Add an action listener for the text field.
    jtf.addActionListener(this);  // ◄──────── Set the action listener for the text field.

    // Add the text field to the content pane.
    jfrm.getContentPane().add(jtf);

    // Create an empty text-based label.
    jlab = new JLabel("");

    // Add the label to the frame.
    jfrm.getContentPane().add(jlab);

    // Display the frame.
    jfrm.setVisible(true);
  }
```

```
   // Handle action events.                          An action event is generated
   public void actionPerformed(ActionEvent ae) {  ←── when the user presses ENTER
                                                      while inside a text field.
     // Obtain the current text and display it in a label.
     jlab.setText("Current contents: " + jtf.getText());
   }

   public static void main(String args[]) {

     // Create the frame on the event dispatching thread.
     SwingUtilities.invokeLater(new Runnable() {
       public void run() {
         new JTextFieldDemo();
       }
     });

   }
}
```

Most of the program should be familiar, but notice this line from within the
actionPerformed( ) method:

```
jlab.setText("Current contents: " + jtf.getText());
```

As explained, when the user presses ENTER, an **ActionEvent** is generated and sent to all
registered action listeners, through the **actionPerformed( )** method. For **TextFieldDemo**,
this method simply obtains the text currently held in the text field by calling **getText( )** on
jtf. It then displays the text through the label referred to by **jlab**.

Like a **JButton**, a **JTextField** has an action command string associated with it. By default,
the action command is the current contents of the text field. However, you can set this to an
action command of your choosing by calling the **setActionCommand( )** method, shown here:

void setActionCommand(String *cmd*)

The string passed in *cmd* becomes the new action command. The text in the text field is
unaffected. Once you set the action command string, it remains the same no matter what is
entered into the text field. One reason that you might want to explicitly set the action command
is to provide a way to recognize the text field as the source of an action event. This is helpful
when another control in the same frame also generates action events and you want to use the
same event handler to process both events. Setting the action command gives you a way to
tell them apart. For example, in the following program, two text fields are used and each is
recognized based on its action command.

```
// Use two text fields.

import java.awt.*;
import java.awt.event.*;
import javax.swing.*;

class TwoTFDemo implements ActionListener {

  JTextField jtf1;
  JTextField jtf2;
  JLabel jlab;

  TwoTFDemo() {

    // Create a new JFrame container.
    JFrame jfrm = new JFrame("Use Two Text Fields");

    // Specify FlowLayout for the layout manager.
    jfrm.getContentPane().setLayout(new FlowLayout());

    // Give the frame an initial size.
    jfrm.setSize(240, 120);

    // Terminate the program when the user closes the application.
    jfrm.setDefaultCloseOperation(JFrame.EXIT_ON_CLOSE);

    // Create two text field instances.
    jtf1 = new JTextField(10);          Create two text fields.
    jtf2 = new JTextField(10);

    // Set the action commands.
    jtf1.setActionCommand("One");       Set the action command
    jtf2.setActionCommand("Two");       strings for the text fields.

    // Add action listeners for the text fields.
    jtf1.addActionListener(this);
    jtf2.addActionListener(this);

    // Add the text fields to the content pane.
    jfrm.getContentPane().add(jtf1);
    jfrm.getContentPane().add(jtf2);

    // Create an empty text-based label.
    jlab = new JLabel("");
```

```
    // Add the label to the frame.
    jfrm.getContentPane().add(jlab);

    // Display the frame.
    jfrm.setVisible(true);
  }

  // Handle action events.
  public void actionPerformed(ActionEvent ae) {

    if(ae.getActionCommand().equals("One"))
      jlab.setText("ENTER pressed in tf1: "
                   + jtf1.getText());
    else
      jlab.setText("ENTER pressed in jtf2: "
                   + jtf2.getText());
  }

  public static void main(String args[]) {

    // Create the frame on the event dispatching thread.
    SwingUtilities.invokeLater(new Runnable() {
      public void run() {
        new TwoTFDemo();
      }
    });

  }
}
```

Use the action command string to determine which text field fired the event.

Sample output is shown in Figure 1-4.

This program creates two **JTextField**s: **jtf1** and **jtf2**. Notice that the action commands associated with **jtf1** and **jtf2** are set using these lines of code:

```
jtf1.setActionCommand("One");
jtf2.setActionCommand("Two");
```

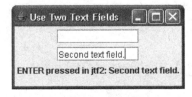

Figure 1-4 Sample output from the two text fields program

Next, inside **actionPerformed( )** notice how the action command is used to determine which text field generated the action event:

```
public void actionPerformed(ActionEvent ae) {

  if(ae.getActionCommand().equals("One"))
    jlab.setText("ENTER pressed in tf1: "
                   + jtf1.getText());
  else
    jlab.setText("ENTER pressed in jtf2: "
                   + jtf2.getText());
}
```

Because the action commands for each text field have been set to a known string, this string can be used to determine which text field generated the event.

Progress Check

1. When using **JTextField**, if the text entered by the user is longer than the text field, the text is truncated. True or false?

2. When the user presses ENTER while within a **JTextField**, what event is generated?

3. Why is it a good idea to explicitly set the action command for a **JTextField**?

Project 1-2 Create a Simple Code Machine

`Coder.java`   This project uses **JLabel**, **JButton**, and **JTextField** to create a simple code machine. The code machine works by implementing a simple substitution cipher in which each character in a string is increased by one. For example, A becomes B, B becomes C, and so on. Of course, such a naive approach is trivially easy to break, but it provides an excellent means of illustrating the ways that push buttons and text fields can interact. It also shows how events generated by different components (in this case a text field and a button) can map to the same event handler.

(continued)

---

1. False. The width of the text can exceed the width of the field.

2. **ActionEvent**

3. If the action command is not set, then by default the action command is the text currently contained within the text field. Setting the action command explicitly identifies the text field independently of what it contains.

Step by Step

1. Create a file called **Coder.java** and then enter the following comment and **import** statements:

```
// Project 1-2: A simple code machine.

import java.awt.*;
import java.awt.event.*;
import javax.swing.*;
```

2. Begin creating the **Coder** class, like this:

```
class Coder implements ActionListener {

    JTextField jtfPlaintext;
    JTextField jtfCiphertext;
```

Notice that **Coder** implements **ActionListener**. It also declares fields for two text fields. **jtfPlaintext** will hold the plain text message entered by the user. **jtfCiphertext** will hold the encoded version of the message.

3. Start the **Coder** constructor, as shown here:

```
Coder() {

    // Create a new JFrame container.
    JFrame jfrm = new JFrame("A Simple Code Machine");

    // Specify FlowLayout for the layout manager.
    jfrm.getContentPane().setLayout(new FlowLayout());

    // Give the frame an initial size.
    jfrm.setSize(340, 120);

    // Terminate the program when the user closes the application.
    jfrm.setDefaultCloseOperation(JFrame.EXIT_ON_CLOSE);
```

This sequence is similar to that used by other examples in this module and should be familiar to you.

4. Add these two **JLabel**s:

```
// Create two labels.
JLabel jlabPlaintext = new JLabel("  Plain Text: ");
JLabel jlabCiphertext = new JLabel("Cipher Text: ");
```

5. Create two **JTextField** instances and assign them to the **jtfPlaintext** and **jtfCiphertext** fields.

```
// Create two text field instances.
jtfPlaintext = new JTextField(20);
jtfCiphertext = new JTextField(20);
```

6. Set the action command for the text fields and then add **this** as an action listener for both fields.

```
// Set the action commands for the text fields.
jtfPlaintext.setActionCommand("Encode");
jtfCiphertext.setActionCommand("Decode");

// Add action listeners for the text fields.
jtfPlaintext.addActionListener(this);
jtfCiphertext.addActionListener(this);
```

It is necessary to set the action command for both **JTextField** instances for three reasons. First, it gives a way to identify each text field. Second, if the action command is not set, then by default the current text is used. If, by happenstance, this text is the same as the action command used by another control, a conflict will arise. Setting the action command prevents this. Third, as you will see shortly, these two action commands are the same as the action commands for two of the push buttons. This means that the same code sequence can be used to handle events from both the push button and the text field.

7. Add the text fields and labels to the content pane.

```
// Add the text fields and labels to the content pane.
jfrm.getContentPane().add(jlabPlaintext);
jfrm.getContentPane().add(jtfPlaintext);
jfrm.getContentPane().add(jlabCiphertext);
jfrm.getContentPane().add(jtfCiphertext);
```

The order in which these components is added is important because the labels describe the text fields.

8. Create three push buttons called Encode, Decode, and Reset, as shown here:

```
// Create push button instances.
JButton jbtnEncode = new JButton("Encode");
JButton jbtnDecode = new JButton("Decode");
JButton jbtnReset =  new JButton("Reset");
```

9. Add **this** as an action listener for these buttons and then add the buttons to the content pane.

```
// Add action listeners for the buttons.
jbtnEncode.addActionListener(this);
```

(continued)

```
jbtnDecode.addActionListener(this);
jbtnReset.addActionListener(this);

// Add the buttons to the content pane.
jfrm.getContentPane().add(jbtnEncode);
jfrm.getContentPane().add(jbtnDecode);
jfrm.getContentPane().add(jbtnReset);
```

10. Conclude the **Coder** constructor with a call to **setVisible( )**, as shown here:

```
// Display the frame.
jfrm.setVisible(true);
}
```

11. Begin coding the **actionPerformed( )** method, as shown here:

```
// Handle action events.
public void actionPerformed(ActionEvent ae) {

  // If action command is "Encode" then encode the string.
  if(ae.getActionCommand().equals("Encode")) {

    // Obtain the plain text and put it into a StringBuilder.
    StringBuilder str = new StringBuilder(jtfPlaintext.getText());

    // Add 1 to each character.
    for(int i=0; i<str.length(); i++)
      str.setCharAt(i, (char)(str.charAt(i) + 1));

    // Set the coded text into the Cipher Text field.
    jtfCiphertext.setText(str.toString());

  }
```

This **if** statement checks the action command against "Encode." The command will be "Encode" if the user pressed the **jbtnEncode** button, or if the user pressed ENTER while entering text inside the **jtfPlaintext** text field. Because the action command for both **jbtnEncode** and **jtfPlaintext** is "Encode," both events are handled by the same code. In other words, events generated by these two controls both map to the same handler because their action commands are the same. This handler encodes the string in the Plain Text field and puts it into the Cipher Text field.

12. Add the following **else if**, which determines if the action command is equal to "Decode":

```
// If action command is "Decode" then decode the string.
else if(ae.getActionCommand().equals("Decode")) {
```

```
// Obtain the cipher text and put it into a StringBuilder.
StringBuilder str = new StringBuilder(jtfCiphertext.getText());

// Subtract 1 from each character.
for(int i=0; i<str.length(); i++)
  str.setCharAt(i, (char)(str.charAt(i) - 1));

// Set the decoded text into the Plain Text field.
jtfPlaintext.setText(str.toString());
}
```

This code works like the "Encode" handler except that it decodes the string in the Cipher Text field and puts it into the Plain Text field.

13. Finish the **actionPerformed( )** method by handling the "Reset" action command, which is linked to **jbtnReset**. Because there are only three action commands, there is no need to explicitly test for "Reset." If execution reaches this point, it is the only option left.

```
// Otherwise, must be "Reset" command.
else {
  jtfPlaintext.setText("");
  jtfCiphertext.setText("");
}
}
```

14. Conclude by adding this **main( )** method:

```
public static void main(String args[]) {

  // Create the frame on the event dispatching thread.
  SwingUtilities.invokeLater(new Runnable() {
    public void run() {
      new Coder();
    }
  });

}
```

15. Here is all the code assembled into a complete program. Sample output is shown here:

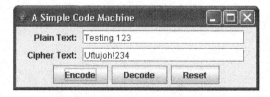

(continued)

```java
// Project 1-2: A simple code machine.

import java.awt.*;
import java.awt.event.*;
import javax.swing.*;

class Coder implements ActionListener {

  JTextField jtfPlaintext;
  JTextField jtfCiphertext;

  Coder() {

    // Create a new JFrame container.
    JFrame jfrm = new JFrame("A Simple Code Machine");

    // Specify FlowLayout for the layout manager.
    jfrm.getContentPane().setLayout(new FlowLayout());

    // Give the frame an initial size.
    jfrm.setSize(340, 120);

    // Terminate the program when the user closes the application.
    jfrm.setDefaultCloseOperation(JFrame.EXIT_ON_CLOSE);

    // Create two labels.
    JLabel jlabPlaintext = new JLabel("   Plain Text: ");
    JLabel jlabCiphertext = new JLabel("Cipher Text: ");

    // Create two text field instances.
    jtfPlaintext = new JTextField(20);
    jtfCiphertext = new JTextField(20);

    // Set the action commands for the text fields.
    jtfPlaintext.setActionCommand("Encode");
    jtfCiphertext.setActionCommand("Decode");

    // Add action listeners for the text fields.
    jtfPlaintext.addActionListener(this);
    jtfCiphertext.addActionListener(this);

    // Add the text fields and labels to the content pane.
    jfrm.getContentPane().add(jlabPlaintext);
    jfrm.getContentPane().add(jtfPlaintext);
    jfrm.getContentPane().add(jlabCiphertext);
    jfrm.getContentPane().add(jtfCiphertext);
```

```
// Create push button instances.
JButton jbtnEncode = new JButton("Encode");
JButton jbtnDecode = new JButton("Decode");
JButton jbtnReset =  new JButton("Reset");

// Add action listeners for the buttons.
jbtnEncode.addActionListener(this);
jbtnDecode.addActionListener(this);
jbtnReset.addActionListener(this);

// Add the buttons to the content pane.
jfrm.getContentPane().add(jbtnEncode);
jfrm.getContentPane().add(jbtnDecode);
jfrm.getContentPane().add(jbtnReset);

// Display the frame.
jfrm.setVisible(true);
}

// Handle action events.
public void actionPerformed(ActionEvent ae) {

  // If action command is "Encode" then encode the string.
  if(ae.getActionCommand().equals("Encode")) {

    // Obtain the plain text and put it into a StringBuilder.
    StringBuilder str = new StringBuilder(jtfPlaintext.getText());

    // Add 1 to each character.
    for(int i=0; i<str.length(); i++)
      str.setCharAt(i, (char)(str.charAt(i) + 1));

    // Set the coded text into the Cipher Text field.
    jtfCiphertext.setText(str.toString());

  }

  // If action command is "Decode" then decode the string.
  else if(ae.getActionCommand().equals("Decode")) {

    // Obtain the cipher text and put it into a StringBuilder.
    StringBuilder str = new StringBuilder(jtfCiphertext.getText());

    // Subtract 1 from each character.
    for(int i=0; i<str.length(); i++)
```

(continued)

1

Swing Fundamentals

Project
1-2

Create a Simple Code Machine

```
        str.setCharAt(i, (char)(str.charAt(i) - 1));

      // Set the decoded text into the Plain Text field.
      jtfPlaintext.setText(str.toString());
    }

    // Otherwise, must be "Reset" command.
    else {
      jtfPlaintext.setText("");
      jtfCiphertext.setText("");
    }
  }

  public static void main(String args[]) {

    // Create the frame on the event dispatching thread.
    SwingUtilities.invokeLater(new Runnable() {
      public void run() {
        new Coder();
      }
    });

  }
}
```

Event Handling Alternatives

The programs in this module have used a simple, straightforward approach to handling events in which the main class of the application has implemented the listener interface itself and all events are sent to an instance of that class. While this is perfectly acceptable, it is not the only way to handle events. Two other approaches are commonly used. First, you can implement separate listener classes. Thus, different classes could handle different events, and these classes would be separate from the main class of the application. Second, you can implement listeners through the use of anonymous inner classes. For example, you could implement an action listener for a button like this:

```
jbnt.addActionListener(new ActionListener() {
  public void actionPerformed(ActionEvent ae) {
    // Handle action event here.
  }
});
```

Here, an anonymous inner class is created that implements the **ActionListener** interface. You will see examples of both alternatives in subsequent modules.

CRITICAL SKILL
1.9 # A Word About Layout Managers

The position of components within a container is controlled by the container's *layout manager*. Java offers several layout managers. Most are provided by the AWT (within **java.awt**), but Swing adds a few of its own. All layout managers are instances of a class that implements the **LayoutManager** interface. (Some will also implement the **LayoutManager2** interface.) Here is a list of a few of the layout managers available to the Swing programmer:

FlowLayout	A simple layout that positions components left-to-right, top-to-bottom. (Positions components right-to-left for some cultural settings.)
BorderLayout	Positions components within the center or the borders of the container. This is the default layout for a content pane.
GridLayout	Lays out components within a grid
GridBagLayout	Lays out different size components within a flexible grid.
BoxLayout	Lays out components vertically or horizontally within a box.
SpringLayout	Lays out components subject to a set of constraints.

So far, you have seen two of these layout managers in action: **BorderLayout** (which is the default layout manager for the content pane) and **FlowLayout**. Other layout managers are described as needed as they are used in examples throughout this book. However, because **BorderLayout** is the default layout, it warrants a closer look at this time.

BorderLayout implements a layout style that defines five locations to which a component can be added. The first is the center. The other four are the sides (i.e., the borders), which are called north, south, east, and west. By default, when you add a component to the content pane, you are adding the component to the center. However, you can specify the location by using this form of **add( )**:

void add(Component *comp*, Object *loc*)

Here, *comp* is the component to add and *loc* specifies the location to which it is added. The *loc* value must be one of the following:

BorderLayout.CENTER	BorderLayout.EAST	BorderLayout.NORTH
BorderLayout.SOUTH	BorderLayout.WEST	

In general, **BorderLayout** is most useful when you are creating a **JFrame** that contains only one component (which is added to the center) or when you are adding a group of components contained within a panel. You will see how this is done in Module 4.

The Swing Packages

Swing is a very large subsystem and makes use of many packages. As of JDK 5, here are the packages used by Swing:

javax.swing	javax.swing.border	javax.swing.colorchooser
javax.swing.event	javax.swing.filechooser	javax.swing.plaf
javax.swing.plaf.basic	javax.swing.plaf.metal	javax.swing.plaf.multi
javax.swing.plaf.synth	javax.swing.table	javax.swing.text
javax.swing.text.html	javax.swing.text.html.parser	javax.swing.text.rtf
javax.swing.tree	javax.swing.undo	

The main package is **javax.swing**. This package must be imported into any program that uses Swing. It contains the classes that implement the basic Swing components, such as push buttons, labels, and check boxes. Several of the other packages will be used throughout the course of this book.

✓
Module 1 Mastery Check

1. Most AWT components translate into native peers. Why is this a problem and how does Swing fix it?

2. Most Swing components are written in 100 percent Java code. True or False?

3. What are the four top-level, heavyweight containers?

4. What is the most commonly used top-level container for an application?

5. **JFrame** contains several panes. To what pane are components added?

6. An event listener must _____ with a source in order to receive event notifications.

7. To receive an action event, a class must implement what interface?

8. When using a **JButton** or a **JTextField**, what method must be called to set the action command?

9. Name three layout managers.

10. The stopwatch example in Project 1-1 uses two buttons, one to start the stopwatch and the other to stop it. However, it is possible to use only one button, which alternates between starting and stopping the stopwatch. One way to do this is to reset the text within the button after each press, alternating between Start and Stop. Because, by default, this text is also the action command associated with the button, you can use the same button for two different purposes. Your job is to rewrite Project 1-1 so that it implements this approach.

To solve this problem, you will use another **JButton** method: **setText( )**. This method sets the text in a button. It is shown here:

    void setText(String *msg*)

Here, *msg* specifies the text that will be shown inside the button. This method lets you set the text inside a button during the execution of a program.

11. If you are using JDK 5 or later, rewrite the code for Project 1-2 so that the explicit calls to **getContentPane( )** are not used.

Module 2

Labels, Buttons, and Borders

This module begins an in-depth examination of the Swing components by looking at two of the most widely used: labels and buttons. It also introduces a feature that is often associated with labels: the border. Adding a border to a label enables you to frame its contents. Along the way, you will also see an alternative event handling technique and learn about another layout manager: **GridLayout**.

Introducing Borders

It is possible to add a border to nearly any Swing component. However, since most components, such as buttons, text fields, and lists, draw their own borders (the style of which is determined by the installed look and feel), normally you will not want to specify a border of your own because it will conflict with the look and feel. However, there are two exceptions to this rule: labels and panels. Panels are described in Module 4. In this module, we will make use of borders to demonstrate certain features of labels. For this reason borders are introduced here.

All Swing borders are instances of the **javax.swing.border.Border** interface. Although it is possible to define your own borders, you won't usually need to because Swing provides several predefined border styles that are available through the **javax.swing.BorderFactory** class. This class defines several factory methods that create various types of borders, ranging from simple line borders to beveled, etched, or matte borders. You can also create a titled border, which includes a short caption embedded in the border, or an empty border, which is an invisible border. Empty borders are useful when a gap around a component is desired.

The three borders used in this chapter are line, etched, and empty. To create a line border, use the following factory method.

static Border createLineBorder(Color *lineColor*)

Here, *lineColor* specifies the color of the line used as the border. For example, to draw a black border, pass **Color.BLACK**. This method creates a line border with the default thickness. You can specify the line thickness by using this form of the method:

static Border createLineBorder(Color *lineColor*, int *width*)

Here, *width* specifies the width of the line in pixels.

An etched border is similar to a line border except that it looks as if the line were etched into the component. There are a number of ways to create an etched border. The one we will use is shown here:

static Border createEtchedBorder( )

This creates an etched border that uses the default configuration.

To create an empty border that provides a gap around the component, use this form of **createEmptyBorder( )**:

static Border createEmptyBorder(int *topWidth*, int *leftWidth*,
int *bottomWidth*, int *rightWidth*)

Here, the parameters specify the gap in pixels for the four sides.

Once you have created a border, you can assign it to a component by calling the **setBorder( )** method defined by **JComponent**. It is shown here:

void setBorder(Border *border*)

Here, *border* specifies the border to use. One thing to understand is that the same border can be used for multiple components. That is, you don't need to create a new **Border** object for each component on which you will be setting the border.

Here is a program that demonstrates line and etched borders. You will see an example of an empty border in the next section. The output produced by the program is shown in Figure 2-1.

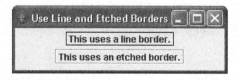

Figure 2-1 The output from the border demonstration program

```java
// Demonstrate a line and an etched border.

import java.awt.*;
import javax.swing.*;

class BorderDemo {

  BorderDemo() {

    // Create a new JFrame container.
    JFrame jfrm = new JFrame("Use Line and Etched Borders");

    // Specify FlowLayout for the layout manager.
    jfrm.getContentPane().setLayout(new FlowLayout());

    // Give the frame an initial size.
    jfrm.setSize(280, 90);

    // Terminate the program when the user closes the application.
    jfrm.setDefaultCloseOperation(JFrame.EXIT_ON_CLOSE);

    // Create a label and give it a line border.
    JLabel jlab = new JLabel(" This uses a line border. ");
    jlab.setBorder(BorderFactory.createLineBorder(Color.BLACK));

    // Create another label and give it an etched border.
    JLabel jlab2 = new JLabel(" This uses an etched border. ");
    jlab2.setBorder(BorderFactory.createEtchedBorder());

    // Add the labels to the content pane.
    jfrm.getContentPane().add(jlab);
    jfrm.getContentPane().add(jlab2);

    // Display the frame.
    jfrm.setVisible(true);
  }

  public static void main(String args[]) {
    // Create the frame on the event dispatching thread.
    SwingUtilities.invokeLater(new Runnable() {
      public void run() {
        new BorderDemo();
      }
    });
  }
}
```

Add a line border to **jlab**.

Add an etched border to **jlab2**.

Progress Check

1. Swing borders are instances of the **javax.swing.border.Border** interface. True or false?

2. It's a good idea to add a border to all of Swing's components. True or false?

3. What factory method creates a line border?

A Closer Look at Labels

Module 1 introduced the label. Here we will examine it in detail. Although they do not respond to user input, Swing labels have a surprising amount of options and features that allow you to tailor them to best fit your needs. Moreover, because of their extraordinary flexibility, you can easily create labels that give your application a distinctive appearance. The careful use of Swing labels enhances the look of nearly any user interface.

Labels are supported by the **JLabel** class. Its constructors are shown in Table 2-1. In Module 1, you saw the simplest form of a label, which is a line of text. However, much more sophisticated labels are possible. For example, you can specify how the contents of the label are aligned. You can create a label that consists of an icon (a graphical image) or a combination of icon and text. You can disable the label. You can associate a label with another component,

Constructor	Description
JLabel( )	Creates a label whose contents are empty.
JLabel(String *str*)	Creates a label that displays the string passed in *str*.
JLabel(Icon *icon*)	Creates a label that displays the image passed in *icon*.
JLabel(String *str*, int *horzAlign*)	Creates a label that displays the string passed in *str* with the horizontal alignment passed in *horzAlign*.
JLabel(Icon *icon*, int *horzAlign*)	Creates a label that displays the image passed in *icon* with the horizontal alignment passed in *horzAlign*.
JLabel(String *str*, Icon *icon*, int *horzAlign*)	Creates a label that displays the string passed in *str* and the image passed in *icon* with the horizontal alignment passed in *horzAlign*.

Table 2-1 The **JLabel** Constructors

1. True

2. False

3. **createLineBorder( )**

such as a text field. You can specify a keyboard mnemonic that is shown in the label. When this key is pressed, the component associated with the label receives focus automatically.

This is an important section because many of the techniques that you will learn (such as loading an icon, disabling a component, or aligning text and images) apply not only to **JLabel**, but also to many other Swing components. Therefore, a careful reading is advised.

CRITICAL SKILL
2.2

Change a Label's Alignment

The simplest way to create a label is by using this **JLabel** constructor:

JLabel(String *str*)

This is the form of the **JLabel** constructor that you have been using since Module 1. Here, *str* specifies the string that will be displayed within the label. This constructor displays *str* on the leading edge of the label (which is the left side for English) and centers the text vertically. However, your labels are not limited to this default behavior, and you can explicitly specify the alignment of text within a label.

There are two ways to specify a horizontal alignment. First, you can use the following constructor:

JLabel(String *str*, int *horzAlign*)

In this form, the string is displayed using the horizontal alignment passed in *horzAlign*. This value must be one of the following:

SwingConstants.LEFT	SwingConstants.RIGHT
SwingConstants.CENTER	SwingConstants.LEADING
SwingConstants.TRAILING	

The **SwingConstants** interface defines several constants that relate to Swing. This interface is implemented by **JLabel** (and several other components). Thus, you can also refer to these constants through **JLabel**, such as **JLabel.RIGHT**. However, this book will continue to refer to them through **SwingConstants** because it most clearly shows where these constants come from.

Although specifying the horizontal alignment when the label is constructed is generally the easiest approach, Swing provides an alternative. You can call the **setHorizontalAlignment( )** method on the label after it has been constructed. It is shown here:

void setHorizontalAlignment(int *horzAlign*)

Here, *horzAlign* must be one of the horizontal alignment constants just described.

To set the vertical alignment, call the **setVerticalAlignment( )** method on the label. It is shown here:

void setVerticalAlignment(int *vertAlign*)

The value passed to *vertAlign* must be one of these vertical alignment constants:

SwingConstants.TOP	SwingConstants.CENTER	SwingConstants.BOTTOM

Of course, text is centered top-to-bottom by default, so you will only use **CENTER** if you are returning the vertical alignment to its default.

There is one important thing to understand when setting a label's alignment: it won't necessarily have an effect. For example, when you use **FlowLayout**, the label will be set to its preferred size, which by default is just large enough to hold its contents. In this case, there is no difference between aligning to the top or bottom of the label. In general, label alignment only affects those labels that are sized larger than their contents. One way this can occur is when using a layout manager, such as **GridLayout**, that automatically adjusts the size of a label to fit an available space. Another way it can happen is when you specify a preferred component size that is larger than that needed to hold its contents. (See "Ask the Expert.")

Here is a program that demonstrates the various vertical and horizontal alignment positions. Notice that it sets the horizontal position by using the **JLabel** constructor and the vertical position by calling **setVerticalPosition( )**. The window produced by the program is shown in Figure 2-2.

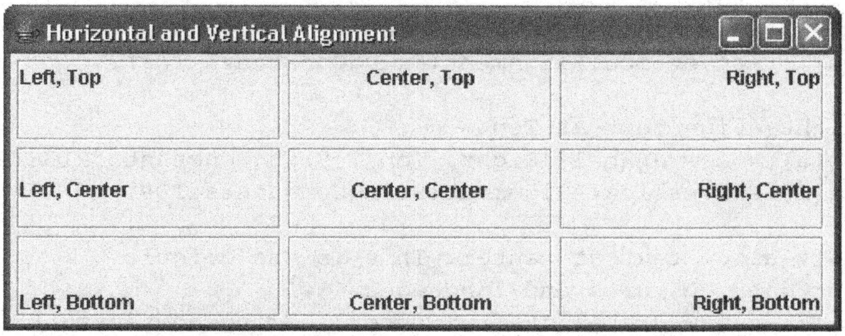

Figure 2-2   The output from the label alignment demonstration program

```
// Demonstrate horizontal and vertical text alignment.

import javax.swing.*;
import java.awt.*;
import javax.swing.border.*;

class AlignLabelDemo {

  AlignLabelDemo() {
    JLabel[] jlabs = new JLabel[9];

    // Create a new JFrame container.
    JFrame jfrm = new JFrame("Horizontal and Vertical Alignment");

    // Specify GridLayout for the layout manager.
    // This specifies a 3 row, 3 column grid with 4 pixels
    // between components.
    jfrm.getContentPane().setLayout(new GridLayout(3, 3, 4, 4));

    // Give the frame an initial size.
    jfrm.setSize(500, 200);

    // Terminate the program when the user closes the application.
    jfrm.setDefaultCloseOperation(JFrame.EXIT_ON_CLOSE);

    // Left-align text at top.
    jlabs[0] = new JLabel("Left, Top", SwingConstants.LEFT);
    jlabs[0].setVerticalAlignment(SwingConstants.TOP);

    // Center text at top.
    jlabs[1] = new JLabel("Center, Top", SwingConstants.CENTER);
    jlabs[1].setVerticalAlignment(SwingConstants.TOP);

    // Right-align text at Top.
    jlabs[2] = new JLabel("Right, Top", SwingConstants.RIGHT);
    jlabs[2].setVerticalAlignment(SwingConstants.TOP);

    // Left-align text at center. This is the default
    // for many cultures and languages.
    jlabs[3] = new JLabel("Left, Center", SwingConstants.LEFT);

    // Center the text.
    jlabs[4] = new JLabel("Center, Center", SwingConstants.CENTER);
```

Use a grid layout.

Specify a horizontal and vertical alignment for each label.

```
    // Right-align text at center.
    jlabs[5] = new JLabel("Right, Center", SwingConstants.RIGHT);

    // Left-align text at bottom.
    jlabs[6] = new JLabel("Left, Bottom", SwingConstants.LEFT);
    jlabs[6].setVerticalAlignment(SwingConstants.BOTTOM);

    // Center text at bottom.
    jlabs[7] = new JLabel("Center, Bottom", SwingConstants.CENTER);
    jlabs[7].setVerticalAlignment(SwingConstants.BOTTOM);

    // Right-align text at bottom.
    jlabs[8] = new JLabel("Right, Bottom", SwingConstants.RIGHT);
    jlabs[8].setVerticalAlignment(SwingConstants.BOTTOM);

    // Add borders so we can see the outline of the labels.
    // First, create an etched border.
    Border border = BorderFactory.createEtchedBorder();

    // Now, add that border to the labels.
    for(int i=0; i<9; i++)
      jlabs[i].setBorder(border);    ◄———— Give each label an etched border.

    // Add the labels to the content pane.
    for(int i=0; i<9; i++)
      jfrm.getContentPane().add(jlabs[i]);

    // Add an empty border around the content pane.
    JPanel cp = ((JPanel) jfrm.getContentPane());
    cp.setBorder(BorderFactory.createEmptyBorder(4, 4, 4, 4));  ◄—┐

    // Display the frame.                    Use an empty border to add a gap
    jfrm.setVisible(true);                   around the interior of the frame.
  }

  public static void main(String args[]) {
    // Create the frame on the event dispatching thread.
    SwingUtilities.invokeLater(new Runnable() {
      public void run() {
        new AlignLabelDemo();
      }
    });
  }
}
```

Ask the Expert

Q: You mention that the size of a component can be set. How is this done?

A: By default, the size of a component is determined by its contents and by the layout manager. However, you can explicitly specify a preferred size for a component by calling **setPreferredSize( )**, which is defined by **JComponent**. It is shown here:

void setPreferredSize(Dimension *newPS*)

newPS specifies the new preferred dimensions for the component. The **Dimension** class is part of the **java.awt** package. Here is one of its constructors:

Dimension(int *w*, int *h*)

Here, *w* specifies the width and *h* specifies the height.

Once you have set the preferred size, a layout manager will use those dimensions as a guide to sizing the component properly. Understand, though, that some layout managers, such as **GridLayout**, will ignore those dimensions.

One last point: you can also specify a minimum size and a maximum size by calling **setMinimumSize( )** and **setMaximumSize( )**, also defined by **JComponent**. These are shown here:

void setMaximumSize(Dimension *newSize*)

As with **setPreferredSize( )**, the dimensions set by these methods are simply suggestions that can be ignored by the layout manager.

In addition to label alignment, there is something else new in the program. It uses a **GridLayout** layout manager. **GridLayout** creates a grid of rectangular cells into which individual components are placed. The size of each cell in the grid is the same, and a component put into a cell is sized to fill the dimensions of the cell. This makes **GridLayout** particularly useful for demonstrating the alignment of a label's contents because the size of the label is larger than the text that it contains. This differs from **FlowLayout**, for example, in which (by default) a label is sized to fit its text precisely.

GirdLayout defines three constructors. The one used in the program is shown here:

GridLayout(int *rows*, int *columns*, int *horzGap*, int *vertGap*)

Here, the number of rows and columns in the grid is specified by *rows* and *columns*. The amount of space (in pixels) between rows and columns is specified by *vertGap* and *horzGap*, respectively. If *rows* is zero, then the number of rows is determined by the number of components added to the grid. If *column* is zero, then the number of columns is determined by the number of components added to the grid. Of course, both *rows* and *columns* cannot be zero.

The program creates a 3-by-3 grid with 4 pixels between cells with the following statement:

```
jfrm.getContentPane().setLayout(new GridLayout(3, 3, 4, 4));
```

By default, components are added to the grid beginning with the upper left corner, filling each row from left to right before moving on the next row. (Actually, whether the grid is filled left-to-right or right-to-left depends upon the container's component orientation setting. For Western languages, the orientation is left-to-right.) You might want to try experimenting with other sized grids, such as 2 by 5, and observing the results.

Add a Graphics Image to a Label

In Swing, labels are not limited to just text. You can also display a graphical image or a combination of image and text. Images are especially useful for displaying corporate logos, icons, or photos. Their careful use can give your GUI a distinctive appearance.

To add an image to a label, you will use one of the following **JLabel** constructors:

JLabel(Icon *icon*)

JLabel(Icon *icon*, int *horzAlign*)

The image is passed through *icon*. This object must be an instance of a class that implements the **javax.swing.Icon** interface. (As you will see shortly, the easiest way to obtain such an object is to use the **javax.swing.ImageIcon** class.) By default, the icon is centered in the label. However, you can set the horizontal alignment by using the second form and passing in the desired alignment, as described in the preceding section.

You can specify both a string and an icon that will be displayed within the same label by using this constructor:

JLabel(String *str*, Icon *icon*, int *horzAlign*)

Here, *str* specifies the string and *icon* specifies the image to be displayed. The horizontal alignment of the combination of text and image is passed in *horzAlign*, as described earlier.

When you construct a label that has both a string and an image, by default, the image is displayed on the leading edge of the text. This can be changed by calling one or both of the following methods:

void setVerticalTextPosition(int *loc*)

void setHorizontalTextPosition(int *loc*)

For **setVerticalTextPosition( )**, *loc* must be one of the vertical alignment constants described earlier. For **SetHorizontalTextPosition( )**, *loc* must be one of the horizontal alignment constants described earlier. For example, to put the label's text above its icon, use a statement like this:

```
jlab.setVerticalTextPosition(SwingConstants.TOP);
```

There are many different ways to obtain an image. Perhaps the easiest is to use Swing's **ImageIcon** class, which is part of **javax.swing**. **ImageIcon** implements the **Icon** interface. Thus, an **ImageIcon** object can be passed as an image to the **JLabel** constructor. **ImageIcon** provides several constructors that create an image. The one we will use here is

ImageIcon(string *filename*)

Here, *filename* specifies the name of a file that contains a graphical image. This file must contain an image in one of the formats supported by Java, such as GIF or JPEG.

The following program demonstrates the use of an image-based label. It also shows how the relative position of the text and image can be changed. The output is shown in Figure 2-3.

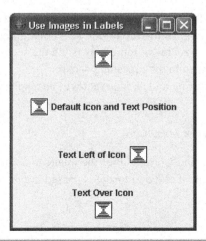

Figure 2-3 The output from the image label demonstration program

```
// Demonstrate labels that use an icon.

import javax.swing.*;
import java.awt.*;
import javax.swing.border.*;

class IconLabelDemo {

  IconLabelDemo() {

    // Create a new JFrame container.
    JFrame jfrm = new JFrame("Use Images in Labels");

    // Specify 4 by 1 GridLayout manager.
    jfrm.getContentPane().setLayout(new GridLayout(4, 1));

    // Give the frame an initial size.
    jfrm.setSize(250, 300);

    // Terminate the program when the user closes the application.
    jfrm.setDefaultCloseOperation(JFrame.EXIT_ON_CLOSE);

    // Load an icon from a file.
    ImageIcon myIcon = new ImageIcon("myIcon.gif");

    // Create an icon-based label.
    JLabel jlabIcon = new JLabel(myIcon);

    // Create an icon- and text-based label.
    JLabel jlabIconTxt = new JLabel("Default Icon and Text Position",
                         myIcon,
                         SwingConstants.CENTER);

    // Create a label with text to left of icon.
    JLabel jlabIconTxt2 = new JLabel("Text Left of Icon", myIcon,
                          SwingConstants.CENTER);
    jlabIconTxt2.setHorizontalTextPosition(SwingConstants.LEFT);

    // Create an icon- and text-based label in which
    // the text is above the icon.
    JLabel jlabIconTxt3 = new JLabel("Text Over Icon", myIcon,
                          SwingConstants.CENTER);
    jlabIconTxt3.setVerticalTextPosition(SwingConstants.TOP);
    jlabIconTxt3.setHorizontalTextPosition(SwingConstants.CENTER);
```

Make an **ImageIcon** from an image stored in a file.

Create an image-based label.

This label has both an image and text.

Put the text to the left of the image.

Put the text above the image.

```
      // Add the labels to the content pane.
      jfrm.getContentPane().add(jlabIcon);
      jfrm.getContentPane().add(jlabIconTxt);
      jfrm.getContentPane().add(jlabIconTxt2);
      jfrm.getContentPane().add(jlabIconTxt3);

      // Display the frame.
      jfrm.setVisible(true);
   }

   public static void main(String args[]) {
      // Create the frame on the event dispatching thread.
      SwingUtilities.invokeLater(new Runnable() {
         public void run() {
            new IconLabelDemo();
         }
      });
   }
}
```

Pay special attention to how the image used by the program is obtained and used to create a label. In the program, the following statement loads an image from a file called **myIcon.gif** and wraps it in an **ImageIcon** called **myIcon**:

```
ImageIcon myIcon = new ImageIcon("myIcon.gif");
```

Next, the following statement uses **myIcon** to create an image-based label:

```
JLabel jlabIcon = new JLabel(myIcon);
```

This instantiates an image-only label in which the image is displayed in its default center position. The program then creates three other labels, which contain both text and image, each having a different text/image alignment. For example, this creates a label in which the text is centered over the image:

```
JLabel jlabIconTxt3 = new JLabel("Text Over Icon", myIcon,
                                  SwingConstants.CENTER);
jlabIconTxt3.setVerticalTextPosition(SwingConstants.TOP);
jlabIconTxt3.setHorizontalTextPosition(SwingConstants.CENTER);
```

Progress Check

1. What does **setHorizontalAlignment( )** do?

2. What layout manager creates a grid?

3. What method controls the vertical position of the text relative to an image in a label?

Disable a Label

Labels are often used to describe other controls, such as text fields or buttons. When the control being described by a label is disabled, it is often a good idea to render the label as disabled, too. Fortunately, this is very easy to do in Swing.

The enabled/disabled state of a label is set by calling the **setEnabled( )** method, which is inherited from **JComponent**. It is shown here:

void setEnabled(boolean *state*)

If *state* is true, the label is enabled. If it is false, the label is disabled.

When a label is disabled, its text is automatically grayed. If the label contains an image, that image is also grayed. However, you can specify a separate image to use when the label is disabled by calling **setDisabledIcon( )**, shown here:

void setDisabledIcon(Icon *icon*)

Here, *icon* is the image shown whenever the label is disabled.

The following program demonstrates disabled labels. To do so, it creates three labels that contain both text and an image. For comparison purposes, the first is not disabled. The second is disabled, but it does not specify a disabled icon, so its default icon is simply grayed. The third is also disabled, but it does specify a disabled icon. The program's output is shown in Figure 2-4.

---

1. It sets the horizontal alignment of the contents of a label within the label's boundaries.
2. **GridLayout**
3. **setVerticalTextPosition( )**

Figure 2-4 The output from the disabled label demonstration program

```
// Demonstrate a disabled label.

import javax.swing.*;
import java.awt.*;
import javax.swing.border.*;

class DisabledLabelDemo {

  DisabledLabelDemo() {

    // Create a new JFrame container.
    JFrame jfrm = new JFrame("Use Images in Labels");

    // Specify 3 by 1 GridLayout manager.
    jfrm.getContentPane().setLayout(new GridLayout(3, 1));

    // Give the frame an initial size.
    jfrm.setSize(240, 250);

    // Terminate the program when the user closes the application.
    jfrm.setDefaultCloseOperation(JFrame.EXIT_ON_CLOSE);

    // Load icons from files.
    ImageIcon myIcon = new ImageIcon("myIcon.gif");
    ImageIcon myDisIcon = new ImageIcon("myDisIcon.gif");

    // Create an icon- and text-based label.
```

Load the icon to be displayed when the label is disabled.

```
        JLabel jlabIconTxt = new JLabel("This label is enabled.",
                                   myIcon,
                                   SwingConstants.CENTER);


        // Create and disable an icon- and text-based label.
        JLabel jlabIconTxt2 = new JLabel("This label is disabled.",
                                   myIcon,
                                   SwingConstants.CENTER);
        jlabIconTxt2.setEnabled(false);
```
                                   ◄─── Disable this label. It will be shown in gray.
```

        // Create and disable an icon- and text-based label.
        // This time, specify a disabled icon.
        JLabel jlabIconTxt3 = new JLabel("Use the disabled icon.",
                                   myIcon,
                                   SwingConstants.CENTER);
        jlabIconTxt3.setDisabledIcon(myDisIcon);
```
                                   ◄──────── Set the disabled icon.
```
        jlabIconTxt3.setEnabled(false);
```
                                   ◄──┐
                                      │ Disable this label. It will be shown
                                        in gray, and the disabled icon will
                                        be displayed.
```

        // Add the labels to the content pane.
        jfrm.getContentPane().add(jlabIconTxt);
        jfrm.getContentPane().add(jlabIconTxt2);
        jfrm.getContentPane().add(jlabIconTxt3);


        // Display the frame.
        jfrm.setVisible(true);
    }

    public static void main(String args[]) {
        // Create the frame on the event dispatching thread.
        SwingUtilities.invokeLater(new Runnable() {
            public void run() {
                new DisabledLabelDemo();
            }
        });
    }
}
```

**CRITICAL SKILL
2.5** # Add a Keyboard Mnemonic to a Label

One common use of labels is to describe the purpose or meaning of another component, such as a text field. For example, a text field that accepts a name might be preceded by a label that displays "Name." In this situation, it is also common for the label to display a keyboard mnemonic that acts as an *accelerator key* (also called a *shortcut key*) that will cause input focus to move to the other component. Thus, for a name field, the mnemonic might be *n*, which stands for *name*. When a mnemonic has been specified, pressing that key in combination with the ALT key causes input focus to move to the text field.

To add a mnemonic to a label involves two steps. First, you must specify the mnemonic character. Second, you must link the component that will receive focus with the label. Fortunately, both steps are very easy to do.

To display a mnemonic within a label, you will use the **setDisplayedMnemonic( )** method defined by **JLabel**:

void setDisplayedMnemonic(int *ch*)

Here, *ch* specifies the character that will be shown as a keyboard accelerator. Typically, this means that the character is underlined. If more than one of the specified characters exists in the label text, then the first occurrence is underlined.

After you have set the mnemonic, you must link the label with the component that will receive focus when the accelerator key is pressed. To do this, use the **setLabelFor( )** method (also defined by **JLabel**):

void setLabelFor(Component *comp*)

Here, *comp* is a reference to the component that will get focus when the mnemonic key is pressed in conjunction with the ALT key.

The following program demonstrates the use of a mnemonic. It creates two text fields, one labeled E-mail Address and the other labeled Name. In the labels describing those fields, the mnemonic for E-mail Address is *e*, and the mnemonic for Name is *n*. When the user presses ALT-N, the Name field receives focus. When the user presses ALT-E, focus is shifted to the E-mail Address field. Sample output is shown in Figure 2-5.

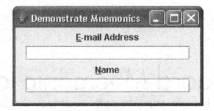

Figure 2-5 Sample output from the mnemonic demonstration program

```
// Demonstrate mnemonics.

import java.awt.*;
import java.awt.event.*;
import javax.swing.*;

class MnemDemo {

  MnemDemo() {

    // Create a new JFrame container.
    JFrame jfrm = new JFrame("Demonstrate Mnemonics");

    // Specify FlowLayout for the layout manager.
    jfrm.getContentPane().setLayout(new FlowLayout());

    // Give the frame an initial size.
    jfrm.setSize(260, 140);

    // Terminate the program when the user closes the application.
    jfrm.setDefaultCloseOperation(JFrame.EXIT_ON_CLOSE);

    // Create two labels.
    JLabel jlab1 = new JLabel("E-mail Address");
    JLabel jlab2 = new JLabel("Name");

    // Assign mnemonics to the labels.
    jlab1.setDisplayedMnemonic('e');
    jlab2.setDisplayedMnemonic('n');
```
    ←— Define the mnemonics.

```
    // Create two text field instances.
    JTextField jtf1 = new JTextField(20);
    JTextField jtf2 = new JTextField(20);

    // Link the labels with the associated components.
    jlab1.setLabelFor(jtf1);
    jlab2.setLabelFor(jtf2);
```
    ←— Set the components associated with the mnemonics.

```
    // Set the action commands for the text fields.
    jtf1.setActionCommand("jtf1");
    jtf2.setActionCommand("jtf2");

    // Add the text fields and labels to the content pane.
    jfrm.getContentPane().add(jlab1);
    jfrm.getContentPane().add(jtf1);
```

```
    jfrm.getContentPane().add(jlab2);
    jfrm.getContentPane().add(jtf2);

    // Display the frame.
    jfrm.setVisible(true);
  }

  public static void main(String args[]) {
    // Create the frame on the event dispatching thread.
    SwingUtilities.invokeLater(new Runnable() {
      public void run() {
        new MnemDemo();
      }
    });
  }
}
```

Get and Set Label Text

As explained in Module 1, you can set the text of a label after it has been created by calling
setText( ), shown here:

void setText(String *str*)

The string that will be displayed within the label is specified by *str*.
    You can obtain the text within a label by calling **getText( )**, shown here:

String getText( )

The text currently displayed by the label is returned.

Using HTML in a Label

Before leaving the topic of labels there is one more feature that needs to be mentioned. You
can use HTML as the label text. To do so, you must begin the text with the sequence **<html>**.
When this is done, the text is automatically formatted as described by the markup. In addition
to other benefits, using HTML enables you to create labels that span two or more lines. For
example, this creates a label that displays two lines of text, with the string "Top" over the
string "Bottom":

```
JLabel jlabhtml = new JLabel("<html>Top<br>Bottom");
```

Ask The Expert

Q: When using a label mnemonic, you state that the first occurrence of the specified letter is underlined. What if the mnemonic is actually associated with the second or third occurrence? For example, if the label is "Enter E-mail Address," how can I have the underline appear beneath the *E* of *E-mail?*

A: You can explicitly specify the index of the mnemonic by using the **setDisplayedMnemonicIndex( )** method, shown here:

void setDisplayedMnemonicIndex(int *idx*) throws IllegalArgumentException

Here, *idx* specifies the index of the character to underline. Thus, given "Enter E-mail Address," to underline the *E* of *E-mail,* you could use a statement like this:

```
jlab.setDisplayedMnemonicIndex(6);
```

Actually, HTML can be used in components other than labels. In general, if a component displays text, then that text can be HTML. In Project 2-1 you will see an example of HTML used in a push button, for example.

Progress Check

1. Because labels simply display information, they cannot be disabled. True or false?

2. When using HTML text inside a label, what character sequence must that text start with?

3. What does **setLabelFor( )** do?

---

1. False
2. **<html>**
3. It associates a label with another field which gets input focus when the label's mnemonic is pressed.

Ask the Expert

Q: I have heard that Swing components are JavaBeans. Is that true?

A: Yes, Swing components are also JavaBeans. If you are unfamiliar with beans and the JavaBeans specification, don't worry because you won't need to know anything about beans in order to use this book. However, if you are familiar with beans then it is useful to know that all Swing components follow the JavaBeans specification and use its naming conventions for properties. Specifically, all read/write properties are supported by *get* and *set* accessor methods. Read-only properties have only a *get* accessor and write-only properties have only a *set* accessor. For example, **JLabel** (and many other components) support the **setText( )** and **getText( )** methods. This means that **JLabel** supports a read/write text property. Beans also support *is* methods, which are read-only **boolean** properties that simply return true or false. For example, the **isEnabled( )** method returns true if the component is enabled. JavaBeans are important to many types of Java programming. If you are unfamiliar with them, it is an area that you will want to learn more about.

CRITICAL SKILL
2.6

Button Fundamentals

Module 1 introduced the button by describing the basics of the **JButton** class. However, **JButton** is just one of several Swing button types. Here is a list of the button classes that Swing provides:

JButton	A standard push button
JToggleButton	A two-state (on/off) button
JCheckBox	A standard check box
JRadioButton	A group of mutually exclusive check boxes

All buttons are subclasses of the **AbstractButton** class, which extends **JComponent**. **AbstractButton** contains many methods that provide basic functionality common to all buttons. For example, **AbstractButton** defines methods that let you set the text within a button, enable or disable the button, specify a mnemonic, and set its alignment. **AbstractButton** also defines the methods that let you set the icon displayed for the button when it is disabled, pressed, selected, or rolled over by the mouse. Of course, **AbstractButton** also defines those methods that add or remove button event listeners. **AbstractButton** defines quite a large number of methods. A sampling is shown in Table 2-2, including those methods used in this module.

NOTE

AbstractButton is also a superclass of **JMenuItem**, but a discussion of menus is deferred until Module 7.

Method	Description
void addActionListener(ActionListener *al*)	Registers a listener for action events.
void addChangeListener(ChangeListener *cl*)	Registers a listener for change events.
void addItemListener(ItemListener *il*)	Registers a listener for item events.
void doClick( )	Presses a button.
String getText( )	Gets the text in the button.
ButtonModule getModel( )	Returns the model for the button.
boolean isSelected( )	Returns true if the button is selected and false otherwise. (Applies only to two-state buttons.)
void setEnabled(boolean *state*)	If *state* is true, the button is enabled. If it is false, the button is disabled.
void setDisabledIcon(Icon *icon*)	Sets the icon shown when the button is disabled to that specified by *icon*.
void setHorizontalAlignment(int *horzAlign*)	Horizontally aligns the contents of the button as specified by *horzAlign*, which must be one of these horizontal alignment constants defined by **SwingConstants**: **CENTER, LEFT, RIGHT, LEADING,** or **TRAILING**.
void setHorizontalTextPosition(int *loc*)	For those buttons containing both text and an image, sets the horizontal position of the text contained within a button relative to the image. The value of *loc* must be one of these constants defined by **SwingConstants**: **CENTER, LEFT, RIGHT, LEADING,** or **TRAILING**.
void setMnemonic(int *ch*)	Sets the mnemonic for the button to that specified by *ch*.
void setPressedIcon(Icon *icon*)	Sets the icon shown when the button is pressed to that specified by *icon*.
void setRolloverIcon(Icon *icon*)	Sets the icon shown when the button is rolled over by the mouse to that specified by *icon*.
void setRolloverSelectedIcon(Icon *icon*)	Sets the icon shown when a selected button is rolled over by the mouse to that specified by *icon*. (Applies only to two-state buttons.)
void setSelected(boolean *state*)	If *state* is true, the button is selected. If *state* is false, the button is deselected. (Applies only to two-state buttons.)

Table 2-2 Several Commonly Used Methods Defined by **AbstractButton**

2

Labels, Buttons, and Borders

Method	Description
void setSelectedIcon(Icon *icon*)	Sets the icon shown when the button is selected to that specified by *icon*. (Applies only to two-state buttons.)
void setText(String *str*)	Sets the text in the button to that specified by *str*.
void setVerticalAlignment(int *vertAlign*)	Vertically aligns the contents of the button as specified by *vertAlign*, which must be one of these vertical alignment constants defined by **SwingConstants**: **CENTER**, **TOP**, or **BOTTOM**.
void setVerticalTextPosition(int *loc*)	For those buttons containing both text and an image, sets the vertical position of the text contained within a button relative to the image. The value of *loc* must be one of these constants defined by **SwingConstants**: **CENTER**, **TOP**, or **BOTTOM**.

Table 2-2 Several Commonly Used Methods Defined by **AbstractButton** *(continued)*

The model used by buttons is defined by the **ButtonModel** interface. The default implementation of this interface is provided in **DefaultButtonModel**. **ButtonModel** defines several properties that are accessed via *get* and *set* methods. In most cases, you won't need to interact with the button model directly. However, it is available to you, if needed, and Project 2-1 shows how to access the button model.

Button events fall into three categories: action events, item events, and change events. An action event is generated when the user performs an action, such as clicking a button. An item event is generated when a button is selected or deselected. A change event is fired when the state of the button changes. Keep in mind that not all three events will necessarily be meaningful to all buttons, or all button applications. For example, a **JButton** does not generate item events. Before looking at the Swing buttons, it is necessary to examine the events that they can generate.

Handling Action Events

An action event is generated when the user clicks a button. As explained in Module 1, an action event is represented by the **ActionEvent** class. Action events are handled by classes that implement the **ActionListener** interface. This interface specifies only one method, **actionPerformed( )**, which is shown here:

void actionPerformed(ActionEvent *ae*)

The action event is received in *ae*.

The **ActionEvent** object passed to **actionPerformed( )** gives you access to several pieces of information. Perhaps most importantly, it enables you to identify what component has generated the event. There are two ways to identify the component: by its action command string (as shown in Module 1) or by its object reference. You can obtain the action comm and string for the component that generated the event by calling **getActionCommand( )** on the **ActionEvent** object. This method is shown here:

String getActionCommand( )

For example, when a button is pressed, an action event is generated that has a command string equal to the text displayed in that button.

The action command is probably the most commonly used way to identify what component generated the action event. However, you can also identify the component by obtaining a reference to it by calling **getSource( )** on the **ActionEvent** object. This method is defined by **EventObject**, the superclass for all event objects. It is shown here:

Object getSource( )

One advantage to using **getSource( )** is that if you need to act directly on the component, you can do so through this reference.

You can find out if the user was pressing any keyboard modifiers (which are the ALT, CTRL, META, and/or SHIFT keys) by calling **getModifiers( )**. It returns an **int** that indicates which modifier keys were pressed when the event was generated. It is shown here:

int getModifiers( )

The value returned will consist of one or more of these values defined by **ActionEvent**: **ALT_MASK, CTRL_MASK, META_MASK,** and **SHIFT_MASK.**

For some applications, the time at which the event was generated may be useful. You can obtain this by calling **getWhen( )**. It returns the time at which the event took place. This is called the event's *timestamp*. The **getWhen( )** method is shown here:

long getWhen( )

Handling Item Events

An item event occurs when an item, such as a check box or radio button, is selected. (This event is not generated by a push button.) Item events are represented by the **ItemEvent** class. Item events are handled by classes that implement the **ItemListener** interface. This interface specifies only one method: **itemStateChanged( )**, which is shown here:

void itemStateChanged(ItemEvent *ie*)

The item event is received in *ie*.

To obtain a reference to the item that changed, call **getItem( )** on the **ItemEvent** object. This method is shown here:

Object getItem( )

The reference returned must be cast to the component class being handled, such as **JCheckBox** or **JRadioButton**.

Calling **getItemSelectable( )** on the **ItemEvent** object obtains an **ItemSelectable** reference to the object that generated an event. Its general form is shown here:

ItemSelectable getItemSelectable( )

ItemSelectable is an interface that is implemented by components that can be selected.

When an item event occurs, the component will be in one of two states: selected or deselected. The **ItemEvent** class defines the following **static int** constants that represent these two states:

SELECTED	DESELECTED

To obtain the new state, call the **getStateChange( )** method defined by **ItemEvent**. It is shown here:

int getStateChange( )

It returns either **ItemEvent.SELECTED** or **ItemEvent.DESELECTED**. You can also determine the selected/deselected state of a button by calling **isSelected( )**, which is defined by **AbstractButton**.

Handling Change Events

A change event occurs when a change takes place to the model of a component. Change events are represented by objects of type **ChangeEvent**. Change events are handled by classes that implement the **ChangeListener** interface. This interface specifies only one method: **stateChanged( )**, which is shown here:

void stateChanged(ChangeEvent *ce*)

The item event is received in *ce*.

To identify the component that generated the **ChangeEvent**, call **getSource( )** on the object passed to **stateChanged( )**. The **getSource( )** method is inherited from **EventObject** as explained earlier.

A Closer Look at JButton

As you know from Module 1, **JButton** implements a standard push button. When the button is pressed, it sends an **ActionEvent** to all registered listeners. It will also send a **ChangeEvent**, but you won't usually need to handle this event because most often your application needs to know only that a button was pressed. Beyond this basic functionality, **JButton** offers a substantial number of options that give you detailed control over the way a push button looks and acts. For example, the button can contain an image; it can be disabled; the horizontal and vertical alignment of its contents can be specified; and icons that appear when it is rolled over by the mouse, selected, or disabled can be specified. Much of this control is inherited from **AbstractButton**. The constructors for **JButton** are shown in Table 2-3.

CRITICAL SKILL
2.7 Add an Image to Push Buttons

The contents of a **JButton** can consist of a string, an image (icon), or both. In addition, different icons can be specified that indicate when the button is rolled-over, disabled, or pressed. In Module 1, only a string-based button was used. Here, you will see how to add an icon to a push button.

To create a push button that contains an icon, you will use one of these **JLabel** constructors:

JButton(Icon *icon*)
JButton(String *str*, Icon *icon*)

Here, *str* and *icon* are the string and icon used for the button. By default, the icon is on the leading edge and the text is on the trailing edge. However, you can change the relative

Constructor	Description
JButton( )	Creates a push button whose contents are empty.
JButton(String *str*)	Creates a push button that displays the string passed in *str*.
JButton(String *str*, Icon *icon*)	Creates a push button that displays the string passed in *str* and the image passed in *icon*.
JButton(Icon *icon*)	Creates a push button that displays the image passed in *icon*.
JButton(Action *act*)	Creates a push button whose text, image, and other properties are defined by the object passed in *act*. Actions are described in Module 7.

Table 2-3 The **JButton** Constructors

positions of image and text. The icon specified in these constructors is the *default icon*. This is the icon that will be used for all purposes if no other icons are specified. An icon can be specified or changed after it has been created by calling **setIcon( )**. The icon can be obtained by calling **getIcon( )**. These methods are defined by **AbstractButton**.

In addition to the default icon specified by the constructor, it is possible to specify icons that are displayed when certain button actions occur. Specifically, you can specify the icon that is displayed when the button is disabled, when it is pressed, and when it is rolled over by the mouse. To set these icons, you will use the following methods:

void setDisabledIcon(Icon *disabledIcon*)
void setPressedIcon(Icon *pressedIcon*)
void setRolloverIcon(Icon *rolloverIcon*)

Once the specified icon has been set, it will be displayed whenever one of the events occurs. Keep in mind, however, that the rollover icon may not be supported by all look-and-feels. You can determine if the rollover icon is enabled by calling **isRolloverEnabled( )**. You can explicitly set the rollover-enabled property by calling **setRolloverEnabled(true)**.

To disable or enable a push button, use the **setEnabled( )** method, shown here:

void setEnabled(boolean *state*)

If *state* is false, the button is disabled. If *state* is true, the button is enabled. When the button is disabled, the button will be displayed in gray. If a disabled icon has been specified, it will be displayed. Otherwise, the default icon is displayed in gray.

You can determine the enabled/disabled status of a button by calling **isEnabled( )**, shown here:

boolean isEnabled( )

This method is inherited from **Component**. It returns true if the button is enabled and false otherwise.

Although they require a bit more work, the addition of the default, rollover, disabled, and pressed icons add visual appeal to your interface. (Of course, adding these icons will also increase download time.) The following program demonstrates their value. It creates two push buttons and assigns icons to each. When you try the program, you will notice that the rollover icon is displayed when the mouse passes over a button. The pressed icon will be displayed when the button is pressed. Each time you press the First button, the Second button toggles between enabled and disabled. When the button is disabled, the disabled icon is displayed. When either button is pressed, the pressed icon is displayed. Sample output is shown in Figure 2-6.

Figure 2-6 Output from the **ButtonIcons** program

```java
// Add icons to a button.

import java.awt.*;
import java.awt.event.*;
import javax.swing.*;

class ButtonIcons implements ActionListener {

  JLabel jlab;
  JButton jbtnFirst;
  JButton jbtnSecond;

  ButtonIcons() {
    ImageIcon myIcon = new ImageIcon("myIcon.gif");
    ImageIcon myDisIcon = new ImageIcon("myDisIcon.gif");
    ImageIcon myROIcon = new ImageIcon("myROIcon.gif");
    ImageIcon myPIcon = new ImageIcon("myPIcon.gif");

    // Create a new JFrame container.
    JFrame jfrm = new JFrame("Use Button Icons");

    // Specify FlowLayout for the layout manager.
    jfrm.getContentPane().setLayout(new FlowLayout());

    // Give the frame an initial size.
    jfrm.setSize(220, 100);

    // Terminate the program when the user closes the application.
    jfrm.setDefaultCloseOperation(JFrame.EXIT_ON_CLOSE);

    // Create a text-based label.
    jlab = new JLabel("Press a button.");

    // Make two buttons.
    jbtnFirst = new JButton("First", myIcon);
    jbtnSecond = new JButton("Second", myIcon);
```

Load all of the icons that are used by a **JButton**.

Set the default icon.

```
    // Set rollover icons.
    jbtnFirst.setRolloverIcon(myROIcon);
    jbtnSecond.setRolloverIcon(myROIcon);

    // Set pressed icons.
    jbtnFirst.setPressedIcon(myPIcon);
    jbtnSecond.setPressedIcon(myPIcon);

    // Set disabled icons.
    jbtnFirst.setDisabledIcon(myDisIcon);
    jbtnSecond.setDisabledIcon(myDisIcon);

    // Add action listeners.
    jbtnFirst.addActionListener(this);
    jbtnSecond.addActionListener(this);

    // Add the buttons to the content pane.
    jfrm.getContentPane().add(jbtnFirst);
    jfrm.getContentPane().add(jbtnSecond);

    // Add the label to the frame.
    jfrm.getContentPane().add(jlab);

    // Display the frame.
    jfrm.setVisible(true);
  }

  // Handle button events.
  public void actionPerformed(ActionEvent ae) {

    if(ae.getActionCommand().equals("First")) {
      jlab.setText("First button was pressed.");
      if(jbtnSecond.isEnabled()) {
        jlab.setText("Second button is disabled.");
        jbtnSecond.setEnabled(false);
      }
      else {
        jlab.setText("Second button is enabled.");
        jbtnSecond.setEnabled(true);
      }
    } else
      jlab.setText("Second button was pressed. ");
  }

  public static void main(String args[]) {
```

— Set the remaining icons.

```
   // Create the frame on the event dispatching thread.
   SwingUtilities.invokeLater(new Runnable() {
     public void run() {
       new ButtonIcons();
     }
   });
  }
}
```

In the program, four icons are created: **myIcon** (default), **myDisIcon** (disabled), **myROIcon** (rollover), and **myPIcon** (pressed). These icons are then linked with the buttons **jbtnFirst** and **jbtnSecond**. Thus, each button has all relevant icons specified. Next, **this** is registered as an action listener for button events, and the buttons are added to the content pane.

Notice that **ButtonIcons** implements the **ActionListener** interface. As explained, the **ActionListener** interface defines only one method: **actionPerformed( )**, and this method is implemented by **ButtonIcons**. Implementing **ActionListener** allows **ButtonIcons** objects to receive action event notifications. This is why **addActionListener( )** can use **this** as an argument.

The **actionPerformed( )** method handles action events for both buttons. Each time the First button is pressed, it toggles the state of the Second button between enabled and disabled. Notice how this is accomplished through the use of these lines of code:

```
if(ae.getActionCommand().equals("First")) {
  jlab.setText("First button was pressed.");
  if(jbtnSecond.isEnabled()) {
    jlab.setText("Second button is disabled.");
    jbtnSecond.setEnabled(false);
  }
  else {
    jlab.setText("Second button is enabled.");
    jbtnSecond.setEnabled(true);
  }
}
```

The action command is obtained, and it is tested against "First," which is the action command of the First button. (Recall that, by default, the action command string for a button is its text.) If this comparison is true, then the status of **jbtnSecond** is obtained by calling **isEnabled( )** on it. If it returns true, the Second button is currently enabled, and it is set to disabled by calling **setEnabled(false)** on **jbtnSecond**. Otherwise, the button is currently disabled, and it is enabled by calling **jbtnSecond.setEnabled(true)**.

Define a Default Button

When using push buttons, it is often useful for one of them to be chosen as the *default button*. This button will be "pressed" when the user presses ENTER on the keyboard. To create a default button, you must call **setDefaultButton( )** on the **JRootPane** object that holds the button. This method is shown here:

void setDefaultButton(JButton *button*)

Here, *button* is the push button that will be selected as the default button.

As mentioned, **setDefaultButton( )** must be called on the root pane of the container. Therefore, in the preceding example, to set **jbtnFirst** as the default button, you will use this statement:

```
jfrm.getRootPane().setDefaultButton(jbtnFirst);
```

This statement can be inserted immediately before the call to **setVisible( )**. After the default button has been specified, pressing ENTER causes that button to fire an **ActionEvent**.

JButton Options

JButton affords the GUI designer several options. For example, you can use HTML for the text in the button in much the same way that it is used in labels. One reason to use HTML is to allow a button to display two or more lines of text. For example, the following constructor creates a **JButton** that displays the word "Press" over the word "Me."

```
JButton jbtn = new JButton("<html>Press<br>Me");
```

You can add a mnemonic to the text displayed within a button. When this key is pressed in conjunction with the ALT key, the button will be pressed. For example, using **jbtn** from the preceding example, to set the keyboard mnemonic to *p*, use this statement:

```
jtbn.setMnemonic('p');
```

Now, you can activate the button by pressing ALT-P.

When using both text and an icon inside a button, you can specify the position of the text relative to an icon by calling **setVerticalTextPosition( )** or **setHorizontalTextPosition( )**.

Progress Check

1. What is **AbstractButton**?

2. What method sets a button's rollover icon?

3. What is a default button?

CRITICAL SKILL
2.9

Use Anonymous Inner Class to Handle Events

Before moving on to check boxes and radio buttons, a small but important digression is needed that describes another way to handle events generated by Swing components. In the preceding program, and in those shown in Module 1, events were handled by a top-level class (that is, a class with package scope) that implemented the **ActionListener** interface. This is a perfectly acceptable technique. However, for some applications, there is another approach that you might find easier. You can use an anonymous inner class to create the event handler. This handler is then passed to the **addActionListener( )** method. For example, using an anonymous inner class, the event handler for the First button in the preceding example can be coded as shown here:

```
jbtnFirst.addActionListener(new ActionListener() {
  public void actionPerformed(ActionEvent ae) {
    if(jbtnSecond.isEnabled()) {
      jlab.setText("Second button is disabled.");
      jbtnSecond.setEnabled(false);
    }
    else {
      jlab.setText("Second button is enabled.");
      jbtnSecond.setEnabled(true);
    }
  }
});
```

---

1. **AbstractButton** is the superclass of all Swing buttons.

2. **setRolloverIcon( )**

3. The default button is the button that is pushed when the user presses the ENTER key on the keyboard.

If you are not familiar with the syntax for anonymous inner classes, then the preceding might seem a bit confusing. Here is how it works. The argument to **addActionListener( )** is a new object of an unnamed class that implements the **ActionListener** interface. Because **ActionListener** defines only one method, that is the only method that the inner class must implement. This instance then becomes the listener for action events that are generated by **jbtnFirst**, and only those action events. It does not receive action events from any other sources. Here is the preceding program reworked for anonymous inner-class event handlers. Notice that **ButtonIcons** no longer implements the **ActionListener** interface. Instead, event handlers based on anonymous inner classes are used. This makes the program a bit shorter and puts the event handler code with the **addActionListener( )** method, which can make it a bit easier to manage. The program works exactly as it did before. The only change is the way that the event handlers are coded.

```
// Use anonymous inner classes as event handlers.

import java.awt.*;
import java.awt.event.*;
import javax.swing.*;

class ButtonIcons {

  JLabel jlab;
  JButton jbtnFirst;
  JButton jbtnSecond;

  ButtonIcons() {
    ImageIcon myIcon = new ImageIcon("myIcon.gif");
    ImageIcon myDisIcon = new ImageIcon("myDisIcon.gif");
    ImageIcon myROIcon = new ImageIcon("myROIcon.gif");
    ImageIcon myPIcon = new ImageIcon("myPIcon.gif");

    // Create a new JFrame container.
    JFrame jfrm = new JFrame("Use Button Icons");

    // Specify FlowLayout for the layout manager.
    jfrm.getContentPane().setLayout(new FlowLayout());

    // Give the frame an initial size.
    jfrm.setSize(220, 100);

    // Terminate the program when the user closes the application.
    jfrm.setDefaultCloseOperation(JFrame.EXIT_ON_CLOSE);

    // Create a text-based label.
```

```java
jlab = new JLabel("Press a button.");

// Make two buttons.
jbtnFirst = new JButton("First", myIcon);
jbtnSecond = new JButton("Second", myIcon);

// Set rollover icons.
jbtnFirst.setRolloverIcon(myROIcon);
jbtnSecond.setRolloverIcon(myROIcon);

// Set pressed icons.
jbtnFirst.setPressedIcon(myPIcon);
jbtnSecond.setPressedIcon(myPIcon);

// Set disabled icons.
jbtnFirst.setDisabledIcon(myDisIcon);
jbtnSecond.setDisabledIcon(myDisIcon);

// Add action listeners.
// Notice that these listeners are implemented
// by using anonymous inner classes.
jbtnFirst.addActionListener(new ActionListener() {
  public void actionPerformed(ActionEvent ae) {
    if(jbtnSecond.isEnabled()) {
      jlab.setText("Second button is disabled.");
      jbtnSecond.setEnabled(false);
    }
    else {
      jlab.setText("Second button is enabled.");
      jbtnSecond.setEnabled(true);
    }
  }
});

jbtnSecond.addActionListener(new ActionListener() {
  public void actionPerformed(ActionEvent ae) {
    jlab.setText("Second button was pressed.");
  }
});

// Add the buttons to the content pane.
jfrm.getContentPane().add(jbtnFirst);
jfrm.getContentPane().add(jbtnSecond);

// Add the label to the frame.
jfrm.getContentPane().add(jlab);
```

Handle events by using anonymous inner classes.

```
    // Display the frame.
    jfrm.setVisible(true);
  }

  public static void main(String args[]) {
    // Create the frame on the event dispatching thread.
    SwingUtilities.invokeLater(new Runnable() {
      public void run() {
        new ButtonIcons();
      }
    });
  }
}
```

In commercial applications, both top-level classes and anonymous inner classes are used for event handling. In some cases, it makes more sense for a top-level class to implement the listener interface because it can prevent code duplication when two or more components share the same code. This approach can also be more efficient because it does not require that separate classes be created. Alternatively, using anonymous inner classes to handle events offers a great deal of convenience and can streamline your source code. However, these handlers cannot be shared, and each implicitly creates a class, which adds overhead. In general, what works best is determined by your application. There is no one hard and fast rule.

Project 2-1 Explore JButton Change Events and ButtonModel

ChangeDemo.java

This project illustrates two important features that relate to **JButton**: change events and **ButtonModel**. As explained earlier, a **JButton** generates two types of events: action and change. Usually, your code relies on action events to know when a button has been pressed. However, you can also monitor change events. These occur when the model underlying a button changes. Handling change events lets your program take actions at various points within the rollover/press/release cycle. For example, you might want to play an audible tone when the user rolls over a button, a different tone when the button is pressed, and a final tone when the button is released.

The button model for **JButton** is defined by the **ButtonModel** interface. Among other things, **ButtonModel** defines five properties that describe the state of a button: enabled, rolled over, armed, pressed, and selected. Of these, only the first four apply to **JButton**. (The selected property pertains specifically to two-state buttons.) These properties are made available by the following methods defined by **ButtonModel**:

boolean isArmed( )	If true, the button has been pressed but not released.
boolean isEnabled( )	If true, the button is available for use.
boolean isPressed( )	If true, the button is pressed.
boolean isRollover( )	If true, the mouse is positioned over the button.
boolean isSelected( )	If true, the button is selected. (Applies only to two-state buttons.)

Using these methods, you can obtain the current state of a button whenever its model changes.

To gain access to the model information for a button, you must first obtain a reference to the button's model by calling **getModel( )**. It is shown here:

ButtonModel getModel( )

Once you have a reference to the model, you can call the aforementioned methods on that model to obtain the current state.

In this project, you will create a program that contains one push button and a change listener for that button. Each time a change event occurs, the current state of the button is displayed.

Step by Step

1. Create a file called **ChangeDemo.java** and then enter the following comment and **import** statements:

```
// Demonstrate a change listener and the button model.

import java.awt.*;
import java.awt.event.*;
import javax.swing.*;
import javax.swing.event.*;
```

2. Begin the **ChangeDemo** class, as shown here:

```
class ChangeDemo {

  JButton jbtn;
  JLabel jlab;
  ChangeDemo() {

    // Create a new JFrame container.
    JFrame jfrm = new JFrame("Button Change Events");

    // Specify FlowLayout for the layout manager.
    jfrm.getContentPane().setLayout(new FlowLayout());
```

(continued)

```
// Give the frame an initial size.
jfrm.setSize(250, 160);

// Terminate the program when the user closes the application.
jfrm.setDefaultCloseOperation(JFrame.EXIT_ON_CLOSE);

// Create an empty label.
jlab = new JLabel();

// Make a button.
jbtn = new JButton("Press for Change Event Test");
```

The preceding code should be familiar territory to you now. It simply sets up a frame and creates a label and a push button.

3. Add this change listener that will respond to change events by displaying the current state of the button:

```
// Add change listener.
jbtn.addChangeListener(new ChangeListener() {
  public void stateChanged(ChangeEvent ce) {
    ButtonModel mod = jbtn.getModel();
    String what = "";

    if(mod.isEnabled()) what += "Enabled<br>";
    if(mod.isRollover()) what += "Rollover<br>";
    if(mod.isArmed()) what += "Armed<br>";
    if(mod.isPressed()) what += "Pressed<br>";

    // Notice that this label's text is HTML.
    jlab.setText("<html>Current state:<br>" + what);
  }
});
```

This listener uses an anonymous inner class to handle change events. Each time it receives an event, it obtains the button model for **jbtn**. Then, based on the results of interrogating the button state, it builds a string that contains those button properties that are true. Finally, it displays those properties in **jlab**. Notice that HTML is used. This makes it easy to present the properties in a list.

4. End **ChangeDemo** with the following lines:

```
// Add the components to the content pane.
jfrm.getContentPane().add(jbtn);
jfrm.getContentPane().add(jlab);

// Display the frame.
jfrm.setVisible(true);
}
```

5. Finally, conclude the program with **main( )**, as shown here:

```
public static void main(String args[]) {
  // Create the frame on the event dispatching thread.
  SwingUtilities.invokeLater(new Runnable() {
    public void run() {
      new ChangeDemo();
    }
  });
}
```

6. When you run the program, you will see the state of the button change when the mouse rolls over it, when it is pressed, and when it is released. Sample output is shown here:

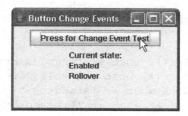

7. The entire program is shown here:

```
// Demonstrate a change listener and the button model.

import java.awt.*;
import java.awt.event.*;
import javax.swing.*;
import javax.swing.event.*;

class ChangeDemo {

  JButton jbtn;
  JLabel jlab;

  ChangeDemo() {

    // Create a new JFrame container.
    JFrame jfrm = new JFrame("Button Change Events");

    // Specify FlowLayout for the layout manager.
    jfrm.getContentPane().setLayout(new FlowLayout());
```

(continued)

```java
    // Give the frame an initial size.
    jfrm.setSize(250, 160);

    // Terminate the program when the user closes the application.
    jfrm.setDefaultCloseOperation(JFrame.EXIT_ON_CLOSE);

    // Create an empty label.
    jlab = new JLabel();

    // Make a button.
    jbtn = new JButton("Press for Change Event Test");

    // Add change listener.
    jbtn.addChangeListener(new ChangeListener() {
      public void stateChanged(ChangeEvent ce) {
        ButtonModel mod = jbtn.getModel();
        String what = "";

        if(mod.isEnabled()) what += "Enabled<br>";
        if(mod.isRollover()) what += "Rollover<br>";
        if(mod.isArmed()) what += "Armed<br>";
        if(mod.isPressed()) what += "Pressed<br>";

        // Notice that this label's text is HTML.
        jlab.setText("<html>Current state:<br>" + what);
      }
    });

    // Add the components to the content pane.
    jfrm.getContentPane().add(jbtn);
    jfrm.getContentPane().add(jlab);

    // Display the frame.
    jfrm.setVisible(true);
  }


  public static void main(String args[]) {
    // Create the frame on the event dispatching thread.
    SwingUtilities.invokeLater(new Runnable() {
      public void run() {
        new ChangeDemo();
      }
    });
  }
}
```

CRITICAL SKILL
2.10 Using JToggleButton

Swing includes a very useful variation on the push button called a *toggle button*. A toggle button looks just like a push button, but it acts differently because it has two states: pushed and released. That is, when you press a toggle button, it stays pressed rather than popping back up as a regular push button does. When you press the toggle button a second time, it releases (pops up). Therefore, each time a toggle button is pushed, it toggles between its two states.

Toggle buttons are objects of the **JToggleButton** class. **JToggleButton** implements **AbstractButton** and defines the constructors shown in Table 2-4. In addition to creating

Constructor	Description
JToggleButton( )	Creates a toggle button that has neither a text nor an image associated with it.
JToggleButton(String *str*)	Creates a toggle button that contains the text passed in *str*.
JToggleButton(Icon *icon*)	Creates a toggle button that contains the image passed in *icon*.
JToggleButton(String *str*, boolean *state*)	Creates a toggle button that contains the text passed in *str*. If *state* is true, the button is initially pressed (selected). Otherwise, it is released (deselected).
JToggleButton(Icon *icon*, boolean *state*)	Creates a toggle button that contains the image passed in *icon*. If *state* is true, the button is initially pressed (selected). Otherwise, it is released (deselected).
JToggleButton(String *str*, Icon *icon*)	Creates a toggle button that contains the text passed in *str* and the image passed in *icon*.
JToggleButton(String *str*, Icon *icon*, boolean *state*)	Creates a toggle button that contains the text passed in *str* and the image passed in *icon*. If *state* is true, the button is initially pressed (selected). Otherwise, it is released (deselected).
JToggleButton(Action *act*)	Creates a toggle button whose text, image, and other properties are defined by the object passed in *act*. Actions are in Module 7.

Table 2-4 The **JToggleButton** Constructors

standard toggle buttons, **JToggleButton** is a superclass for two other Swing components that also represent two-state controls. These are **JCheckBox** and **JRadioButton**, which are described later in this module. Thus, **JToggleButton** defines the basic functionality of all two-state components.

JToggleButton uses a different model than **JButton**. The model used by **JToggleButton** is defined by a nested class called **JToggleButton.ToggleButtonModel**. Normally, you won't need to interact directly with the model to use a standard toggle button.

Like **JButton**, **JToggleButton** generates an action event and a change event each time it is pressed. Unlike **JButton**, however, **JToggleButton** also generates an item event. This event is used by those components that support the concept of selection. When a **JToggleButton** is pressed in, it is selected. When it is popped out, it is deselected.

To handle item events, you must implement the **ItemListener** interface. Each time an item event is generated, it is passed to the **itemStateChanged( )** method defined by **ItemListener**. Inside **itemStateChanged( )**, the **getItem( )** method can be used to obtain a reference to the **JToggleButton** object that generated the event. Next, you can call **getStateChange( )** to determine if the button was pressed in or popped out. If the button was pressed in, **ItemEvent.SELECTED** is returned. Otherwise, **ItemEvent.DESELECTED** is returned. Alternatively, you can call the **isSelected( )** method (inherited from **AbstractButton**) on the button that generated the event to determine its status.

Here is an example that uses a toggle button. Sample output is shown in Figure 2-7. Notice how the item listener works. It simply calls **isSelected( )** to determine the button's state.

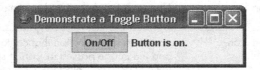

Figure 2-7 Sample output from the toggle button example

```
// Demonstrate a toggle button.

import java.awt.*;
import java.awt.event.*;
import javax.swing.*;

class ToggleDemo {

  JLabel jlab;
  JToggleButton jtbn;

  ToggleDemo() {
    // Create a new JFrame container.
    JFrame jfrm = new JFrame("Demonstrate a Toggle Button");

    // Specify a flow layout.
    jfrm.getContentPane().setLayout(new FlowLayout());

    // Give the frame an initial size.
    jfrm.setSize(290, 80);

    // Terminate the program when the user closes the application.
    jfrm.setDefaultCloseOperation(JFrame.EXIT_ON_CLOSE);

    // Create a label.
    jlab = new JLabel("Button is off.");

    // Make a toggle button.
    jtbn =  new JToggleButton("On/Off");          ◀───── Create a toggle button.

    // Add item listener for jtbn by using
    // an anonymous inner class.
    jtbn.addItemListener(new ItemListener() {     ◀───── Use an ItemListener to handle
      public void itemStateChanged(ItemEvent ie) {          toggle button events.
        if(jtbn.isSelected()) ◀─────────────┐
          jlab.setText("Button is on.");     │
        else                                 Use isSelected() to determine
          jlab.setText("Button is off.");    which state the button is in.
      }

    });
```

```
      // Add toggle button and label to the content pane.
      jfrm.getContentPane().add(jtbn);
      jfrm.getContentPane().add(jlab);

      // Display the frame.
      jfrm.setVisible(true);
   }

   public static void main(String args[]) {
      // Create the frame on the event dispatching thread.
      SwingUtilities.invokeLater(new Runnable() {
        public void run() {
          new ToggleDemo();
        }
      });
   }
}
```

Use getItem( ) to Determine the Source of an Item Event

The preceding example handled the item event generated when the button was toggled by using an anonymous inner class. This meant that the handler received events only for that specific button, and there was no need to further identify the button that generated the event because it was already known. However, in cases in which two or more components share the same **ItemEvent** handler, your handler will need to identify which component generated the event. The easiest way to do this is by calling **getItem( )** on the **ItemEvent** object passed to the **itemStateChanged( )** method. The **getItem( )** method obtains a reference to the component that generated the event. You can then compare this reference to the components defined by your program.

The following program demonstrates using **getItem( )**. It creates a class called **TwoTBDemo** that implements the **ItemListener** interface. It then creates two toggle buttons called **jtbnAlpha** and **jtbnBeta**. The item events generated by these buttons are both handled by the same **itemStateChanged( )** method. Output is shown in Figure 2-8.

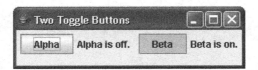

Figure 2-8 The output from the **TwoTBDemo** program

```java
// Use two toggle buttons.

import java.awt.*;
import java.awt.event.*;
import javax.swing.*;

class TwoTBDemo implements ItemListener {

  JLabel jlabAlpha;
  JLabel jlabBeta;
  JToggleButton jtbnAlpha;
  JToggleButton jtbnBeta;

  TwoTBDemo() {
    // Create a new JFrame container.
    JFrame jfrm = new JFrame("Two Toggle Buttons");

    // Specify a flow layout.
    jfrm.getContentPane().setLayout(new FlowLayout());

    // Give the frame an initial size.
    jfrm.setSize(290, 80);

    // Terminate the program when the user closes the application.
    jfrm.setDefaultCloseOperation(JFrame.EXIT_ON_CLOSE);

    // Create two labels.
    jlabAlpha = new JLabel("Alpha is off.  ");
    jlabBeta = new JLabel("Beta is off.");

    // Make two toggle buttons.
    jtbnAlpha =  new JToggleButton("Alpha");
    jtbnBeta =  new JToggleButton("Beta");

    // Add item listener for buttons.
    jtbnAlpha.addItemListener(this);
    jtbnBeta.addItemListener(this);

    // Add toggle buttons and labels to the content pane.
    jfrm.getContentPane().add(jtbnAlpha);
    jfrm.getContentPane().add(jlabAlpha);
    jfrm.getContentPane().add(jtbnBeta);
    jfrm.getContentPane().add(jlabBeta);
```

Create two toggle buttons.

```
   // Display the frame.
   jfrm.setVisible(true);
}

// Handle item events for both buttons.
public void itemStateChanged(ItemEvent ie) {

   // Get a reference to the button.
   JToggleButton tb = (JToggleButton) ie.getItem();

   // Determine which button was toggled.
   if(tb == jtbnAlpha)
     if(tb.isSelected())
       jlabAlpha.setText("Alpha is on.   ");
     else
       jlabAlpha.setText("Alpha is off.   ");

   else if(tb == jtbnBeta)
     if(tb.isSelected())
       jlabBeta.setText("Beta is on.");
     else
       jlabBeta.setText("Beta is off.");
}

public static void main(String args[]) {
   // Create the frame on the event dispatching thread.
   SwingUtilities.invokeLater(new Runnable() {
     public void run() {
       new TwoTBDemo();
     }
   });
}
}
```

Obtain a reference to the button that fired the event.

Use that reference to determine which button was changed.

Inside **itemStateChanged( )**, notice how **getItem( )** is used to obtain a reference to the item that generated the event:

```
JToggleButton tb = (JToggleButton) ie.getItem();
```

This reference is then tested against the button references **jtbnAlpha** and **jtbnBeta** to determine which button caused the event. This same general procedure can be used to determine the source of any item event.

JToggleButton Options

JToggleButton can be configured and customized in much the same way as **JButton**. For example, you can specify icons that indicate the pressed and unpressed states. You can also specify a rollover icon. To add the default icon, you will use this form of the **JToggleButton** constructor:

JToggleButton(String *str*, Icon *icon*)

It creates a toggle button that contains the text passed in *str* and the image passed in *icon*. To add the other icons, use these methods: **setDisabledIcon( )**, **setPressedIcon( )**, **setRolloverIcon( )**, **setRolloverSelectedIcon( )**, and **setSelectedIcon( )**. Keep in mind that you must supply a default icon in order for the other icons to be used. You can specify the position of the text relative to an icon by calling **setVerticalTextPosition( )** or **setHorizontalTextPosition( )**.

You can add a mnemonic to the text displayed within the button. When this key is pressed in conjunction with the ALT key, the button will change states. For example, in the preceding example, to set the keyboard mnemonic for **jtbnAlpha** to *A*, add the following line:

```
jtbnAlpha.setMnemonic('a');
```

Now, you can toggle the button by pressing ALT-A.

You can disable/enable a **JToggleButton** in the same way that you disable a **JButton**: by calling **setEnabled( )**.

Progress Check

1. What is a two-state button?

2. What method determines if a **JToggleButton** is pressed or released?

3. What listener interface is typically implemented to manage **JToggleButton** events?

---

1. A two-state button has two states: pressed (selected) or released (deselected).
2. **getStateChange( )** or **isSelected( )**
3. **ItemListener**

CRITICAL SKILL

2.11 Create Check Boxes with JCheckbox

After the push button, perhaps the next most widely used control is the check box. In Swing, a check box is an object of type **JCheckBox**. **JCheckBox** inherits **AbstractButton** and **JToggleButton**. Thus, the same techniques that you used to manage a toggle button apply to a check box.

JCheckBox supports the constructors shown in Table 2-5.

Like all two-state buttons, a check box can have its state changed in two ways. First, through user interaction. Second, under program control. To change the state of a check box (or any two-state button) programmatically, use **setSelected( )**, shown here:

void setSelected(boolean *state*)

If *state* is true, the check box will be checked. If *state* is false, the check box will be cleared.

When a check box is selected or deselected, an item event is generated. This is handled by **itemStateChanged( )**. Inside **itemStateChanged( )**, the **getItem( )** method can be used to obtain a reference to the **JCheckBox** object that generated the event. Next, you can call **getStateChange( )** to determine if the box was selected or cleared. If the box was selected, **ItemEvent.SELECTED** is returned. Otherwise, **ItemEvent.DESELECTED** is returned. Alternatively, you can call **isSelected( )** (inherited by **AbstractButton**) on the check box that generated the event.

Check boxes generate an item event whenever the state of a check box changes. Check boxes also generate action events when a selection changes, but it is easier to use an **ItemListener** because it gives you direct access to the **getStateChange( )** method.

The following program demonstrates check boxes. It creates a window that contains four check boxes. Only the first, which is labeled Enable Options, is initially enabled. The three remaining boxes, which display various options, are disabled. When the Enable Options box is checked, the Options check boxes are enabled. Each time an Options check box is changed, the current action is displayed. Also, the list of currently selected options is updated. Sample output is shown in Figure 2-9.

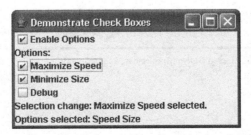

Figure 2-9 Sample output from the check box program

Constructor	Description
JCheckBox( )	Creates a check box that has neither a text nor an image associated with it.
JCheckBox(String *str*)	Creates a check box that is associated with the text specified by *str*.
JCheckBox(Icon *icon*)	Creates a check box that is associated with the image passed in *icon*.
JCheckBox(String *str*, boolean *state*)	Creates a check box that is associated with the text passed in *str*. If *state* is true, the box is initially checked. Otherwise, it is cleared.
JCheckBox(Icon *icon*, boolean *state*)	Creates a check box that is associated with the image passed in *icon*. If *state* is true, the box is initially checked. Otherwise, it is cleared.
JCheckBox(String *str*, Icon *icon*)	Creates a check box that is associated with the text passed in *str* and the image passed in *icon*.
JCheckBox(String *str*, Icon *icon*, boolean *state*)	Creates a check box that is associated with the text passed in *str* and the image passed in *icon*. If *state* is true, the box is initially checked. Otherwise, it is cleared.
JCheckBox(Action *act*)	Creates a check box whose text, image, and other properties are defined by the object passed in *act*. Actions are described later in this book.

Table 2-5 The **JCheckBox** Constructors

```
// Demonstrate check boxes.

import java.awt.*;
import java.awt.event.*;
import javax.swing.*;

class CBDemo implements ItemListener {

  JLabel jlabOptions;
  JLabel jlabWhat;
  JLabel jlabChange;
  JCheckBox jcbOptions;
  JCheckBox jcbSpeed;
  JCheckBox jcbSize;
  JCheckBox jcbDebug;

  CBDemo() {
```

```
// Create a new JFrame container.
JFrame jfrm = new JFrame("Demonstrate Check Boxes");

// Specify a 1 column, 7 row grid layout.
jfrm.getContentPane().setLayout(new GridLayout(7, 1));

// Give the frame an initial size.
jfrm.setSize(300, 150);

// Terminate the program when the user closes the application.
jfrm.setDefaultCloseOperation(JFrame.EXIT_ON_CLOSE);

// Create two labels.
jlabOptions = new JLabel("Options:");
jlabChange = new JLabel("");
jlabWhat = new JLabel("Options selected:");

// Make check boxes.
jcbOptions = new JCheckBox("Enable Options");
jcbSpeed = new JCheckBox("Maximize Speed");
jcbSize = new JCheckBox("Minimize Size");
jcbDebug = new JCheckBox("Debug");

// Initially disable option check boxes.
jcbSpeed.setEnabled(false);
jcbSize.setEnabled(false);
jcbDebug.setEnabled(false);

// Add item listener for jcbOptions.
jcbOptions.addItemListener(new ItemListener() {
  public void itemStateChanged(ItemEvent ie) {
    if(jcbOptions.isSelected()) {
      jcbSpeed.setEnabled(true);
      jcbSize.setEnabled(true);
      jcbDebug.setEnabled(true);
    }
    else {
      jcbSpeed.setEnabled(false);
      jcbSize.setEnabled(false);
      jcbDebug.setEnabled(false);
    }
  }
});

// Events generated by the Options check boxes
// are handled in common by the itemStateChanged( )
```

Create four check boxes.

Disable all option check boxes.

Toggle option check boxes between enabled and disabled status each time an Options check box fires an item event.

```
    // method implemented by CBDemo.
    jcbSpeed.addItemListener(this);
    jcbSize.addItemListener(this);
    jcbDebug.addItemListener(this);

    // Add check boxes and labels to the content pane.
    jfrm.getContentPane().add(jcbOptions);
    jfrm.getContentPane().add(jlabOptions);

    jfrm.getContentPane().add(jcbSpeed);
    jfrm.getContentPane().add(jcbSize);
    jfrm.getContentPane().add(jcbDebug);
    jfrm.getContentPane().add(jlabChange);
    jfrm.getContentPane().add(jlabWhat);

    // Display the frame.
    jfrm.setVisible(true);
  }

  // This is the handler for all of the Options check boxes.
  public void itemStateChanged(ItemEvent ie) {
    String opts = "";

    // Obtain a reference to the check box that
    // caused the event.
    JCheckBox cb = (JCheckBox) ie.getItem();

    // Tell the user what they did.
    if(ie.getStateChange() == ItemEvent.SELECTED)
      jlabChange.setText("Selection change: " +
                         cb.getText() + " selected.");
    else
      jlabChange.setText("Selection change: " +
                         cb.getText() + " cleared.");

    // Build a string that contains all selected options.
    if(jcbSpeed.isSelected()) opts += "Speed ";
    if(jcbSize.isSelected()) opts += "Size ";
    if(jcbDebug.isSelected()) opts += "Debug ";

    // Display the currently selected options.
    jlabWhat.setText("Options selected: " + opts);
  }


  public static void main(String args[]) {
```

Use **getStateChange( )** to determine if the box was selected or deselected.

```
// Create the frame on the event dispatching thread.
SwingUtilities.invokeLater(new Runnable() {
  public void run() {
    new CBDemo();
  }
});
  }
}
```

There are several things of interest to notice about this program. First, the handler for **jcbOptions** uses an anonymous inner class. This makes sense because it is the only handler that uses this sequence of code. However, the handler for the remaining three check boxes uses the **itemStateChanged( )** method implemented by **CBDemo**. This also make sense because each check box uses the same sequence of code. Thus, it can be shared. This avoids unnecessary duplication. As this example shows, you can handle events in whatever manner is most appropriate to your application.

Check Box Options

Like push buttons and toggle buttons, check boxes offer a rich array of options and features that let you create a custom look easily. For example, you can specify an unchecked and checked icon that will be used instead of an empty or checked box. The unchecked icon is most easily specified using one of the **JCheckBox** constructors that takes an image as a parameter. The checked icon is set by calling **setSelectedIcon( )**. Because these icons work together as a pair, both need to be specified. You cannot use one without the other.

You can set the alignment of the check box and the alignment of the text relative to the icon. The methods that handle this are the same as for all buttons: **setVerticalAlignment( )**, **setHorizontalAlignment( )**, **setVerticalTextPosition( )**, and **setHorizontalTextPosition( )**. You can set a mnemonic that is shown in the check box label by calling **setMnemonic( )**.

Ask the Expert

Q: Is there a way to generate a button "click" under program control?

A: Yes, you can call the **doClick( )** method on the button. This method is defined by **AbstractButton**, and it causes the appropriate events to be fired in the same way as if the button were clicked by a user.

CRITICAL SKILL
2.12 Create Radio Buttons with JRadioButton

The last component we will examine in this module is the radio button. Radio buttons are used to manage sets of mutually exclusive options. Radio buttons are supported by the **JRadioButton** class, which implements **AbstractButton**. Its immediate superclass is **JToggleButton**, which provides support for two-state buttons. The **JRadioButton** constructors are shown in Table 2-6.

Within a group of radio buttons, each time one button is selected, the previously selected button is deselected. Thus, within a group, only one radio button can be selected at any given time. Groups of radio buttons are created by adding them to a **ButtonGroup**. This class is in **javax.swing**, and it provides only a default constructor. Elements are then added to the button group via the following method:

void add(AbstractButton *button*)

Constructor	Description
JRadioButton( )	Creates a radio button that has neither a text nor an image associated with it.
JRadioButton(String *str*)	Creates a radio button that is associated with the text passed in *str*.
JRadioButton(Icon *icon*)	Creates a radio button that is associated with the image passed in *icon*.
JRadioButton(String *str*, boolean *state*)	Creates a radio button that is associated with the text passed in *str*. If *state* is true, the button is initially selected. Otherwise, it is deselected.
JRadioButton(Icon *icon*, boolean *state*)	Creates a radio button that is associated with the image passed in *icon*. If *state* is true, the button is initially selected. Otherwise, it is deselected.
JRadioButton(String *str*, Icon *icon*)	Creates a radio button that is associated with the text passed in *str* and the image passed in *icon*.
JRadioButton(String *str*, Icon *icon*, boolean *state*)	Creates a radio button that is associated with the text passed in *str* and the image passed in *icon*. If *state* is true, the button is initially selected. Otherwise, it is deselected.
JCheckBox(Action *act*)	Creates a check box whose text, image, and other properties are defined by the object passed in *act*. Actions are described later in this book.

Table 2-6 The **JRadioButton** Constructors

Here, *button* is a reference to the button to be added to the group. Although you can use **ButtonGroup** to create a group of any type of two-state button, it is used mostly with radio buttons.

A **JRadioButton** generates action events, item events, and change events each time the button selection changes. Most often it is the action event that is handled, which means that you will normally implement the **ActionListener** interface. Recall that the only method defined by **ActionListener** is **actionPerformed( )**. Inside this method, you can use a number of different ways to determine which button was selected. First, you can check its action command by calling **getActionCommand( )**. By default, the action command is the same as the button label, but you can set the action command to something else by calling **setActionCommand( )** on the radio button. Second, you can call **getSource( )** on the **ActionEvent** object and check that reference against the buttons. Finally, you can simply check each radio button to find out which one is currently selected by calling **isSelected( )** on each button. Remember, each time an action event occurs, it means that the button being selected has changed and that one and only one button will be selected.

When using radio buttons, you will normally want to initially select one of the buttons. This is done by calling **setSelected( )**.

The following program reworks the preceding check box example by substituting radio buttons for check boxes in the option selection. Now, only one option can be chosen. Sample output is shown in Figure 2-10.

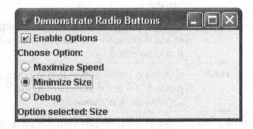

Figure 2-10 Output from the **RBDemo** program

```java
// Demonstrate radio buttons.

import java.awt.*;
import java.awt.event.*;
import javax.swing.*;

class RBDemo implements ActionListener {

  JLabel jlabOptions;
  JLabel jlabWhat;
  JCheckBox jcbOptions;
  JRadioButton jrbSpeed;
  JRadioButton jrbSize;
  JRadioButton jrbDebug;

  RBDemo() {
    // Create a new JFrame container.
    JFrame jfrm = new JFrame("Demonstrate Radio Buttons");

    // Specify a 1 column, 6 row grid layout.
    jfrm.getContentPane().setLayout(new GridLayout(6, 1));

    // Give the frame an initial size.
    jfrm.setSize(300, 150);

    // Terminate the program when the user closes the application.
    jfrm.setDefaultCloseOperation(JFrame.EXIT_ON_CLOSE);

    // Create two labels.
    jlabOptions = new JLabel("Choose Option:");
    jlabWhat = new JLabel("Option selected: Speed");

    // Make one check box.
    jcbOptions = new JCheckBox("Enable Options");

    // Make three radio buttons. Notice that
    // jrbSpeed is initially selected.
    jrbSpeed = new JRadioButton("Maximize Speed", true);
    jrbSize = new JRadioButton("Minimize Size");
    jrbDebug = new JRadioButton("Debug");

    // Add radio buttons to a group.
```

Create three radio buttons. Select the first button.

```
ButtonGroup bg = new ButtonGroup();
bg.add(jrbSpeed);
bg.add(jrbSize);                              Add the radio buttons to a button group.
bg.add(jrbDebug);

// Initially disable option buttons.
jrbSpeed.setEnabled(false);
jrbSize.setEnabled(false);
jrbDebug.setEnabled(false);

// Add item listener for jcbOptions.
jcbOptions.addItemListener(new ItemListener() {
  public void itemStateChanged(ItemEvent ie) {
    if(jcbOptions.isSelected()) {
      jrbSpeed.setEnabled(true);
      jrbSize.setEnabled(true);
      jrbDebug.setEnabled(true);
    }
    else {
      jrbSpeed.setEnabled(false);
      jrbSize.setEnabled(false);
      jrbDebug.setEnabled(false);
    }
  }
});

// Events generated by the radio buttons
// are handled in common by the actionPerformed()
// method implemented by RBDemo.
jrbSpeed.addActionListener(this);
jrbSize.addActionListener(this);
jrbDebug.addActionListener(this);

// Add check box and labels to the content pane.
jfrm.getContentPane().add(jcbOptions);
jfrm.getContentPane().add(jlabOptions);

jfrm.getContentPane().add(jrbSpeed);
jfrm.getContentPane().add(jrbSize);
jfrm.getContentPane().add(jrbDebug);
jfrm.getContentPane().add(jlabWhat);

// Display the frame.
jfrm.setVisible(true);
```

```
    }

    // This is the handler for all of the radio buttons.
    public void actionPerformed(ActionEvent ie) {
      String opts = "";

      // Create a string that describes the selected option.
      if(jrbSpeed.isSelected()) opts = "Speed ";
      else if(jrbSize.isSelected()) opts = "Size ";
      else opts = "Debug ";

      // Display the currently selected option.
      jlabWhat.setText("Option selected: " + opts);
    }


    public static void main(String args[]) {
      // Create the frame on the event dispatching thread.
      SwingUtilities.invokeLater(new Runnable() {
        public void run() {
          new RBDemo();
        }
      });
    }
  }
```

Only one option can be selected at any given time.

Progress Check

1. What class implements a check box?

2. Mutually exclusive buttons are typically objects of type **JRadioButton**. True or False?

3. To create a group of mutually exclusive buttons, you should add the buttons to an object of type _____.

1. **JCheckBox**
2. True
3. **ButtonGroup**

Project 2-2 Build a Simple Phone List

Phonebook.java
This projects builds a simple telephone list utility that stores names and phone numbers. Using the program, you can look up a number given a name, or look up a name given a number. It supports several options. First, you can ignore case differences when searching for a name. You can require an exact match between the search name and the names in the list. Alternatively, you can find a number given just the beginning or ending of a name. This project uses radio buttons, check boxes, text fields, and labels.

Step by Step

1. Create a file called **ChangeDemo.java**, and then enter the following comment and **import** statements:

```
// Project 2-2: A simple phone list.

import java.awt.*;
import java.awt.event.*;
import javax.swing.*;
```

2. Begin creating the **Phonebook** class as shown here:

```
class Phonebook {

  JTextField jtfName;
  JTextField jtfNumber;

  JRadioButton jrbExact;
  JRadioButton jrbStartsWith;
  JRadioButton jrbEndsWith;

  JCheckBox jcbIgnoreCase;

  // A short list of names and phone numbers.
  String[][] phonelist = {
    {"Jon", "555-8765"},
    {"Jessica", "555-5643"},
    {"Adam", "555-1212" },
    {"Rachel", "555-3435"},
    {"Tom & Jerry", "555-1001"}
  };
```

Notice the two-dimensional array **phonelist**. It contains a list of names and phone numbers. For a real application, you would probably want to use one of Java's Collection classes to hold the phone list, but this simple approach is sufficient for our purposes.

3. Begin coding the **Phonebook** constructor like this. It sets up the frame using the familiar sequence.

```
Phonebook() {

   // Create a new JFrame container.
   JFrame jfrm = new JFrame("A Simple Phone List");

   // Specify a GridLayout for the layout manager.
   jfrm.getContentPane().setLayout(new GridLayout(0, 1));

   // Give the frame an initial size.
   jfrm.setSize(240, 220);

   // Terminate the program when the user closes the application.
   jfrm.setDefaultCloseOperation(JFrame.EXIT_ON_CLOSE);
```

4. Add the following components to the **Phonebook** constructor:

```
   // Create labels.
   JLabel jlabName = new JLabel("Name");
   JLabel jlabNumber = new JLabel("Number");
   JLabel jlabOptions = new JLabel("Search Options");

   // Create text fields.
   jtfName = new JTextField(10);
   jtfNumber = new JTextField(10);

   // Create check box for Ignore Case.
   jcbIgnoreCase = new JCheckBox("Ignore Case");

   // Create radio buttons.
   jrbExact = new JRadioButton("Exact Match", true);
   jrbStartsWith = new JRadioButton("Starts With");
   jrbEndsWith = new JRadioButton("Ends With");
```

5. Now, add the radio buttons to a button group.

```
   // Add radio buttons to button group.
   ButtonGroup bg = new ButtonGroup();
   bg.add(jrbExact);
   bg.add(jrbStartsWith);
   bg.add(jrbEndsWith);
```

Recall that radio buttons only take on their mutually exclusive characteristics after they have been added to a button group.

(continued)

2

Labels, Buttons, and Borders

Project 2-2

Build a Simple Phone List

6. The only event handlers needed by the program are those that respond to the action events fired by the two text fields. (There is no reason to handle the events generated by the check box and radio buttons because their settings are simply obtained as needed.) Recall from Module 1 that text fields generate an **ActionEvent** when the user presses ENTER when a text field has input focus.

```
// Add action listener for the Name text field.
jtfName.addActionListener(new ActionListener() {
  public void actionPerformed(ActionEvent ae) {
    jtfNumber.setText(lookupName(jtfName.getText()));
  }
});

// Add action listener for the Number text field.
jtfNumber.addActionListener(new ActionListener() {
  public void actionPerformed(ActionEvent ae) {
    jtfName.setText(lookupNumber(jtfNumber.getText()));
  }
});
```

Because anonymous inner classes are used, the text field that generated the event is already known. The only thing that these handlers need to do is call the appropriate lookup method.

7. Finish **Phonebook( )** by adding the components to the content pane. Notice that two empty labels are added. These help the spacing of the components.

```
// Add components to the content pane.
jfrm.getContentPane().add(jlabName);
jfrm.getContentPane().add(jtfName);
jfrm.getContentPane().add(jlabNumber);
jfrm.getContentPane().add(jtfNumber);
jfrm.getContentPane().add(new JLabel());
jfrm.getContentPane().add(jlabOptions);
jfrm.getContentPane().add(jcbIgnoreCase);
jfrm.getContentPane().add(new JLabel());
jfrm.getContentPane().add(jrbExact);
jfrm.getContentPane().add(jrbStartsWith);
jfrm.getContentPane().add(jrbEndsWith);

// Display the frame.
jfrm.setVisible(true);
}
```

8. Next, add the **lookupName( )** and **lookupNumber( )** methods, shown next:

```
// Look up a name and return the number.
String lookupName(String n) {
```

```
    for(int i=0; i < phonelist.length; i++) {
      if(jrbStartsWith.isSelected()) {
        if(jcbIgnoreCase.isSelected()) {
          if(phonelist[i][0].toLowerCase().startsWith(n.toLowerCase()))
            return phonelist[i][1];
        } else {
          if(phonelist[i][0].startsWith(n))
            return phonelist[i][1];
        }
      }
      else if(jrbEndsWith.isSelected()) {
        if(jcbIgnoreCase.isSelected()) {
          if(phonelist[i][0].toLowerCase().endsWith(n.toLowerCase()))
            return phonelist[i][1];
        } else {
          if(phonelist[i][0].endsWith(n))
            return phonelist[i][1];
        }
      }
      else {
        if(jcbIgnoreCase.isSelected()) {
          if(phonelist[i][0].toLowerCase().equals(n.toLowerCase()))
            return phonelist[i][1];
        } else {
          if(phonelist[i][0].equals(n))
            return phonelist[i][1];
        }
      }
    }

    return "Not Found";
}

// Look up a number and return the name.
String lookupNumber(String n) {
  for(int i=0; i < phonelist.length; i++) {
    if(phonelist[i][1].equals(n))
      return phonelist[i][0];
  }
  return "Not Found";
}
```

The **lookupName( )** method looks for the specified name and, if found, returns its phone number. The **lookupNumber( )** method looks for the specified number. If found, it returns

(continued)

the name associated with that number. Pay special attention to **lookupName( )**. How the search is conducted is determined by the Ignore Case check box and the radio buttons.

9. End the program in the usual way, as shown here:

```
public static void main(String args[]) {
  // Create the frame on the event dispatching thread.
  SwingUtilities.invokeLater(new Runnable() {
    public void run() {
      new Phonebook();
    }
  });
}
}
```

10. Sample output from the program is shown here:

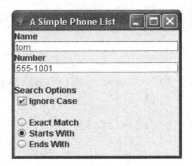

11. The entire phone list program is shown here:

```
// Project 2-2: A simple phone list.

import java.awt.*;
import java.awt.event.*;
import javax.swing.*;

class Phonebook {

  JTextField jtfName;
  JTextField jtfNumber;

  JRadioButton jrbExact;
  JRadioButton jrbStartsWith;
  JRadioButton jrbEndsWith;
```

```
JCheckBox jcbIgnoreCase;

// A short list of names and phone numbers.
String[][] phonelist = {
  {"Jon", "555-8765"},
  {"Jessica", "555-5643"},
  {"Adam", "555-1212" },
  {"Rachel", "555-3435"},
  {"Tom & Jerry", "555-1001"}
};

Phonebook() {

  // Create a new JFrame container.
  JFrame jfrm = new JFrame("A Simple Phone List");

  // Specify a GridLayout for the layout manager.
  jfrm.getContentPane().setLayout(new GridLayout(0, 1));

  // Give the frame an initial size.
  jfrm.setSize(240, 220);

  // Terminate the program when the user closes the application.
  jfrm.setDefaultCloseOperation(JFrame.EXIT_ON_CLOSE);

  // Create labels.
  JLabel jlabName = new JLabel("Name");
  JLabel jlabNumber = new JLabel("Number");
  JLabel jlabOptions = new JLabel("Search Options");

  // Create text fields.
  jtfName = new JTextField(10);
  jtfNumber = new JTextField(10);

  // Create check box for Ignore Case.
  jcbIgnoreCase = new JCheckBox("Ignore Case");

  // Create radio buttons.
  jrbExact = new JRadioButton("Exact Match", true);
  jrbStartsWith = new JRadioButton("Starts With");
  jrbEndsWith = new JRadioButton("Ends With");

  // Add radio buttons to button group.
  ButtonGroup bg = new ButtonGroup();
```

(continued)

```
      bg.add(jrbExact);
      bg.add(jrbStartsWith);
      bg.add(jrbEndsWith);

      // Add action listener for the Name text field.
      jtfName.addActionListener(new ActionListener() {
        public void actionPerformed(ActionEvent ae) {
          jtfNumber.setText(lookupName(jtfName.getText()));
        }
      });

      // Add action listener for the Number text field.
      jtfNumber.addActionListener(new ActionListener() {
        public void actionPerformed(ActionEvent ae) {
          jtfName.setText(lookupNumber(jtfNumber.getText()));
        }
      });

      // Add components to the content pane.
      jfrm.getContentPane().add(jlabName);
      jfrm.getContentPane().add(jtfName);
      jfrm.getContentPane().add(jlabNumber);
      jfrm.getContentPane().add(jtfNumber);
      jfrm.getContentPane().add(new JLabel());
      jfrm.getContentPane().add(jlabOptions);
      jfrm.getContentPane().add(jcbIgnoreCase);
      jfrm.getContentPane().add(new JLabel());
      jfrm.getContentPane().add(jrbExact);
      jfrm.getContentPane().add(jrbStartsWith);
      jfrm.getContentPane().add(jrbEndsWith);

      // Display the frame.
      jfrm.setVisible(true);
    }

    // Look up a name and return the number.
    String lookupName(String n) {
      for(int i=0; i < phonelist.length; i++) {
        if(jrbStartsWith.isSelected()) {
          if(jcbIgnoreCase.isSelected()) {
            if(phonelist[i][0].toLowerCase().startsWith(n.toLowerCase()))
              return phonelist[i][1];
          } else {
            if(phonelist[i][0].startsWith(n))
              return phonelist[i][1];
```

```
        }
      }
      else if(jrbEndsWith.isSelected()) {
        if(jcbIgnoreCase.isSelected()) {
          if(phonelist[i][0].toLowerCase().endsWith(n.toLowerCase()))
            return phonelist[i][1];
        } else {
          if(phonelist[i][0].endsWith(n))
            return phonelist[i][1];
        }
      }
      else {
        if(jcbIgnoreCase.isSelected()) {
          if(phonelist[i][0].toLowerCase().equals(n.toLowerCase()))
            return phonelist[i][1];
        } else {
          if(phonelist[i][0].equals(n))
            return phonelist[i][1];
        }
      }
    }

    return "Not Found";
  }

  // Look up a number and return the name.
  String lookupNumber(String n) {
    for(int i=0; i < phonelist.length; i++) {
      if(phonelist[i][1].equals(n))
        return phonelist[i][0];
    }
    return "Not Found";
  }

  public static void main(String args[]) {
    // Create the frame on the event dispatching thread.
    SwingUtilities.invokeLater(new Runnable() {
      public void run() {
        new Phonebook();
      }
    });
  }
}
```

Module 2 Mastery Check

1. What method sets a component's border?

2. By default, the contents of a label are centered vertically and aligned horizontally on the _____ edge.

3. In a label, what method sets the vertical position of the text relative to the icon?

4. Why is **ImageIcon** useful?

5. By default, when a component is disabled, it is shown in gray. True or False?

6. What is a keyboard mnemonic?

7. Name the four types of buttons provided by Swing.

8. What method must be provided in order to implement the **ItemListener** interface?

9. **JToggleButton** is the superclass for what other two-state buttons?

10. What is **setDefaultButton( )** used for?

11. To what object must radio buttons be added in order for their mutually exclusive behavior to be exhibited?

12. Extra Challenge: Rework and improve the **StopWatch** program in Project 1-1 from Module 1 in the following ways:

   - Instead of using the **Calendar** class and **getTimeInMillis( )** to obtain the current system time, use the timestamp provided when an action event is generated. Recall that this timestamp is available through **getWhen( )**.

   - Disable the Stop button until the Start button is pressed. Then, disable the Start button until the Stop button is pressed.

   - Add a check box that controls whether a log of elapsed times is displayed. If it is checked, have the times added to the log. When the box is cleared, have the log erased. Only store and display the last three times. When the log is full (contains three entries), have an old time drop off the end of the list each time a new time is added.

Module 3

Scroll Bars, Sliders, and Progress Bars

This chapter examines three related GUI controls: the scroll bar, the slider, and the progress bar. These are familiar components to virtually all readers because they are widely used in modern computing. Of these, the scroll bar is arguably the most important because it is integral to the operation of many applications. Moreover, it was one of the original controls that helped define the GUI revolution decades ago. Although GUIs have advanced greatly from those early days, the scroll bar still works today the same as it did then. It has stood the test of time.

The success of the scroll bar led to several adaptations. One is the slider. A slider is a variation on the scroll bar that is used to set an integer value. Another variation is the progress bar, which is used to display the progress of a task. Although different in their look and purpose, all three components have one thing in common: they share the concept of a visual indicator moving through a predefined range. In Swing, this type of action is governed by the model specified by the **BoundedRangeModel** interface. Thus, the scroll bar, slider, and progress bar all use **BoundedRangeModel** to define their state information. For this reason, it makes sense to cover all three here.

CRITICAL SKILL
3.1 # BoundedRangeModel

The model for all Swing components that operate within a predefined integer range is defined by the **BoundedRangeModel** interface. This interface defines four key values:

- The minimum value

- The maximum value

- The current value

- The extent

The minimum and maximum values define the endpoints of the range over which a component based on **BoundedRangeModel** can operate. The current value of the component will be within that range. In general, the extent represents the conceptual "width" of a sliding element that moves between the endpoints of the component. For example, in the scroll bar, the extent corresponds to the width (or "thickness") of the scroll bar's slider box.

BoundedRangeModel enforces a relationship between these four values. First, the minimum must be less than or equal to the maximum. The current value must be greater than or equal to the minimum value. The current value *plus the extent* must be less than or equal to the maximum value. Thus, if you specify a maximum value of 100 and an extent of 20, then the current value can never be greater than 80 (which is 100 − 20). You can specify an extent of 0, which enables the current value to be anywhere within the range specified by the minimum and maximum, inclusive.

BoundedRangeModel also defines a property that indicates when the component is in the process of being changed. This value, referred to as the *is-adjusting* property, is accessed through the **getValueIsAdjusting( )** and **setValueIsAdjusting( )** methods. This property is quite useful because both scroll bars and sliders generate many events when they are in the process of being dragged to a new setting. Your event handler can wait until **getValueIsAdjusting( )** returns false before it takes action. Alternatively, you can respond to all events, as they happen in real time. The choice is yours. The property accessor methods for **BoundedRangeModel** are shown in Table 3-1.

BoundedRangeModel specifies the **addChangeListener( )** and **removeChangeListener( )** methods. As these methods suggest, change events are fired whenever the data changes. As you will see, however, the scroll bar converts these change events into adjustment events.

In general, you don't need to interact directly with **BoundedRangeModel** when using a scroll bar, slider, or progress bar because these individual classes provide methods that interface with the model. However, the model is available to you, should you want to access it.

Method	Description
int getExtent( )	Returns the extent.
int getMaximum( )	Returns the maximum.
int getMinimum( )	Returns the minimum.
int getValue( )	Returns the current value.
boolean getValueIsAdjusting( )	Returns true if the control is in the process of being changed by the user. Returns false otherwise.
void setExtent(int *val*)	Sets the extent to *val*.
void setMaximum(int *max*)	Sets the maximum value to *max*.
void setMinimum(int *min*)	Sets the minimum value to *min*.
void setRangeProperties(int *val*, int *ext*, int *min*, int *max*, boolean is *isAdj*)	Sets all properties.
void setValue(int *val*)	Sets the current value to *val*.
void setValueIsAdjusting(boolean *val*)	If *val* is true, indicates that a sequence of changes (such as when a scroll bar is being dragged) is taking place.

Table 3-1 The Accessor Methods Defined by **BoundedRangeModel**

The default implementation of the **BoundedRangeModel** interface is provided in **DefaultBoundedRangeModel**. In this implementation, the default values for the current value, minimum, maximum, and extent are as shown here:

Current value	0
Minimum	0
Maximum	100
Extent	0

Given these defaults, the current value can range from 0 to 100.

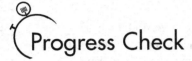

Progress Check

1. What are the four properties specified by **BoundedRangeModel**?

2. When the user has finished moving a scroll bar or slider, what will **getValueIsAdjusting( )** return?

3. Can the current value ever exceed the maximum value?

CRITICAL SKILL
3.2 Scroll Bars

In Swing, a scroll bar is an object of the **JScrollBar** class. Its behavior is governed by its model (which is the **BoundedRangeModel** just described) and the **java.awt.Adjustable** interface, which it implements. (As a point of interest, **Adjustable** is the same interface used by the original AWT **Scrollbar** class.) Given the importance and widespread use of scroll bars, they are surprisingly easy to program. For example, even though they do offer a significant amount of flexibility, their default implementations are often exactly what you want.

A scroll bar is actually a composite of several individual parts. At each end are arrows that you can click to change the current value of the scroll bar one unit in the direction of the arrow. The current value of the scroll bar relative to its minimum and maximum values is indicated by position of the *thumb*. The thumb can be dragged by the user to a new position. This new position then becomes the current value of the scroll bar. The scroll bar's model will then reflect this value. Clicking the bar (which is also called the *paging area*) causes the thumb to

---

1. Current value, maximum, minimum, and extent
2. False
3. No

Ask the Expert

Q: I have heard that JScrollBar **is not as widely used in Swing programming as one might expect. Is this true?**

A: Make no mistake, scroll bars are a very important part of Swing programming. However, the scroll bars are not often used in their stand-alone configuration. The reason is that Swing provides a special component called a **JScrollPane** that creates a *scroll pane*. A scroll pane is, essentially, a container that automatically provides vertical and horizontal scroll bars. The contents of the scroll pane can be scrolled by moving the scroll bars. Thus, for many applications the scroll pane is a more convenient choice than stand-alone scroll bars because it automates the scrolling process. **JScrollPane** is just one of several special containers provided by Swing. It is described in Module 4.

jump in that direction by some increment that is usually larger than 1 unit. Typically, this action translates into some form of page up and page down.

JScrollbar defines the constructors shown in Table 3-2. Scroll bars have two orientations: vertical or horizontal. The default constructor creates a vertical scroll bar. The other two constructors allow you to specify the orientation. Notice that the orientation value must be either **JScrollBar.VERTICAL** or **JScrollBar.HORIZONTAL**. (These values are inherited from **java.awt.Adjustable**.) The first two constructors use the default settings. The third constructor lets you explicitly set the minimum, maximum, extent, and current value when the scroll bar is created. For scroll bars, the extent specifies the size of the thumb. However, the physical size of the thumb on the screen will never drop below a certain point because it must remain large enough to be dragged. It is important to understand that the largest value that the

Constructor	Description
JScrollBar( )	Creates a vertical scroll bar that uses the default settings.
JScrollBar(int *VorH*)	Creates a scroll bar that is oriented as specified by *VorH*. The value of *VorH* must be either **JScrollBar.VERTICAL** or **JScrollBar.HORIZONTAL**. The default settings are used.
JScrollBar(int *VorH*, int *initialValue*, int *extent*, int *min*, int *max*)	Creates a scroll bar oriented as specified by *VorH*, with the specified initial value, extent, minimum, and maximum values. The value of *VorH* must be either **JScrollBar.VERTICAL** or **JScrollBar.HORIZONTAL**.

Table 3-2 The **JScrollBar** Constructors

scroll bar can have is equal to the maximum value minus the extent. By default, a scroll bar has a range of 0 to 100, inclusive. The extent is 10 and the initial value is 0. Thus, by default, the value can range between 0 and 90 (100 – 10).

CRITICAL SKILL
3.3

JScrollBar Properties

JScrollBar defines several properties that determine its behavior. First, it supports the minimum, maximum, extent, and current value properties defined by **BoundedRangeModel**. The minimum and maximum values can be accessed by the following methods:

int getMinimum( )
void setMinimum(int *val*)

int getMaximum( )
void setMaximum(int *val*)

By default, the minimum is 0 and the maximum is 100.
The accessors for the current value are

int getValue( )
void setValue(int *val*)

By default, the value is 0.
The accessors for the extent are shown here:

int getVisibleAmount( )
void setVisibleAmount(int *val*)

Notice that these use the name **VisibleAmount**. This is because these methods are defined by the **Adjustable** interface (which predates Swing). However, they still refer to the extent property defined by **BoundedRangeModel**. The default value for the extent is 10.

JScrollBar also defines a convenience method called **setValues( )**, which lets you set the value, visible amount (extent), minimum, and maximum values in a single call. It is shown here:

void setValues(int v*alue*, int *visibleAmount*, int *min*, int *max*)

JScrollBar supports the is-adjusting property defined by **BoundedRangeModel** by providing these accessors:

boolean getValueIsAdjusting( )
void setValueIsAdjusting( )

If the scroll bar is in the process of being dragged or in the middle of a sequence of page-up or page-down commands, then **getValueIsAdjusting( )** will return true. This property lets you wait until the user has stopped changing the scroll bar before you respond to the changes. For example, dragging the thumb results in a series of events. If all you care about is the final value, then you can simply ignore those events until the user completes the drag operation.

In addition to dragging the thumb, a scroll bar's position can be changed by clicking the arrows at its ends or the paging area of the bar. When the arrows are clicked, the scroll bar changes its position by the value contained in the *unit increment* property. Its accessors are shown here:

int getUnitIncrement( )
void setUnitIncrement(int *val*)

By default, this property is 1.

When the paging area is clicked, the position of the thumb changes by the value contained in the *block increment* property.

int getBlockIncrement( )
void setBlockIncrement(int *val*)

By default, this property is 10.

NOTE

There is a second version of **getUnitIncrement( )** and **getBlockIncrement( )** that lets you specify the direction of the increment. These versions are mostly for overriding by subclasses that compute a different increment based on the direction of scroll.

CRITICAL SKILL
3.4 Handling JScrollBar Adjustment Events

JScrollBar generates adjustment events, which are objects of type **java.awt.event.AdjustmentEvent**. To process an adjustment event, you will need to implement the **AdjustmentListener** interface. It defines only one method, **adjustmentValueChanged( )**, shown here:

void adjustmentValueChanged(AdjustmentEvent *ae*)

This method is called whenever a change is made to the value of the scroll bar.

You can obtain a reference to the scroll bar that generated the event by calling **getAdjustable( )** on the **AdjustmentEvent** object. It is shown here:

Adjustable getAdjustable( )

Most of the properties supported by **JScrollBar** are defined by **Adjustable**, so you can operate directly on those properties through the reference returned by this method.

AdjustmentEvent defines two methods that are very convenient when working with scroll bars. First, you can obtain the current value of the scroll bar by calling **getValue( )**:

int getValue( )

Second, you can determine if the scroll bar is still having its value adjusted by calling

boolean getValueIsAdjusting( )

These methods perform the same function as their counterparts in **JScrollBar**. They simply offer the advantage of not having to explicitly obtain a reference to the scroll bar.

Progress Check

1. In addition to the properties defined by **BoundedRangeModel**, what two other properties define the characteristics of a scroll bar?

2. When a scroll bar is moved, an _____ event is generated.

3. Scroll bars can be vertical, but not horizontal. True or False?

Use Scroll Bars

Given their power, scroll bars are surprisingly easy to use. To understand the process, we will begin with a simple example that creates two scroll bars that each use the default property values. One scroll bar is vertical. The other is horizontal. Therefore, the two bars differ only in their orientation. The program displays the current value of each scroll bar. When you move a bar, the output is updated. The program also displays the default property values, which apply to both scroll bars. Sample output is shown in Figure 3-1.

---

1. Unit increment and block increment
2. Adjustment
3. False, both vertical and horizontal scroll bars are supported.

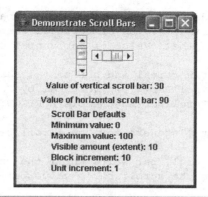

Figure 3-1 Sample output from the **SBDemo** program

```java
// Demonstrate JScrollBar.

import java.awt.*;
import java.awt.event.*;
import javax.swing.*;
import javax.swing.event.*;

class SBDemo {

  JLabel jlabVert;
  JLabel jlabHoriz;
  JLabel jlabSBInfo;

  JScrollBar jsbVert;
  JScrollBar jsbHoriz;

  SBDemo() {
    // Create a new JFrame container.
    JFrame jfrm = new JFrame("Demonstrate Scroll Bars");

    // Specify a flow layout.
    jfrm.getContentPane().setLayout(new FlowLayout());

    // Give the frame an initial size.
    jfrm.setSize(260, 260);

    // Terminate the program when the user closes the application.
    jfrm.setDefaultCloseOperation(JFrame.EXIT_ON_CLOSE);
```

```java
// These labels display the current scroll bar value.
jlabVert = new JLabel("Value of vertical scroll bar: 0");
jlabHoriz = new JLabel("Value of horizontal scroll bar: 0");

// Create default vertical and horizontal scroll bar.
jsbVert = new JScrollBar(); // vertical by default
jsbHoriz = new JScrollBar(Adjustable.HORIZONTAL);

// Add adjustment listeners for the scroll bars.

// The vertical scroll bar waits until the user
// stops changing the scroll bar's value before
// it responds.
jsbVert.addAdjustmentListener(new AdjustmentListener() {
  public void adjustmentValueChanged(AdjustmentEvent ae) {
    // If the scroll bar is in the process of being
    // changed, simply return.
    if(jsbVert.getValueIsAdjusting()) return;

    // Display the new value.
    jlabVert.setText("Value of vertical scroll bar: "
                  + ae.getValue());
  }
});

// The horizontal scroll bar handler responds to all
// adjustment events, including those generated while
// the scroll bar is in the process of being changed.
jsbHoriz.addAdjustmentListener(new AdjustmentListener() {
  public void adjustmentValueChanged(AdjustmentEvent ae) {
    // Display the new value.
    jlabHoriz.setText("Value of horizontal scroll bar: "
                  + ae.getValue());
  }
});

// Display the scroll bar defaults.
jlabSBInfo = new JLabel("<html>Scroll Bar Defaults<br>" +
                "Minimum value: " +
                jsbVert.getMinimum() + "<br>" +
                "Maximum value: " +
                jsbVert.getMaximum() + "<br>" +
                "Visible amount (extent): " +
                jsbVert.getVisibleAmount() + "<br>" +
                "Block increment: " +
```

Create vertical and horizontal scroll bars.

Scroll bars generate adjustment events.

If the scroll bar is in the process of being adjusted, return without taking any action.

This handler responds to all scroll bar adjustment events.

```
                              jsbVert.getBlockIncrement() + "<br>" +
                              "Unit increment: " +
                              jsbVert.getUnitIncrement());

    // Add components to the content pane.
    jfrm.getContentPane().add(jsbVert);
    jfrm.getContentPane().add(jsbHoriz);
    jfrm.getContentPane().add(jlabVert);
    jfrm.getContentPane().add(jlabHoriz);
    jfrm.getContentPane().add(jlabSBInfo);

    // Display the frame.
    jfrm.setVisible(true);
  }

  public static void main(String args[]) {
    // Create the frame on the event dispatching thread.
    SwingUtilities.invokeLater(new Runnable() {
      public void run() {
        new SBDemo();
      }
    });
  }
}
```

There are several things of interest in this program. First, notice that each scroll bar has a maximum of 100 and an extent (visible area) of 10. This means that the largest current value that can be reached by each bar is 90. Recall that the current value will always be less than or equal to the maximum minus the extent. This is 100 – 10, or 90, in this case. To confirm this, run the program and then move the thumb as far as it will go in the maximum direction. The value will 90. If you want the current value to be able to reach the maximum value, the extent must be set to 0. Alternatively, you can set the maximum value to *maximum* + *extent*, so that the current value can reach the desired value.

Now, look at how the scroll bars handle adjustment events. The handler for the vertical scroll bar simply returns if **getValueIsAdjusting( )** is true. This means that when the thumb in the vertical scroll bar is dragged, the current value is not updated in **jlabVert** until after the drag has ended. Thus, you cannot watch the values change. This technique is useful for those applications in which you don't care about the intermediary values that the thumb passes through on the way to its final destination.

The handler for the horizontal scroll bar updates the output in **jlabHoriz** each time an event occurs. Therefore, when a drag event occurs, each value that the thumb passes through is displayed. For many applications, such as scrolling through a text file, this is the way that you want the scroll bar to act because it enables you to scroll the text in a smooth manner.

As the output from the program shows, the block increment is 10 and the unit increment is 1. These are the defaults, and they are often what you will want. However, for scrolling through large values, such as 0 to 10,000, you may want a larger block increment or even a larger unit increment.

There is one other thing to notice about the scroll bars: they are somewhat small. As the next example shows, it is easy to specify the size of a scroll bar.

Some Scroll Bar Options

Although the default scroll bar settings are often useful as-is, sometimes the demands of your application will require different values. For example, you might want a scroll bar that scrolls between a range other than 0 to 100, or you might want the scroll bar's value to be able to reach its maximum value. You might also want to set the size of the block increment or unit increment to best fit the range being scrolled. Finally, you might want to specify a preferred size for the scroll bar that best fits your visual design. Fortunately, all of these are easy to implement.

As just described, you can set the values of a scroll bar's extent, value, minimum, and maximum by using accessor methods provided by **JScrollBar**. However, it's usually easier to specify these values when you create the scroll bar by using this constructor:

JScrollBar(int *VorH*, int *initialValue*, int *extent*, int *min*, int *max*)

Recall that *VorH* must be either **JScrollBar.VERTICAL** or **JScrollBar.HORIZONTAL**. When using this constructor, the unit increment will be set to 1 and the block increment will be set equal to *extent*. However, if *extent* is 0, then the block increment will be 1. For example, this creates a vertical scroll bar with a minimum of 0 and a maximum of 500, an extent of 25, and an initial value of 250.

```
JScrollBar sb = new JScrollBar(ScrollBar.VERTICAL, 250, 25, 0, 500);
```

This scroll bar's value can range from 0 to 475 (*maximum – extent*). Its block increment will be 25 and its unit increment will be 1. To set the block increment or the unit increment to a different value, you must use the accessor methods **setBlockIncrement( )** or **setUnitIncrement( )**.

One way (and often the best way) to enable a scroll bar's value to reach the maximum is to specify an extent (visible amount) of 0. Because the value must be less than or equal to *maximum – extent*, using an extent of 0 lets the value reach the maximum. As mentioned, the physical size of the thumb is proportional to the extent unless the extent drops below the thumb's minimum size. Thus, specifying an extent of 0 still results in a normal-sized thumb. A second way to enable the value to reach a desired upper limit is to specify a maximum that is equal to the desired endpoint plus the extent. Frankly, unless you want to increase the size of the thumb beyond its normal (default) size, then the easiest way to create a scroll bar whose value can reach the maximum is to specify an extent of 0. If you use an extent of 0, you will probably also want to set the block increment because it will be 1 by default.

To set the size of a scroll bar, use the **setPreferredSize( )** method defined by **JComponent**. Recall from Module 2 that it is declared like this:

void setPreferredSize(Dimension *size*)

You can set the size of a scroll bar as appropriate for your application. If you want a scroll bar that is longer than the default but uses the default width, you can obtain the default scroll bar dimensions by calling **getPreferredSize( )** and then use that width when setting the size.

Here is a program that creates two custom scroll bars. Both scroll bars are longer than the default length. The vertical scroll bar is wider and the horizontal scroll bar is narrower than the default. Sample output is shown in Figure 3-2.

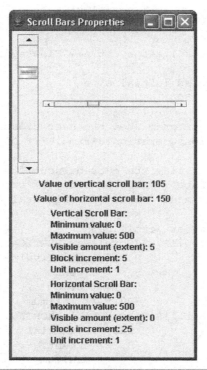

Figure 3-2 Output from the **CustomSBDemo** program

```java
// Specify scroll bar properties.

import java.awt.*;
import java.awt.event.*;
import javax.swing.*;
import javax.swing.event.*;

class CustomSBDemo {

  JLabel jlabVert;
  JLabel jlabHoriz;
  JLabel jlabVSBInfo;
  JLabel jlabHSBInfo;

  JScrollBar jsbVert;
  JScrollBar jsbHoriz;

  CustomSBDemo() {
    // Create a new JFrame container.
    JFrame jfrm = new JFrame("Scroll Bars Properties");

    // Specify a flow layout.
    jfrm.getContentPane().setLayout(new FlowLayout());

    // Give the frame an initial size.
    jfrm.setSize(260, 500);

    // Terminate the program when the user closes the application.
    jfrm.setDefaultCloseOperation(JFrame.EXIT_ON_CLOSE);

    // These labels display the current scroll bar value.
    jlabVert = new JLabel("Value of vertical scroll bar: 0");
    jlabHoriz = new JLabel("Value of horizontal scroll bar: 250");

    // Specify values for scroll bars.
    jsbVert = new JScrollBar(JScrollBar.VERTICAL,
                       0, // initial value
                       5, // extent
                       0, // minimum
                       500); // maximum
    jsbHoriz = new JScrollBar(Adjustable.HORIZONTAL,
                       250, // initial value
                       0, // extent
                       0, // minimum
                       500); // maximum
```

Specify the range, extent, and initial value of the scroll bars.

```
// Specify preferred size for scroll bars.
//
// The vertical scroll bar will be wide.
jsbVert.setPreferredSize(new Dimension(30, 200));
// The horizontal scroll bar will be narrow.
jsbHoriz.setPreferredSize(new Dimension(200, 10));

// Set the block increment size for the horizontal bar.
jsbHoriz.setBlockIncrement(25);

// Add adjustment listeners for the scroll bars.

// The vertical scroll bar waits until the user
// stops changing the scroll bar's value before
// it responds.
jsbVert.addAdjustmentListener(new AdjustmentListener() {
  public void adjustmentValueChanged(AdjustmentEvent ae) {
    // If the scroll bar is in the process of being
    // changed, simply return.
    if(jsbVert.getValueIsAdjusting()) return;

    // Display the new value.
    jlabVert.setText("Value of vertical scroll bar: "
                    + ae.getValue());
  }
});

// The horizontal scroll bar handler responds to all
// adjustment events, including those generated while
// the scroll bar is in the process of being changed.
jsbHoriz.addAdjustmentListener(new AdjustmentListener() {
  public void adjustmentValueChanged(AdjustmentEvent ae) {
    // Display the new value.
    jlabHoriz.setText("Value of horizontal scroll bar: "
                    + ae.getValue());
  }
});

// Display the scroll bar values
jlabVSBInfo = new JLabel("<html>Vertical Scroll Bar:<br>" +
                "Minimum value: " +
                jsbVert.getMinimum() + "<br>" +
                "Maximum value: " +
                jsbVert.getMaximum() + "<br>" +
                "Visible amount (extent): " +
                jsbVert.getVisibleAmount() + "<br>" +
```

— Set the size of the scroll bars.

— Set the block increment for the horizontal scroll bar.

```
                              "Block increment: " +
                              jsbVert.getBlockIncrement() + "<br>" +
                              "Unit increment: " +
                              jsbVert.getUnitIncrement());

          jlabHSBInfo = new JLabel("<html>Horizontal Scroll Bar:<br>" +
                              "Minimum value: " +
                              jsbHoriz.getMinimum() + "<br>" +
                              "Maximum value: " +
                              jsbHoriz.getMaximum() + "<br>" +
                              "Visible amount (extent): " +
                              jsbHoriz.getVisibleAmount() + "<br>" +
                              "Block increment: " +
                              jsbHoriz.getBlockIncrement() + "<br>" +
                              "Unit increment: " +
                              jsbHoriz.getUnitIncrement());

      // Add components to the content pane.
      jfrm.getContentPane().add(jsbVert);
      jfrm.getContentPane().add(jsbHoriz);
      jfrm.getContentPane().add(jlabVert);
      jfrm.getContentPane().add(jlabHoriz);
      jfrm.getContentPane().add(jlabVSBInfo);
      jfrm.getContentPane().add(jlabHSBInfo);

      // Display the frame.
      jfrm.setVisible(true);
    }

    public static void main(String args[]) {
      // Create the frame on the event dispatching thread.
      SwingUtilities.invokeLater(new Runnable() {
        public void run() {
          new CustomSBDemo();
        }
      });
    }
  }
```

Let's first look at how the scroll bars are created. The vertical scroll bar specifies a minimum of 0 and a maximum of 500. Its extent is 5 and its initial value is 0. Because its extent is 5, it has a scrollable range of 0 to 495. Its block increment is automatically set to the value of its extent, which makes it 5. The vertical scroll bar has its preferred size set as 30 units wide and 200 units tall. This makes it a bit wider than normal.

The horizontal scroll bar specifies a minimum of 0 and a maximum of 500. Its extent is 0 and its initial value is 250. Because its extent is 0, it has a scrollable range of 0 to 500. The horizontal scroll bar has its preferred size set as 10 units tall and 200 units wide. This makes it a bit narrower than normal. Because the extent is 0, the block increment is set to 1 by the constructor. However, this is changed to 25 with a call to **setBlockIncrement( )**.

Progress Check

1. To use the full range of a scroll bar, the extent (visible amount) must be set to what value?

2. To set the block increment, you use what accessor method?

CRITICAL SKILL
3.6 Sliders

A *slider* is conceptually similar to a scroll bar because both move a box through a range of values and both use **BoundedRangeModel** for their model. However, a slider is designed to fill a different need, and its operation, events, and configuration differ from the scroll bar. In general, a scroll bar is used to move information (such as text or an image) through a window. A slider is used to set a value within a range. For example, a slider might be used as a volume control for a media player. The Swing class that creates a slider is **JSlider**.

A slider is composed of a bar through which the slider box, called the *knob,* moves. Usually, a slider has *tick marks* that evenly divide the range, and labels that indicate the value associated with each tick mark. The tick marks and labels are optional, however. Thus, it is possible to create a slider without either or both.

JSlider defines the constructors shown in Table 3-3. Sliders have two orientations: vertical or horizontal. By default, the slider will be horizontal, but you can specify a vertical orientation, if desired. By default, a slider has a range of 0 to 100, inclusive. The extent is 0, and the initial value is 50. However, you can specify the range and the initial value. Usually, the default extent value of 0 is used.

JSlider generates a change event when its knob is moved. (Notice that this differs from **JScollBar**, which generates an adjustment event.) Recall that change events are handled by implementing **ChangeListener**. This interface defines only one method, **stateChanged( )**, shown here.

void stateChanged(ChangeEvent *ce*)

1. 0
2. **setBlockIncrement( )**

Constructor	Description
JSlider( )	Creates a horizontal slider. The range is 0 to 100. The extent is 0. The initial value is 50.
JSlider(int *min*, int *max*)	Creates a horizontal slider. The range is passed in *min* and *max*. The extent is 0. The initial value is the midpoint between *min* and *max*.
JSlider(int *min*, int *max*, int *val*)	Creates a horizontal slider. The range is passed in *min* and *max*. The extent is 0. The initial value is passed in *val*.
JSlider(int *VorH*)	Creates a slider that is oriented as specified by *VorH*, which must be either **JSlider.VERTICAL** or **JSlider.HORIZONTAL**. The range is 0 to 100. The extent is 0. The initial value is 50.
JSlider(int *VorH*, int *min*, int *max*, int *val*)	Creates a slider that is oriented as specified by *VorH*, which must be either **JSlider.VERTICAL** or **JSlider.HORIZONTAL**. The range is passed in *min* and *max*. The extent is 0. The initial value is passed in *val*.
JSlider(BoundedRangeModel *model*)	Creates a slider that uses the model passed in *model*.

Table 3-3 The **JSlider** Constructors

To obtain a reference to the slider that generated the event, call **getSource( )** on *ce*. A steady stream of events is generated when the slider is moved. If all you care about is the knob's final destination, then you can ignore the changes until **getValueIsAdjusting( )** returns false.

Because the slider uses the **BoundedRangeModel**, it defines properties that represent the minimum and maximum values in its range, its current value, and its extent. Conceptually, the extent is the width of the knob. However, by default, this value is 0 and this is the value that you will normally want it to be. This value enables the knob to move through the entire range. If the extent is greater than 0, then the knob will only be able to move to a point that is less than or equal to *maximum − extent*. (Recall that this relationship is defined by **BoundedRangeModel**.)

The minimum, maximum, current value, and extent properties defined by **BoundedRangeModel** are available through accessor methods defined by **JSlider**. They are shown here:

int getMinimum( )
void setMinimum(int *val*)

int getMaximum( )
void setMaximum(int *val*)

int getValue( )
void setValue(int *val*)

int getExtent( )
void setExtent(int *val*)

As mentioned, normally you will not need to set the extent because its default value of 0 is what is usually required.

CRITICAL SKILL
3.7 # Setting Tick Marks and Labels

Although you can create a slider that does not have tick marks or numeric labels that indicate the value of the slider, normally you will want both of these elements. When a slider is first created, it has neither, so you must explicitly add them. We will begin with the tick marks.

Sliders support two sets of tick marks: major and minor. The minor tick marks go between the major ones. Often, only the major tick marks are used. To add tick marks, you must first specify their spacing. For the major tick marks, this is done by calling **setMajorTickSpacing( )**, shown here:

void setMajorTickSpacing(int *incr*)

Here, *incr* specifies the number of units between marks. For example, a spacing of 10 produces a major tick mark every 10 units. Thus, assuming the default range of 0 to 100, the tick marks will be on the numbers 0, 10, 20, and so on up to 100.

To set the minor tick spacing, use **setMinorTickSpacing( )**, shown next:

void setMinorTickSpacing(int *incr*)

Here, *incr* specifies the number of units between marks.

Before the tick marks will be visible, they must be turned on by calling **setPaintTicks( )**. It is shown here:

void setPaintTicks(boolean *on*)

Here, if *on* is true, the tick marks are displayed. If it is false, the tick marks are not shown.

Setting and displaying the tick marks causes the tick marks to be shown, but they won't be labeled with values. Thus, by themselves, the tick marks simply show increments, but no scale. Usually, you will want each major tick mark labeled with the value that it represents. To do this, you will need to call **setLabelTable( )**, shown here:

void setLabelTable(Dictionary *labs*)

Here, *labs* is a collection of key/value pairs that link the value of each major tick mark with a label, such as a **JLabel**. Although it is not hard to create such a collection, Swing offers a more convenient alternative for many cases. Often, you will want to label the major tick marks with the values that the marks represent. You can obtain a collection of such labels by calling **createStandardLabels( )**, shown next:

Hashtable createStandardLabels(int *incr*)

Here, *incr* specifies the increments at which you want the labels. Normally, this will be the same as the increment for the major tick marks.

Before the labels will display, you must call **setPaintLabels( )**, shown here:

void setPaintLabels(boolean *on*)

If *on* is true, the labels will be displayed. If *on* is false, no labels are shown.

You can obtain the current settings for tick marks and labels, and determine if these items will be painted, by using these get accessors provided by **JSlider**.

Dictionary getLabelTable( )

int getMajorTickSpacing( )

int getMinorTickSpacing( )

boolean getPaintLabels( )

boolean getPaintTicks( )

Progress Check

1. What is a slider's default range?

2. What are the two types of tick marks used by a slider?

3. What method causes the tick marks to be painted?

Demonstrate Sliders

The following program demonstrates slider controls. Output is shown in Figure 3-3.

---

1. 0 to 100

2. Major and minor

3. **setPaintTicks( )**

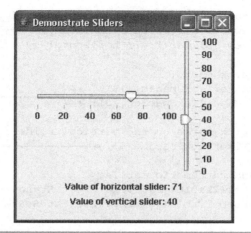

Figure 3-3 Output from the **JSlider** demonstration program

```java
// Demonstrate sliders.

import java.awt.*;
import javax.swing.*;
import javax.swing.event.*;

class SliderDemo {

  JLabel jlabVert;
  JLabel jlabHoriz;

  JSlider jsldrHoriz;
  JSlider jsldrVert;

  SliderDemo() {
    // Create a new JFrame container.
    JFrame jfrm = new JFrame("Demonstrate Sliders");

    // Specify a flow layout.
    jfrm.getContentPane().setLayout(new FlowLayout());

    // Give the frame an initial size.
    jfrm.setSize(300, 300);

    // Terminate the program when the user closes the application.
    jfrm.setDefaultCloseOperation(JFrame.EXIT_ON_CLOSE);
```

```
// Create default vertical and horizontal sliders.
jsldrVert = new JSlider(JSlider.VERTICAL);          ◄──────   Create vertical
jsldrHoriz = new JSlider(); // horizontal by default ◄──────   and horizontal
                                                               sliders.

// Add major tick marks.
jsldrVert.setMajorTickSpacing(10);   ◄──────
jsldrHoriz.setMajorTickSpacing(20);  ◄──────   Set the major tick spacing
                                               for both sliders.

// Use minor tick marks on the vertical slider.
jsldrVert.setMinorTickSpacing(5);   ◄──────    Set the minor tick spacing
                                               for the vertical slider.

// Create standard numeric labels.
jsldrVert.setLabelTable(jsldrVert.createStandardLabels(10));   ◄──
jsldrHoriz.setLabelTable(jsldrHoriz.createStandardLabels(20)); ◄──

                                               Add standard labels.

// Cause the tick marks to be displayed.
jsldrVert.setPaintTicks(true);   ◄──────
jsldrHoriz.setPaintTicks(true);  ◄──────   Cause the tick marks to be displayed.

// Cause the labels to be displayed.
jsldrVert.setPaintLabels(true);   ◄──────
jsldrHoriz.setPaintLabels(true);  ◄──────   Cause the labels to be displayed.

// These labels display the current slider value.
jlabHoriz = new JLabel("Value of horizontal slider: " +
                       jsldrHoriz.getValue());
jlabVert = new JLabel("Value of vertical slider: " +
                      jsldrVert.getValue());

// Add change listeners for the sliders.
//
// The horizontal slider waits until the user
// stops changing the slider's value before
// it responds.
jsldrHoriz.addChangeListener(new ChangeListener() {
  public void stateChanged(ChangeEvent ce) {
    // If the slider is in the process of being
    // changed, simply return.
    if(jsldrHoriz.getValueIsAdjusting()) return;

    // Display the new value.
    jlabHoriz.setText("Value of horizontal slider: "
                    + jsldrHoriz.getValue());
  }
```

```
        });

        // The vertical slider handler responds to all
        // change events, including those generated while
        // the slider is in the process of being changed.
        jsldrVert.addChangeListener(new ChangeListener() {
          public void stateChanged(ChangeEvent ce) {
            // Display the new value.
            jlabVert.setText("Value of vertical slider: "
                            + jsldrVert.getValue());
          }
        });

        // Add components to the content pane.
        jfrm.getContentPane().add(jsldrHoriz);
        jfrm.getContentPane().add(jsldrVert);
        jfrm.getContentPane().add(jlabHoriz);
        jfrm.getContentPane().add(jlabVert);

        // Display the frame.
        jfrm.setVisible(true);
    }

    public static void main(String args[]) {
        // Create the frame on the event dispatching thread.
        SwingUtilities.invokeLater(new Runnable() {
          public void run() {
            new SliderDemo();
          }
        });
    }
}
```

The program creates two sliders. One is vertical, the other is horizontal. Both use the default range (0 to 100). The horizontal slider has major tick marks every 20 units. The vertical slider has major tick marks every 10 units with minor tick marks every 5 units.

As explained, sliders generate change events when they are moved. The horizontal slider uses **getValueIsAdjusting( )** to skip all intervening events that are generated prior to the slider reaching its new position. Thus, the contents of the label referred to by **jlabHoriz** won't be updated until after you stop moving the slider. However, the vertical slider handles all events. This means that you will be able to watch the current value change in **jlabVert** as you move the vertical slider.

Ask the Expert

Q: Can a slider be run using the keyboard rather than the mouse?

A: Yes, a slider can be run by using the keyboard. Once a slider has input focus, it can be moved incrementally using the arrow keys. Pressing PGUP or PGDN causes a slider to move by an increment that is equal to one tenth of its range.

CRITICAL SKILL
3.8 # Some Slider Options

Although tick marks and labels are technically optional, they really are mandatory for most slider uses. However, **JSlider** does offer two other options that you might find appealing. First, when the knob is moved, you can have it land automatically on the closest tick mark. This behavior is called "snap-to," and it is set by calling the **setSnapToTicks( )** method, shown here:

void setSnapToTicks(boolean *on*)

If *on* is true, then the knob moves to the nearest tick mark automatically when movement stops. If it is false, the knob stays in the position at which the user left it. To obtain the current snap-to-ticks setting, call **getSnapToTicks( )**, shown here:

boolean getSnapToTicks( )

It returns true if snap-to-ticks is on.

To see the effect of enabling snap-to-ticks, try adding this line immediately after the sliders have been created in the previous program.

```
jsldrVert.setSnapToTicks(true);
```

Next, try moving the vertical slider's knob. As you will see, it will always land on a tick mark.

A second option that is sometimes useful is to reverse the range of the slider. This is done by calling **setInverted( )**, shown here:

void setInverted(boolean *on*)

If *on* is true, then the range is inverted. If it is false, the range is normal. Keep in mind that what constitutes normal and inverted is governed by language and cultural settings. For North

America, the range will normally read left to right. When inverted, it will read from right to left. To determine if the range is inverted, call **getInverted( )**:

boolean getInverted( )

It returns true if the range is inverted.

   To see the effect of an inverted range, add this line to the previous program immediately after the sliders have been created.

```
jsldrHoriz.setInverted(true);
```

   One last point: like all Swing components, you can set the preferred size of the slider by calling **setPreferredSize( )**. Thus, if you don't like its default size, you can specify one more compatible with your application.

Progress Check

1. To cause a slider to always land on a tick mark, what method must you call?

2. Can a slider's range be inverted? If so, how?

Project
3-1

Project 3-1   Use Custom Slider Labels to Build an Audio Player Interface

`AudioPlayer.java`

In addition to using the standard labels provided by **JSlider**'s **createStandardLabels( )** method, you can create your own table of labels. Not only do custom labels give your application a unique, individualized appearance, but also they can enhance its usability by making it clear precisely what a slider's position indicates. This project shows how to add custom labels to your sliders. As you will see, the process is quite easy, although it does require a couple of extra steps.

   The custom slider labels are used to create the GUI for a simple audio player control panel. The panel uses five sliders. Three set the bass, midrange, and treble frequencies. A fourth slider sets the left/right balance, and the fifth sets the volume. As you will see, the labels are designed to best fit each slider's purpose.

(continued)

1. **setSnapToTicks( )**
2. Yes. You can invert a slider's range by calling **setInverted( )**.

In addition to demonstrating custom slider labels, this project illustrates two other aspects of Swing. First, it demonstrates how two different types of controls can cooperate in a GUI. In this case, radio buttons select from various presets that are used to initialize the sliders. Second, it offers a sense of what it takes to begin creating Swing GUIs for real applications. Although the GUI presented here is still quite simple (a commercial application would definitely want it to be more stylish), it does show the level of effort needed to construct real interfaces. As you will see, although small as interfaces go, it still requires a fair amount of code to implement.

The GUI produced by this example is shown in Figure 3-4. As explained, this GUI represents the interface to a control panel for the audio portion of a media player. The GUI lets you set the bass, midrange, treble, balance, and volume by using sliders. It also lets you select between three presets. The first is the default setting. The other two can be set by you. To do so, first select either Preset 1 or Preset 2. Then, adjust the audio settings as desired. Finally, press the Store Settings button. This causes the current audio settings to be stored into the selected preset.

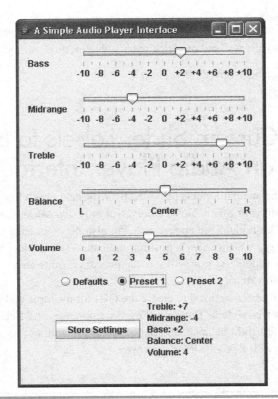

Figure 3-4 The GUI produced by Project 3-1

Step By Step

1. Create a file called **AudioPlayer.java** and add the following comment and **import** statements:

```
// Project 3-1: A Swing interface for an audio player.

import java.awt.*;
import java.awt.event.*;
import javax.swing.*;
import javax.swing.event.*;
import java.text.*;
import java.util.*;
```

2. This project contains two classes. The first is a small class called **Presets** that stores the values used by a preset. This class is shown here. Enter it now.

```
// A class that holds the audio settings.
class Presets {
  int bass;
  int midrange;
  int treble;
  int balance;
  int volume;

  Presets(int b, int m, int t, int bl, int v) {
    bass = b;
    midrange = m;
    treble = t;
    balance = bl;
    volume = v;
  }
}
```

3. The main class is called **AudioPlayer**. Begin coding it with the following lines:

```
// The main audio interface class.
class AudioPlayer implements ChangeListener {

  JLabel jlabBass;
  JLabel jlabMidrange;
  JLabel jlabTreble;
  JLabel jlabBalance;
  JLabel jlabVolume;
  JLabel jlabInfo;
```

(continued)

```
JSlider jsldrBass;
JSlider jsldrMidrange;
JSlider jsldrTreble;
JSlider jsldrBalance;
JSlider jsldrVolume;

JRadioButton jrbPreset1;
JRadioButton jrbPreset2;
JRadioButton jrbDefaults;

JButton jbtnStore;

DecimalFormat df;

Presets[] presets;
```

There are three things to notice. First, **AudioPlayer** implements the **ChangeListener**
interface. Recall that sliders generate change events. **AudioPlayer** provides the
stateChanged( ) method to handle those events. Second, a **DecimalFormat** reference
called **df** is declared. This formatter will be used to format the values of the sliders.
Third, an array of **Presets** objects is declared. This array will store the preset values.

4. Begin coding the **AudioPlayer** constructor as shown here:

```
AudioPlayer() {
  // Create a new JFrame container.
  JFrame jfrm = new JFrame("A Simple Audio Player Interface");

  // Specify a flow layout.
  jfrm.getContentPane().setLayout(new FlowLayout());

  // Give the frame an initial size.
  jfrm.setSize(340, 520);

  // Terminate the program when the user closes the application.
  jfrm.setDefaultCloseOperation(JFrame.EXIT_ON_CLOSE);

  // Create a decimal format that shows both + and - signs.
  df = new DecimalFormat("+#;-#");
```

Most of this is familiar. The one new item is the creation of a **DecimalFormat** object.
It specifies a format in which a positive value is shown with a + sign and a negative
value is shown with a – sign. You will see how this is used, shortly.

5. Continue coding **AudioPlayer( )** with these statements:

```
// Set presets.
setupPresets();
```

```
// Create the sliders.
setupSliders();

// Create the labels that describe the sliders.
setupLabels();

// Create the presets radio buttons.
setupRButtons();

// Create the Store Settings button.
jbtnStore = new JButton("Store Settings");
```

This sequence sets up the components. Because the code needed to create and initialize the presets, sliders, labels, and radio buttons is fairly long, it is organized into methods, which are called from within the **AudioPlayer** constructor.

6. Next, add event listeners.

```
// Add change listeners for the sliders.
jsldrBass.addChangeListener(this);
jsldrMidrange.addChangeListener(this);
jsldrTreble.addChangeListener(this);
jsldrBalance.addChangeListener(this);
jsldrVolume.addChangeListener(this);

// Handle Store Settings button.
jbtnStore.addActionListener(new ActionListener() {
  public void actionPerformed(ActionEvent ae) {
    if(jrbPreset1.isSelected())
      storePreset(presets[1]);
    else if(jrbPreset2.isSelected())
      storePreset(presets[2]);
  }
});

// Handle Defaults radio button.
jrbDefaults.addActionListener(new ActionListener() {
  public void actionPerformed(ActionEvent ae) {
    loadPreset(presets[0]);
  }
});

// Handle Preset 1 radio button.
jrbPreset1.addActionListener(new ActionListener() {
  public void actionPerformed(ActionEvent ae) {
    loadPreset(presets[1]);
  }
```

(continued)

```
  });

  // Handle Preset 2 radio button.
  jrbPreset2.addActionListener(new ActionListener() {
    public void actionPerformed(ActionEvent ae) {
      loadPreset(presets[2]);
    }
  });
```

The event handler for the change events generated by sliders is implemented as a stand-alone method. The handlers for the radio buttons and the push button are coded inline using anonymous inner classes.

When a radio button is selected, the presets associated with that button are loaded by calling **loadPreset( )**. When the Store Settings button is pressed, the current settings are stored by calling **storePreset( )**. Both of these methods are passed a reference to the element in the **presets** array that corresponds to the radio button that is currently selected. However, you can only store the setting if Preset 1 or Preset 2 is selected. Pressing Store Settings has no effect if the Defaults radio button is selected.

7. Finish **AudioPlayer( )** like this:

```
  // Add components to the content pane.
  Container cp = jfrm.getContentPane();
  cp.add(jlabBass);
  cp.add(jsldrBass);
  cp.add(jlabMidrange);
  cp.add(jsldrMidrange);
  cp.add(jlabTreble);
  cp.add(jsldrTreble);
  cp.add(jlabBalance);
  cp.add(jsldrBalance);
  cp.add(jlabVolume);
  cp.add(jsldrVolume);
  cp.add(jrbDefaults);
  cp.add(jrbPreset1);
  cp.add(jrbPreset2);
  cp.add(jbtnStore);
  cp.add(new JLabel(""));
  cp.add(jlabInfo);

  // Display the frame.
  jfrm.setVisible(true);
}
```

8. Add the **stateChanged( )** event handler for the sliders.

```
// Handle slider events.
public void stateChanged(ChangeEvent ce) {
  showSettings(); // update the info display
}
```

Notice that it simply calls **showSettings( )**, which displays the current audio settings in a label.

9. Add the **showSettings( )** method.

```
// Display the current settings.
void showSettings() {
  String bal;

  // Get balance setting.
  int b = jsldrBalance.getValue();
  if(b > 0)
    bal = "Right " + df.format(jsldrBalance.getValue());
  else if(b==0)
    bal = "Center";
  else
    bal = "Left " + df.format(-jsldrBalance.getValue());

  jlabInfo.setText("<html>Treble: " +
            df.format(jsldrTreble.getValue()) +
            "<br>Midrange: " +
            df.format(jsldrMidrange.getValue()) +
            "<br>Base: " +
            df.format(jsldrBass.getValue()) +
            "<br>Balance: " + bal +
            "<br>Volume: " +
            jsldrVolume.getValue());
}
```

This method sets the text in the **jlabInfo** label so that it reflects the current settings of the sliders.

10. Add the **setupSliders( )** method, which creates, customizes, and initializes the sliders.

```
// Create and initialize sliders.
void setupSliders() {
  // Create the sliders.
  jsldrBass = new JSlider(-10, 10);
  jsldrMidrange = new JSlider(-10, 10);
```

(continued)

3

Scroll Bars, Sliders, and Progress Bars

Project
3-1

Use Custom Slider Labels to Build an Audio Player Interface

```
jsldrTreble = new JSlider(-10, 10);
jsldrVolume = new JSlider(0, 10, 0);
jsldrBalance = new JSlider(-5, 5);

// Add major tick marks.
jsldrBass.setMajorTickSpacing(2);
jsldrMidrange.setMajorTickSpacing(2);
jsldrTreble.setMajorTickSpacing(2);
jsldrVolume.setMajorTickSpacing(1);
jsldrBalance.setMajorTickSpacing(1);

// Add minor tick marks.
jsldrBass.setMinorTickSpacing(1);
jsldrMidrange.setMinorTickSpacing(1);
jsldrTreble.setMinorTickSpacing(1);

// Create labels for Bass, Midrange, and Treble sliders.
Hashtable table = new Hashtable();
for(int i = -10; i <= 0; i += 2)
  table.put(new Integer(i), new JLabel("" + i));
for(int i = 2; i <= 10; i += 2)
  table.put(new Integer(i), new JLabel("+" + i));
jsldrTreble.setLabelTable(table);
jsldrMidrange.setLabelTable(table);
jsldrBass.setLabelTable(table);

// Create labels for the Balance slider.
table = new Hashtable();
table.put(new Integer(0), new JLabel("Center"));
table.put(new Integer(-5), new JLabel("L"));
table.put(new Integer(5), new JLabel("R"));
jsldrBalance.setLabelTable(table);

// Create standard numeric labels for Volume slider.
jsldrVolume.setLabelTable(jsldrVolume.createStandardLabels(1));

// Cause the tick marks to be displayed.
jsldrBass.setPaintTicks(true);
jsldrMidrange.setPaintTicks(true);
jsldrTreble.setPaintTicks(true);
jsldrVolume.setPaintTicks(true);
jsldrBalance.setPaintTicks(true);

// Cause the slider labels to be displayed.
jsldrBass.setPaintLabels(true);
jsldrMidrange.setPaintLabels(true);
jsldrTreble.setPaintLabels(true);
```

```
jsldrVolume.setPaintLabels(true);
jsldrBalance.setPaintLabels(true);

// Move to closest tick mark.
jsldrBass.setSnapToTicks(true);
jsldrMidrange.setSnapToTicks(true);
jsldrTreble.setSnapToTicks(true);
jsldrVolume.setSnapToTicks(true);
jsldrBalance.setSnapToTicks(true);

// Set the preferred slider size.
Dimension sldrSize = new Dimension(240, 60);
jsldrBass.setPreferredSize(sldrSize);
jsldrMidrange.setPreferredSize(sldrSize);
jsldrTreble.setPreferredSize(sldrSize);
jsldrVolume.setPreferredSize(sldrSize);
jsldrBalance.setPreferredSize(sldrSize);
}
```

There is quite a bit of code here, but much of it will be familiar. There are two key things to notice. First, except for the volume slider, the range of the other sliders includes both positive and negative values. The use of such a range is not uncommon when working with sliders.

Second, this method contains the code that creates the slider labels. Three different approaches are used. First, the three frequency sliders use custom labels that are created by the following code:

Project
3-1

Use Custom Slider Labels to Build an Audio Player Interface

```
// Create labels for Bass, Midrange, and Treble sliders.
Hashtable table = new Hashtable();
for(int i = -10; i <= 0; i += 2)
  table.put(new Integer(i), new JLabel("" + i));
for(int i = 2; i <= 10; i += 2)
  table.put(new Integer(i), new JLabel("+" + i));
jsldrTreble.setLabelTable(table);
jsldrMidrange.setLabelTable(table);
jsldrBass.setLabelTable(table);
```

Recall that slider labels are set by calling **setLabelTable( )**. This method takes as its only argument a reference to a **Dictionary**, which must contain a table of labels and the values to which they correspond. The table is organized into pairs that have the following form:

value, *label*

Normally, *value* will be an instance of **Integer** and *label* will be an instance of **JLabel**. However, you can use other components for the label if it suits your need. As you may know, **Dictionary** is an abstract class, which means that you can't create a **Dictionary**

(continued)

object directly. However, **Hashtable** is a concrete class that inherits the abstract class **Dictionary**. This means that it can be used in a call to **setLabelTable( )**. Next, the table is loaded with the values −10 to +10. Notice that the positive values are preceded by the + sign.

The custom labels for the Balance slider are created using this code:

```
// Create labels for the Balance slider.
table = new Hashtable();
table.put(new Integer(0), new JLabel("Center"));
table.put(new Integer(-5), new JLabel("L"));
table.put(new Integer(5), new JLabel("R"));
jsldrBalance.setLabelTable(table);
```

Notice that in this case, the labels are not numbers. Rather, they are the strings "L," "Center," and "R." When using a slider, the labels can be whatever is appropriate to your application.

Note that the preceding code will work for all versions of Java. However, if you are using JDK 5 or later, then you will want to use the following generic declaration for **Hashtable**, which is shown here:

```
Hashtable<Integer, JLabel> table = new Hashtable<Integer, JLabel>();
```

You will also want to use this line when allocating the new **Hashtable** for the Balance slider:

```
table = new Hashtable<Integer, JLabel>();
```

Using the generic code will avoid warning messages when compiling with JDK 5 or later. It also makes your code type-safe.

11. Add the **setupLabels( )** method. This method creates the labels that describe the sliders with the words Bass, Midrange, Treble, Balance, and Volume. It also creates the label that displays the current settings.

```
// Create the labels that describe the sliders.
void setupLabels() {
  // Create the labels.
  jlabTreble = new JLabel("Treble");
  jlabMidrange = new JLabel("Midrange");
  jlabBass = new JLabel("Bass");
  jlabVolume = new JLabel("Volume");
  jlabBalance = new JLabel("Balance");

  // Set preferred size for slider labels.
  Dimension labSize = new Dimension(60, 25);
```

```
jlabTreble.setPreferredSize(labSize);
jlabMidrange.setPreferredSize(labSize);
jlabBass.setPreferredSize(labSize);
jlabVolume.setPreferredSize(labSize);
jlabBalance.setPreferredSize(labSize);

// Create and size the audio info label.
jlabInfo = new JLabel("");
jlabInfo.setPreferredSize(new Dimension(110, 100));

// Load jlabInfo with the default settings.
showSettings();
}
```

12. Add the code that initializes the radio buttons that select the presets.

```
// Create and initialize the presets radio buttons.
void setupRButtons() {
  // Create the presets radio buttons.
  jrbDefaults = new JRadioButton("Defaults");
  jrbPreset1 = new JRadioButton("Preset 1");
  jrbPreset2 = new JRadioButton("Preset 2");

  // Add the radio buttons to a button group.
  ButtonGroup bg = new ButtonGroup();
  bg.add(jrbDefaults);
  bg.add(jrbPreset1);
  bg.add(jrbPreset2);

  // Select the Defaults button.
  jrbDefaults.setSelected(true);
}
```

13. Add the **loadPreset( )** method that sets the values of the sliders based on the information passed to it. This method is called by the event handlers for radio buttons.

```
// Load a preset.
void loadPreset(Presets info) {
  jsldrBass.setValue(info.bass);
  jsldrMidrange.setValue(info.midrange);
  jsldrTreble.setValue(info.treble);
  jsldrBalance.setValue(info.balance);
  jsldrVolume.setValue(info.volume);
}
```

Notice that the parameter to **loadPreset( )** is of type **Presets**.

Project
3-1

Use Custom Slider Labels to Build an Audio Player Interface

(continued)

14. Add **storePreset( )**, which is used to store the current settings into the **presets** array. This method is called by the event handler for the Store Settings button.

```
// Store a preset.
void storePreset(Presets info) {
  info.bass = jsldrBass.getValue();
  info.midrange = jsldrMidrange.getValue();
  info.treble = jsldrTreble.getValue();
  info.balance = jsldrBalance.getValue();
  info.volume = jsldrVolume.getValue();
}
```

This method simply obtains the current settings for the sliders and copies them into the array element referred to by **info**.

15. Enter the code for **setupPresets( )**, shown next. This method initializes the **presets** array with the default settings and two custom settings.

```
// Initialize presets.
void setupPresets() {
  presets = new Presets[3];
  presets[0] = new Presets(0, 0, 0, 0, 0);
  presets[1] = new Presets(2, -4, 7, 0, 4);
  presets[2] = new Presets(3, 3, -2, 1, 7);
}
```

The values given to **presets[1]** and **presets[2]** are arbitrary. You can use any values you like, except that they must be within range.

16. Finish **AudioPlayer** with the following **main( )** method:

```
public static void main(String args[]) {
  // Create the frame on the event dispatching thread.
  SwingUtilities.invokeLater(new Runnable() {
    public void run() {
      new AudioPlayer();
    }
  });
}
```

17. The entire program is shown here. You should experiment with this program, trying different slider labels, for example. As you can see, the code is fairly long. This gives you an idea of what is involved when developing real Swing interfaces.

```
// Project 3-1: A Swing interface for an audio player.

import java.awt.*;
import java.awt.event.*;
```

```
import javax.swing.*;
import javax.swing.event.*;
import java.text.*;
import java.util.*;

// A class that holds the audio settings.
class Presets {
  int bass;
  int midrange;
  int treble;
  int balance;
  int volume;

  Presets(int b, int m, int t, int bl, int v) {
    bass = b;
    midrange = m;
    treble = t;
    balance = bl;
    volume = v;
  }
}

// The main audio interface class.
class AudioPlayer implements ChangeListener {

  JLabel jlabBass;
  JLabel jlabMidrange;
  JLabel jlabTreble;
  JLabel jlabBalance;
  JLabel jlabVolume;
  JLabel jlabInfo;

  JSlider jsldrBass;
  JSlider jsldrMidrange;
  JSlider jsldrTreble;
  JSlider jsldrBalance;
  JSlider jsldrVolume;

  JRadioButton jrbPreset1;
  JRadioButton jrbPreset2;
  JRadioButton jrbDefaults;

  JButton jbtnStore;

  DecimalFormat df;
```

(continued)

3

Scroll Bars, Sliders, and Progress Bars

Project
3-1

Use Custom Slider Labels to Build an Audio Player Interface

```
    Presets[] presets;

    AudioPlayer() {
      // Create a new JFrame container.
      JFrame jfrm = new JFrame("A Simple Audio Player Interface");

      // Specify a flow layout.
      jfrm.getContentPane().setLayout(new FlowLayout());

      // Give the frame an initial size.
      jfrm.setSize(340, 520);

      // Terminate the program when the user closes the application.
      jfrm.setDefaultCloseOperation(JFrame.EXIT_ON_CLOSE);

      // Create a decimal format that shows both + and - signs.
      df = new DecimalFormat("+#;-#");

      // Set presets.
      setupPresets();

      // Create the sliders.
      setupSliders();

      // Create the labels that describe the sliders.
      setupLabels();

      // Create the presets radio buttons.
      setupRButtons();

      // Create the Store Settings button.
      jbtnStore = new JButton("Store Settings");

      // Add change listeners for the sliders.
      jsldrBass.addChangeListener(this);
      jsldrMidrange.addChangeListener(this);
      jsldrTreble.addChangeListener(this);
      jsldrBalance.addChangeListener(this);
      jsldrVolume.addChangeListener(this);

      // Handle Store Settings button.
      jbtnStore.addActionListener(new ActionListener() {
        public void actionPerformed(ActionEvent ae) {
          if(jrbPreset1.isSelected())
            storePreset(presets[1]);
          else if(jrbPreset2.isSelected())
```

```
        storePreset(presets[2]);
    }
});

// Handle Defaults radio button.
jrbDefaults.addActionListener(new ActionListener() {
  public void actionPerformed(ActionEvent ae) {
    loadPreset(presets[0]);
  }
});

// Handle Preset 1 radio button.
jrbPreset1.addActionListener(new ActionListener() {
  public void actionPerformed(ActionEvent ae) {
    loadPreset(presets[1]);
  }
});

// Handle Preset 2 radio button.
jrbPreset2.addActionListener(new ActionListener() {
  public void actionPerformed(ActionEvent ae) {
    loadPreset(presets[2]);
  }
});

// Add components to the content pane.
Container cp = jfrm.getContentPane();
cp.add(jlabBass);
cp.add(jsldrBass);
cp.add(jlabMidrange);
cp.add(jsldrMidrange);
cp.add(jlabTreble);
cp.add(jsldrTreble);
cp.add(jlabBalance);
cp.add(jsldrBalance);
cp.add(jlabVolume);
cp.add(jsldrVolume);
cp.add(jrbDefaults);
cp.add(jrbPreset1);
cp.add(jrbPreset2);
cp.add(jbtnStore);
cp.add(new JLabel(""));
cp.add(jlabInfo);

// Display the frame.
jfrm.setVisible(true);
```

(continued)

```java
  }

  // Handle slider events.
  public void stateChanged(ChangeEvent ce) {
    showSettings(); // update the info display
  }

  // Create and initialize sliders.
  void setupSliders() {
    // Create the sliders.
    jsldrBass = new JSlider(-10, 10);
    jsldrMidrange = new JSlider(-10, 10);
    jsldrTreble = new JSlider(-10, 10);
    jsldrVolume = new JSlider(0, 10, 0);
    jsldrBalance = new JSlider(-5, 5);

    // Add major tick marks.
    jsldrBass.setMajorTickSpacing(2);
    jsldrMidrange.setMajorTickSpacing(2);
    jsldrTreble.setMajorTickSpacing(2);
    jsldrVolume.setMajorTickSpacing(1);
    jsldrBalance.setMajorTickSpacing(1);

    // Add minor tick marks.
    jsldrBass.setMinorTickSpacing(1);
    jsldrMidrange.setMinorTickSpacing(1);
    jsldrTreble.setMinorTickSpacing(1);

    // Create labels for Bass, Midrange, and Treble sliders.
    Hashtable table = new Hashtable();
    for(int i = -10; i <= 0; i += 2)
      table.put(new Integer(i), new JLabel("" + i));
    for(int i = 2; i <= 10; i += 2)
      table.put(new Integer(i), new JLabel("+" + i));
    jsldrTreble.setLabelTable(table);
    jsldrMidrange.setLabelTable(table);
    jsldrBass.setLabelTable(table);

    // Create labels for the Balance slider.
    table = new Hashtable();
    table.put(new Integer(0), new JLabel("Center"));
    table.put(new Integer(-5), new JLabel("L"));
    table.put(new Integer(5), new JLabel("R"));
    jsldrBalance.setLabelTable(table);
```

```
    // Create standard numeric labels for Volume slider.
    jsldrVolume.setLabelTable(jsldrVolume.createStandardLabels(1));

    // Cause the tick marks to be displayed.
    jsldrBass.setPaintTicks(true);
    jsldrMidrange.setPaintTicks(true);
    jsldrTreble.setPaintTicks(true);
    jsldrVolume.setPaintTicks(true);
    jsldrBalance.setPaintTicks(true);

    // Cause the slider labels to be displayed.
    jsldrBass.setPaintLabels(true);
    jsldrMidrange.setPaintLabels(true);
    jsldrTreble.setPaintLabels(true);
    jsldrVolume.setPaintLabels(true);
    jsldrBalance.setPaintLabels(true);

    // Move to closest tick mark.
    jsldrBass.setSnapToTicks(true);
    jsldrMidrange.setSnapToTicks(true);
    jsldrTreble.setSnapToTicks(true);
    jsldrVolume.setSnapToTicks(true);
    jsldrBalance.setSnapToTicks(true);

    // Set the preferred slider size.
    Dimension sldrSize = new Dimension(240, 60);
    jsldrBass.setPreferredSize(sldrSize);
    jsldrMidrange.setPreferredSize(sldrSize);
    jsldrTreble.setPreferredSize(sldrSize);
    jsldrVolume.setPreferredSize(sldrSize);
    jsldrBalance.setPreferredSize(sldrSize);
}

// Create the labels that describe the sliders.
void setupLabels() {
    // Create the labels.
    jlabTreble = new JLabel("Treble");
    jlabMidrange = new JLabel("Midrange");
    jlabBass = new JLabel("Bass");
    jlabVolume = new JLabel("Volume");
    jlabBalance = new JLabel("Balance");

    // Set preferred size for slider labels.
    Dimension labSize = new Dimension(60, 25);
    jlabTreble.setPreferredSize(labSize);
```

3

Scroll Bars, Sliders, and Progress Bars

Project
3-1

Use Custom Slider Labels to Build an Audio Player Interface

(continued)

```java
      jlabMidrange.setPreferredSize(labSize);
      jlabBass.setPreferredSize(labSize);
      jlabVolume.setPreferredSize(labSize);
      jlabBalance.setPreferredSize(labSize);

      // Create and size the audio info label.
      jlabInfo = new JLabel("");
      jlabInfo.setPreferredSize(new Dimension(110, 100));

      // Load jlabInfo with the default settings.
      showSettings();
    }

    // Create and initialize the presets radio buttons.
    void setupRButtons() {
      // Create the presets radio buttons.
      jrbDefaults = new JRadioButton("Defaults");
      jrbPreset1 = new JRadioButton("Preset 1");
      jrbPreset2 = new JRadioButton("Preset 2");

      // Add the radio buttons to a button group.
      ButtonGroup bg = new ButtonGroup();
      bg.add(jrbDefaults);
      bg.add(jrbPreset1);
      bg.add(jrbPreset2);

      // Select the Defaults button.
      jrbDefaults.setSelected(true);
    }

    // Display the current settings.
    void showSettings() {
      String bal;

      // Get balance setting.
      int b = jsldrBalance.getValue();
      if(b > 0)
        bal = "Right " + df.format(jsldrBalance.getValue());
      else if(b==0)
        bal = "Center";
      else
        bal = "Left " + df.format(-jsldrBalance.getValue());

      jlabInfo.setText("<html>Treble: " +
                df.format(jsldrTreble.getValue()) +
```

```
               "<br>Midrange: " +
               df.format(jsldrMidrange.getValue()) +
               "<br>Base: " +
               df.format(jsldrBass.getValue()) +
               "<br>Balance: " + bal +
               "<br>Volume: " +
               jsldrVolume.getValue());
  }

  // Initialize presets.
  void setupPresets() {
    presets = new Presets[3];
    presets[0] = new Presets(0, 0, 0, 0, 0);
    presets[1] = new Presets(2, -4, 7, 0, 4);
    presets[2] = new Presets(3, 3, -2, 1, 7);
  }

  // Store a preset.
  void storePreset(Presets info) {
    info.bass = jsldrBass.getValue();
    info.midrange = jsldrMidrange.getValue();
    info.treble = jsldrTreble.getValue();
    info.balance = jsldrBalance.getValue();
    info.volume = jsldrVolume.getValue();
  }

  // Load a preset.
  void loadPreset(Presets info) {
    jsldrBass.setValue(info.bass);
    jsldrMidrange.setValue(info.midrange);
    jsldrTreble.setValue(info.treble);
    jsldrBalance.setValue(info.balance);
    jsldrVolume.setValue(info.volume);
  }

  public static void main(String args[]) {
    // Create the frame on the event dispatching thread.
    SwingUtilities.invokeLater(new Runnable() {
      public void run() {
        new AudioPlayer();
      }
    });
  }
}
```

Progress Bars

Progress bars are commonly used GUI components with which you are no doubt familiar. A progress bar indicates the degree of completion of some task. As the task moves towards completion, the bar grows longer. The length of the bar keeps the user apprised of the progress of the operation. Although a very simple component, a progress bar adds value to many applications because it provides important information to the user in a visually appealing fashion. Progress bars are instances of **JProgressBar**. They use **BoundedRangeModel** for their model.

JProgressBar defines the constructors shown in Table 3-4. Progress bars have two orientations: vertical or horizontal. By default, the progress bar will be horizontal, but you can specify a vertical orientation, if desired. The default range is 0 to 100, inclusive, and the initial value is 0.

Progress bars do not generate events based on user interaction. Instead, they simply display output. Of course, like all components, a progress bar generates a change event when its state changes. However, you will seldom monitor those events.

Because the progress bar uses the **BoundedRangeModel**, it defines properties that represent the minimum and maximum values in its range and its current value. However, progress bars do not use the extent property. The minimum, maximum, and current values defined by **BoundedRangeModel** are available through accessor methods defined by **JProgressBar**. They are shown here.

int getMinimum( )
void setMinimum(int *val*)

int getMaximum( )
void setMaximum(int *val*)

int getValue( )
void setValue(int *val*)

As you can see, no accessors are provided for the extent because it is not used. By default, the minimum is 0, the maximum is 100, and the value 0. Although you can set these to other values, usually the defaults are what you want because they offer an easy-to-use range.

The value property determines the length of the bar displayed within the progress bar component. Therefore, to use a progress bar, your application will increase the value as the operation advances. The idea is to have the value increase smoothly, reaching its maximum when the operation completes. This is not always easy to achieve, but it is the goal for which you should strive.

Constructor	Description
JProgressBar( )	Creates a horizontal progress bar. The range is 0 to 100. The initial value is 0.
JProgressBar(int *min*, int *max*)	Creates a horizontal progress bar. The range is passed in *min* and *max*. The initial value is *min*.
JProgressBar(int *VorH*)	Creates a progress bar that is oriented as specified by *VorH*, which must be either **JProgressBar.VERTICAL** or **JProgressBar.HORIZONTAL**. The range is 0 to 100. The initial value is 0.
JProgressBar(int *VorH*, int *min*, int *max*)	Creates a progress bar that is oriented as specified by *VorH*, which must be either **JProgressBar.VERTICAL** or **JProgressBar.HORIZONTAL**. The range is passed in *min* and *max*. The initial value is *min*.
JProgressBar(BoundedRangeModel *model*)	Creates a progress bar that uses the model passed in *model*.

Table 3-4 The **JProgressBar** Constructors

JProgressBar offers an option that you will often want to use: it can display a string inside the progress bar. By default, this string displays a percentage that corresponds to the degree of completion. This option is initially off. To turn it on, call **setStringPainted( )**, shown here:

void setStringPainted(boolean *on*)

If *on* is true, the string will be displayed. Otherwise, no string is displayed. You can determine the setting of the string-painted property by calling **isStringPainted( )**, shown here:

boolean isStringPainted( )

If it returns true, the string is displayed. Otherwise, the string is not displayed.

Demonstrate Progress Bars

The following program demonstrates **JProgressBar**. It creates two progress bars, one horizontal and one vertical. They use the default range of 0 to 100. The program turns on the display-string property, which causes the percentage of completion to be displayed inside the bar. The program also adds a button called Push Me. Each time this button is pressed, the bars will be advanced by 10 units. Sample output is shown in Figure 3-5.

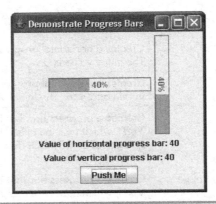

Figure 3-5 Sample output from the Progress Bar demonstration program

```
// Demonstrate a progress bar.

import java.awt.*;
import java.awt.event.*;
import javax.swing.*;

class ProgressDemo {

  JLabel jlabVert;
  JLabel jlabHoriz;

  JProgressBar jprogHoriz;
  JProgressBar jprogVert;

  JButton jbtn;

  ProgressDemo() {
    // Create a new JFrame container.
    JFrame jfrm = new JFrame("Demonstrate Progress Bars");

    // Specify a flow layout.
    jfrm.getContentPane().setLayout(new FlowLayout());

    // Give the frame an initial size.
    jfrm.setSize(280, 270);

    // Terminate the program when the user closes the application.
    jfrm.setDefaultCloseOperation(JFrame.EXIT_ON_CLOSE);

    // Create default vertical and horizontal progress bars.
```

```
jprogVert = new JProgressBar(JProgressBar.VERTICAL);
jprogHoriz = new JProgressBar(); // horizontal by default

// Display the percentage string.
jprogVert.setStringPainted(true);
jprogHoriz.setStringPainted(true);

jbtn = new JButton("Push Me");

// These labels display the current progress bar value.
jlabHoriz = new JLabel("Value of horizontal progress bar: " +
                          jprogHoriz.getValue());
jlabVert = new JLabel("Value of vertical progress bar: " +
                          jprogVert.getValue());

// Increment the progress bars each time the
// Push Me button is pressed.  When the value
// reaches the maximum, no further action is taken.
jbtn.addActionListener(new ActionListener() {
  public void actionPerformed(ActionEvent ae) {
    int hVal = jprogHoriz.getValue();
    int vVal = jprogVert.getValue();

    if(hVal >= jprogHoriz.getMaximum())
      return;
    else
      jprogHoriz.setValue(hVal + 10);

    if(vVal >= jprogHoriz.getMaximum())
      return;
    else
      jprogVert.setValue(vVal + 10);

    jlabHoriz.setText("Value of horizontal progress bar: " +
                      jprogHoriz.getValue());
    jlabVert.setText("Value of vertical progress bar: " +
                      jprogVert.getValue());
  }
});

// Add components to the content pane.
jfrm.getContentPane().add(jprogHoriz);
jfrm.getContentPane().add(jprogVert);
jfrm.getContentPane().add(jlabHoriz);
jfrm.getContentPane().add(jlabVert);
jfrm.getContentPane().add(jbtn);
```

Create vertical and horizontal progress bars.

Cause the percentage of completion to be shown.

Advance the progress bars each time the Push Me button is pressed.

```
    // Display the frame.
    jfrm.setVisible(true);
  }

  public static void main(String args[]) {
    // Create the frame on the event dispatching thread.
    SwingUtilities.invokeLater(new Runnable() {
      public void run() {
        new ProgressDemo();
      }
    });
  }
}
```

Notice how the value of the progress bars is incremented within the action event handler for the Push Me push button. First, the current value for each bar is obtained. Then, if that value is greater than or equal to the maximum, no action is taken. Otherwise, the progress bar is advanced by 10 units.

Some JProgressBar Options

Sometimes you may not know how long an operation will take but you want to give the user feedback that indicates that the operation is underway. To handle this situation, you can put a progress bar into an *indeterminate* state by calling **setIndeterminate( )**, shown here:

void setIndeterminate(boolean *on*)

If *on* is true, the progress bar enters an indeterminate state. In this state, a short bar bounces between the two ends of the progress bar. This animation indicates that activity is occurring, but does not indicate a degree of completion. To return the progress bar to normal, pass false to *on*. In general, you should return the progress bar to normal as soon as you can determine when the operation will complete. Also, you will not normally show the percentage string when the indeterminate property is on because the point of the indeterminate state is that you don't know how much of the operation has been completed. You can determine the setting of the indeterminate property by calling **isIndeterminate( )**, shown here:

boolean isIndeterminate( )

It returns true if the progress bar is in an indeterminate state and false otherwise.

You can easily see what an indeterminate progress bar looks like. In the preceding program, add these lines after the progress bars are created:

```
jprogVert.setIndeterminate(true);
jprogHoriz.setIndeterminate(true);
```

You should also remove the lines that turn on the percentage string. After making these changes, both progress bars will be animated.

By default, progress bars have borders. This is what you will normally want. However, you can turn the border off by calling **setBorderPainted( )**, shown here:

void setBorderPainted(boolean on)

If *on* is true, the border is painted. If it is false, the border is removed. You can determine the setting of the border-painted property by calling **isBorderPainted( )**, shown next:

boolean isBorderPainted( )

It returns true if the border is painted and false otherwise.

It is possible to display a string inside the bar that contains something other than the percentage. To do this, call **setString( )**, shown here:

void setString(String *str*)

Here, *str* is the string displayed. For most uses, the automatically generated percentage string is a better choice, but **JProgressBar** does give you the option of using a custom string. You can obtain the current string by calling **getString( )**, shown next:

String getString ( )

It returns the current string.

As with other components, you can specify the preferred size of a progress bar by calling **setPreferredSize( )** defined by **JComponent**.

Progress Check

1. If you choose to show a string inside a progress bar, what is shown by default?

2. What does the progress bar display when it is in an indeterminate state?

3. What is the default range of a progress bar?

---

1. The percentage of completion
2. A short bar that bounces between the two endpoints of the progress bar
3. 0 to 100

✓

Module 3 Mastery Check

1. Scroll bars, sliders, and progress bars all use the _____ model.

2. Describe the relationship between the current value and the minimum, maximum, and extent.

3. When the user clicks on the paging area of a scroll bar, the thumb is advanced by the amount specified by the block increment. True or false?

4. To receive scroll bar events, what event listener must your program implement?

5. Explain the difference between the major and minor tick marks in a slider.

6. What type of event is generated by a slider?

7. Having a slider display labels is a three-step process. Describe the steps.

8. Do progress bars generate events based on user input?

9. Is it possible to create a progress bar that does not have a border? If so, how is this achieved?

10. If you want to monitor the state of a progress bar, what event listener must be implemented?

11. Create a program that contains a slider and a scroll bar that are linked together. That is, each time the slider is moved, the scroll bar will move the same amount and vice versa.

12. Project 2-2 creates a simple phone list. Add a scroll bar to the program that scrolls through the list of names and numbers. To do this, add a label that displays a name and number. Each time the scroll bar is moved, show the next name and number.

Module 4

Managing Components with Panels, Panes, and Tooltips

Before looking at any more Swing controls, such as lists, spinners, trees, and so on, it is useful to examine the containers and techniques that help organize and manage those controls. As mentioned in Module 1, in addition to top-level containers, such as **JFrame**, Swing provides a number of other containers. One of the most commonly used is **JPanel**. Others include **JScrollPane**, **JTabbedPane**, and **JSplitPane**. Each of these adds important capabilities that enable you to conveniently manage what might otherwise be difficult situations. This module also shows how to add tooltips to your GUI components. As you will see, Swing's built-in support of tooltips makes this an easy task.

CRITICAL SKILL
4.1 # Work with JPanel

In commercial Swing applications, it is common to find that most components are not added directly to the content pane of the top-level container. Instead, the components are added to one or more panels and these panels are then added to the content pane. Using this approach helps organize the GUI, giving you the ability to treat related controls as a group, which often aids in layout. The commonly used container for this purpose is **JPanel**.

JPanel is a general-purpose container that can be used to hold other components. Recall that **JPanel** inherits **JComponent**, which means that it is also a component. Thus, **JPanel** is a lightweight container that can also be used to hold other **JPanel**s. This makes **JPanel** perfect for creating a multilayered containment system.

JPanel defines the constructors shown in Table 4-1. Notice that, by default, a **JPanel** is created with flow layout and uses double buffering. Double buffering is a mechanism that is commonly employed to achieve a better user experience when screen refreshes take place. Instead of drawing each component on the screen directly, which can lead to "flicker," the components are rendered to a separate buffer. When the rendering is complete, the buffer is copied to the screen in one fast, uninterrupted operation. In this way, the complete contents of a panel appear instantaneously, rather than slowly and in pieces. You can turn off double buffering if desired, although you will seldom want to do so. Support for double buffering is inherited from **JComponent**.

Notice that **JPanel** lets you specify the layout manager. This ability offers a major advantage when handling some types of GUIs because it lets you organize components into panels, with each panel using the layout manager that best fits your needs. This is another reason that organizing parts of a larger GUI into panels is such a useful and common technique.

JPanels can be given borders. The process is the same as that used to give a label a border and is described in Module 2. By giving a panel a border, you make its extent visible. Of course, you don't have to give a panel a border.

Constructor	Description
JPanel( )	Creates a default panel. It uses double buffering and flow layout.
JPanel(LayoutManager *lm*)	Creates a panel that uses the layout manager specified by *lm*. The panel is double-buffered.
JPanel(boolean *doubleBuf*)	Creates a panel that uses flow layout. If *doubleBuf* is true, the panel is double-buffered. If *doubleBuf* is false, it is not double-buffered.
JPanel(LayoutManager *lm*, boolean *doubleBuf*)	Creates a panel that uses the layout specified by *lm*. If *doubleBuf* is true, the panel is double-buffered. If *doubleBuf* is false, it is not double-buffered.

Table 4-1 The **JPanel** Constructors

In general, most panels should be opaque, especially if used as content panes. Swing defines two visual component types: *opaque* and *transparent*. An opaque component overwrites (that is, paints over) anything that is beneath it. A transparent component does not paint its background color. This allows anything underneath to show through. In most look-and-feels, **JPanel**s are opaque by default. However, this is not the case with GTK+.

Ask the Expert

Q: You said that double buffering was inherited by JPanel from JComponent. How can I determine if a component is double-buffered? How can I activate or deactivate this feature?

A: You can determine if a component is double-buffered by calling **isDoubleBuffered( )**, shown here:

boolean isDoubleBuffered( )

It returns true if the component is double-buffered and false otherwise. You can turn double buffering on and off by calling **setDoubleBuffered( )**, which is defined like this:

void setDoubleBuffered(boolean *DBon*)

If *DBon* is true, the component will be double-buffered. If *DBon* is false, double buffering is deactivated.

Thus, if you want an opaque panel (which is normally the case) and you want that behavior to be consistent across all look-and-feels, then you should explicitly set its opaque property to true by calling **setOpaque( )**, which is defined for all components. It is shown here:

void setOpaque(boolean *opaqueOn*)

If *opaqueOn* is true, the panel will be opaque. If *opaqueOn* is false, the panel will be transparent. You can determine if a panel (or any other component) is opaque by calling **isOpaque( )**, shown next:

boolean isOpaque( )

It returns true if the component is opaque and false if it is transparent.

The remainder of this section examines two applications of **JPanel**. The first shows how panels can be used to organize components into subgroups, which gives you greater control over layout. The second shows a common technique in which a custom **JPanel** is used as the content pane.

CRITICAL SKILL
4.2 # Use Panels to Organize Components

As just explained, **JPanel** inherits **JComponent**. This means that **JPanel** is also a component that can be added to a container. Furthermore, it means that a **JPanel** can be added as a component to another **JPanel**, thus allowing nested panels. In practice, one of the most common places this will occur is when you add a **JPanel** instance to the content pane of a **JFrame**. As you know from Module 1, the content pane of a **JFrame** is a **JPanel**. Therefore, you can add one or more **JPanel**s to the content pane of a **JFrame**. This offers several advantages.

First, you can use a separate **JPanel** to hold a related group of components, letting the layout manager used by the content pane treat them as a unit, instead of positioning each component separately. This often provides an easy way to keep components together when the frame is resized. (This is especially important when a flow layout is used by the content pane.) Second, it lets you specify a different layout manager for each panel. Third, it gives you a way to add or remove groups of components to or from the content pane in a single operation.

The following program shows how to organize components into panels. It creates two **JPanel** instances. It then adds two push buttons and a label to the first and three labels to the second. Borders are added to both panels so that their boundaries can be seen. The panels are then added to the content pane. Sample output is shown in Figure 4-1.

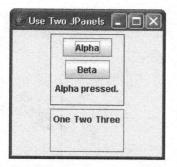 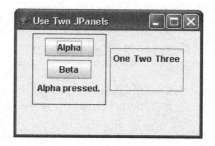

Figure 4-1 Sample output from the **PanelDemo** program. Notice that even when the frame is resized, the organization of the contents of the two panels remains unchanged.

```java
// Create two JPanels and add them to the content pane.

import java.awt.*;
import java.awt.event.*;
import javax.swing.*;

class PanelDemo {

  JLabel jlab;
  JButton jbtnAlpha;
  JButton jbtnBeta;

  PanelDemo() {

    // Create a new JFrame container. Use the default
    // border layout.
    JFrame jfrm = new JFrame("Use Two JPanels");

    // Specify FlowLayout manager.
    jfrm.getContentPane().setLayout(new FlowLayout());

    // Give the frame an initial size.
    jfrm.setSize(210, 210);

    // Terminate the program when the user closes the application.
    jfrm.setDefaultCloseOperation(JFrame.EXIT_ON_CLOSE);
```

```java
// Create the first JPanel.
JPanel jpnl = new JPanel();

// Set the preferred size of the first panel.
jpnl.setPreferredSize(new Dimension(100, 100));

// Make the panel opaque.
jpnl.setOpaque(true);

// Add a blue border to the panel.
jpnl.setBorder(
    BorderFactory.createLineBorder(Color.BLUE));

// Create the second JPanel.
JPanel jpnl2 = new JPanel();

// Set the preferred size of the second panel.
jpnl2.setPreferredSize(new Dimension(100, 60));

// Make the panel opaque.
jpnl2.setOpaque(true);

// Add a red border to the panel.
jpnl2.setBorder(
    BorderFactory.createLineBorder(Color.RED));

// Create a label.
jlab = new JLabel("Press a button.");

// Make two buttons.
jbtnAlpha = new JButton("Alpha");
jbtnBeta = new JButton("Beta");

// Add action listeners for the buttons.
jbtnAlpha.addActionListener(new ActionListener() {
  public void actionPerformed(ActionEvent ae) {
    jlab.setText("Alpha pressed.");
  }
});

jbtnBeta.addActionListener(new ActionListener() {
  public void actionPerformed(ActionEvent ae) {
    jlab.setText("Beta pressed.");
  }
});
```

— Create and initialize the first **JPanel**.

— Create and initialize the second **JPanel**.

```
      // Add the buttons and label to the panel.
      jpnl.add(jbtnAlpha);
      jpnl.add(jbtnBeta);              Add buttons and label to first JPanel.
      jpnl.add(jlab);

      // Add some labels to the second JPanel.
      jpnl2.add(new JLabel("One"));
      jpnl2.add(new JLabel("Two"));           Add labels to second JPanel.
      jpnl2.add(new JLabel("Three"));

      // Add the panels to the frame.
      jfrm.getContentPane().add(jpnl);
      jfrm.getContentPane().add(jpnl2);       Add the panels to the content pane.

      // Display the frame.
      jfrm.setVisible(true);
    }

  public static void main(String args[]) {
    // Create the frame on the event dispatching thread.
    SwingUtilities.invokeLater(new Runnable() {
      public void run() {
        new PanelDemo();
      }
    });
  }
}
```

Let's look closely at this program. First, notice that the top-level container is a **JFrame** called **jfrm**. Its layout manager is set to flow layout. As you know, when using a flow layout, the contents of the window will move around when the window is resized. Keep this fact in mind.

Next, two **JPanel** instances called **jpnl** and **jpnl2** are created. Each panel has its preferred size set. This effectively fixes the dimensions of the panel. Each panel then has its opaque property set to true, and each panel is given a border. For **jpnl**, the border is blue; for **jpn2**, the border is red. The borders enable the boundaries of the panels to be seen. They are not necessary otherwise. Both panels use their default flow layout.

Next, components are added to each panel. In the case of **jpnl**, two push buttons and a label are added. Three labels are added to **jpnl2**. Finally, the two panels are added to the content pane of the frame, and the frame is displayed.

When you try the program, you will see that the layout of the components within the panels is fixed no matter how the outer frame is resized. For example, if you make the frame wider, the position of the two panels relative to each other will change, but the position of the components within the panels will not. This is an example of how **JPanel** makes the organization and management of the GUI easier.

CRITICAL SKILL
4.3 Use a Custom JPanel as the Content Pane

In all of the previous examples, components have been added to the existing content pane of a **JFrame** top-level container. While there is nothing wrong with this approach, there is an alternative technique that can be very effective. Instead of using the content pane provided by **JFrame**, construct a panel of your own and then make that panel the content pane of the **JFrame**. Recall that the content pane of a **JFrame** is an instance of **JPanel**. Thus, you can use any **JPanel** for the content pane, not just the one provided automatically when you create an instance of **JFrame**. The advantage of this approach is that it lets you a create a custom **JPanel** that contains the desired content automatically.

To set the content pane of a **JFrame**, you must use the **setContentPane( )** method, shown here:

void setContentPane(Container *panel*)

Here, *panel* must be an opaque container derived from **JComponent**. (Recall that **JComponent** inherits **Container**.)

One of the most common ways to create custom content panes is to define a class that extends **JPanel**. An object of this class will be able to be used as a content pane. The extending class can populate the pane with components so that it is fully initialized before it becomes the content pane. The following program shows this technique. It defines a custom content pane that contains two push buttons and a label. The push buttons are labeled Red and Blue. When one is pushed, the color of the border around the content pane is changed to the indicated color. Sample output is shown in Figure 4-2.

Figure 4-2 Sample output from the **CustomCPDemo** program

```
// Create a custom JPanel and use it for the content pane.

import java.awt.*;
import java.awt.event.*;
import javax.swing.*;

// This class creates a panel by extending JPanel.
// It adds no new functionality, but the
// object that it constructs can be used
// anywhere that a JPanel can be used.
class MyContentPanel extends JPanel {
```
◄———— Create a custom **JPanel** that will be used as the content pane.

```
  JLabel jlab;
  JButton jbtnRed;
  JButton jbtnBlue;

  MyContentPanel() {

    // Ensure that the panel is opaque.
    setOpaque(true);
```
◄———— Remember, content panes must be opaque.

```
    // Start with a green, 5-pixel border.
    setBorder(
      BorderFactory.createLineBorder(Color.GREEN, 5));

    // Create a label.
    jlab = new JLabel("Select Border Color");

    // Make two buttons.
    jbtnRed = new JButton("Red");
    jbtnBlue = new JButton("Blue");

    // Add action listeners for the buttons.
    jbtnRed.addActionListener(new ActionListener() {
      public void actionPerformed(ActionEvent ae) {
        setBorder(
          BorderFactory.createLineBorder(Color.RED, 5));
      }
    });

    jbtnBlue.addActionListener(new ActionListener() {
      public void actionPerformed(ActionEvent ae) {
```

```
        setBorder(
          BorderFactory.createLineBorder(Color.BLUE, 5));
      }
    });

    // Add the buttons and label to the panel.
    add(jbtnRed);   ─┐
    add(jbtnBlue);   ├──────── Add the components to the custom panel.
    add(jlab);      ─┘

  }
}


// Create a top-level container and use the panel
// created by MyContentPanel as the content pane.
class CustomCPDemo {
  CustomCPDemo() {
    // Create a new JFrame container. Use the default
    // border layout.
    JFrame jfrm = new JFrame("Set the Content Pane");

    // Give the frame an initial size.
    jfrm.setSize(240, 150);

    // Terminate the program when the user closes the application.
    jfrm.setDefaultCloseOperation(JFrame.EXIT_ON_CLOSE);

    // Create an instance of the custom content pane.
    MyContentPanel mcp = new MyContentPanel();

    // Make mcp the content pane.
    jfrm.setContentPane(mcp);  ◄──────── Make the custom panel the content pane.

    // Display the frame.
    jfrm.setVisible(true);
  }

  public static void main(String args[]) {
    // Create the frame on the event dispatching thread.
    SwingUtilities.invokeLater(new Runnable() {
      public void run() {
        new CustomCPDemo();
      }
    });
  }
}
```

The program contains two classes. The first is **MyContentPanel**, which extends **JPanel**. This class does not add any new functionality to **JPanel**. It simply creates a **JPanel** that contains the components that are added to it. In this case, the components are two push buttons and a label. Notice that the panel is explicitly set to opaque. This is necessary. All content panes should be opaque. Also notice how methods such as **setOpaque( )** and **setBorder( )** are called. Because **MyContentPanel** extends **JPanel**, these methods are called directly, without being qualified by a **JPanel** object. This is because these methods operate on the **JPanel** instance that is being created.

Now, look at the second class, **CustomCPDemo**. In its constructor, a **JFrame** called **jfrm** is set up. Then, an instance of **MyContentPanel** called **mcp** is created. This instance is then used as the **jfrm**'s content pane. When the call to **setVisible( )** occurs, it is the contents of **mcp** that are displayed.

Progress Check

1. What is the benefit of double buffering?

2. Is **JPanel** double-buffered by default?

3. When a panel is transparent, what is beneath the panel shows through. True or false?

Ask the Expert

Q: When compiling the custom content pane program, if I specify the –Xlint option (which enables recommended warnings), I get the following warning message:

warning: [serial] serializable class MyContentPanel has no
            definition of serialVersionUID

What does this mean, why do I get it, and how can I get rid of it?

A: This warning is issued because **MyContentPanel** extends **JPanel**, and **JPanel** implements the **Serializable** interface. **Serializable** is a marker interface that simply

(continued)

---

1. Double buffering improves the user experience by preventing flicker. It also improves the apparent performance of the GUI by "snapping" a completed image to the screen in one uninterrupted operation.

2. Yes

3. True

indicates that a class may be serialized. Each serializable class has associated with it a serial version ID, which is stored in a static final variable called **serialVersionUID**. If the class does not explicitly declare this ID, then one is automatically generated. However, the Java API documentation states that it is better for you to provide this value explicitly. This is why the warning message is issued. In cases in which serialization is not an issue, such as in the sample programs shown in this book, it is perfectly fine to ignore this warning. However, for real applications you should define a serial ID explicitly. Doing so will also keep the warning messages from being displayed.

To declare the **serialVersionUID** variable, use a statement similar to the following:

```
static final long serialVersionUID = 10101;
```

Of course, you must pick your own ID value.

CRITICAL SKILL

4.4 Use JScrollPane

Swing defines several specialized containers that help organize your GUI. These include the scroll pane, the tabbed pane, and the split pane, and these containers are the subject of the next few sections. This section examines the scroll pane, which is supported by the class **JScrollPane**. The scroll pane automatically handles the scrolling of the component that it is passed. Because all lightweight containers are also components, a **JScrollPane** can also scroll the contents of a **JPanel**, for example. As mentioned in Module 3, because the **JScrollPane** automates scrolling, it usually eliminates the need to manage individual scroll bars separately.

The layout of a **JScrollPane** is managed by the **ScrollPaneLayout** layout manager. It organizes the window of a scroll pane into nine separate parts, which are depicted in Figure 4-3.

Typically, the largest part of a **JScrollPane** is the *viewport*, which is the window in which the component being scrolled is displayed. Thus, the viewport displays the visible portion of the component being scrolled. The scroll bars scroll the component through the viewport. In its default behavior, a **JScrollPane** will dynamically add or remove a scroll bar as needed. For example, if the component is taller than the viewport, a vertical scroll bar is added. If the component will fit within the viewport completely, the scroll bars are removed. You can add row and column headers, which usually describe the view or supply additional functionality. Finally, there are the four corners into which you can be put components that also add functionality.

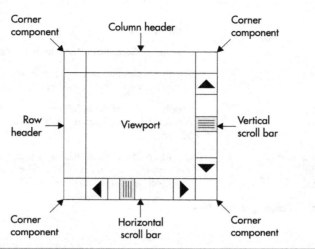

Figure 4-3 The layout of a **JScrollPane**

At first, you might think that, given the number of parts, a **JScrollPane** would be difficult to use. Fortunately, this is not the case. Although a **JScrollPane** does offer these nine parts, you don't need to use them all. In its default configuration, a **JScrollPane** provides only the viewport and the dynamic scroll bars. For many applications, this default configuration is all that you will need. Furthermore, this default configuration is trivially easy to use: simply pass to **JScrollPane** the component that you want to scroll and it does the rest automatically. Thus, even though **JScrollPane** gives you the ability to create highly customized scroll panes, you don't necessarily have to do so.

JScrollPane defines the constructors shown in Table 4-2. As the table shows, you can create a **JScrollPane** that does not contain a component to be scrolled. In these cases, you will set the component after the scroll pane has been created. Most often, however, you will specify the component when the scroll pane is constructed. Also notice that you can set the scroll bar policy. The scroll bar policy determines when the scroll bars are displayed. Scroll bar policies are described later in this section. If you don't specify a policy, then the scroll bars will be shown as needed. This is usually what you want.

The scrollable area within a **JScrollPane** is managed by an object of type **JViewport**. When you pass a component to a **JScrollPane** constructor, a **JViewport** is automatically constructed for that component. For most uses of **JScrollPane**, you won't need to interact with **JViewport** directly.

Constructor	Description
JScrollPane( )	Creates a **JScrollPane** for which no view has been defined.
JScrollPane(Component *comp*)	Creates a **JScrollPane** that scrolls automatically through the component specified by *comp*.
JScrollPane(int *vertSBP*, int *horizSBP*)	Creates a **JScrollPane** for which no view has been defined. The scroll bar policies are specified by *vertSBP* and *horizSBP*.
JScrollPane(Component *comp*, int *vertSBP*, int *horizSBP*)	Creates a **JScrollPane** that scrolls automatically through the component specified by *comp*. The scroll bar policies are specified by *vertSBP* and *horizSBP*.

Table 4-2 The **JScrollPane** Constructors

A Simple JScrollPane Example

Despite its power, **JScrollPane** is very easy to use, especially in its default configuration. In general, you can use **JScrollPane** to provide scrolling for any component by simply passing a reference to the component when the scroll pane is constructed. Once that has been done, **JScrollPane** does the rest automatically. Here is a simple example that illustrates the process. It creates a scroll pane that scrolls through the contents of a **JLabel**, which contains several lines of HTML. Sample output is shown in Figure 4-4.

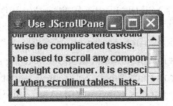

Figure 4-4 Sample output from the **ScrollPaneDemo** program

```java
// A simple JScrollPane example.

 import javax.swing.*;

class ScrollPaneDemo {

  ScrollPaneDemo() {

    // Create a new JFrame container. Use the default
    // border layout.
    JFrame jfrm = new JFrame("Use JScrollPane");

    // Give the frame an initial size.
    jfrm.setSize(200, 120);

    // Terminate the program when the user closes the application.
    jfrm.setDefaultCloseOperation(JFrame.EXIT_ON_CLOSE);

    // Create a long, HTML-based label.
    JLabel jlab =
      new JLabel("<html>JScrollPane simplifies what would<br>" +
                 "otherwise be complicated tasks.<br>" +
                 "It can be used to scroll any component<br>" +
                 "or lightweight container. It is especially<br>" +
                 "useful when scrolling tables, lists,<br>" +
                 "or images.");

    // Create a scroll pane and have it scroll the label.
    JScrollPane jscrlp = new JScrollPane(jlab);   // ◄——— Create a scroll pane that
                                                  //      contains a long label.
    // Add the scroll pane to the frame.
    jfrm.getContentPane().add(jscrlp);   // ◄——— Add the scroll pane to the content pane.

    // Display the frame.
    jfrm.setVisible(true);
  }

  public static void main(String args[]) {
    // Create the frame on the event dispatching thread.
    SwingUtilities.invokeLater(new Runnable() {
      public void run() {
```

```
        new ScrollPaneDemo();
      }
    });
  }
}
```

In the program, pay special attention to this line:

```
JScrollPane jscrlp = new JScrollPane(jlab);
```

Here, the label **jlab** is passed as the view component to **JScrollPane**. Once this has been done, **jscrlp** displays the contents of **jlab** through the viewport automatically, adding scrollbars as needed.

Add Headers

As explained previously, for many applications, the default behavior of **JScrollPane** is exactly what you want. However, it is also very easy to customize. One common enhancement is the addition of headers. **JScrollPane** supports both a column header and a row header. You can use either or both. A header can consist of any type of component. This means that you are not limited to only passive labels; a header can also contain active controls, such as a push button.

The easiest way to set a row header is to call **setRowHeaderView( )**, shown here:

void setRowHeaderView(Component *comp*)

Here, *comp* is the component that will be used as a header.

The easiest way to set a column header is to call **setColumnHeaderView( )**, shown next:

void setColumnHeaderView(Component *comp*)

Here, *comp* is the component that will be used as a header.

When using headers, it is sometimes useful to include a border around the viewport. This is easily accomplished by calling **setViewportBorder( )**, which is defined by **JScrollPane**. It is shown here:

void setViewportBorder(Border *border*)

Recall that you can construct standard borders by using the **BorderFactory** class. (See Module 2.)

The following example shows how to add row and column headers to a scroll pane. It also puts a border around the viewport. Notice how easy it is to add the headers. (Of course, you can create much more sophisticated headers than the simple ones shown here, but the basic procedure is the same.) Sample output is shown in Figure 4-5.

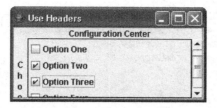

Figure 4-5 Sample output from the **AddHeadersDemo** program

```
// Add headers and a border to a scroll pane.

import java.awt.*;
import javax.swing.*;

class AddHeadersDemo {

  JCheckBox jcbOpt1;
  JCheckBox jcbOpt2;
  JCheckBox jcbOpt3;
  JCheckBox jcbOpt4;
  JCheckBox jcbOpt5;

  AddHeadersDemo() {
    // Create a new JFrame container. Use the default
    // border layout.
    JFrame jfrm = new JFrame("Use Headers");

    // Give the frame an initial size.
    jfrm.setSize(280, 140);

    // Terminate the program when the user closes the application.
    jfrm.setDefaultCloseOperation(JFrame.EXIT_ON_CLOSE);

    // Create a label.
    JLabel jlabOptions = new
      JLabel("Select one or more options: ");

    // Make some check boxes.
    jcbOpt1 = new JCheckBox("Option One");
    jcbOpt2 = new JCheckBox("Option Two");
    jcbOpt3 = new JCheckBox("Option Three");
    jcbOpt4 = new JCheckBox("Option Four");
    jcbOpt5 = new JCheckBox("Option Five");

    // No event handlers needed for this example.
```

```java
    // Create a JPanel to hold the options check boxes.
    JPanel  jpnl = new JPanel();
    jpnl.setLayout(new GridLayout(6, 1));
    jpnl.setOpaque(true);

    // Add check boxes and label to the JPanel.
    jpnl.add(jlabOptions);
    jpnl.add(jcbOpt1);
    jpnl.add(jcbOpt2);
    jpnl.add(jcbOpt3);
    jpnl.add(jcbOpt4);
    jpnl.add(jcbOpt5);

    // Create a scroll pane that will scroll the panel.
    JScrollPane jscrlp = new JScrollPane(jpnl);

    // Put a border around the viewport.
    jscrlp.setViewportBorder(
            BorderFactory.createLineBorder(Color.BLACK));

    // Create labels for the row and column headers.
    JLabel jlabCH = new JLabel("Configuration Center",
                              SwingConstants.CENTER);
    JLabel jlabRH = new JLabel("<html>C<br>h<br>o<br>o<br>s<br>e",
                              SwingConstants.CENTER);
    jlabRH.setPreferredSize(new Dimension(20, 200));

    // Add row and column headers.
    jscrlp.setColumnHeaderView(jlabCH);
    jscrlp.setRowHeaderView(jlabRH);

    // Add the scroll pane to the frame.
    jfrm.getContentPane().add(jscrlp);

    // Display the frame.
    jfrm.setVisible(true);
  }

  public static void main(String args[]) {
    // Create the frame on the event dispatching thread.
    SwingUtilities.invokeLater(new Runnable() {
      public void run() {
        new AddHeadersDemo();
      }
    });
  }
}
```

These labels are used for the headers.

Add the headers to the scroll pane.

CRITICAL SKILL
4.6 # Some Scroll Pane Options

In addition to setting the headers and adding a border around the viewport, **JScrollPane** offers several other options and customizations. Perhaps the most commonly used option is the scroll bar policy. The scroll bar policy determines when the scroll bars are shown. By default, a **JScrollPane** displays a scroll bar only when it is needed. For example, if the information being scrolled is too long for the viewport, a vertical scroll bar is automatically displayed to enable the viewport to be scrolled up and down. When the information all fits within the viewport, then no scroll bars are shown. Although the default scroll bar policy is appropriate for many scroll panes, it might be a problem when the corners are used, as explained a bit later. One other point: each scroll bar has its own policy. This lets you specify a separate policy for the vertical and the horizontal scroll bars.

You can specify scroll bar policies when a **JScrollPane** is created by passing the policy using one of these constructors:

JScrollPane(int *vertSBP*, int *horizSBP*)

JScrollPane(Component *comp*, int *vertSBP*, int *horizSBP*)

Here, *vertSBP* specifies the policy for the vertical scroll bar and *horizSBP* specifies the policy for the horizontal scroll bar. The scroll bar policies are specified using constants defined by the interface **ScrollPaneConstants**. The scroll bar policies are shown here:

Constant	Policy
HORIZONTAL_SCROLLBAR_AS_NEEDED	Horizontal scroll bar shown when needed. This is the default.
HORIZONTAL_SCROLLBAR_NEVER	Horizontal scroll bar never shown.
HORIZONTAL_SCROLLBAR_ALWAYS	Horizontal scroll bar always shown.
VERTICAL_SCROLLBAR_AS_NEEDED	Vertical scroll bar shown when needed. This is the default.
VERTICAL_SCROLLBAR_NEVER	Vertical scroll bar never shown.
VERTICAL_SCROLLBAR_ALWAYS	Vertical scroll bar always shown.

You can set the scroll bar policies after a scroll pane has been created by calling these methods:

void setVerticalScrollBarPolicy(int *vertSBP*)

void setHorizontalScrollBarPolicy(int *horizSBP*)

Here, *vertSBP* and *horizSBP* specify the scroll bar policy.

You can gain access to the scroll bars by calling these methods:

JScrollBar getHorizontalScrollBar( )

JScrollBar getVerticalScrollBar( )

These methods return a reference to the specified scroll bar. Using that reference, you can adjust the attributes of the scroll bar, such as setting the block or unit increment, as described in Module 3.

Another popular customization is to use the corners of a **JScrollPane**. These corners are created when the scroll bars intersect with each other or with the row or column headers. These corners can contain any component, such as a label or push button. However, be aware of two issues concerning the use of these corners. First, the size of the corners depends entirely on the thickness of the scroll bars or the headers. Therefore, they are often very small. Second, the corners will be visible only if the scroll bars and headers are shown. For example, there will be a lower right corner only if both the horizontal and vertical scroll bars are both shown. If you want to put a control in that corner, then the scroll bars will need to remain visible at all times. (This is one reason why you might need to set the scroll bar policies to "always.")

To put a component into a corner, call **setCorner( )** shown here:

void setCorner(String *which*, Component *comp*)

Here, *which* specifies which corner. It must be one of the following constants defined by the **ScrollPaneConstants** interface, which is implemented by **JScrollPane**.

LOWER_LEADING_CORNER

LOWER_LEFT_CORNER

LOWER_RIGHT_CORNER

LOWER_TRAILING_CORNER

UPPER_LEADING_CORNER

UPPER_LEFT_CORNER

UPPER_RIGHT_CORNER

UPPER_TRAILING_CORNER

Ask the Expert

Q: What is the Scrollable **interface? Is it important to** JScrollPane?

A: The **Scrollable** interface defines the scrolling attributes used by **JScrollPane**, such as the preferred size of the viewport, the block increment, and the unit increment. If this interface is not implemented by a component, then **JScrollPane** uses defaults for these values. In general, if you want to scroll a component with sophisticated or complicated scrolling needs, then you should implement **Scrollable** for it. For very simple components, it's not necessary.

Frankly, to make good use of the corners requires a bit of effort. It's not something that every use of **JScrollPane** will require or benefit from. However, if you are striving for a highly customized look to your scroll panes, then consider utilizing the corners.

Progress Check

1. **JScrollPane** can scroll any lightweight Swing component. True or False?

2. What scroll bar policy causes the vertical scroll bars to be always shown?

3. Can a row or column header contain an active component such as a push button?

Project 4-1 Scrolling a JPanel

`ScrollJPanelDemo.java`   Because **JPanel** is a lightweight container that implements **JComponent**, it too can be scrolled using **JScrollPane**. This capability makes it possible to scroll the entire contents of a **JPanel** with almost no effort on your part. When screen space is in short supply, scrolling a panel might be the solution to an otherwise difficult situation.

This project demonstrates how to scroll a **JPanel**. The panel contains a label and series of check boxes. This panel is then passed to the **JScrollPane** constructor. This causes a **JScrollPane**

(continued)

---

1. True
2. VERTICAL_SCROLLBAR_ALWAYS
3. Yes

object to be created that provides automatic scrolling for the panel. You can use this basic technique whenever you need to scroll the contents of a panel. Sample output is shown here:

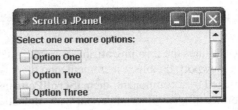

Step by Step

1. Create a file called **ScrollJPanelDemo.java** and add the following comment and **import** statements:

```
// Project 4-1: Use a JScrollPane to scroll a JPanel.

import java.awt.*;
import javax.swing.*;
```

2. Begin the **ScrollJPanelDemo** class with the following declaration:

```
class ScrollJPanelDemo {
```

3. Start the **ScrollJPanelDemo** constructor in the usual way:

```
ScrollJPanelDemo() {
  // Create a new JFrame container. Use the default
  // border layout.
  JFrame jfrm = new JFrame("Scroll a JPanel");

  // Give the frame an initial size.
  jfrm.setSize(280, 130);

  // Terminate the program when the user closes the application.
  jfrm.setDefaultCloseOperation(JFrame.EXIT_ON_CLOSE);
```

4. Add the following lines, which create the label and check boxes:

```
// Create a label.
JLabel jlabOptions = new
  JLabel("Select one or more options: ");

// Make some check boxes.
JCheckBox jcbOpt1 = new JCheckBox("Option One");
JCheckBox jcbOpt2 = new JCheckBox("Option Two");
JCheckBox jcbOpt3 = new JCheckBox("Option Three");
```

```
JCheckBox jcbOpt4 = new JCheckBox("Option Four");
JCheckBox jcbOpt5 = new JCheckBox("Option Five");

// No event handlers needed for this example.
```

Because the point of this program is to demonstrate scrolling a **JPanel**, no event handlers are included because the check boxes are simply used for their appearance.

5. Add the code that constructs the **JPanel** that will be scrolled and then add the label and check boxes to it.

```
// Create a JPanel to hold the options check boxes.
JPanel  jpnl = new JPanel();
jpnl.setLayout(new GridLayout(6, 1));
jpnl.setOpaque(true);

// Add check boxes and label to the JPanel.
jpnl.add(jlabOptions);
jpnl.add(jcbOpt1);
jpnl.add(jcbOpt2);
jpnl.add(jcbOpt3);
jpnl.add(jcbOpt4);
jpnl.add(jcbOpt5);
```

6. Create the **JScrollPane**, using the panel as the object to be scrolled. Then add the scroll pane to the content pane. Finally, make the frame visible.

```
   // Create a scroll pane that will scroll the panel.
   JScrollPane jscrlp = new JScrollPane(jpnl);

   // Add that scroll pane to the frame.
   jfrm.getContentPane().add(jscrlp);

   // Display the frame.
   jfrm.setVisible(true);
 }
```

7. End the class in the usual way.

```
   public static void main(String args[]) {
     // Create the frame on the event dispatching thread.
     SwingUtilities.invokeLater(new Runnable() {
       public void run() {
         new ScrollJPanelDemo();
       }
     });
   }
 }
```

(continued)

8. The entire program is shown here:

```java
// Project 4-1: Use a JScrollPane to scroll a JPanel.

import java.awt.*;
import javax.swing.*;

class ScrollJPanelDemo {

  ScrollJPanelDemo() {
    // Create a new JFrame container. Use the default
    // border layout.
    JFrame jfrm = new JFrame("Scroll a JPanel");

    // Give the frame an initial size.
    jfrm.setSize(280, 130);

    // Terminate the program when the user closes the application.
    jfrm.setDefaultCloseOperation(JFrame.EXIT_ON_CLOSE);

    // Create a label.
    JLabel jlabOptions = new
      JLabel("Select one or more options: ");

    // Make some check boxes.
    JCheckBox jcbOpt1 = new JCheckBox("Option One");
    JCheckBox jcbOpt2 = new JCheckBox("Option Two");
    JCheckBox jcbOpt3 = new JCheckBox("Option Three");
    JCheckBox jcbOpt4 = new JCheckBox("Option Four");
    JCheckBox jcbOpt5 = new JCheckBox("Option Five");

    // No event handlers needed for this example.

    // Create a JPanel to hold the options check boxes.
    JPanel  jpnl = new JPanel();
    jpnl.setLayout(new GridLayout(6, 1));
    jpnl.setOpaque(true);

    // Add check boxes and label to the JPanel.
    jpnl.add(jlabOptions);
    jpnl.add(jcbOpt1);
    jpnl.add(jcbOpt2);
    jpnl.add(jcbOpt3);
    jpnl.add(jcbOpt4);
    jpnl.add(jcbOpt5);

    // Create a scroll pane that will scroll the panel.
    JScrollPane jscrlp = new JScrollPane(jpnl);
```

```
    // Add that scroll pane to the frame.
    jfrm.getContentPane().add(jscrlp);

    // Display the frame.
    jfrm.setVisible(true);
  }

  public static void main(String args[]) {
    // Create the frame on the event dispatching thread.
    SwingUtilities.invokeLater(new Runnable() {
      public void run() {
        new ScrollJPanelDemo();
      }
    });
  }
}
```

CRITICAL SKILL

4.7 Work with JTabbedPane

Another specialized container is **JTabbedPane**. It manages a set of components by linking them with tabs. Selecting a tab causes the component associated with that tab to come to the forefront. Tabbed panes are very common in the modern GUI, and you have no doubt used them many times. Given the complex nature of a tabbed pane, they are surprisingly easy to create and use. They are one of Swing's most powerful components.

JTabbedPane defines the constructors shown in Table 4-3. The parameterless constructor creates a tabbed pane in which the tabs are across the top of the control. If the number and/or size of the tabs exceeds what can be displayed in a single line, the tabs are wrapped (that is, stacked) on top of one another.

The second constructor allows you to specify the location of tabs. There are four possible positions: top, bottom, left, or right. The constants that represent these locations are **TOP**, **BOTTOM**, **LEFT**, and **RIGHT**. These are defined by the **SwingConstants** interface, which is implemented by **JTabbedPane**. Thus, you can refer to them through either name. For example, **JTabbedPane.TOP** and **SwingConstants.TOP** are both valid.

The third constructor enables you to define the location of the tabs and the policy that is used if the tabs won't all fit on one line. There are two options. First, you can let the tabs wrap, in which case they will be stacked on top of one another. This policy is specified by the constants **JTabbedPane.WRAP_TAB_LAYOUT**. (This is the default policy for the other two constructors.) The second policy, specified by **JTabbedPane.SCROLL_TAB_LAYOUT**, keeps all tabs on a single line but adds a means to scroll the tabs.

JTabbedPane uses the **SingleSelectionModel** model. However, you won't usually need to interact with the model to use a tabbed pane.

Constructor	Description
JTabbedPane( )	Creates a tabbed pane in which the tabs are on the top of the control.
JTabbedPane(int *where*)	Creates a tabbed pane in which the placement of the tabs is specified by *where*. The value of *where* must be one of these: **JTabbedPane.TOP JTabbedPane.BOTTOM** **JTabbedPane.LEFT JTabbedPane.RIGHT**
JTabbedPane(int *where*, int *sclrOrWrap*)	Creates a tabbed pane in which the placement of the tabs is specified by *where*. The value of *where* must be one of these: **JTabbedPane.TOP JTabbedPane.BOTTOM** **JTabbedPane.LEFT JTabbedPane.RIGHT** When there are too many tabs for a single line, the value of *sclrOrWrap* controls how the tabs are organized. It must be either **JTabbedPane.WRAP_TAB_LAYOUT** or **JTabbedPane.SCROLL_TAB_LAYOUT**

Table 4-3 The **JTabbedPane** Constructors

JTabbedPane generates a change event whenever the user switches to a new tab. However, most of the time you won't need to handle this event because **JTabbedPane** handles the switching between tabs for you. Of course, if the component associated with a tab must perform some action when it is selected, such as read updated information from a file, then your program must handle the change events generated by a tab switch and take appropriate action. But again, this is the exception, not the rule.

Using a tabbed pane is amazingly simple. First, create an instance of **JTabbedPane**. Second, add components to it, with each component specifying the name of the tab. To add groups of components to a single tab, organize them into a **JPanel** first. (Remember, **JPanel** is a lightweight container that inherits **JComponent**, so it is both a container and a component.)

To add tabs, you will use the **addTab( )** method. It has the three forms. The simplest one is shown here:

void addTab(String *name*, Component *comp*)

This first form creates a tab with the name specified by *name* that contains the component passed in *comp*.

The following program constructs a simple tabbed pane that contains four tabs. For simplicity, the tabs contain only labels, but a tab can hold any component, including groups of components organized into a lightweight container. Sample output is shown in Figure 4-6.

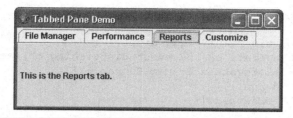

Figure 4-6 Sample output from the **TabbedPaneDemo** program

```java
// Demonstrate a simple JTabbedPane.

import javax.swing.*;

class TabbedPaneDemo {

  TabbedPaneDemo() {
    // Create a new JFrame container. Use the default
    // border layout.
    JFrame jfrm = new JFrame("Tabbed Pane Demo");

    // Give the frame an initial size.
    jfrm.setSize(380, 150);

    // Terminate the program when the user closes the application.
    jfrm.setDefaultCloseOperation(JFrame.EXIT_ON_CLOSE);

    // Create a tabbed pane.
    JTabbedPane jtp = new JTabbedPane();              Create the tabbed pane.

    // Add tabs to the tabbed pane
    jtp.addTab("File Manager",
            new JLabel(" This is the File Manager tab."));
    jtp.addTab("Performance",
            new JLabel(" This is the Performance tab."));     Add the
    jtp.addTab("Reports",                                     tabs.
            new JLabel(" This is the Reports tab."));
    jtp.addTab("Customize",
            new JLabel(" This is the Customize tab."));

    // Add the tabbed pane to the content pane.
    jfrm.getContentPane().add(jtp);

    // Display the frame.
    jfrm.setVisible(true);
```

```
    }

    public static void main(String args[]) {
      // Create the frame on the event dispatching thread.
      SwingUtilities.invokeLater(new Runnable() {
        public void run() {
          new TabbedPaneDemo();
        }
      });
    }
}
```

Notice how little code is required to create a fully functional tabbed pane. Also notice that no effort is required on the part of the program to manage the tabbed pane. This is one of the best things about Swing's specialized containers: they supply an amazing amount of functionality, but require very little programming effort on your part.

JTabbedPane Options

JTabbedPane supports many options. Two have already been mentioned when **JTabbedPane** constructors were described. First, you can specify the location of the tabs and second, you can specify the policy used when there are too many tabs to fit on a single line. For example, in the preceding program, try substituting this line when constructing the tabbed pane.

```
JTabbedPane jtp = new JTabbedPane(SwingConstants.TOP,
                                  JTabbedPane.SCROLL_TAB_LAYOUT);
```

Then, when the window is reduced in width, scroll bar arrows will automatically be displayed that enable you to scroll through the tabs, as shown here:

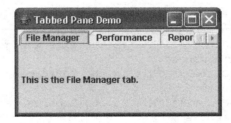

For many applications scrolling tabs rather than wrapping tabs is a better alternative.

Often it is helpful to include an image in the tab along with a string. To do this, use this form of **addTab( )**:

void addTab(String *name*, Icon *image*, Component *comp*)

Here, *image* is the graphics image that will be shown in the tab. Recall that you can create an image easily from a file by using the **ImageIcon** class (as described in Module 2). If you want to use an image but not a string, simply pass **null** for the string.

Another very common customization is to add tooltips to the tabs. A *tooltip* is a string that will be displayed when the mouse hovers over the tab. This is easy to accomplish by using this form of **addTab( )**:

void addTab(String *name*, Icon *image*, Component *comp*, String *tooltip*)

This form adds the tooltip specified by *tooltip*. In the previous example, if you add the Reports tab as shown here:

```
jtp.addTab("Reports", null,
          new JLabel(" This is the Reports tab."),
          "This is the Reports tab.");
```

then the tooltip "This is the Reports tab." will be displayed when the mouse hovers over the Reports tab, as shown here:

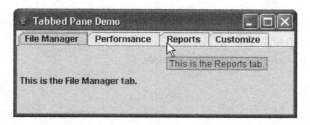

If you want to add a tooltip, but not an image, simply pass **null** for *image*. (As you will see later in this module, you can add a tooltip to any component, not just tabs.)

You can insert a tab at a specific location using the method **insertTab( )**, shown here:

void insertTab(String *name*, Icon *image*, Component *comp*,
                String *tooltip*, int *idx*)

This method works the same as **addTab( )** except that it inserts the tab at the index passed in *idx*. Tab indexing starts at zero. Thus, if you added the following line to the previous program, it would insert a new tab after the Performance tab, shifting the remaining tabs right:

```
jtp.insertTab("New Tab", null, new JLabel("New Tab"),
             "New Tab Tooltip", 2);
```

You can remove a tab by using **remove( )**, shown here:

void remove(int *idx*)

Here, *idx* specifies the zero-based index of the tab to remove. Removing a tab also removes the component associated with the tab.

In addition to the options described here, **JTabbedPane** supports several more. It is beyond the scope of this book to discuss them. **JTabbedPane** is a component that you will definitely want to examine in detail. To help you get started, here are few of its features that you will want to try:

- Set the foreground color of a tab by calling **setForegroundAt( )**.
- Set the background color by calling **setBackgroundAt( )**.
- Set a keyboard mnemonic for a tab by calling **setMnemonicAt( )**.
- Select a tab under program control by calling **setSelectedIndex( )**.
- Enable or disable a tab under program control by calling **setEnabledAt( )**.
- Determine the enabled state by calling **isEnabledAt( )**.
- When a tab is disabled, it is grayed-out and cannot be selected. You can specify a disabled icon for a tab by calling **setDisabledIconAt( )**.

Progress Check

1. Each tab in a tabbed pane must hold a lightweight container, such as **JPanel**. True or false?

2. What method do you call to add a component to a tab?

3. If there are too many tabs for one line, what policy causes the tabs to be scrolled rather than wrapped?

---

1. False. A tabbed pane can hold any component, which includes the lightweight containers.
2. To add a component to a tab call **addTab( )**.
3. **JTabbedPane.SCROLL_TAB_LAYOUT**

Project 4-2 Use JPanels with a JTabbedPane

`TabbedPaneWithPanels.java`

Although the **JTabbedPane** example shown earlier does demonstrate the mechanics of using a **JTabbedPane**, it does not show its power. In most cases, you will not use a tab to hold a single control, such as a label or push button. Instead, you will use a tab to hold a lightweight container, such as **JPanel**, in which two or more controls are stored. Thus, you will normally construct a container that holds a group of related components and then create a tab that holds that container. In this project, you will see how to implement such a strategy.

This project creates a three-tab **JTabbedPane** that holds components that simulate what a customer might use when shopping for a new computer. The first tab is called Style. It lets the user specify the type of computer, which will be either a tower, a notebook, or a handheld. The second tab is called Options, and it lets the user specify various options, such as a DVD burner. The third tab lets the user select software, such as word processing or program development. Although the program does not do anything with the user's selections, it demonstrates how to use **JTabbedPane** to display **JPanels**.

Here is what the program looks like when run:

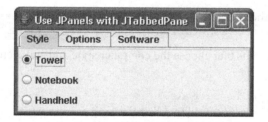

Step by Step

1. Create a file called **TabbedPaneWithPanels.java** and add the following comment and **import** statements:

```
// Project 4-2: Demonstrate using JPanels with JTabbedPane.

import java.awt.*;
import javax.swing.*;
```

2. Begin the **TabbedPaneWithPanels** class like this:

```
class TabbedPaneWithPanels {

   JCheckBox jcbDVD;
```

(continued)

```
JCheckBox jcbScanner;
JCheckBox jcbNtwrkRdy;

JCheckBox jcbWordProc;
JCheckBox jcbCompiler;
JCheckBox jcbDatabase;

JRadioButton jrbTower;
JRadioButton jrbNotebook;
JRadioButton jrbHandheld;
```

This defines the components that will be used in the panels.

3. Begin coding the **TabbedPaneWithPanels** constructor in the usual way as shown here:

```
// Create a new JFrame container. Use the default
// border layout.
JFrame jfrm = new JFrame("Use JPanels with JTabbedPane");

// Give the frame an initial size.
jfrm.setSize(280, 140);

// Terminate the program when the user closes the application.
jfrm.setDefaultCloseOperation(JFrame.EXIT_ON_CLOSE);
```

4. Create the radio buttons that choose the computer style and add them to a **JPanel**, as shown here:

```
// Make Style radio buttons.
jrbTower = new JRadioButton("Tower");
jrbNotebook = new JRadioButton("Notebook");
jrbHandheld = new JRadioButton("Handheld");
ButtonGroup bg = new ButtonGroup();
bg.add(jrbTower);
bg.add(jrbNotebook);
bg.add(jrbHandheld);

// Create a JPanel to hold the Style radio buttons.
JPanel  jpnl = new JPanel();
jpnl.setLayout(new GridLayout(3, 1));
jpnl.setOpaque(true);

// Add Style radio buttons to first panel.
jpnl.add(jrbTower);
jpnl.add(jrbNotebook);
jpnl.add(jrbHandheld);
```

Notice that a grid layout is used. This makes the components lay out nicely in the panel in this example. However, you can use whatever type of layout is best suited to your application.

5. Create the components for the Options and Software tabs in the same way, as shown next:

```
// Make options check boxes.
jcbDVD = new JCheckBox("DVD Burner");
jcbScanner = new JCheckBox("Scanner");
jcbNtwrkRdy = new JCheckBox("Network Ready");

// Create a JPanel to hold the options check boxes.
JPanel  jpnl2 = new JPanel();
jpnl2.setLayout(new GridLayout(3, 1));
jpnl2.setOpaque(true);

// Add check boxes and label to the second JPanel.
jpnl2.add(jcbDVD);
jpnl2.add(jcbScanner);
jpnl2.add(jcbNtwrkRdy);

// Make Software check boxes.
jcbWordProc = new JCheckBox("Word Processing");
jcbCompiler = new JCheckBox("Program Development");
jcbDatabase = new JCheckBox("Database");

// Create a JPanel to hold the options check boxes.
JPanel  jpnl3 = new JPanel();
jpnl3.setLayout(new GridLayout(3, 1));
jpnl3.setOpaque(true);

// Add check boxes and label to the third JPanel.
jpnl3.add(jcbWordProc);
jpnl3.add(jcbCompiler);
jpnl3.add(jcbDatabase);
```

6. Because this project does nothing with the choices entered by the user, add this comment as a reminder:

```
// No event handlers are included in this example.
```

In a real program, you would need to have event handlers to handle each component in each panel.

7. Create the **JTabbedPane** that will hold the three panels and then add the three panels to it, as shown here:

```
// Create a tabbed pane that uses a scroll policy.
JTabbedPane jtp = new JTabbedPane(JTabbedPane.TOP,
JTabbedPane.SCROLL_TAB_LAYOUT);

// Add the panels to the tabbed pane.
```

(continued)

```
jtp.addTab("Style", jpnl);
jtp.addTab("Options", jpnl2);
jtp.addTab("Software", jpnl3);
```

8. End the constructor by adding the tabbed pane to the content pane and then making it visible.

```
// Add the tabbed pane to the content pane.
jfrm.getContentPane().add(jtp);

// Display the frame.
jfrm.setVisible(true);
}
```

9. Finally, end **TabbedPaneWithPanels** in the usual way.

```
public static void main(String args[]) {
  // Create the frame on the event dispatching thread.
  SwingUtilities.invokeLater(new Runnable() {
    public void run() {
      new TabbedPaneWithPanels();
    }
  });
}
}
```

10. The entire **TabbedPaneWithPanels** program is shown here:

```
// Project 4-2: Demonstrate using JPanels with JTabbedPane.

import java.awt.*;
import javax.swing.*;

class TabbedPaneWithPanels {

  JCheckBox jcbDVD;
  JCheckBox jcbScanner;
  JCheckBox jcbNtwrkRdy;

  JCheckBox jcbWordProc;
  JCheckBox jcbCompiler;
  JCheckBox jcbDatabase;

  JRadioButton jrbTower;
  JRadioButton jrbNotebook;
  JRadioButton jrbHandheld;
```

```
TabbedPaneWithPanels() {

    // Create a new JFrame container. Use the default
    // border layout.
    JFrame jfrm = new JFrame("Use JPanels with JTabbedPane");

    // Give the frame an initial size.
    jfrm.setSize(280, 140);

    // Terminate the program when the user closes the application.
    jfrm.setDefaultCloseOperation(JFrame.EXIT_ON_CLOSE);

    // Make Style radio buttons.
    jrbTower = new JRadioButton("Tower");
    jrbNotebook = new JRadioButton("Notebook");
    jrbHandheld = new JRadioButton("Handheld");
    ButtonGroup bg = new ButtonGroup();
    bg.add(jrbTower);
    bg.add(jrbNotebook);
    bg.add(jrbHandheld);

    // Create a JPanel to hold the Style radio buttons.
    JPanel  jpnl = new JPanel();
    jpnl.setLayout(new GridLayout(3, 1));
    jpnl.setOpaque(true);

    // Add Style radio button to first panel.
    jpnl.add(jrbTower);
    jpnl.add(jrbNotebook);
    jpnl.add(jrbHandheld);

    // Make Options check boxes.
    jcbDVD = new JCheckBox("DVD Burner");
    jcbScanner = new JCheckBox("Scanner");
    jcbNtwrkRdy = new JCheckBox("Network Ready");

    // Create a JPanel to hold the Options check boxes.
    JPanel  jpnl2 = new JPanel();
    jpnl2.setLayout(new GridLayout(3, 1));
    jpnl2.setOpaque(true);

    // Add check boxes and label to the second JPanel.
    jpnl2.add(jcbDVD);
    jpnl2.add(jcbScanner);
    jpnl2.add(jcbNtwrkRdy);
```

(continued)

4

Managing Components with Panels, Panes, and Toolips

Project
4-2

Use JPanels with a JTabbedPane

```java
      // Make Software check boxes.
      jcbWordProc = new JCheckBox("Word Processing");
      jcbCompiler = new JCheckBox("Program Development");
      jcbDatabase = new JCheckBox("Database");

      // Create a JPanel to hold the Options check boxes.
      JPanel  jpnl3 = new JPanel();
      jpnl3.setLayout(new GridLayout(3, 1));
      jpnl3.setOpaque(true);

      // Add check boxes and label to the third JPanel.
      jpnl3.add(jcbWordProc);
      jpnl3.add(jcbCompiler);
      jpnl3.add(jcbDatabase);

      // No event handlers are included in this example.

      // Create a tabbed pane that uses a scroll policy.
      JTabbedPane jtp = new JTabbedPane(JTabbedPane.TOP,
                            JTabbedPane.SCROLL_TAB_LAYOUT);

      // Add the panels to the tabbed pane.
      jtp.addTab("Style", jpnl);
      jtp.addTab("Options", jpnl2);
      jtp.addTab("Software", jpnl3);

      // Add the tabbed pane to the content pane.
      jfrm.getContentPane().add(jtp);

      // Display the frame.
      jfrm.setVisible(true);
   }

   public static void main(String args[]) {
      // Create the frame on the event dispatching thread.
      SwingUtilities.invokeLate (new Runnable() {
         public void run() {
            new TabbedPaneWithPanels();
         }
      });
   }
}
```

CRITICAL SKILL
4.9 Use JSplitPane

JSplitPane is another specialized container that provides a convenient solution to an otherwise difficult problem. It creates a two-piece window that lets you display two components. The components are separated by a divider, which allows the relative size of the components to be changed dynamically by the user.

JSplitPane defines the constructors shown in Table 4-4. Notice that split panes come in two basic styles: horizontal and vertical. This orientation refers to whether the two components

Constructor	Description
JSplitPane( )	Creates an empty, horizontal split pane that does not continuously redraw its components when the divider changes position.
JSplitPane(int *vertOrHoriz*)	Creates an empty, noncontinuously updating split pane that is oriented as specified by *vertOrHoriz*. The value of *vertOrHoriz* must be either **JSplitPane.HORIZONTAL_SPLIT** or **JSplitPane.VERTICAL_SPLIT**.
JSplitPane(int *vertOrHoriz*, boolean *contRedraw*)	Creates an empty split pane that is oriented as specified by *vertOrHoriz* and updates its components when the divider is moved as specified by *contRedraw*. The value of *vertOrHoriz* must be either **JSplitPane.HORIZONTAL_SPLIT** or **JSplitPane.VERTICAL_SPLIT**. If *contRedraw* is true, then the components are redrawn as the divider moves. Otherwise, they are redrawn after the divider stops moving.
JSplitPane(int *vertOrHoriz*, Component *leftOrTop*, Component *rightOrBottom*)	Creates a noncontinuously updating split pane that is oriented as specified by *vertOrHoriz* that contains the components passed in *leftOrTop* and *rightOrBottom*. The position of the components depends on whether the pane is oriented horizontally or vertically. The value of *vertOrHoriz* must be either **JSplitPane.HORIZONTAL_SPLIT** or **JSplitPane.VERTICAL_SPLIT**.
JSplitPane(int *vertOrHoriz*, boolean *contRedraw*, Component *leftOrTop*, Component *rightOrBottom*)	Creates a split pane that is oriented as specified by *vertOrHoriz* that contains the components passed in *leftOrTop* and *rightOrBottom*. The position of the components depends on whether the pane is oriented horizontally or vertically. When the divider is moved, the components are updated as specified by *contRedraw*. The value of *vertOrHoriz* must be one of **JSplitPane.HORIZONTAL_SPLIT** or **JSplitPane.VERTICAL_SPLIT**. If *contRedraw* is true, then the components are redrawn as the divider moves. Otherwise, they are redrawn after the divider stops moving.

Table 4-4 The Constructors of **JSplitPane**

Ask the Expert

Q: It seems to me that using continuous layout with a split pane is much better than using noncontinuous layout. Why wouldn't I want to always use continuous layout?

A: In cases in which the component or components being affected take a long time to repaint, using continuous layout may make your application appear sluggish. In these cases, using noncontinuous layout may offer a better user experience. However, given the modern computing environment, such cases are growing rarer.

are displayed side by side, or one above the other. A split pane also offers two ways in which the redrawing of the components can be accomplished when the divider position is changed. First, it can continuously update (that is, continuously redraw) the components as the divider moves. This is called *continuous layout*. Second, it can simply wait to update the components until after the divider has stopped moving. Notice that you can add the components to the split pane when it is created. Of course, you can also add the components afterward.

When using a split pane, you will normally need to set the minimum size of the components displayed within it. The reason is that the divider in the split pane won't reduce a component below its minimum size. Therefore, to get the most utility out of a split pane, you need to specify the smallest minimum size that is reasonable for a component. You may also want to set the preferred size. The preferred size of a component governs how the initial split between the two components will be determined.

Here is a simple example that illustrates **JSplitPane**. It displays two labels in separate windows. Sample output is shown in Figure 4-7.

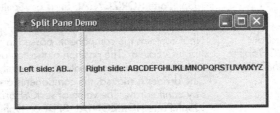

Figure 4-7 Sample output from the **SplitPaneDemo** program

```java
// Demonstrate a simple JSplitPane.

import javax.swing.*;
import java.awt.*;

class SplitPaneDemo {

  SplitPaneDemo() {
    // Create a new JFrame container. Use the default
    // border layout.
    JFrame jfrm = new JFrame("Split Pane Demo");

    // Give the frame an initial size.
    jfrm.setSize(380, 150);

    // Terminate the program when the user closes the application.
    jfrm.setDefaultCloseOperation(JFrame.EXIT_ON_CLOSE);

    // Make two labels to show in the split pane.
    JLabel jlab =
      new JLabel(" Left side: ABCDEFGHIJKLMNOPQRSTUVWXYZ");
    JLabel jlab2 =
      new JLabel(" Right side: ABCDEFGHIJKLMNOPQRSTUVWXYZ");

    // Set the minimum size for each label. This step is
    // not technically needed to use a split pane, but
    // it enables the split pane resizing features to be
    // used to their maximum extent.
    jlab.setMinimumSize(new Dimension(90, 30));
    jlab2.setMinimumSize(new Dimension(90, 30));

    // Create a split pane.
    JSplitPane jsp =
      new JSplitPane(JSplitPane.HORIZONTAL_SPLIT, true, jlab, jlab2);

    // Add the split pane to the content pane.
    jfrm.getContentPane().add(jsp);

    // Display the frame.
    jfrm.setVisible(true);
  }

  public static void main(String args[]) {
```

Set the minimum size for the labels.

Create a split pane that holds the labels.

```
      // Create the frame on the event dispatching thread.
      SwingUtilities.invokeLater(new Runnable() {
        public void run() {
          new SplitPaneDemo();
        }
      });
    }
}
```

The program creates two labels and both are given a minimum width of 90 and a minimum height of 30. This means that when displayed within a horizontal split pane, the divider will be able to reduce the size of a window up to the point at which this minimum width is encountered. If the minimum size had not been set, then the minimum size would have been, by default, the size of the entire label, and the divider would not be moveable. (You might want to prove this to yourself by removing the calls to **setMinimumSize( )** and observing the results.) Next, a horizontal split pane is created and the two labels are added to it. When you try the program, you will see that you can move the divider, changing the size of the labels.

Some JSplitPane Options

JSplitPane offers many options that let you customize a split pane to best suit your needs. Several are described here. One of the most important options that **JSplitPane** offers is the ability to control the orientation of the split. As explained, you can create panes that are split horizontally or vertically and the orientation of the split can be specified when you construct a split pane. You can also change the orientation of a split pane after it is constructed by calling **setOrientation( )**, which is shown here:

void setOrientation(int *vertOrHoriz*)

Here, *vertOrHoriz* must be either **JSplitPane.HORIZONTAL_SPLIT** or **JSplitPane.VERTICAL_SPLIT**.

Although it is usually easier to pass the components to be displayed to the split pane when it is being constructed, you can specify these components after the fact by calling one of these methods:

void setBottomComponent(Component *comp*)

void setLeftComponent(Component *comp*)

void setRightComponent(Component *comp*)

void setTopComponent(Component *comp*)

In all cases, *comp* specifies the component to be displayed in the indicated location. Although four separate methods are provided, only two are actually needed because calling **setBottomComponent( )** on a split pane with horizontal orientation causes the right component to be set, calling **setLeftComponent( )** on a split pane with vertical orientation causes the top component to be set, and so on.

You can turn on or off continuous layout during the execution of a program by calling **setContinuousLayout( )**, shown here:

void setContinuousLayout(boolean *CLon*)

If *CLon* is true, the continuous layout is turned on. Otherwise, it is turned off.

One especially useful option you might want consider taking advantage of adds buttons that support the "one-touch-expandable" feature. Be aware, however, that this feature may not be available in all look-and-feels. It is off by default in the Metal look and feel, although it can be turned on. The one-touch-expandable option creates two small buttons within the divider. Pressing one of these buttons causes one side of the split pane to be expanded to the full size of the window and the other side to be removed from view. The hidden side can be brought back into view by pressing the other button. The one-touch-expandable feature is false by default. It can be turned on by calling **setOneTouchExpandable( )**, shown here:

void setOneTouchExpandable(boolean *OTEon*)

If *OTEon* is true, then buttons are added to the divider and the feature is activated. If *OTEon* is false, then the buttons are removed and the feature is turned off. To see the effect of this option, try adding the following line to the preceding program immediately after the **JSplitPane** constructor is called:

```
jsp.setOneTouchExpandable(true);
```

When you run the program, you will now see that the one-touch-expandable buttons have been added to the divider, as shown in Figure 4-8.

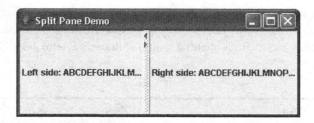

Figure 4-8 The one-touch-expandable buttons

Here are a few more options that you might want to look at. You can specify how the split between the two panes is adjusted when the split pane is resized by calling **setResizeWeight( )**. You can set the size of the divider by calling **setDividerSize( )**. You can set the position of the divider under program control by calling **setDividerLocation( )**.

Progress Check

1. What value must be passed to create a vertical split pane?

2. Is it usually necessary to set the minimum size of the components being displayed by a split pane?

3. What method do you call to activate the one-touch-expandable feature?

4.11 Add Tooltips

In the discussion of tabbed panes, you saw that it was possible to add a tooltip to a tab. This represents a special case of a more general concept. In Swing, it is possible to add a tooltip to any lightweight component. The reason is that **JComponent** (which is, of course, the base class for all Swing lightweight components) supplies the method **setToolTipText( )**. This method lets you set a string that is displayed when the mouse hovers over a component. In most cases, adding tooltips is so easy that there is virtually no reason not to use them when appropriate. Their inclusion helps manage the user experience and greatly adds to the usability of nearly any GUI.

The **setToolTipText( )** method is shown here:

void setToolTipText(String *tip*)

Here, *tip* specifies the text that will be shown.

Here is an example that shows just how easy it is to incorporate tooltips into your application. It creates two buttons and then associates a tooltip with each. Figure 4-9 shows one of the tooltips in action.

---

1. **JSplitPane.VERTICAL_SPLIT**
2. Yes
3. **setOneTouchExpandable( )**

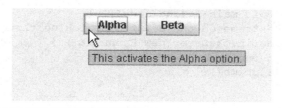

Figure 4-9 The tooltip demonstration

```java
// Demonstrate tooltips.

import javax.swing.*;
import java.awt.*;

class ToolTipDemo {

  ToolTipDemo() {
    // Create a new JFrame container. Use the default
    // border layout.
    JFrame jfrm = new JFrame("Add Tooltips");

    // Specify FlowLayout for the layout manager.
    jfrm.getContentPane().setLayout(new FlowLayout());

    // Give the frame an initial size.
    jfrm.setSize(300, 150);

    // Terminate the program when the user closes the application.
    jfrm.setDefaultCloseOperation(JFrame.EXIT_ON_CLOSE);

    // Make two buttons.
    JButton jbtnAlpha = new JButton("Alpha");
    JButton jbtnBeta = new JButton("Beta");

    // Set tooltips.
    jbtnAlpha.setToolTipText("This activates the Alpha option.");
    jbtnBeta.setToolTipText("This activates the Beta option.");

    jfrm.getContentPane().add(jbtnAlpha);
    jfrm.getContentPane().add(jbtnBeta);

    // Display the frame.
    jfrm.setVisible(true);
  }
```

Add tooltips to the buttons.

```
public static void main(String args[]) {
  // Create the frame on the event dispatching thread.
  SwingUtilities.invokeLater(new Runnable() {
    public void run() {
      new ToolTipDemo();
    }
  });
}
```

✓

Module 4 Mastery Check

1. What is double buffering and why is it important?

2. What method do you call to make a **JPanel** opaque?

3. Can you set the content pane of a **JFrame** to a **JPanel** that your program creates?

4. Although very powerful, **JScrollPane** can be tricky to use properly. True or False?

5. What are the nine parts of **JScrollPane**?

6. What method do you call to set a row header in a **JScrollPane**?

7. What method is used to add components to a **JTabbedPane**?

8. How do you add a tooltip to a tab in a **JTabbedPane**?

9. In what two orientations can a **JSplitPane** be shown?

10. Explain the one-touch-expandable feature of **JSplitPane**. What method is called to turn it on?

11. Can a tooltip be added to any lightweight Swing control? If so, how?

12. It's best not to use too many tooltips because they clutter the GUI. True or false?

13. Add tooltips to the buttons in the **CustomCPDemo** program shown earlier in this chapter.

14. Modify the split pane example so that it contains the scroll pane shown in Project 4-1 on the left side.

Module 5

Lists

This module resumes our examination of Swing's components by examining its support for lists. Swing provides three list components: **JList**, **JComboBox**, and **JSpinner**. Each provides a different approach to handling the situation in which a user must select from a list of choices. Although each of these is easy to use, they all offer a significant number of options that enable you to tailor them to your specific application.

Work with JList

In Swing, the basic list class is called **JList**. It supports the selection of one or more items from a list. Although often the list consists of strings, it is possible to create a list of just about any object that can be displayed. **JList** is so widely used in Java that it is highly unlikely that you have not seen one before.

JList is based on two models. The first is **ListModel**. This interface defines how access to the list data is achieved. Swing provides a default implementation of **ListModel** called **DefaultListModel**. It defines a large number of methods that enable the list to be manipulated. The second model is the **ListSelectionModel** interface, which defines methods that determine what list item or items are selected. The default implementation of **ListSelectionModel** used by **JList** is **DefaultListSelectionModel**. Often, you won't need to interact directly with either of these two models because **JList** provides methods that give you access to much of the model's functionality. However, you will need to access the list model if you want to listen for **ListDataEvent**s, which are generated when the contents of the list change.

JList provides the constructors shown in Table 5-1. If you create an empty **JList**, then you must explicitly assign a model to it after the fact. The two constructors that take an array or a vector automatically create a model. For most simple **JList** applications, these are easiest to use. However, they create an immutable list, the contents of which cannot be altered at runtime (although you can assign a new model to the list). The fourth constructor lets you specify the model when you are creating the list.

Although a **JList** will work properly by itself, most of the time you will wrap a **JList** inside a **JScrollPane**. This way, long lists will automatically be scrollable. This simplifies GUI design. It also makes it easy to change the number of entries in a list without having to

Constructor	Description
JList( )	Creates an empty **JList**.
JList(Object[ ] *items*)	Creates a **JList** that contains the items specified by *items*.
JList(Vector<?> *items*)	Creates a **JList** that contains the items in the vector specified by *items*.
JList(ListModel *lm*)	Creates a **JList** that uses the model specified by *lm*.

Table 5-1 The **JList** Constructors

change the size of the **JList** component. In this book, all **JList** components are wrapped within a **JScrollPane** because it is the common approach.

A **JList** generates a **ListSelectionEvent** when the user makes or changes a selection. This event is also generated when the user deselects an item. It is handled by implementing **ListSelectionListener**. This listener specifies only one method, called **valueChanged( )**, which is shown here:

void valueChanged(ListSelectionEvent *le*)

Here, *le* is a reference to the object that generated the event. Although **ListSelectionEvent** does provide some methods of its own, normally you will interrogate the **JList** object itself to determine what has occurred.

By default, a **JList** allows the user to select multiple ranges of items within the list, but you can set this behavior by calling **setSelectionMode( )**, which is defined by **JList**. It is shown here:

void setSelectionMode(int *mode*)

Here, *mode* specifies the selection mode. It must be one of these values defined by **ListSelectionModel**:

SINGLE_SELECTION

SINGLE_INTERVAL_SELECTION

MULTIPLE_INTERVAL_SELECTION

By default, a **JList** supports multiple-interval selection. In this mode, the user can select multiple ranges of items within a list. With single-interval selection, the user can select one range of items. With single selection, the user can select only a single item. Of course, a single item can be selected in the other two modes, too. It's just that they also allow a range to be selected.

You can obtain the index of the first item selected, which will also be the index of the only selected item when using single-selection mode, by calling **getSelectedIndex( )**, shown here:

int getSelectedIndex( )

Indexing begins at zero. So, if the first item is selected, this method will return 0. If no item is selected, –1 is returned.

Before going into any more details, here is a program that demonstrates a simple **JList**. It displays a list of apple varieties. When the user selects an apple, the selection is shown in a label. When the user presses the Buy Apple button, the selection is obtained and a purchase confirmation is shown. Sample output is shown in Figure 5-1.

Figure 5-1 Sample output from the **ListDemo** program

```
// Demonstrate a simple JList.

import javax.swing.*;
import javax.swing.event.*;
import java.awt.*;
import java.awt.event.*;

class ListDemo {

  JList jlst;
  JLabel jlab;
  JScrollPane jscrlp;
  JButton jbtnBuy;

  // Create an array of apple varieties.
  String apples[] = { "Winesap", "Cortland", "Red Delicious",
                      "Golden Delicious", "Gala", "Fuji",
                      "Granny Smith", "Jonathan" };

  ListDemo() {
    // Create a new JFrame container.
    JFrame jfrm = new JFrame("JList Demo");

    // Specify FlowLayout manager.
    jfrm.getContentPane().setLayout(new FlowLayout());

    // Give the frame an initial size.
    jfrm.setSize(204, 200);

    // Terminate the program when the user closes the application.
    jfrm.setDefaultCloseOperation(JFrame.EXIT_ON_CLOSE);
```

```
// Create a JList.
jlst = new JList(apples);  ◄─────────── Create a JList from an array of strings.

// Set the list selection mode to single selection.
jlst.setSelectionMode(ListSelectionModel.SINGLE_SELECTION); ◄┐
                                   Set the selection mode to single selection.
// Add list to a scroll pane.
jscrlp = new JScrollPane(jlst); ◄─────── Put the JList inside a JScrollPane.

// Set the preferred size of the scroll pane.
jscrlp.setPreferredSize(new Dimension(120, 90));

// Make a label that displays the selection.
jlab = new JLabel("Please choose an apple.");
                                     Listen for selection events.
// Add selection listener for the list.
jlst.addListSelectionListener(new ListSelectionListener() { ◄┐
  public void valueChanged(ListSelectionEvent le) {
    // Get the index of the changed item.
    int idx = jlst.getSelectedIndex(); ◄─────── Get the index of the
                                                 current selection.
    // Display selection, if item was selected.
    if(idx != -1)
      jlab.setText("Current selection " + apples[idx]);
    else // Otherwise, reprompt.
      jlab.setText("Please choose an apple.");

  }
});


// Make a button that "buys" the selected apple.
jbtnBuy = new JButton("Buy Apple");

// Add action listener for Buy Apple button.
jbtnBuy.addActionListener(new ActionListener() {
  public void actionPerformed(ActionEvent ae) {
    // Get the index of the changed item.
    int idx = jlst.getSelectedIndex();

    // Display purchase selection if item was selected.
    if(idx != -1) jlab.setText("You purchased " +
                                   apples[idx]);
    else // Otherwise, explain.
      jlab.setText("No apple has been selected.");
  }
});
```

```
    // Add the list and label to the content pane.
    jfrm.getContentPane().add(jscrlp);
    jfrm.getContentPane().add(jbtnBuy);
    jfrm.getContentPane().add(jlab);

    // Display the frame.
    jfrm.setVisible(true);
  }

  public static void main(String args[]) {
    // Create the frame on the event dispatching thread.
    SwingUtilities.invokeLater(new Runnable() {
      public void run() {
        new ListDemo();
      }
    });
  }
}
```

Let's look closely at this program. First, notice the **apples** array near the top of the program. It is initialized to a list of strings that contain the names of various varieties of apples. Inside **ListDemo( )**, a **JList** is constructed using the **apples** array. As mentioned, when the array constructor is used (as it is in this case) a model is automatically created that contains the contents of the array. Thus, the list will contain the names of the apples.

Next, the selection mode is set to single selection. This means that only one type of apple can be selected at any one time. (You will see how to handle multiple selections in the next section.) Then, the **JList** is wrapped inside a **JScrollPane**, and the preferred size of the scroll pane is set to 120 by 90. This makes for a compact, but easy-to-use size.

A label that will display the user's actions is then created followed by the event handler for list selection events. A list selection event occurs whenever the user selects an item or changes the item selected. Inside this event handler, the index of the item selected is obtained by calling **getSelectedIndex( )**. Because the list has been set to single selection mode, this is the index of the only item selected. This index is then used to index the **apples** array to obtain the name of the item selected. Notice that this index value is tested against −1. Recall that this is the value returned if no item has been selected. This will be the case when the selection event handler is called if the user has deselected an item. Remember: a selection event is generated when the user selects or deselects an item.

Next, the Buy Apple button is created followed by the action event handler that processes button presses. This event handler works the same way as the list selection event handler, and it also checks that the index is not −1. If no item has been selected, as it won't be when the program first starts or if the user deselects an item, then a message is displayed informing the user of this fact.

CRITICAL SKILL
5.2 Handle Multiple Selections

The previous program allowed only one item to be selected from the list. However, it is possible for a list to allow several items to be selected and, as explained, this is the default behavior of **JList**. The main difference between handling a **JList** that allows multiple items to be selected and one that allows only a single item to be selected is found in the way events are handled. When multiple items can be selected, you need some way to obtain the indices of all selected items. The easiest way to do this is to call **getSelectedIndices( )**, shown here:

int [ ] getSelectedIndices( )

It returns an array of the indices of the selected items, starting with the lowest index. Remember, when using multiple-interval selection (which is the default), the indices in the array may be discontinuous. If no items have been selected, the length of the returned array will be zero.

Here is a reworked version of the preceding program that shows one way to handle the selection of multiple ranges of items. Sample output is shown in Figure 5-2.

```
// Handle multiple list selections.

import javax.swing.*;
import javax.swing.event.*;
import java.awt.*;
import java.awt.event.*;

class MultiRangeList {

  JList jlst;
  JLabel jlab;
  JScrollPane jscrlp;
  JButton jbtnBuy;

  // Create an array of apple varieties.
  String apples[] = { "Winesap", "Cortland", "Red Delicious",
                      "Golden Delicious", "Gala", "Fuji",
                      "Granny Smith", "Jonathan" };

  MultiRangeList() {
    // Create a new JFrame container.
    JFrame jfrm = new JFrame("Multiple Range");

    // Specify FlowLayout manager.
    jfrm.getContentPane().setLayout(new FlowLayout());
```

```
// Give the frame an initial size.
jfrm.setSize(180, 240);

// Terminate the program when the user closes the application.
jfrm.setDefaultCloseOperation(JFrame.EXIT_ON_CLOSE);

// Create a JList. By default, this list allows
// multiple ranges to be selected.
jlst = new JList(apples);
```
◄─────── This time the default multiple selection mode is used.

```
// Add list to a scroll pane.
jscrlp = new JScrollPane(jlst);

// Set the preferred size of the scroll pane.
jscrlp.setPreferredSize(new Dimension(120, 90));

// Make a label that displays the selection.
jlab = new JLabel("Please choose an apple.");

// Add selection listener for the list.
jlst.addListSelectionListener(new ListSelectionListener() {
  public void valueChanged(ListSelectionEvent le) {
    String what = "";
```
Get an array that contains the indices of the selected items.
```
    // Get the index of the changed item.
    int indices[] = jlst.getSelectedIndices();
```
◄─┐
```
    // Confirm that one or more items have been selected.
    if(indices.length == 0) {
```
◄─────── If the array length is zero, then no items are selected.
```
      jlab.setText("Please choose an apple.");
      return;
    }

    // Display the selected items.
    for(int i = 0; i < indices.length; i++)
      what += apples[indices[i]] + "<br>";

    jlab.setText("<html>Current selection:<br>" + what);
  }
});
```

```java
      // Make a button that "buys" the selected apple.
      jbtnBuy = new JButton("Buy Apple");

      // Add action listener for Buy Apple button.
      jbtnBuy.addActionListener(new ActionListener() {
        public void actionPerformed(ActionEvent ae) {
          String what = "";

          // Get the index of the changed item.
          int indices[] = jlst.getSelectedIndices();

          // Confirm that one or more items have been selected.
          if(indices.length == 0) {
            jlab.setText("No apple has been selected.");
            return;
          }

          // Display the selected items.
          for(int i = 0; i < indices.length; i++)
            what += apples[indices[i]] + "<br>";

          jlab.setText("<html>Apples purchased:<br>" + what);
        }
      });

    // Add the list and label to the content pane.
    jfrm.getContentPane().add(jscrlp);
    jfrm.getContentPane().add(jbtnBuy);
    jfrm.getContentPane().add(jlab);

    // Display the frame.
    jfrm.setVisible(true);
  }

  public static void main(String args[]) {
    // Create the frame on the event dispatching thread.
    SwingUtilities.invokeLater(new Runnable() {
      public void run() {
        new MultiRangeList();
      }
    });
  }
}
```

Figure 5-2 Sample output from the **MultiRangeList** program that allows multiple items in a **JList** to be selected

There are two main differences between this version of the program and the previous one. First, the default multiple-interval selection mode is used. Therefore, there is no call to **setSelectionMode( )**. Second, notice how selection and action events are handled. An array of the currently selected indices is obtained by calling **getSelectedIndices( )**. Then, the length of the array is tested to ensure that it is greater than zero. If it isn't, then no items have been selected and **jlab** is updated to reflect this fact and the handler returns. Recall that a selection event is generated when items are selected or deselected, so it is possible for **valueChanged( )** to be called when there are no selected items. (It is also possible for **actionPerformed( )** to be called if the user presses the Buy Apple button before making a selection.) Therefore, it is necessary to confirm that a selection has actually been made when handling the events by testing the length of the array. Finally, an HTML string containing the names of the selected apples is constructed and displayed.

CRITICAL SKILL
5.3 JList Options

JList supports many options and features and it is beyond the scope of this book to examine all of them. However, several commonly used ones are discussed here, beginning with an alternative way to determine which item or items have been selected. Instead of obtaining the index of a selection, you can obtain the value associated with the selection by calling one of these methods:

Object getSelectedValue( )

Object[ ] getSelectedValues( )

getSelectedValue( ) returns a reference to the first selected value. If no value has been selected, then it returns **null**. **getSelectedValues( )** returns an array that contains references to all of the items selected. It returns a zero-length array if no items are selected. The values are in list order.

Using **getSelectedValues( )**, it is possible to rewrite the list selection handler for the preceding program as shown here:

```
// Add selection listener for the list.
jlst.addListSelectionListener(new ListSelectionListener() {
  public void valueChanged(ListSelectionEvent le) {
    String what = "";

    // Get the index of the changed item.
    Object[] strs = jlst.getSelectedValues();

    if(strs.length == 0) {
      jlab.setText("Please choose an apple.");
      return;
    }

    // Display the selected item.
    for(int i= 0; i < strs.length; i++)
      what += strs[i] + "<br>";

    jlab.setText("<html>Current selection:<br>" + what);
  }
});
```

Remember that **getSelectedValues( )** returns an array of **Object**, so you may need to cast the elements of that array into the type of items actually stored in the list. In this case, this is not necessary because **Object** provides the **toString( )** method, which is automatically called to obtain the string representation of the object. However, other applications may need to employ explicit casts.

You can select an item under program control by calling **setSelectedIndex( )**, shown here:

void setSelectedIndex(int *idx*)

Here, *idx* is the index of the item to be selected. This method is commonly used to preselect an item when the list is first displayed. For example, if you add this line to the preceding program, the first item in the list, which is Winesap, will be selected when the program starts.

```
jlst.setSelectedIndex(0);
```

If the list supports multiple selection then you can select more than one item by calling **setSelectedIndices( )**, shown here:

void setSelectedIndices(int[ ] *idxs*)

Here, the array passed through *idxs* contains the indices of the items to be selected. For example, if you add these lines to the preceding program, then the first, third, and fifth items are selected:

```
int indices[] = {0, 2, 4 };
jlst.setSelectedIndices(indices);
```

You can select an item by value instead of by index if you call **setSelectedValue( )**:

void setSelectedValue(Object *item*, boolean *scrollToItem*)

Here, *item* specifies the value to be selected. If *scrollToItem* is true, and the selected item is not currently in view, it is scrolled into view. For example, again using the preceding program, this statement

```
jlst.setSelectedValue("Gala", true);
```

selects Gala and scrolls it into view.

You can deselect any and all selections by calling **clearSelection( )**, shown here:

void clearSelection( )

After this method executes, all selections are cleared.

You can determine if a selection is available by calling **isSelectionEmpty( )**, shown here:

boolean isSelectionEmpty( )

It returns true if no selections have been made and false otherwise.

When using a list that supports multiple selection, sometimes you will want to know which item was selected first and which item was selected last. In the language of **JList**, the first item is called the *anchor*. The last item is called the *lead*. Understand that the anchor will not be less than the lead if the user selected items in reverse order. You can obtain these indices by calling **getAnchorSelectionIndex( )** and **getLeadSelectionIndex( )**, shown here:

void getAnchorSelectionIndex( )

void getLeadSelectionIndex( )

Both return −1 if no selection has been made.

Ask The Expert

Q: Can I select a range of values under program control?

A: Yes. To select a range, call **setSelectionInterval( )**, shown here:

void setSelectionInterval(int *idxStart*, int *idxStop*)

The range selected is inclusive. Thus, both *idxStart* and *idxStop*, and all items in between, will be selected. One other point: the value of *idxStart* does not need to be less than *idxStop*. Instead, *idxStart* specifies the anchor and *idxStop* specifies the lead, as described earlier.

You can set the items in a **JList** by calling **setListData( )**. It has the following two forms:

void setListData(Object[ ] *items*)

void setListData(Vector<?> *items*)

Here, *items* is an array or vector that contains the items that you want to be displayed in the invoking list.

Instead of creating a list by passing an array or vector to a **JList** constructor, you can construct a list by first creating a model. You then populate that model and use it to construct a **JList**. This has two advantages. First, you can create custom list models, if desired. Second, you can alter the contents of the list at runtime by adding or removing elements from the model. This technique is shown in Project 5-1.

A **JList** may generate several list selection events when the user is in the process of selecting or deselecting one or more items. You can use the **getValueIsAdjusting( )** method to determine if selections are occurring. It will return true if the selection process is ongoing and false when the user stops the selection process. (This method works in much the same way that the method by the same name does for scroll bars and sliders, as described in Module 3.)

One final option that you may find useful is the ability of **JList** to use a custom cell renderer. A custom cell renderer determines how each entry in the list gets drawn. It must be an object of a class that implements the **ListCellRenderer** interface. This interface defines only one method, called **getListCellRendererComponent( )**, which must return a component that will display the information in the list entry. To specify a custom cell renderer, call **setCellRenderer( )** on the list.

Progress Check

1. What form of the **JList** constructor do you use to construct a list from an array?

2. What event is generated when the user selects an item?

3. What method is called to obtain the indices of all selected items? What method is called to obtain the values of all selected items?

Project 5-1 | Work with a List Model

ListModelDemo.java

For many applications of **JList** there is no reason to create or interact with a list model directly. As the preceding examples have shown, the model provided by **JList** when a list is constructed from an array or a **Vector** is easy to use and full featured. However, if you want to interact with the data directly, such as by adding one or more items, then you will need to access the model directly. Fortunately, this is easy to do. This project demonstrates how to work with a list model. It uses the model to construct a **JList**, add items to the list, and remove items from the list.

In general, to work with the list model, usually you follow three steps:

1. Create a model.

2. Populate the model with list items.

3. Create a **JList** that uses the model.

By far the easiest way to create a list model is to use **DefaultListModel**. This model implements the **ListModel** interface. It also provides many methods that enable you to manage the data in the list, including methods that add and remove items. You can either use **DefaultListModel** directly (which is what this project does) or create a custom version of the model by subclassing it.

After the list has been created, you can obtain a reference to the model by calling **getModel( )**, shown here:

ListModel getModel( )

It returns a reference to the model used by the list.

---

1. **JList(Object[ ] items)**
2. **ListSelectionEvent**
3. **getSelectedIndices( )** and **getSelectedValues( )**

As mentioned, the model used by this project is **DefaultListModel**. It defines several methods (which are similar in function to those defined by the original **Vector** class). Here is a sampling of its methods, including the ones used by this project:

Method	Description
void add(int *idx*, Object *item*)	Adds *item* at the index specified by *idx*.
void addElement(Object *item*)	Adds *item* to the end of the list.
void clear( )	Removes all items from the list.
Object get(int *idx*)	Returns the item at the index specified by *idx*.
int getSize( )	Returns the number of items in the list.
Object remove(int *idx*)	Removes the item at the index specified by *idx*, returning the item in the process.
void removeRange(int *start*, int *end*)	Removes the range of elements specified by *start* and *end*, inclusive. Also, *start* must not be greater than *end*.

Using these methods you can add items to or remove items from the list. You can also determine how many items are in the list. Keep in mind that **DefaultListModel** defines other methods that help manage the list. It is a class that you will want to explore fully on your own.

This project creates a variation on the apples list used by the preceding **JList** examples. It uses the list model to allow apple varieties to be added to or removed from the list of apple types. It supports this action by adding another button. When the program starts up, this button is called Add More Varieties. When pressed, it causes additional apple varieties to be added to the list. Then, the label in the button is changed to Remove Extra Varieties. Pressing the button a second time causes the additional varieties to be removed from the list. All list interaction is performed through the model. Sample output is shown here:

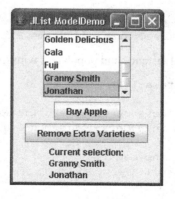

Project
5-1

Work with a List Model

(continued)

Step by Step

1. Create a file called **ListModelDemo.java** and add the following comment and **import** statements:

```
// Project 5-1: Use the ListModel interface.

import javax.swing.*;
import javax.swing.event.*;
import java.awt.*;
import java.awt.event.*;
```

2. Begin coding the **ListModelDemo** class and its constructor in the usual way, as shown here:

```
class ListModelDemo {

  JList jlst;
  JLabel jlab;
  JScrollPane jscrlp;
  JButton jbtnBuy;
  JButton jbtnAddDel;

  ListModelDemo() {
    // Create a new JFrame container.
    JFrame jfrm = new JFrame("JList ModelDemo");

    // Specify FlowLayout manager.
    jfrm.getContentPane().setLayout(new FlowLayout());

    // Give the frame an initial size.
    jfrm.setSize(180, 240);

    // Terminate the program when the user closes the application.
    jfrm.setDefaultCloseOperation(JFrame.EXIT_ON_CLOSE);
```

3. Create a **DefaultListModel** instance and populate it with five apple varieties, like this:

```
// Create and populate a list model.
//
// First, create an instance of DefaultListModel.
DefaultListModel lm = new DefaultListModel();

// Now, add items to the model.
lm.addElement("Winesap");
lm.addElement("Cortland");
lm.addElement("Red Delicious");
```

```
lm.addElement("Golden Delicious");
lm.addElement("Gala");
```

This creates a new list model called **lm** and then adds five items to the model. In other words, after the preceding code executes, **lm** will contain data for five apple varieties.

4. Create a **JList** instance, passing in the model.

```
// Create a JList by specifying the model.
jlst = new JList(lm);
```

After this line executes, **jlst** will be a fully initialized list that contains the data specified by **lm**.

5. Wrap the **JList** in a **JScrollPane** and set its preferred size.

```
// Add list to a scroll pane.
jscrlp = new JScrollPane(jlst);

// Set the preferred size of the scroll pane.
jscrlp.setPreferredSize(new Dimension(120, 90));
```

6. Add a label that will display messages to the user.

```
// Make a label that displays the selection.
jlab = new JLabel("Please choose an apple.");
```

7. Add a list selection event handler as shown next. Notice that it uses **getSelectedValues( )** to obtain an array of the values, rather than using **getSelectedIndices( )**. It is otherwise similar to the same sequence used by the preceding example programs.

```
// Add selection listener for the list.
jlst.addListSelectionListener(new ListSelectionListener() {
  public void valueChanged(ListSelectionEvent le) {
    String what = "";

    // Get the index of the changed item.
    Object values[] = jlst.getSelectedValues();

    // Confirm that one or more items have been selected.
    if(values.length == 0) {
      jlab.setText("Please choose an apple.");
      return;
    }

    // Display the selected items.
    for(int i = 0; i < values.length; i++)
      what += values[i] + "<br>";
```

(continued)

```
     jlab.setText("<html>Current selection:<br>" + what);
   }
});
```

8. Add the Buy Apple button and its action event handler. This sequence is similar to the example programs shown earlier except that it uses **getSelectedValues( )** rather than **getSelectedIndices( )** to obtain the selections.

```
// Make a button that "buys" the selected apple.
jbtnBuy = new JButton("Buy Apple");

// Add action listener for Buy Apple button.
jbtnBuy.addActionListener(new ActionListener() {
  public void actionPerformed(ActionEvent ae) {
    String what = "";

    // Get the index of the changed item.
    Object values[] = jlst.getSelectedValues();

    // Confirm that one or more items have been selected.
    if(values.length == 0) {
      jlab.setText("No apple has been selected.");
      return;
    }

    // Display the selected items.
    for(int i = 0; i < values.length; i++)
      what += values[i] + "<br>";

    jlab.setText("<html>Apples purchased:<br>" + what);
  }
});
```

9. Create the Add More Varieties button and its action event handler. This handler uses the list model to add or remove items from the list. Pay special attention to it.

```
// Make a button that adds more apple selections.
jbtnAddDel = new JButton("Add More Varieties");

// Add action listener for Add More Varieties button.
jbtnAddDel.addActionListener(new ActionListener() {
  public void actionPerformed(ActionEvent ae) {

    // Get a reference to the model.
    DefaultListModel lm = (DefaultListModel) jlst.getModel();
```

```
      // See if extra varieties already added.
      if(lm.getSize() > 5) {
        // If so, remove extra varieties.
        for(int i=7; i > 4; i-) lm.remove(i);

        jbtnAddDel.setText("Add More Varieties");
      } else {
        // Add extra varieties.
        lm.addElement("Fuji");
        lm.addElement("Granny Smith");
        lm.addElement("Jonathan");
        jbtnAddDel.setText("Remove Extra Varieties");
      }
    }
  });
```

The event handler begins by obtaining a reference to the model by calling **getModel( )**.
It then uses this model to obtain the current size of the list. If the list has more than five
entries, then it removes all entries past the fifth one by using the **remove( )** method. (The
removal of the varieties could also be accomplished with a single call to **removeRange( )**.
You might want to try this alternative on your own.) Otherwise, it adds three apple varieties
to the list by calling **addElement( )**.

10. End the **ListModelDemo( )** constructor by adding the components to the content pane and
then making the frame visible.

```
    // Add the list and label to the content pane.
    jfrm.getContentPane().add(jscrlp);
    jfrm.getContentPane().add(jbtnBuy);
    jfrm.getContentPane().add(jbtnAddDel);
    jfrm.getContentPane().add(jlab);

    // Display the frame.
    jfrm.setVisible(true);
  }
```

11. Finally, end the **ListModelDemo** class in the usual way:

```
  public static void main(String args[]) {
    // Create the frame on the event dispatching thread.
    SwingUtilities.invokeLater(new Runnable() {
      public void run() {
        new ListModelDemo();
      }
    });
  }
}
```

(continued)

Project
5-1

Work with a List Model

12. The entire **ListModelDemo** program is shown here:

```
// Project 5-1: Use the ListModel interface.

import javax.swing.*;
import javax.swing.event.*;
import java.awt.*;
import java.awt.event.*;

class ListModelDemo {

  JList jlst;
  JLabel jlab;
  JScrollPane jscrlp;
  JButton jbtnBuy;
  JButton jbtnAddDel;

  ListModelDemo() {
    // Create a new JFrame container.
    JFrame jfrm = new JFrame("JList ModelDemo");

    // Specify FlowLayout manager.
    jfrm.getContentPane().setLayout(new FlowLayout());

    // Give the frame an initial size.
    jfrm.setSize(180, 240);

    // Terminate the program when the user closes the application.
    jfrm.setDefaultCloseOperation(JFrame.EXIT_ON_CLOSE);

    // Create and populate a list model.
    //
    // First, create an instance of DefaultListModel.
    DefaultListModel lm = new DefaultListModel();

    // Now, add items to the model.
    lm.addElement("Winesap");
    lm.addElement("Cortland");
    lm.addElement("Red Delicious");
    lm.addElement("Golden Delicious");
    lm.addElement("Gala");

    // Create a JList by specifying the model.
    jlst = new JList(lm);

    // Add list to a scroll pane.
```

```
jscrlp = new JScrollPane(jlst);

// Set the preferred size of the scroll pane.
jscrlp.setPreferredSize(new Dimension(120, 90));

// Make a label that displays the selection.
jlab = new JLabel("Please choose an apple.");

// Add selection listener for the list.
jlst.addListSelectionListener(new ListSelectionListener() {
  public void valueChanged(ListSelectionEvent le) {
    String what = "";

    // Get the index of the changed item.
    Object values[] = jlst.getSelectedValues();

    // Confirm that one or more items have been selected.
    if(values.length == 0) {
      jlab.setText("Please choose an apple.");
      return;
    }

    // Display the selected items.
    for(int i = 0; i < values.length; i++)
      what += values[i] + "<br>";

    jlab.setText("<html>Current selection:<br>" + what);
  }
});

// Make a button that "buys" the selected apple.
jbtnBuy = new JButton("Buy Apple");

// Add action listener for Buy Apple button.
jbtnBuy.addActionListener(new ActionListener() {
  public void actionPerformed(ActionEvent ae) {
    String what = "";

    // Get the index of the changed item.
    Object values[] = jlst.getSelectedValues();

    // Confirm that one or more items have been selected.
    if(values.length == 0) {
      jlab.setText("No apple has been selected.");
```

(continued)

```
        return;
      }

      // Display the selected items.
      for(int i = 0; i < values.length; i++)
        what += values[i] + "<br>";

      jlab.setText("<html>Apples purchased:<br>" + what);
    }
  });

  // Make a button that adds more apple selections.
  jbtnAddDel = new JButton("Add More Varieties");

  // Add action listener for Add More Varieties button.
  jbtnAddDel.addActionListener(new ActionListener() {
    public void actionPerformed(ActionEvent ae) {

      // Get a reference to the model.
      DefaultListModel lm = (DefaultListModel) jlst.getModel();

      // See if extra varieties already added.
      if(lm.getSize() > 5) {
        // If so, remove extra varieties.
        for(int i=7; i > 4; i-) lm.remove(i);

        jbtnAddDel.setText("Add More Varieties");
      } else {
        // Add extra varieties.
        lm.addElement("Fuji");
        lm.addElement("Granny Smith");
        lm.addElement("Jonathan");
        jbtnAddDel.setText("Remove Extra Varieties");
      }
    }
  });

  // Add the list and label to the content pane.
  jfrm.getContentPane().add(jscrlp);
  jfrm.getContentPane().add(jbtnBuy);
  jfrm.getContentPane().add(jbtnAddDel);
  jfrm.getContentPane().add(jlab);

  // Display the frame.
  jfrm.setVisible(true);
}

public static void main(String args[]) {
```

```
    // Create the frame on the event dispatching thread.
    SwingUtilities.invokeLater(new Runnable() {
      public void run() {
        new ListModelDemo();
      }
    });
  }
}
```

Use JComboBox

A variation on the list is the *combo box*. The combo box gets its name from the fact that it combines two components. There are two types of combo boxes. The first combines a drop-down list (also referred to as a pop-up list) and a button that activates the drop-down list. The second combines a drop-down list with an edit field. Because combo boxes work with a drop-down list, they are very compact and are excellent when screen space is in short supply or when the GUI is very crowded. The combo box is supported by the Swing class **JComboBox**.

JComboBox uses the **ComboBoxModel**. This interface extends **ListModel** and supplies two additional methods: **getSelectedItem( )** and **setSelectedItem( )**. Combo boxes that are mutable (in which the contents can be changed) use the **MutableComboBoxModel**, which extends **ComboBoxModel**. There is a default implementation of **MutableComboBoxModel** called **DefaultComboBoxModel**. This class also provides methods that add and remove items from the list and works in a manner similar to **DefaultListModel** described in Project 5-1. For many uses, you will not need to interact with the model directly because **JComboBox** supplies methods that interface to the model.

JComboBox provides the constructors shown in Table 5-2.

JComboBox generates an action event when the user selects an item from the list (or, when the user enters a string into the edit field, if the combo box uses an edit field). Therefore, when an action command is received, it means that the user selected an item. **JComboBox** also generates an item event when the state of selection changes, which occurs when an item

Constructor	Description
JComboBox( )	Creates an empty combo box.
JComboBox(Object[ ] *items*)	Creates a combo box that contains the items specified by *items*.
JComboBox(Vector<?> *items*)	Creates a combo box that contains the items in the vector specified by *items*.
JComboBox(ComboBoxModel *cbm*)	Creates a combo box that uses the model specified by *cbm*.

Table 5-2 The **JComboBox** Constructors

is selected or deselected. Thus, changing a selection means that two item events will occur: one for the deselected item and another for the selected item. Often, it is sufficient to simply listen for action events, but both event types are available for your use.

You can determine the current selection two ways. First, you can call **getSelectedItem( )**, which returns a reference to the item. It is shown here:

Object getSelectedItem( )

If no item is selected, **null** is returned.

The second way to determine what item has been selected is to call **getSelectedIndex( )**, shown next:

int getSelectedIndex( )

It returns the zero-based index of the selected item in the list. If no item is selected, −1 is returned.

You can select an item in the list under program control by calling either **setSelectedItem( )** or **setSelectedIndex( )**. Both are shown here:

void setSelectedItem(Object *item*)

void setSelectedIndex(int *idx*)

Here, *item* specifies the item to select and *idx* specifies the index to select. Remember that indexing starts at zero.

For most applications, **JComboBox** is very easy to use. Simply pass to its constructor an array containing the items that you want shown in the drop-down list and register an action listener. Each time the user makes or changes a selection, the action listener is notified of the selection. The following program demonstrates the process. Sample output is shown in Figure 5-3.

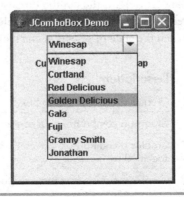

Figure 5-3 Sample output from the **ComboBoxDemo** program

```
// Demonstrate a simple combo box.

import javax.swing.*;
import java.awt.*;
import java.awt.event.*;

class ComboBoxDemo {

  JComboBox jcbb;
  JLabel jlab;

  // Create an array of apple varieties.
  String apples[] = { "Winesap", "Cortland", "Red Delicious",
                      "Golden Delicious", "Gala", "Fuji",
                      "Granny Smith", "Jonathan" };

  ComboBoxDemo() {
    // Create a new JFrame container.
    JFrame jfrm = new JFrame("JComboBox Demo");

    // Specify FlowLayout manager.
    jfrm.getContentPane().setLayout(new FlowLayout());

    // Give the frame an initial size.
    jfrm.setSize(220, 240);

    // Terminate the program when the user closes the application.
    jfrm.setDefaultCloseOperation(JFrame.EXIT_ON_CLOSE);

    // Create a JComboBox.
    jcbb = new JComboBox(apples);          ◄─────── Create combo box that
                                                   contains an array of strings.

    // Make a label that displays the selection.
    jlab = new JLabel();

    // Add action listener for the combo box.
    jcbb.addActionListener(new ActionListener() {   ◄─────── Listen for combo
      public void actionPerformed(ActionEvent le) {           box events.
        // Get a reference to the item selected.
        String item = (String) jcbb.getSelectedItem();   ◄─┐

        // Display the selected item.                      Get the item selected
        jlab.setText("Current selection: " + item);        in the combo box.
      }
```

```
    });

    // Initially select the first item in the list.
    jcbb.setSelectedIndex(0);    ◄──────────────── Initially select the first item.

    // Add the combo box and label to the content pane.
    jfrm.getContentPane().add(jcbb);
    jfrm.getContentPane().add(jlab);

    // Display the frame.
    jfrm.setVisible(true);
  }

  public static void main(String args[]) {
    // Create the frame on the event dispatching thread.
    SwingUtilities.invokeLater(new Runnable() {
      public void run() {
        new ComboBoxDemo();
      }
    });
  }
}
```

This program displays the same list of apple varieties as the **JList** examples did. However, it uses a combo box to render this functionality in a smaller space. Notice that the combo box is created by passing it the **apples** array. This causes a **ComboBoxModel** to be automatically created that contains the array.

An action listener is registered for the **jcbb** combo box. Recall that each time the user selects an item from the list, an action event is generated. The event handler **actionPerformed( )** processes the event by obtaining the selected item by calling **getSelectedItem( )**. Because an action event is generated only when the user selects an item, an item will always be selected when the action event is received. The handler then displays the selection.

Notice that the first item in the list is selected by the program by calling **setSelectedIndex( )**. This is not technically necessary, but adding this step effectively gives the combo box a default selection. It also triggers an action event.

CRITICAL SKILL
5.5 Create an Editable Combo Box

As mentioned, it is possible to add an edit control to a combo box. When this is done, the user can either select an item from the drop-down list or enter something not in the list.

Furthermore, it is also possible to select an item from the drop-down list and then edit it to create the desired name. If you press ENTER when the edit field has focus, whatever has been entered becomes the current selection and an action event is generated. Be aware, however, that entering a new name or editing an existing name does not alter the list.

To create an editable combo box, first create an instance of **JComboBox** and then call **setEditable(true)** on that instance. The **setEditable( )** method has this general form:

void setEditable(boolean *canEdit*)

If *canEdit* is true, then an edit field is included in the combo box. If *canEdit* is false, then the edit field is removed.

To make the combo box used by the preceding program editable, simply add these lines immediately after the call to the **JComboBox( )** constructor:

```
// Make the combo box editable.
jcbb.setEditable(true);
```

After making this change, the combo box will now look like the one shown in Figure 5-4. To make an edited string the current selection, simply press ENTER while focus is in the edit field. Remember that whatever you edit will not become part of the list, however.

Figure 5-4 An editable combo box

Some JComboBox Options

Like **JList**, **JComboBox** supports many options—-more than can be described in this module. However, a few of the more popular options are examined here. One very useful combo box feature is its ability to add or remove items from the drop-down list dynamically, during program execution. This feature is supported by the methods **addItem( )** and **removeItem( )**, shown here:

void addItem(Object *item*)

void removeItem(Object *item*)

Here, *item* is the item to be added or removed. One important point: These methods are available only to combo boxes that are mutable. Fortunately, **DefaultComboBoxModel** is mutable, so these methods work with the default model used by **JComboBox**. When an item is added to the default model, it is added to the end of the list.

You can also remove an item at a specific index by using the **removeItemAt( )** method. You can remove all items by calling **removeAllItems( )**. These methods are shown here:

void removeItemAt(int *idx*)

void removeAllItems( )

Here, *idx* specifies the zero-based index of the item to remove.

You can obtain the size of the list (that is, the number of items in the list) by calling **getItemCount( )**, shown here:

int getItemCount( )

If the list is empty, the value returned will be zero.

The following program shows how to use several of these methods. It is a variation on the first combo box example with the following changes. First, it creates an editable combo box. Second, if the user enters an item that is not in the list, the item is added to the list. Third, it adds a button called Remove Selection. When pressed, the current selection from the list is removed. Sample output is shown in Figure 5-5.

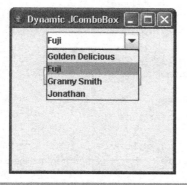

Figure 5-5 Sample output from **DynamicComboBox**, which adds and removes list items dynamically. Notice that several apple varieties have been removed.

```java
// Demonstrate how to add and remove items
// to and from a list dynamically.

import javax.swing.*;
import java.awt.*;
import java.awt.event.*;

class DynamicComboBox {

  JComboBox jcbb;
  JLabel jlab;
  JButton jbtnRemove;

  // Create an array of apple varieties.
  String apples[] = { "Winesap", "Cortland", "Red Delicious",
                      "Golden Delicious", "Gala", "Fuji",
                      "Granny Smith", "Jonathan" };

  DynamicComboBox() {
    // Create a new JFrame container.
    JFrame jfrm = new JFrame("Dynamic JComboBox");

    // Specify FlowLayout manager.
    jfrm.getContentPane().setLayout(new FlowLayout());
```

```
// Give the frame an initial size.
jfrm.setSize(220, 240);

// Terminate the program when the user closes the application.
jfrm.setDefaultCloseOperation(JFrame.EXIT_ON_CLOSE);

// Create a JComboBox.
jcbb = new JComboBox(apples);

// Make the combo box editable.
jcbb.setEditable(true);  ◄──────── Make the combo box editable.

// Make a label that displays the selection.
jlab = new JLabel();

// Add action listener for the combo box.
// If the user enters a new item, it is added
// to the list.
jcbb.addActionListener(new ActionListener() {
  public void actionPerformed(ActionEvent le) {
    // Get a reference to the item selected.
    String item = (String) jcbb.getSelectedItem();

    // Ignore if nothing is selected.
    if(item==null) return;

    // Display the selected item.
    jlab.setText("Current selection: " + item);

    // Add the item to the list if it's not already on it.
    int i;

    // See if it is in the list.
    for(i=0; i < jcbb.getItemCount(); i++)  ◄──── 
      if(item.equals(jcbb.getItemAt(i))) break; // in list

    // If not, then add it.
    if(i==jcbb.getItemCount()) jcbb.addItem(item); ◄──
  }
});

// Initially select the first item in the list.
jcbb.setSelectedIndex(0);
```

See if item in the edit field
is already in the list.

If it is a new item, add it to the list.

```
      // Create the Remove Selection button.
      jbtnRemove = new JButton("Remove Selection");

      // Add action listener for the button.
      jbtnRemove.addActionListener(new ActionListener() {
        public void actionPerformed(ActionEvent le) {
          // Get a reference to the item selected.
          String item = (String) jcbb.getSelectedItem();

          // Ignore if nothing is selected.
          if(item==null) return;

          // Remove the item.
          jcbb.removeItem(item);  ◄─────────── Remove the selected item.

          // Display the selected item.
          jlab.setText("Removed " + item);
        }
      });

      // Add the combo box, label, and button to the content pane.
      jfrm.getContentPane().add(jcbb);
      jfrm.getContentPane().add(jlab);
      jfrm.getContentPane().add(jbtnRemove);

      // Display the frame.
      jfrm.setVisible(true);
    }

    public static void main(String args[]) {
      // Create the frame on the event dispatching thread.
      SwingUtilities.invokeLater(new Runnable() {
        public void run() {
          new DynamicComboBox();
        }
      });
    }
  }
```

A key part of the program is the code that adds an item entered by the user in the edit field to the list. The item is only added if it is not already in the list. (Thus, no duplicates will appear in the list.) The code that handles this is inside the action event handler for the combo box. It is shown here:

```
// Add the item to the list if it's not already in it.
int i;

// See if it is in the list.
for(i=0; i < jcbb.getItemCount(); i++)
  if(item.equals(jcbb.getItemAt(i))) break; // in list

// If not, then add it.
if(i==jcbb.getItemCount()) jcbb.addItem(item);
```

Let's look at this closely. First, a **for** loop is set up that cycles through the items in the list. Notice that the loop runs from zero to one less than the number of items in the list. This value is obtained by calling **getItemCount( )**. During each pass through the loop, the currently selected item is tested against an item in the list by calling **getItemAt( )**. If a match is found, the loop stops early. Otherwise, if the loop runs to completion, then **i** will be equal to the value returned by **getItemCount( )**, which means that the item is not yet on the list. If this is the case, the item is added to the list by calling **addItem( )**.

The other interesting part of the program occurs in the handler for the Remove Selection button. This handler removes the currently selected item from the list. It is shown in its entirety here:

```
jbtnRemove.addActionListener(new ActionListener() {
  public void actionPerformed(ActionEvent le) {
    // Get a reference to the item selected.
    String item = (String) jcbb.getSelectedItem();

    // Ignore if nothing is selected.
    if(item==null) return;

    // Remove the item.
    jcbb.removeItem(item);

    // Display the selected item.
    jlab.setText("Removed " + item);
  }
});
```

The handler begins by obtaining a reference to the currently selected item. If this reference is **null** (which it will be if the list is empty), the handler simply returns. Otherwise, it removes the currently selected item by calling **removeItem( )**.

Here are a few other options that you might find interesting. You can expand the pop-up list under program control by calling **setPopupVisible( )**, shown here:

void setPopupVisible(boolean *show*)

If *show* is true, then the list is displayed; otherwise it is hidden. You can also hide the pop-up list by calling **hidePopup( )**.

You can disable/enable a combo box by calling **setEnabled( )**, shown here:

void setEnabled(boolean *enable*)

If *enable* is true, the combo box is enabled. If it is false, the combo box is disabled.

You can obtain a reference to the combo box model by calling **getModel( )**, shown next:

ComboBoxModel getModel( )

You can set the model by calling **setModel( )**, shown next:

void setModel(ComboBoxModel *cbm*)

As mentioned, for many uses of **JComboBox** you won't need to access or set the model directly.

Progress Check

1. When the user selects an item from a combo box, what event is generated?

2. What method obtains the current selection from a combo box?

3. What method must be called to create an editable combo box?

---

1. **ActionEvent**
2. **getSelectedItem( )**
3. **setEditable( )**

Ask the Expert

Q: Is there a way to determine if the pop-up list is currently displayed?

A: Yes! Just call **isPopupVisible( )**. It returns true if the pop-up list is currently displayed and false otherwise.

CRITICAL SKILL
5.7 Work with JSpinner

Another Swing component that makes use of a list is the spinner. A spinner is a control that incorporates a list with arrows (similar to the arrows on a scroll bar) that allow the list to be scrolled through an edit field. You can also scroll through the list by using the up and down arrow keys on the keyboard. The item shown in the edit field is the currently selected item from the list. Spinners were added by Java version 1.4 and are supported by the **JSpinner** class.

The model used by **JSpinner** is based on the **SpinnerModel** interface. This interface defines the methods shown in Table 5-3. Notice that it gives you access to the current item (which is the one being shown in the edit field), the previous item (if one exists), and the next item (if one exists). It does not let you access any arbitrary element. Thus, the data in a spinner is best thought of as a sequential list of ordered data. Because the operation of **JSpinner** is highly dependent upon the data being managed (for example, different editors are required for different types of data), you will usually need to create a model for each spinner that you use. This differs from many of the other Swing controls in which a default model is often sufficient.

AbstractSpinnerModel is an abstract class that partially implements **SpinnerModel**. It is used as a base class for the following standard spinner models:

SpinnerDateModel	Manages a list of dates.
SpinnerListModel	Manages a list of items defined by an array or a **List** collection.
SpinnerNumberModel	Manages a list of numbers.

In general, to create a spinner that scrolls through a sequence of numeric values, use **SpinnerNumberModel**. To create a spinner that scrolls through a list of dates, use **SpinnerDateModel**. All other lists are handled by **SpinnerListModel**. This is the model that you would use to scroll through a list of strings, for example.

Method	Description
void addChangeListener(ChangeListener *cl*)	Adds *cl* as a listener for change events.
Object getNextValue( )	Returns the value that is one beyond the current value. Returns **null** if the current value is the last value in the list.
Object getPreviousValue( )	Returns the value that is one before the current value. Returns **null** if the current value is the first value in the list.
Object getValue( )	Returns the current value. This is the value shown in the edit field.
void removeChangeListener(ChangeListener *cl*)	Removes *cl* as a listener for change events.
void setValue(Object *val*)	Sets the current value to *val*. If *val* represents an invalid value, **IllegalArgumentException** is thrown.

Table 5-3 The Methods Defined by **SpinnerModel**

JSpinner provides the constructors shown in Table 5-4. Although the first constructor does create what is, in essence, a default spinner that is capable of spinning through a list of integers, it is of little real use because it is unbounded. Usually, when spinning through a list of numbers, you will need to specify an upper and/or lower bound. To do this, or to spin through other types of data, you will need to specify the model when constructing the spinner.

JSpinner generates a change event whenever the value of the spinner (which is the current selection) changes. Understand that the current value can change when the user scrolls a new value into view, or if the user enters a new value by hand.

Constructor	Description
JSpinner( )	Creates a spinner that spins through an unbounded list of integers.
JSpinner(SpinnerModel *spm*)	Creates a spinner based on the model passed via *spm*.

Table 5-4 The **JSpinner** Constructors

JSpinner provides methods that give you access to the current, previous, and next values. They are shown here:

Object getValue( )

Object getPreviousValue( )

Object getNextValue( )

These methods are provided by **JSpinner** as a convenience so that you don't need to access the model directly to obtain the values.

CRITICAL SKILL
5.8 # Use the SpinnerListModel

The **SpinnerListModel** is the most general of the three built-in spinner models because it can be used to spin through a list of any type of values, including strings. This model defines the constructors shown in Table 5-5. It implements the methods defined by **SpinnerModel** and adds these two methods:

List<?> getList( )

void setList(List<?> *items*)

The **getList( )** method returns a reference to the list. The **setList( )** method makes the **List** referred to by *items* the new list. Understand that a copy of the list is not made. Rather, just a reference to the list is stored.

The following program demonstrates a **JSpinner** that uses **SpinnerListModel**. The spinner manages a list of strings that represent the RGB colors Red, Green, and Blue. The selected color is used to set the color of the border that is shown around a label that displays the current selection. Sample output is shown in Figure 5-6.

Constructor	Description
SpinnerListModel( )	Creates a model that contains no data.
SpinnerListModel(Object[ ] *items*)	Creates a model that contains the data passed in the array specified by *items*.
SpinnerListModel(List<?> *items*)	Creates a model that contains the data passed in the **List** specified by *items*.

Table 5-5 The **SpinnerListModel** Constructors

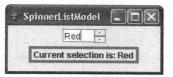

Figure 5-6 Sample output from the **SpinnerListModel** program

```java
// Demonstrate a spinner based on SpinnerListModel.

import javax.swing.*;
import javax.swing.event.*;
import java.awt.*;

class SpinnerDemo {

  JSpinner jspin;
  JLabel jlab;

  // Create an array of RGB colors.
  String colors[] = { "Red", "Green", "Blue" };

  SpinnerDemo() {
    // Create a new JFrame container.
    JFrame jfrm = new JFrame("SpinnerListModel");

    // Specify FlowLayout manager.
    jfrm.getContentPane().setLayout(new FlowLayout());

    // Give the frame an initial size.
    jfrm.setSize(220, 100);

    // Terminate the program when the user closes the application.
    jfrm.setDefaultCloseOperation(JFrame.EXIT_ON_CLOSE);

    // Create spinner list model.
    SpinnerListModel spm = new SpinnerListModel(colors);

    // Create a JSpinner and specify the model.
    jspin = new JSpinner(spm);

    // Set the preferred size of the spinner.
```

Create a spinner model that holds a list of strings.

Create a spinner that uses the model.

```
jspin.setPreferredSize(new Dimension(60, 20));

// Make a label that displays the selection
// and set its border color. Because Red is the
// first string in the list, it will be selected
// by default when the spinner is created.
jlab = new JLabel(" Current selection is: Red ");
jlab.setBorder(BorderFactory.createLineBorder(Color.RED, 4));

// Add change listener for the spinner.                    Listen for changes to the selection.
jspin.addChangeListener(new ChangeListener() {  ◄─────┘
  public void stateChanged(ChangeEvent ce) {
    // Obtain the current selection.
    String color = (String) jspin.getValue();  ◄─────── Get the value selected.

    // Report the selection in the label.
    jlab.setText(" Current selection is: " +
                 color + " ");

    // Set the label's border color based on
    // the selection.
    if(color.equals("Red"))  ◄─────── Use the value to set the color of the label's border.
      jlab.setBorder(
        BorderFactory.createLineBorder(Color.RED, 4));
    else if(color.equals("Green"))
      jlab.setBorder(
        BorderFactory.createLineBorder(Color.GREEN, 4));
    else
      jlab.setBorder(
        BorderFactory.createLineBorder(Color.BLUE, 4));
  }
});

// Add the spinner and label to the content pane.
jfrm.getContentPane().add(jspin);
jfrm.getContentPane().add(jlab);

// Display the frame.
jfrm.setVisible(true);
}

public static void main(String args[]) {
  // Create the frame on the event dispatching thread.
  SwingUtilities.invokeLater(new Runnable() {
```

```
      public void run() {
         new SpinnerDemo();
      }
   });
   }
}
```

In the program, an array of strings called **colors** is created that contains the strings "Red," "Green," and "Blue." This array is used to create a **SpinnerListModel** instance. This model is then passed to the **JSpinner** constructor. When the spinner is displayed, the first item in the list, which is Red in this case, is displayed automatically and is the currently selected value. When the user changes the selection, the change event handler obtains the new selection by calling **getValue( )**. It displays that selection in the label and then changes the color of the label's border to that specified by the selection.

CRITICAL SKILL
5.9 # Use the SpinnerNumberModel

If you want to spin through a list of numeric values, then you will want to create a **SpinnerNumberModel**. This model specifies properties that determine the minimum and maximum values in the range of values, the *step size* (which is the increment between numbers), and the value (which is inherited from **SpinnerModel**). It defines the constructors shown in Table 5-6.

Constructor	Description
SpinnerNumberModel( )	Creates a default model that is unbounded. Its initial value is 0 and its step size is 1.
SpinnerNumberModel(int *val*, int *min*, int *max*, int *stepSize*)	Creates a model that sets the initial value to *val*, the minimum value to *min*, the maximum value to *max*, and the step size to *stepSize*.
SpinnerNumberModel(double *val*, double *min*, double *max*, double *stepSize*)	Creates a model that sets the initial value to *val*, the minimum value to *min*, the maximum value to *max*, and the step size to *stepSize*.
SpinnerNumberModel(Number *val*, Comparable *min*, Comparable *max*, Number *stepSize*)	Creates a model that sets the initial value to *val* and the step size to *stepSize*. The minimum and maximum bounds are determined by the objects referenced by *min* and *max*.

Table 5-6 The **SpinnerNumberModel** Constructors

SpinnerNumberModel implements the methods defined by **SpinnerModel** and adds these additional methods, which provide access to the minimum, maximum, and step size properties:

Comparable getMaximum( )

void setMaximum(Comparable *max*)

Comparable getMinimum( )

void setMinimum(Comparable *min*)

Number getStepSize( )

void setStepSize(Number *stepSize*)

Even though **setMaximum( )** and **setMinimum( )** specify parameters of type **Comparable**, normally you will pass numeric objects. (All of Java's numeric types implement **Comparable**, so objects of all numeric types are valid as arguments.) **SpinnerNumberModel** also supplies the **getNumber( )** method, shown next:

Number getNumber( )

It returns the current value as a **Number** rather than an **Object**.

Here is an example that demonstrates **SpinnerNumberModel**. It creates a spinner that spins integers from 1 to 10. The value is used to set the thickness of the border that surrounds a label that displays the current value. Thus, as you change the value of the spinner, the thickness of the border changes. Sample output is shown in Figure 5-7.

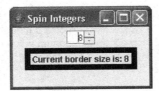

Figure 5-7 Sample output from the **SpinInts** program

```
// Spin integers.

import javax.swing.*;
import javax.swing.event.*;
import java.awt.*;


class SpinInts {

  JSpinner jspin;
  JLabel jlab;

  SpinInts() {
    // Create a new JFrame container.
    JFrame jfrm = new JFrame("Spin Integers");

    // Specify FlowLayout manager.
    jfrm.getContentPane().setLayout(new FlowLayout());

    // Give the frame an initial size.
    jfrm.setSize(200, 120);

    // Terminate the program when the user closes the application.
    jfrm.setDefaultCloseOperation(JFrame.EXIT_ON_CLOSE);

    // Create an integer spinner model.
    SpinnerNumberModel spm =
          new SpinnerNumberModel(1, 1, 10, 1);

    // Create a JSpinner using the model.
    jspin = new JSpinner(spm);

    // Set the preferred size of the spinner.
    jspin.setPreferredSize(new Dimension(40, 20));

    // Make a label that displays the selection.
    jlab = new JLabel(" Current border size is: 1 ");
    jlab.setBorder(BorderFactory.createLineBorder(Color.BLACK));

    // Add change listener for the spinner.
    jspin.addChangeListener(new ChangeListener() {
      public void stateChanged(ChangeEvent ce) {
```

Create a spinner model for the integers 1 through 10.

Create a spinner that uses that model.

```
              // Get the current size.
              Integer bSize = (Integer) jspin.getValue();
```
◄——— Get the current value.

```
              // Report the current size.
              jlab.setText(" Current border size is: " +
                        bSize + " ");

              // Set the label's border size based on
              // the value selected.
              jlab.setBorder(
                BorderFactory.createLineBorder(Color.BLACK,
                                        bSize.intValue())));
```
└— Set the border size based on that value.
```
            }
          });

          // Add the spinner and label to the content pane.
          jfrm.getContentPane().add(jspin);
          jfrm.getContentPane().add(jlab);

          // Display the frame.
          jfrm.setVisible(true);
        }

        public static void main(String args[]) {
          // Create the frame on the event dispatching thread.
          SwingUtilities.invokeLater(new Runnable() {
            public void run() {
              new SpinInts();
            }
          });
        }
      }
```

In the program, notice how the **SpinnerNumberModel** is created by this line:

```
SpinnerNumberModel spm =
      new SpinnerNumberModel(1, 1, 10, 1);
```

This creates a model that ranges from 1 to 10, with an step increment of 1, and an initial value of 1. This model is then used to construct the spinner. On your own, you might want to try using different step sizes and observe the results.

Whenever the current value of the spinner changes, the change event listener uses the new value to set the size of the border around the label. Thus, each time you change the value of the spinner, the border of the label will also change. If you press and hold one of the spinner's arrows, the border size will change continually (up or down to its limit) in real time, in an animated way.

Use the SpinnerDateModel

One of the more frequent uses for a spinner is to allow the user to choose a date. To accommodate this common task, Swing provides **SpinnerDateModel**. It defines the constructors shown in Table 5-7. **SpinnerDateModel** specifies properties that determine the beginning and ending dates that define the bounds of the date range. It also has a property, called **calendarField**, that defines how the date is changed. For example, you can specify that the date change by day, month, hour, or minute. In general, when allowing the user to select dates, you will use a day increment. When selecting time, you will often use a minute increment. Of course, the increment is dictated by your application. Be aware, however, because **calendarField** can be ignored by the look and feel. In these cases, the field selected by the user is changed. Therefore, it's best not to rely on the **calendarField** property.

The value of the **calendarField** property must be one of these values defined by **Calendar**:

AM_PM	DAY_OF_MONTH	DAY_OF_WEEK
DAY_OF_WEEK_IN_MONTH	DAY_OF_YEAR	ERA
HOUR	HOUR_OF_DAY	MILLISECOND
MINUTE	MONTH	SECOND
WEEK_OF_MONTH	WEEK_OF_YEAR	YEAR

As mentioned, the look and feel might ignore the increment value.

Constructor	Description
SpinnerDateModel( )	Creates an unbounded model that uses the current date as the initial value and changes dates by day.
SpinnerDateModel(Date *val*, Comparable *begin*, Comparable *end*, int *calField*)	Creates a model that has the initial date specified by *val*. It is bounded by the dates passed via *begin* and *end*. The **calendarField** value is passed in *calField*. See text for details on this value.

Table 5-7 The Constructors for **SpinnerDateModel**

SpinnerDateModel implements the methods defined by **SpinnerModel** and adds these additional methods, which provide access to the beginning and ending dates and **calendarField**:

int getCalendarField( )

Comparable getEnd( )

Comparable getStart( )

void setCalendarField(int *calField*)

void setEnd(Comparable *end*)

void setStart(Comparable *begin*)

Even though **setEnd( )** and **setStart( )** use parameters of type **Comparable**, you will usually pass **Date** objects. (**Date** implements **Comparable**.) **SpinnerDateModel** also supplies the **getDate( )** method, shown next:

Date getDate( )

It returns the current value as a **Date** rather than an **Object**.

Here is a program the demonstrates **SpinnerDateModel**. It creates a spinner that lets you choose any date and time from one month prior to the current date to one month after the current date. Sample output is shown in Figure 5-8.

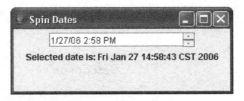

Figure 5-8 Sample output from the **SpinDates** program

```
// Spin Dates.

import javax.swing.*;
import javax.swing.event.*;
import java.awt.*;
import java.util.*;

class SpinDates {

  JSpinner jspin;
  JLabel jlab;

  SpinDates() {
    // Create a new JFrame container.
    JFrame jfrm = new JFrame("Spin Dates");

    // Specify FlowLayout manager.
    jfrm.getContentPane().setLayout(new FlowLayout());

    // Give the frame an initial size.
    jfrm.setSize(300, 120);

    // Terminate the program when the user closes the application.
    jfrm.setDefaultCloseOperation(JFrame.EXIT_ON_CLOSE);

    // Create a Calendar object that contains the
    // current date.
    GregorianCalendar g = new GregorianCalendar();

    // Get the current date.
    Date curDate = new Date();

    // Set start date one month prior to
    // current date and end date one month
    // after current date.
    g.add(Calendar.MONTH, -1);
    Date begin = g.getTime();
    g.add(Calendar.MONTH, 2);
    Date end = g.getTime();

    // Create a date spinner model.
    SpinnerDateModel spm =
      new SpinnerDateModel(curDate, begin, end, Calendar.HOUR);
```

Obtain the initial date and then construct the endpoint dates.

Create a spinner model that uses those dates.

```
      // Create a JSpinner using the model.
      jspin = new JSpinner(spm);  ◄───────── Create a spinner that uses that model.

      // Make a label that displays the selected date.
      jlab = new JLabel(" Selected date is: " + curDate);

      // Add change listener for the spinner.
      jspin.addChangeListener(new ChangeListener() {
        public void stateChanged(ChangeEvent ce) {
          // Get the date.
          Date date = (Date) jspin.getValue();  ◄───────── Get the selected date.

          // Report the date.
          jlab.setText(" Selected date is: " + date + " ");
        }
      });

      // Add the spinner and label to the content pane.
      jfrm.getContentPane().add(jspin);
      jfrm.getContentPane().add(jlab);

      // Display the frame.
      jfrm.setVisible(true);
  }

  public static void main(String args[]) {
    // Create the frame on the event dispatching thread.
    SwingUtilities.invokeLater(new Runnable() {
      public void run() {
        new SpinDates();
      }
    });
  }
}
```

In the program, the current date is obtained by constructing a default **Date** object. The begin and end dates are constructed by creating a default **GregorianCalendar** object called **g**, which contains the current date. Next, this object is increased by one month and the result is stored in **begin**. Then **g** is decreased by two months and the result is stored in **end**. These two dates will form the boundaries of the date spinner. Next, a **SpinnerDateModel** is created that specifies the current date as the initial value, **begin** and **end** as the boundaries, and a

calendarField value of **Calendar.HOUR**. (Keep in mind that **calendarField** is ignored by some look-and-feels.) Thus, the date can be changed, but only within plus or minus one month from the current date. Each time the date is changed, the date is displayed in the label.

Progress Check

1. A spinner is similar to an editable combo box with an important exception. What is that exception?

2. What model spins numbers?

3. What model spins any type of list?

Ask the Expert

Q: In SpinnerDateModel, the setStart( ) and setEnd( ) **methods specify parameters of type** Comparable. **Why don't they just specify objects of type** Date? **This same question applies in a different way to** SpinnerNumberModel. **Why don't that model's** setMinimum( ) **and** setMaximum( ) **methods specify parameters of type** Number **rather than of type** Comparable?

A: By specifying these parameters as objects of type **Comparable**, you can supply your own date or numeric comparison class that lets you define precisely what the bounds mean. Recall that **Comparable** is implemented easily because it defines only one method called **compareTo( )**, shown here:

int compareTo(T *obj*)

which compares the invoking object against the object passed as a parameter. Here, **T** is a generic type specifier that will be replaced by the actual type used in your program.

---

1. The list of items does not pop up. Rather, the items are simply scrolled through the edit field.
2. **SpinnerNumberModel**
3. **SpinnerListModel**

Module 5 Mastery Check

1. A **JList** provides a mechanism by which a user selects one or more items from a list. True or False?

2. If you want a **JList** to be scrollable, what must you do?

3. What type of event is generated by a **JList** when the user makes a selection? What method is called to obtain the index of the first selected item?

4. What model does **JList** use?

5. What Swing component provides a pop-up list?

6. What method obtains the selected item in a **JComboBox**?

7. What method do you call to create an editable combo box?

8. Can you add items to a combo box dynamically at runtime? If so, what method do you call?

9. Can you display and remove the pop-up list of a combo box under program control? If so, what method do you call?

10. A spinner is supported by what Swing class?

11. What spinner method obtains the current value? What method obtains the previous value?

12. Can a spinner manage a list of strings?

13. Create a program that spins a set of **double** values between the range of 0.0 to 9.9. Set the increment at 0.1.

14. Starting with the **DynamicComboBox** program, add a **JList** component. Each time the user removes an apple variety from the combo box, have this variety be inserted into the **JList**. Thus, the **JList** will contain a record of the varieties removed.

Module 6
Text Components

This module examines the components that enable a user to enter, display, and edit text. Because text controls are such an important part of the user interface, Swing provides extensive support for them. In Module 1, you were introduced to one text component: **JTextField**. This is Swing's simplest text control. In addition to **JTextField**, Swing provides several others. Here is a list of Swing's text components, which are packaged in **javax.swing**:

JTextField

JPasswordField

JFormattedTextField

JTextArea

JEditorPane

JTextPane

This book covers the first four. These are the text components that you will use most frequently. They provide the ability to edit plain (that is, nonstyled) text and are easy to use. The last two, **JEditorPane** and **JTextPane**, are substantially more sophisticated because they support the editing of styled documents, such as those that use HTML and RTF. They can also contain images and other components. As a result, they are much more complicated and are beyond the scope of this book.

It is important to state at the outset that even the simple text controls are some of Swing's most powerful and feature-rich components. They allow many customizations and support several options. Fortunately, their standard configurations are often exactly what you want and, as you will see, they are quite easy to use as-is in your applications. However, if the creation of customized text components is in your programming future, then this is an area of Swing that you will want to examine more on your own.

CRITICAL SKILL
6.1 # JTextComponent

At the foundation of Swing's text components is the abstract class **JTextComponent**. This class is a superclass for all other text controls, and it defines the functionality that is common to all. **JTextComponent** is defined in the **javax.swing.text** package.

The model used by **JTextComponent** (and thus all of Swing's text components) is specified by the **Document** interface, also defined in **javax.swing.text**. There is an abstract implementation of **Document** called **AbstractDocument**. From **AbstractDocument** are derived the following concrete implementations: **PlainDocument** and **DefaultStyledDocument**. From **DefaultStyledDocument** is derived **HTMLDocument**. For most simple uses of Swing's text components, you won't need to deal with the model directly.

JTextComponent defines a feature called the *caret*. In this context, caret is essentially another word for *cursor*. Therefore, the position of the caret within a document determines where the next action will occur. You can obtain or set the location of the caret, set its color, or even change the caret itself (although normally you won't need to). Carets are represented by an instance of the **Caret** interface, which is packaged in **javax.swing.text**. The default caret implementation is **DefaultCaret**.

JTextComponent supports the concept of *selected text*. **JTextComponent** allows you to obtain the text that has been selected by the user. You can also select a region of text under program control.

One facility supported by **JTextComponent** that you will find especially helpful in some circumstances is its ability to cut, copy, and paste to and from the clipboard.

There are other aspects of **JTextComponent**, such as navigation filters that restrict the movement of the caret, input methods and their corresponding input method events, and key bindings and key maps. These are beyond the scope of this book, but you might want to explore them on your own.

Table 6-1 shows a sampling of the methods defined by **JTextComponent**. These will be available for use in all of Swing's text components. Pay special attention to the methods that support clipboard actions: **copy( )**, **cut( )**, and **paste( )**. These methods make it very easy to move text to and from other applications. Also notice that there are methods that let you obtain the current selection or set the selection under program control. For example, to get the currently selected text, you can call **getSelectedText( )**. To select text, your program can either call **select( )** or call **setCaretPosition( )** followed by a call to **moveCaretPosition( )**. (The second approach is the recommended technique, and the method used in this book.)

Each time the caret changes location, a **CaretEvent** is generated. Your program can choose to listen for these events by implementing a **CaretListener**. **CaretListener** is packaged in **javax.swing.event**. It defines only one method, called **caretUpdate( )**, which is shown here:

void caretUpdate(CaretEvent *ce*)

CaretEvent defines two methods, shown next:

int getDot( )

int getMark( )

The **getDot( )** method returns the current location of the caret. This is called the *dot*. The **getMark( )** method returns the beginning point of a selection. This is called the *mark*. Thus, a selection is bound by the mark and the dot. If no selection has been made, then the dot and mark will be the same value.

Method	Description
void addCaretListener(CaretListener *cl*)	Adds a listener for caret events.
void copy( )	Copies to the clipboard the text currently selected.
void cut( )	Copies to the clipboard the text currently selected. In the process, the selected text is deleted.
int getCaretPosition( )	Returns the current location of the caret. This value represents the number of characters the caret is from the start of the text.
Document getDocument( )	Returns the model.
Insets getMargin( )	Returns an **Insets** object that contains the margins.
String getSelectedText( )	Returns a string that contains the text that is currently selected.
int getSelectionEnd( )	Returns the position of the last character selected. This value represents the number of characters that the end character is from the start of the text.
int getSelectionStart( )	Returns the position of the first character selected. This value represents the number of characters that the start character is from the start of the text.
String getText( )	Returns all of the text contained in the component.
String getText(int *start*, int *num*)	Returns as a string the text that begins at *start* and runs for *num* characters.
boolean isEditable( )	Returns true if the text can be edited. Returns false if the text is read-only.
void moveCaretPosition(int *newLoc*)	Sets the position of the caret to *newLoc*, which is specified in terms of characters from the start of the text. The text between the current position and the new position is selected.
void paste( )	Copies the contents (if any) of the clipboard into the component. If text in the component has been selected, then the clipboard contents replace the selected text. Otherwise, the clipboard contents are inserted immediately before the caret.
void read(Reader *input*, Object *what*) throws IOException	Copies data from *input* to the text component. The value of *what* describes the input stream. It can be **null**.
void select(int *start*, int *end*)	Selects the text between *start* and *end*, which is specified in terms of characters from the start of the text. In all cases, *start* must be less than or equal to *end* and both must be within the text.
void selectAll( )	Selects all of the text within the component.

Table 6-1 A Sampling of Methods Defined by **JTextComponent**

Method	Description
void setCaretPosition(int *newLoc*)	Sets the position of the caret to *newLoc,* which is specified in terms of characters from the start of the text.
void setEditable(boolean *canEdit*)	If *canEdit* is true, the component's text can be changed. If *canEdit* is false, the text is read-only.
void setMargin(Insets *margins*)	Sets the text margins to those specified by *margins.*
void setText(String *str*)	Sets the text to the string specified by *str.*
void write(Writer *output*) throws IOException	Writes the contents of the component to the specified stream.

Table 6-1 A Sampling of Methods Defined by **JTextComponent** *(continued)*

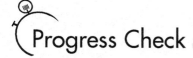

Progress Check

1. Is **JTextComponent** the superclass of all Swing text components?

2. What does the position of the caret signify?

3. What type of event is generated when the caret changes its location?

CRITICAL SKILL
6.2 JTextField

The simplest text component is **JTextField**. It allows the user to enter a single line of text and is widely used. You were introduced to **JTextField** in Module 1. Here we will examine it in a bit more detail.

JTextField defines the constructors shown in Table 6-2. Notice that several of the constructors allow you to specify a column width. Remember, you can enter a string that is longer than the number of columns. It's just that the physical size of the text field on the screen will be *cols* columns wide. By default, **JTextField** uses the **PlainDocument** model.

As explained in Module 2, when a user presses ENTER while inputting into a text field, an **ActionEvent** is generated. To handle action events, you must implement the **ActionListener** interface. A **JTextField** has an action command string associated with it. By default, the

1. Yes

2. The caret position indicates the location of the next edit event, such as the point at which text will be inserted.

3. **CaretEvent**

Constructor	Description
JTextField( )	Creates an empty text component.
JTextField(int *cols*)	Creates an empty text component that has the column width specified by *cols*.
JTextField(String *str*)	Creates a text component that contains the string specified by *str*. The control will be wide enough to display *str*.
JTextField(String *str*, int *cols*)	Creates a text component that contains the string specified by *str*. The control will have the column width specified by *cols*.
JTextField(Document *model*, String *str*, int *cols*)	Creates a text component that uses the model specified by *model*. The component will contain the string specified by *str* and have the column width specified by *cols*.

Table 6-2 The **JTextField** Constructors

action command is the current contents of the text field. However, you can set this to an action command of your choosing by calling the **setActionCommand( )** method, shown here:

void setActionCommand(String *cmd*)

The string passed in *cmd* becomes the new action command. The text in the text field is unaffected. Once you set the action command string, it remains the same no matter what is entered into the text field. One reason that you might want to set the action command explicitly is to provide a way to recognize the text field as the source of an action event. This is helpful when another control in the same frame also generates action events and you want to use the same event handler to process both events. Of course, this is not an issue if you use anonymous inner classes to handle events.

Because **JTextField** inherits **JTextComponent**, you can use any of the methods defined by **JTextComponent** to access or manipulate the text within a **JTextField**. Here are some examples. To obtain the string that is currently displayed in the text field, call **getText( )** on the **JTextField** instance. It is shown here:

String getText( )

You can set the text in a **JTextField** by calling **setText( )**, shown next:

void setText(String *text*)

Here, *text* is the string that will be put into the text field.

You can obtain the portion of the text that has been selected by calling **getSelectedText( )**, shown here:

String getSelectedText( )

If no text has been selected, then **null** is returned.

You can position the caret under program control by calling **setCaretPosition( )**, shown here:

void setCaretPosition(int *newLoc*)

You can select a portion of text under program control by calling **moveCaretPosition( )**, shown next:

void moveCaretPosition(int *newLoc*)

The text between the original caret location and the new position is selected.

You can move text to or from the clipboard under program control by using the methods **cut( )**, **copy( )**, and **paste( )**, shown here:

void cut( )

void copy( )

void paste( )

The **cut( )** method removes any text that is selected within the text field and copies it to the clipboard. The **copy( )** method simply copies, but does not remove, the selected text. The **paste( )** method copies any text that may be in the clipboard to the text field. If the text field contains selected text, then that text is replaced by what is in the clipboard. Otherwise, the clipboard text is inserted immediately before the current caret position.

The following program demonstrates **JTextField** and several of the methods just discussed. It creates a text field that is 15 columns wide. Whenever you press ENTER while in the text field, the current contents are displayed. If any part of the field has been selected, the selected text is also displayed. The program has two buttons called Cut and Paste. These buttons show how the standard cut and paste functions can be utilized under program control. If text has been selected, then pressing Cut removes the selected text and puts it on the clipboard. Pressing Paste copies any text in the clipboard to the text field. Of course, you can also perform cut and paste through standard keyboard commands, such as CTRL-X and CTRL-V in the Windows environment. Sample output is shown in Figure 6-1.

Figure 6-1 Sample output from the **JTextFieldDemo** program

```java
// Demonstrate various features of a text field.

import java.awt.*;
import java.awt.event.*;
import javax.swing.*;
import javax.swing.event.*;

class JTextFieldDemo {

  JLabel jlabAll;
  JLabel jlabSelected;

  JTextField jtf;

  JButton jbtnCut;
  JButton jbtnPaste;

  public JTextFieldDemo() {

    // Create a new JFrame container.
    JFrame jfrm = new JFrame("Use JTextField");

    // Specify FlowLayout for the layout manager.
    jfrm.getContentPane().setLayout(new FlowLayout());

    // Give the frame an initial size.
    jfrm.setSize(200, 150);

    // Terminate the program when the user closes the application.
    jfrm.setDefaultCloseOperation(JFrame.EXIT_ON_CLOSE);

    // Create labels.
    jlabAll = new JLabel("All text: ");
    jlabSelected = new JLabel("Selected text: ");
```

```
// Create the text field.
jtf = new JTextField("This is a test.", 15);  ◄─────── Create a text field.

// Add an action listener for the text field.
// Each time the user presses enter, the contents
// of the field are displayed. Any currently
// selected text is also displayed.
jtf.addActionListener(new ActionListener() {
  public void actionPerformed(ActionEvent le) {
    jlabAll.setText("All text: " + jtf.getText());  ◄─
    jlabSelected.setText("Selected text: " +
                  jtf.getSelectedText());  ◄─
  }
});
```

Each time the user presses ENTER, display the entire text and any selected text.

```
// Create the Cut and Paste buttons.
jbtnCut = new JButton("Cut");
jbtnPaste = new JButton("Paste");

// Add action listener for the Cut button.
jbtnCut.addActionListener(new ActionListener() {
  public void actionPerformed(ActionEvent le) {
    // Cut any selected text and put it
    // on the clipboard.
    jtf.cut();  ◄────────────────── Cut text and place
    jlabAll.setText("All text: " + jtf.getText());   on the clipboard.
    jlabSelected.setText("Selected text: " +
                  jtf.getSelectedText());
  }
});

// Add action listener for the Paste button.
jbtnPaste.addActionListener(new ActionListener() {
  public void actionPerformed(ActionEvent le) {
    // Paste text from the clipboard into
    // the text field.
    jtf.paste();  ◄─┐
  }                  Copy text from the clipboard.
});

// Add a caret listener. This lets the application
// respond in real time to changes in the text field.
jtf.addCaretListener(new CaretListener() {
  public void caretUpdate(CaretEvent ce) {
    jlabAll.setText("All text: " + jtf.getText());
    jlabSelected.setText("Selected text: " +
                  jtf.getSelectedText());
```

Each time the caret changes position, display the entire text and any selected text.

```
      }
   });

   // Add the components to the content pane.
   jfrm.getContentPane().add(jtf);
   jfrm.getContentPane().add(jbtnCut);
   jfrm.getContentPane().add(jbtnPaste);
   jfrm.getContentPane().add(jlabAll);
   jfrm.getContentPane().add(jlabSelected);

   // Set the caret to just after the 5th character.
   jtf.setCaretPosition(5);
   // Now, move the caret just after the 7th character.
   // This sequence causes the word "is" to be selected.
   jtf.moveCaretPosition(7);

   // Display the frame.
   jfrm.setVisible(true);
}

public static void main(String args[]) {
   // Create the frame on the event dispatching thread.
   SwingUtilities.invokeLater(new Runnable() {
     public void run() {
       new JTextFieldDemo();
     }
   });
}
}
```

Select the word "is."

Much of this program will be familiar, but there are a few key points that warrant a close look. First, when the text field **jtf** is created, it is given both an initial size of 15 and initial contents consisting of the string "This is a test." Next, notice that just before the window is made visible, the characters between the 5th and 7th characters are selected using the following sequence:

```
// Set the caret to just after the 5th character.
jtf.setCaretPosition(5);
// Now, move the caret just after the 7th character.
// This sequence causes the word "is" to be selected.
jtf.moveCaretPosition(7);
```

As explained, setting and then moving the caret position causes the text in between to be selected. Thus, when the program starts up, the word "is" will automatically be selected.

Each time the user presses ENTER when inside the **jtf** text field, an **ActionEvent** is generated and sent to the **actionPerformed( )** method of **jtf**'s action listener. This method obtains the text currently held in the text field by calling **getText( )** on **jtf**. It then displays the text through the label referred to by **jlabAll**. It also obtains any selected text by calling **getSelectedText( )** and displays it through the **jlabSelected** label.

Now, notice that a caret listener has been added. Each time the caret position changes, a **CaretEvent** is fired and this causes **caretUpdate( )** to be called. This method updates the two labels (**jlabAll** and **jlabSelected**) so that they reflect the current contents and selected text inside **jtf**. Thus, as you make changes to the text field, those changes are echoed in real time in the labels.

Next, look at the event handlers for the Cut and Paste buttons. The Cut button calls **cut( )** to remove any selected text and put it onto the clipboard. The Paste button copies text from the clipboard into the text field by calling **paste( )**. Of course, you can use the standard editing keys, such as CTRL-X and CTRL-V when using Windows, to achieve the same results, but these handlers show how to perform these actions under program control.

Progress Check

1. What methods inherited from **JTextComponent** enable **JTextField** to operate on the clipboard?

2. When the user presses ENTER while inside a text field, what event is generated?

3. What method can you call to obtain just the text that has been selected within a **JTextField**?

---

1. The clipboard methods are **copy( )**, **cut( )**, and **paste( )**.
2. **ActionEvent**
3. **getSelectedText( )**

Ask the Expert

Q: Can I change the font used to display text in a JTextField?

A: Yes. You can change the font in a **JTextField** (or any other Swing component) by calling **setFont( )**. You can obtain the current font by calling **getFont( )**. These methods are provided by **JComponent** and are shown here:

void setFont(Font *newFont*)

Font getFont( )

Font is a class packaged in **java.awt**. Although an in-depth discussion of **Font** and all of its features cannot be given in this book, it is still possible for you to begin experimenting with different fonts because it is actually quite easy to create a font. For example, here is one of **Font**'s constructors:

Font(String *fontName*, int *fontStyle*, int *pointSize*)

Here, *fontName* is the name of a font, such as Dialog or Serif. The *fontStyle* must be one or more of the following values:

Font.PLAIN	Font.BOLD	Font.ITALIC

The point size is determined by *pointSize*. To try a new font, add this line to the **JTextFieldDemo** program, after the text field has been created.

```
jtf.setFont(new Font("monospaced", Font.PLAIN, 20));
```

After making this change, the program will display text in a 20-point, monospaced font, as shown here:

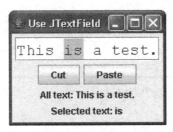

CRITICAL SKILL
6.3 JPasswordField

There is a subclass of **JTextField** that is designed expressly for obtaining passwords from the user. It is called **JPasswordField**. When the user enters text into a password field, the characters typed are not echoed to the field. Instead, a placeholder character, such as an asterisk (*) character, is shown. This makes it possible to enter a password without having it displayed on the screen.

JPasswordField defines the constructors shown in Table 6-3. As with **JTextField**, **JPasswordField** fires an action event when the user presses ENTER while in the field. It also generates caret events each time the caret is moved. Although **JPasswordField** inherits **JTextField**, the clipboard methods **cut( )** and **copy( )** are disabled for security reasons. Also, **getText( )** is deprecated, also for security reasons.

To obtain the password entered by the user, call **getPassword( )**, shown here:

char [ ] getPassword( )

Notice that the password is returned as an array of characters rather than as a string. The reason is easy to understand if you put it into the context of security. Strings are immutable, which means that they can't be changed. Thus, there is no way to clear the password from the string after it has been used. This means that the contents of a discarded password string will remain unchanged in memory until it is garbage-collected, reallocated, and overwritten (which might take a long time or not happen at all). Therefore, it is theoretically possible for

Constructor	Description
JPasswordField( )	Creates an empty password component.
JPasswordField(int *cols*)	Creates an empty password component that has the column width specified by *cols*.
JPasswordField(String *str*)	Creates a password component that contains the string specified by *str*. The control will be wide enough to display *str*.
JPasswordField(String *str*, int *cols*)	Creates a password component that contains the string specified by *str*. The control will have the column width specified by *cols*.
JPasswordField(Document *model*, String *str*, int *cols*)	Creates a password component that uses the model specified by *model*. The component will contain the string specified by *str* and have the column width specified by *cols*.

Table 6-3 The Constructors Defined by **JPasswordField**

the password to be obtained by another process that searches memory for passwords. Fortunately, there is a solution to this problem. Because **getPassword( )** returns an array of characters (which, of course, are mutable), it is possible to clear the array after it has been used, thus closing this potential security hole. In general, after using a **JPasswordField**, you should clear both the array obtained from the field and the array that holds the password that you are testing against. Normally, the best way to clear an array is to fill it with zeros. This is usually referred to as "zeroing out" the array.

In general, the character displayed when you enter characters into a **JPasswordField** is the asterisk (*). However, you can change this by calling **setEchoChar( )**, shown here:

void setEchoChar(char *echr*)

Here, *echr* becomes the character echoed. Be aware, however, that the echo character is under the control of the look-and-feel, and a different echo character might be used.

The following program demonstrates **JPasswordField**. Notice how the password arrays are cleared after use. Sample output is shown in Figure 6-2.

```
// Demonstrate JPasswordField.

import java.awt.*;
import java.awt.event.*;
import javax.swing.*;
import java.util.*;

class JPasswordFieldDemo {

  JLabel jlabPW;

  JPasswordField jpswd;

  public JPasswordFieldDemo() {

    // Create a new JFrame container.
    JFrame jfrm = new JFrame("Use JPasswordField");

    // Specify FlowLayout for the layout manager.
    jfrm.getContentPane().setLayout(new FlowLayout());

    // Give the frame an initial size.
    jfrm.setSize(240, 100);

    // Terminate the program when the user closes the application.
    jfrm.setDefaultCloseOperation(JFrame.EXIT_ON_CLOSE);
```

```
      // Create a label.
      jlabPW = new JLabel("Enter Password");

      // Create the password field.
      jpswd = new JPasswordField(15); ◄─────── Create a password field.

      // Add an action listener for the password field.
      // Each time the user presses enter, the contents
      // of the password field are checked against
      // the password.
      jpswd.addActionListener(new ActionListener() {
        public void actionPerformed(ActionEvent le) {
          char pw[] = { 't', 'e', 's', 't' };

          char [] userSeq = jpswd.getPassword();

          // Test for valid password.
          if(Arrays.equals(userSeq, pw)) ◄────── Check the string entered by the
            jlabPW.setText("Password Valid");       user against the password.
          else
            jlabPW.setText("Password Invalid -- Try Again");

          // Clear both arrays on exit.
          Arrays.fill(pw, (char) 0); ◄───┐
          Arrays.fill(userSeq, (char) 0); ◄─┘──── Clear the arrays for security purposes.
        }
      });

      // Add the components to the content pane.
      jfrm.getContentPane().add(jpswd);
      jfrm.getContentPane().add(jlabPW);

      // Display the frame.
      jfrm.setVisible(true);
    }

    public static void main(String args[]) {
      // Create the frame on the event dispatching thread.
      SwingUtilities.invokeLater(new Runnable() {
        public void run() {
          new JPasswordFieldDemo();
        }
      });
    }
  }
```

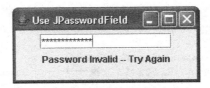

Figure 6-2 Sample output from the **JPasswordFieldDemo** program

Notice that the **pw** array (which holds the password string) and the **userSeq** array, which holds the array returned from **jpswd**, are both cleared by calling **Arrays.fill( )**. **Arrays** is a class in **java.util** that provides many **static** utility methods that operate on arrays. The **fill( )** method fills the array passed as the first argument with the value passed in the second argument. It provides a highly efficient way to fill an array with a known value.

CRITICAL SKILL
6.4 # JFormattedTextField

Swing offers another subclass of **JTextField** that enables you to enforce a specific format for the text. This component is called **JFormattedTextField** and was added to Swing by Java 1.4. Although **JFormattedTextField** offers a lot of features that can give you fine-grained control over the editing of formatted fields, you won't need to use them often because its default configuration is both quite powerful and easy to use.

JFormattedTextField provides the constructors shown in Table 6-4. Notice the constructors that take an **AbstractFormatter** or an **AbstractFormatterFactory** for an argument. These are two nested classes defined by **JFormattedTextField**. An instance of **AbstractFormatter** is used to format the text. This instance is provided on demand by an instance of **AbstractFormatterFactory**. However, for many straightforward uses of **JFormattedTextField**, you do not need to interact with these classes directly. The reason is that the following two constructors handle the details for you, behind the scenes:

JFormattedTextField(Object *contents*)

JFormattedTextField(Format *fmt*)

These constructors automatically create an abstract formatter and an abstract formatter factory that is compatible with the type of data specified by *contents* or with the format specified by *fmt*. Let's examine these two constructors a bit more closely.

Constructor	Description
JFormattedTextField( )	Creates an empty formatted text field that does not have a formatter associated with it.
JFormattedTextField(Object *contents*)	Creates a formatted text field that displays the data specified by *contents*. It uses a formatter compatible with the type of data passed via *contents*.
JFormattedTextField(Format *fmt*)	Creates an empty formatted text field that uses the formatter compatible with *fmt*.
JFormattedTextField(JFormattedTextField. AbstractFormatter *absFmt*)	Creates an empty formatted text field that uses the abstract formatter specified by *absFmt*.
JFormattedTextField(JFormattedTextField. AbstractFormatterFactory *absFmtFact*)	Creates an empty formatted text field that uses the abstract formatter factory specified by *absFmtFact*.
JFormattedTextField(JFormattedTextField. AbstractFormatterFactory *absFmtFact*, Object *contents*)	Creates a formatted text field that displays the data specified by *contents*. It uses the abstract formatter factory specified by *absFmtFact*.

Table 6-4 The Constructors Offered by **JFormattedTextField**

CRITICAL SKILL

6.5

Create a JFormattedTextField Based on Data Type

For simple formats, the easiest way to create a **JFormattedTextField** is to use this constructor:

JFormattedTextField(Object *contents*)

It automatically constructs an **AbstractFormatterFactory** based on the type of data referred to by *contents*. For example, the following creates a **JFormattedTextField** that will handle integer values:

```
JFormattedTextField jtf = new JFormattedTextField(10);
```

Because *contents* refers to a numeric value, a formatter for numbers will be created. As convenient as this approach can be, it might not give you the level of control that you require. For these cases, it is better to specify the format, as described in the next section.

CRITICAL SKILL
6.6 # Create a JFormattedTextField Based on a Format

You can specify the precise format for a **JFormattedTextField** by using this constructor:

JFormattedTextField(Format *fmt*)

In this case, the format specified by *fmt* is automatically used to construct an **AbstractFormatter**, which is then placed inside an **AbstractFormatterFactory**. **Format** is an abstract class that defines the basic nature of a format. Java provides two important classes derived from **Format**: **DateFormat** and **NumberFormat**, both of which are also abstract. However, both provide factory methods that create various date and numeric formats. The example in this module uses the following two factory methods:

static final NumberFormat getCurrencyInstance( )

static final DateFormat getDateInstance(int *dateStyle*)

The **getCurrencyInstance( )** method is provided by **NumberFormat**, and it returns a format that handles currency values for the default locale. It displays two decimal places and includes the currency sign and thousand separators. The **getDateInstance( )** method is provided by **DateFormat** and it returns a format that handles dates. The value of *dateStyle* must be one of the following values:

DateFormat.SHORT	DateFormat.MEDIUM
DateFormat.LONG	DateFormat.FULL

As the names imply, each supports a different style of date format. The short form uses an approach such as 9/12/09. The remaining ones show progressively longer formats. The medium form is used by the example program in this section. It produces a date format like this: Sep 12, 2009.

You can also easily produce one other type of format, called a *mask format*. A mask format lets you specify the general form of the format that you want. It is supported by the **MaskFormatter** class, which is packaged in **javax.swing.text**. It is a subclass of **JFormattedTextField.AbstractFormatter**. Thus, when using **MaskFormatter**, you will use this **JFormattedTextField** constructor:

JFormattedTextField(JFormattedTextField.AbstractFormatter *absFmt*)

MaskFormatter provides two constructors. One is the default constructor. The other is the one used in this section and is shown here:

MaskFormatter(String *fmtMask*)

Here, *fmtMask* is a string that specifies the general form of the format that you want the formatted text field to match. This string can consist of literal characters, which will be skipped, and the following placeholder characters:

Character	Accepts
A	Alphanumeric characters
H	Hexadecimal characters
L	Letters, which are translated to lowercase
U	Letters, which are translated to uppercase
#	Digits
*	All characters
?	All letters
'	Escape code to specify one of the format characters as a literal

For example, the following

```
new MaskFormatter("ID: AA-LL-UU");
```

creates a **MaskFormatter** that accepts three two-letter sequences. The first sequence can be any letter. The second can be any letter, but the letters are translated to lowercase. The third sequence can be any letter, but the letters are translated to uppercase. The first four characters "ID: " are literals that cannot be edited. One other point: if you specify an invalid format when creating a **MaskFormatter**, a **ParseException** is thrown.

CRITICAL SKILL
6.7

Handle Property Change Events for a JFormattedTextField

Just like **JTextField**, which it extends, **JFormattedTextField** generates an action event when the user presses ENTER. However, you will often want to listen for a property change event, instead. The reason is easy to understand once you know how **JFormattedTextField** works.

Let's begin with a key concept: A **JFormattedTextField** maintains a value. This value relates to what is shown in the text field, but is independent from it. Basically, when a user enters text into the component, the formatter converts that formatted text into the value. Alternatively, if the value is set under program control, then the formatter is used to convert the value into a string, which is displayed within the component. Thus, the value of a formatted text field is reflected in its text field, but text in the field is separate from value of the component. This leads to the following question: when the user enters a new string into a formatted text field, when and under what circumstances does the value get updated to agree with the text?

In its default configuration, when you edit text inside a formatted text field, the changes that you make do not become the value of the text field until you *either* press ENTER *or* move input focus to another field. When one of these actions occurs, the changes that you have made will then be "committed," and the value of the formatted text field will be updated to reflect the changes. (Assuming, of course, that you entered valid input relative to the specified format.) Thus, the *text* shown in the component and the *value* of the component will not be the same until the commit phase has occurred. Furthermore, the changes will commit when you move out of the formatted text field whether you have pressed ENTER or not. Therefore, to watch for a change in a formatted text field's value, you must listen for a property change event (rather than an action event) because one will be generated each time the value of a formatted text field actually changes.

Property change events are objects of the **PropertyChangeEvent** class, which is packaged in **java.beans**. To listen for property change events, you must implement the **PropertyChangeListener** interface. It defines only the **propertyChange( )** method shown here:

void propertyChange(PropertyChangeEvent *pe*)

Among other things, **PropertyChangeEvent** defines methods that let you get the old value and the new value of the property that changed along with the name of the property that changed. Usually, however, you will simply operate on the formatted text field when a property change event occurs on the field.

There are two ways to add a listener for a property change event. Both are shown here:

void addPropertyChangeListener(PropertyChangeEvent *pl*)

void addPropertyChangeListener(String *propName*, PropertyChangeEvent *pl*)

The first form listens for all property change events. The second listens just for changes to the property named by *propName*. For **JFormattedTextField**, the property that maintains the value is called **value**.

You can set the value of a formatted text field under program control by calling **setValue( )**. You can obtain the current value by calling **getValue( )**. These methods are shown here:

void setValue(Object *val*)

Object getValue( )

Here, *val* becomes the new value of the formatted text field. Setting the value also causes the text displayed in the field to be updated. Of course, the value must be compatible with the format of the field.

A JFormattedTextField Demonstration Program

The following program demonstrates **JFormattedTextField**. It creates three formatted text fields, with each using a different format. The first uses a mask formatter to edit an employee ID that consists of a two-digit department code followed by a three-digit employee number. The two parts are separated by a hyphen, as in 12-576. The second field uses a number format to edit the employee's monthly salary. The third uses a date format to edit the date hired. Sample output is shown in Figure 6-3.

Figure 6-3 Sample output from the **FormattedTFDemo** program

```
// Demonstrate formatted text fields.

import java.beans.*;
import java.awt.*;
import java.awt.event.*;
import javax.swing.*;
import java.text.*;
import javax.swing.text.*;
import java.util.*;

class FormattedTFDemo {

  NumberFormat cf;
  DateFormat df;

  JLabel jlab;

  JFormattedTextField jftfSalary;
  JFormattedTextField jftfDate;
  JFormattedTextField jftfEmpID;

  JButton jbtnShow;

  public FormattedTFDemo() {

    // Create a new JFrame container.
    JFrame jfrm = new JFrame("JFormattedTextField");

    // Specify FlowLayout for the layout manager.
    jfrm.getContentPane().setLayout(new FlowLayout());

    // Give the frame an initial size.
    jfrm.setSize(240, 270);

    // Terminate the program when the user closes the application.
    jfrm.setDefaultCloseOperation(JFrame.EXIT_ON_CLOSE);

    // Create a label.
    jlab = new JLabel();

    // Create a formatted text field for employee ID.
    // This uses a mask formatter.
    try {
      MaskFormatter mf = new MaskFormatter("##-###");
      jftfEmpID = new JFormattedTextField(mf);
    } catch (ParseException exc) {
```

Create a formatted text field based on a mask format.

```
      System.out.println("Invalid Format");
      return;
   }
   jftfEmpID.setColumns(15);
   jftfEmpID.setValue("24-895");

   // Create a formatted text field for money.
   // This uses a currency formatter.
   cf = NumberFormat.getCurrencyInstance();
   cf.setMaximumIntegerDigits(5);
   cf.setMaximumFractionDigits(2);
   jftfSalary = new JFormattedTextField(cf);
   jftfSalary.setColumns(15);
   jftfSalary.setValue(new Integer(7000));

   // Create a formatted text field for date.
   // This uses a date formatter.
   df = DateFormat.getDateInstance(DateFormat.MEDIUM);
   jftfDate = new JFormattedTextField(df);
   jftfDate.setColumns(15);
   jftfDate.setValue(new Date()); // init to current date

   // Add property change listener for the employee ID field.
   jftfEmpID.addPropertyChangeListener("value",
                    new PropertyChangeListener() {
     public void propertyChange(PropertyChangeEvent pe) {
       jlab.setText("Employee ID changed.");
     }
   });

   // Add property change listener for the salary field.
   jftfSalary.addPropertyChangeListener("value",
   new PropertyChangeListener() {
     public void propertyChange(PropertyChangeEvent pe) {
       jlab.setText("Monthly salary changed.");
     }
   });

   // Add property change listener for the date field.
   jftfDate.addPropertyChangeListener("value",
   new PropertyChangeListener() {
     public void propertyChange(PropertyChangeEvent pe) {
       jlab.setText("Date hired changed.");
     }
   });
```

Create a formatted text field based on a currency format.

Create a formatted text field based on a date format.

Listen for changes to the value of the formatted text field.

```
    // Create the Show Updates button.
    jbtnShow = new JButton("Show Updates");

    // Add action listener for the Show Updates button.
    jbtnShow.addActionListener(new ActionListener() {
      public void actionPerformed(ActionEvent le) {
        // Display formatted contents. Note that the
        // salary and date info is formatted using the
        // same formatters as the edit fields.  The
        // value retrieved from the employee ID field is
        // already formatted.
        jlab.setText("<html>Employee ID: " +
                    jftfEmpID.getValue() +
                    "<br>Monthly Salary: " +
                    cf.format(jftfSalary.getValue()) +
                    "<br>Date Hired: " +
                    df.format(jftfDate.getValue())));
      }
    });

    // Add the components to the content pane.
    jfrm.getContentPane().add(new JLabel("Employee ID"));
    jfrm.getContentPane().add(jftfEmpID);
    jfrm.getContentPane().add(new JLabel("Monthly Salary"));
    jfrm.getContentPane().add(jftfSalary);
    jfrm.getContentPane().add(new JLabel("Date Hired"));
    jfrm.getContentPane().add(jftfDate);
    jfrm.getContentPane().add(jbtnShow);
    jfrm.getContentPane().add(jlab);

    // Display the frame.
    jfrm.setVisible(true);
  }

  public static void main(String args[]) {
    // Create the frame on the event dispatching thread.
    SwingUtilities.invokeLater(new Runnable() {
      public void run() {
        new FormattedTFDemo();
      }
    });
  }
}
```

Display the values using the same formats as the formatted text fields.

This program shows several important aspects of using **JFormattedTextField**. After the usual starting sequence, the program creates three formatted text fields. The first uses a

MaskFormatter that allows the input of employee ID numbers. The format string "##-###" specifies the form of these numbers. Therefore, a number such as 12-465 is valid, but AB-934 is not, because letters can't be used. The second formatted text field uses a numeric currency format for the monthly salary. The third uses a medium-length date format for the date hired. Notice that all three fields are initialized using valid values. This is important. Initializing with invalid values will cause runtime problems.

Next, property change listeners are added for each of the formatted text fields. As explained, whenever the value of one of these fields changes, a property change event is fired. These listeners simply report that a change occurred, but your programs can handle these events in more useful ways.

Finally, a button called Show Updates is created and an action event listener for it is added. When the button is pressed, the contents of the three formatted text fields are obtained and displayed. Notice that the salary and the date hired are displayed using the same format as that used by the edit fields. This makes the displayed data look just like that shown in the formatted text fields.

Ask the Expert

Q: You mention that the behavior of JFormattedTextField **when input focus is lost can be changed. How is this done?**

A: By default, when a **JformattedTextField** loses input focus, the changes made by the user are *committed*, which means that the value of the component is updated. However, this occurs only if the changes are valid. If the changes are invalid, the field reverts back to its previous value. This default behavior is often what you will want. However, you can change it by calling **setFocusLostBehavior( )**, shown here:

void setFocusLostBehavior(int *what*)

Here, *what* must be one of these static values defined by **JFormattedTextField**:

COMMIT	REVERT	COMMIT_OR_REVERT	PERSIST

COMMIT_OR_REVERT is the default value. Setting the focus-lost policy to **COMMIT** causes a valid entry to be committed. An invalid entry is retained in the text field, but no change to the value is made. **REVERT** causes the current value to be obtained and displayed. **PERSIST** maintains the current edit, but no change to the value occurs.

One last point: No matter which focus-lost policy is used, if you press ENTER within a formatted text field, then the current contents of that field will become the new value of the field if it constitutes a valid value.

Before moving on, you might want to experiment a bit with **JFormattedTextField**. For example, try different mask or numeric formats. Try specifying different behavior when input focus is lost. (See the preceding "Ask the Expert.") **JFormattedTextField** is a powerful component. It is worth a little extra effort to get familiar with it.

CRITICAL SKILL
6.8 # Use JTextArea

JTextField and its subclasses **JPasswordField** and **JFormattedTextField** are specifically designed for situations in which only a single line of text is needed, such as when the user must enter a filename or a URL. For cases in which multiple lines of text are needed, you must use another of Swing's text components. For many situations, this will be **JTextArea**.

JTextArea enables the user to enter and edit multiple lines of text. It is simple to use, but it works with only plain text. It does not support any formatting or styling of text and its default model is **PlainDocument**. Therefore, it is best suited for situations in which plain text is appropriate. For example, you might use a text area when you want to allow the user to attach specific shipping instructions to an online order form. **JTextArea** supports the standard keyboard editing commands as implemented by the installed look-and-feel.

Although **JTextArea** can hold multiple lines of text, it does not provide any scrolling capabilities. Instead, when scrolling is needed (or might be needed), you should put a **JTextArea** inside a **JScrollPane**. This is the way that **JTextArea** is commonly handled within an application.

JTextArea provides the constructors shown in Table 6-5. If you will be creating a text area that will not be wrapped inside a scroll pane, then you will usually want to specify the number of rows and columns. For text areas inside scroll panes, it is the preferred size of the scroll pane that determines the size of the text area. Be aware of one point: when used outside of a scroll pane, the size of the text area will grow as needed to accommodate the text that it contains. This can cause layout problems, which is another reason why it's usually best to wrap a text area within a scroll pane. (Of course, you can also set the text area's preferred size, but again, using a scroll pane is usually just a better idea.)

Unlike **JTextField**, **JTextArea** does not generate action events. Instead, it simply generates those events that it inherits from **JTextComponent**, such as caret events. It will also generate document events when its model changes. Of course, for most applications, listening for caret events is sufficient. Moreover, you will not often even need to listen for events when using a text area. Instead, your application will simply retrieve the text in the component as needed. For example, if your application uses a text area to allow a user to compose a remark that is passed along to a supervisor, then that remark is simply obtained when the user presses the Send button.

As with all text components, **JTextArea** inherits **JTextComponent**. Thus, you can use all of the methods defined by **JTextComponent**. For example, as with **JTextField**, you can easily obtain the current text by calling **getText( )**. You can obtain selected text by calling

Constructor	Description
JTextArea( )	Creates an empty text area whose dimensions are zero.
JTextArea(String *str*)	Creates a text area that initially contains the string passed in *str*.
JTextArea(int *numRows*, int *numCols*)	Creates an empty text area whose dimensions are determined by *numRows* and *numCols*, which specify the number of rows and columns, respectively.
JTextArea(*String* str, int *numRows*, int *numCols*)	Creates a text area that initially contains the string passed in *str*. Its dimensions are determined by *numRows* and *numCols*, which specify the number of rows and columns, respectively.
JTextArea(Document *model*)	Creates a text area that uses the model specified by *model*.

Table 6-5 The Constructors for **JTextArea**

getSelectedText( ). You can select text under program control by calling **setCaretPosition( )** followed by **moveCaretPosition( )**. Of course, you can access the clipboard through the methods **cut( )**, **copy( )**, and **paste( )**.

By default, when you enter text, long lines can exceed the width of the text area. If you have put the text area into a scroll pane, then a scroll bar will be shown automatically, which lets you horizontally scroll the long line. However, this does not offer a pleasant user-experience. As an alternative, you can cause the text to wrap when the edge of the window is reached by turning on line wrapping using the **setLineWrap( )** method shown here:

void setLineWrap(boolean *wrapOn*)

If *wrapOn* is true, then the lines will wrap automatically when the edge of the text area is reached. If it is false, no wrapping takes place. This property is false by default. You can obtain the current line-wrap setting by calling **getLineWrap( )**. It returns true if line wrapping is on.

Once line wrapping is on, it can occur in one of two ways. First, a line can break between characters when it is wrapped. Second, the line can break between words. By default, lines break between characters. However, you can cause lines to be broken on word boundaries by calling **setWrapStyleWord( )**, shown here:

void setWrapStyleWord(boolean *breakOnWord*)

If *breakOnWord* is true, then long lines will break at word boundaries when wrapped. Before looking at any more of **JTextArea**'s features, it is useful to see a simple example of one in action. Here is a program that demonstrates **JTextArea**. It creates a small text area that is wrapped in a scroll pane. Each time a caret event occurs, the number of words in the text are counted and displayed. Despite its power, notice how little code is required to handle the text area. Sample output is shown in Figure 6-4.

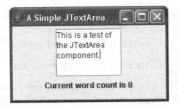

Figure 6-4 Sample output from **SimpleTextAreaDemo**

```java
// Demonstrate a simple text area.

import java.io.*;

import java.awt.*;
import java.awt.event.*;
import javax.swing.*;
import javax.swing.event.*;

class SimpleTextAreaDemo {

  JLabel jlabWC;

  JTextArea jta;

  public SimpleTextAreaDemo() {

    // Create a new JFrame container.
    JFrame jfrm = new JFrame("A Simple JTextArea");

    // Specify FlowLayout for the layout manager.
    jfrm.getContentPane().setLayout(new FlowLayout());

    // Give the frame an initial size.
    jfrm.setSize(240, 150);

    // Terminate the program when the user closes the application.
    jfrm.setDefaultCloseOperation(JFrame.EXIT_ON_CLOSE);

    // Create the word count label.
    jlabWC = new JLabel("Current word count is 0");

    // Create the text field.
    jta = new JTextArea();          Create a text area.
```

```
    // Set line wrap on word boundaries.
    jta.setLineWrap(true);              Turn on line wrapping on word boundaries.
    jta.setWrapStyleWord(true);

    // Put the text area into a scroll pane.
    JScrollPane jscrlp = new JScrollPane(jta);        Wrap the text area
    jscrlp.setPreferredSize(new Dimension(100, 75));   in a scroll pane.

    // Add a caret listener. This handler displays
    // the word count in real time.
    jta.addCaretListener(new CaretListener() {        Each time a caret
      public void caretUpdate(CaretEvent ce) {        event occurs, display
        int wc; // this will hold the word count      the word count.

        // Get the current text.
        String str = jta.getText();

        if(str.length() == 0)
          wc = 0; // if no text present, word count is 0.
        else {
          // Split the string into words based on nonword
          // characters, such as whitespace and punctuation.
          String [] strsplit = str.split("\\W+");

          // The word count will equal the number of
          // strings returned by split().
          wc = strsplit.length;

          // Handle the case of a leading nonword character.
          if(strsplit.length > 0 &&
             strsplit[0].length() == 0) wc--;
        }

        // Display the word count
        jlabWC.setText("Current word count is " + wc);
      }
    });

    // Add the components to the content pane.
    jfrm.getContentPane().add(jscrlp);
    jfrm.getContentPane().add(jlabWC);

    // Display the frame.
    jfrm.setVisible(true);
  }
```

```
public static void main(String args[]) {

    // Create the frame on the event dispatching thread.
    SwingUtilities.invokeLater(new Runnable() {
      public void run() {
        new SimpleTextAreaDemo();
      }
    });

  }
}
```

Let's look closely at parts of this program. First, notice how the text area **jta** is constructed and prepared for use by the following code sequence:

```
// Create the text field.
jta = new JTextArea();

// Set line wrap on word boundaries.
jta.setLineWrap(true);
jta.setWrapStyleWord(true);
```

Because many applications require line wrapping on word boundaries, this sequence is often found in code that uses **JTextArea**. Of course, there will be some applications in which neither line wrapping nor breaking on word boundaries is appropriate, but for text areas used for things such as memos, notes, and comments, turning on these two features gives your text area a more professional look.

The next code sequence stores **jta** within a scroll pane and gives the scroll pane a preferred size:

```
// Put the text area into a scroll pane.
JScrollPane jscrlp = new JScrollPane(jta);
jscrlp.setPreferredSize(new Dimension(100, 75));
```

Setting the preferred size of the scroll pane is important because it determines the size of the text area. Moreover, this preferred size overrides any row or column dimensions that might have been specified when the text area was created.

The program then registers a caret event handler. Caret events work the same in a **JTextArea** as they do in a **JTextField**: each time a caret event occurs, the **caretUpdate( )** method is called. In this program, the handler obtains the string currently contained within the text area by calling **getText( )**. It then counts the number of words in the text by calling split( ), which is defined by **String**. This method splits a string into substrings. The substrings are delimited by characters that match a regular expression. In this case, the regular expression \W+ is used. This is a predefined expression that matches any sequence of nonword characters. Therefore, the call to **split( )** breaks the text into an array of words, and this array is returned. The length of this array equals the number of words in the text. This value is displayed in a label. Because a caret event is fired each time the caret changes position, the word count is updated in real time, as the user types.

Some JTextArea Options

In addition to the functionality it inherits from **JTextComponent**, **JTextArea** provides several options of its own. For example, the default tab size of **JTextArea** is 8, but you can set the tab size by calling **setTabSize( )**, shown here:

void setTabSize(int *newSize*)

Here, *newSize* specifies the new tab size.

    JTextArea offers several methods that let you add text under program control. They are shown here:

void append(String *str*)

void insert(String *str*, int *idx*)

void replaceRange(String *str*, int *begin*, int *end*)

Here, *str* is the text that is being inserted into the text area. The **append( )** method adds the string to the end. The **insert( )** method adds the string at the location specified by *idx*, which is a character-offset from the start of the text. You can replace one substring with another by calling **replaceRange( )**. The range to be replaced extends from *begin* to *end* – 1. Both *begin* and *end* are character offsets from the start of the text.

    One other thing: You can obtain a count of the lines in the text field by calling **getLineCount( )**:

int getLineCount( )

It is important to understand, however, that this method counts lines that end with a newline. Thus, "lines" that are created because of automatic wrapping are not counted as separate lines.

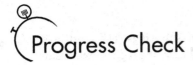

Progress Check

1. How does **JTextArea** differ from **JTextField**?

2. Does **JTextArea** automatically scroll text?

3. What method do you call to make **JTextArea** wrap lines at word boundaries?

Project 6-1 Create a Simple Text Editor

`SimpleTextEditor.java`

This project shows the power of Swing's text components by creating a simple text editor. You can load a file from disk or save the current file to disk. You can also search for a string. The editor uses a **JTextArea** to edit a file. Thus, the editor automatically supports the basic editing commands such as cut and paste. It uses **JTextField**s to hold the name of the file being edited and to hold a string that can be searched for. As you will see, it is amazing how little code is required to create a fully functional text editor. Here is what the editor looks like:

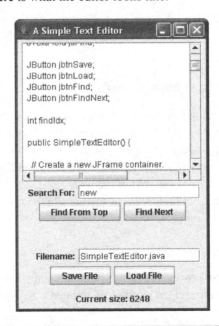

---

1. **JTextField** allows the user to enter just one line of text. **JTextArea** allows the user to enter multiple lines of text.
2. No, it must be put into a scroll pane to enable automatic scrolling.
3. **setWrapStyleWord(true)**

Because the editor uses **JTextArea**, it can handle only plain text, such as program files or configuration files. However, such an editor can still be quite useful. For example, you could use this example as the starting point for your own source code editor or as the basis for a simple note-keeping utility. You might also enjoy enhancing the editor and customizing it for your own uses. ("Mastery Check" questions 13–15 suggest some things for you to try.)

Step by Step

1. Create a file called **SimpleTextEditor.java** and add the following comment and **import** statements:

```
// Project 6-1: Create a simple text editor using Swing.

import java.io.*;
import java.awt.*;
import java.awt.event.*;
import javax.swing.*;
import javax.swing.event.*;
```

2. Begin the **SimpleTextEditor** class with the following declaration:

```
class SimpleTextEditor {

  JLabel jlabMsg;

  JTextArea jta;

  JTextField jtfFName;
  JTextField jtfFind;

  JButton jbtnSave;
  JButton jbtnLoad;
  JButton jbtnFind;
  JButton jbtnFindNext;

  int findIdx;
```

Here is what the instance variables do. The **jlabMsg** label is used to display messages related to the operation of the editor, such as the current character count or the result of a search. The text area that provides the editing is referred to by **jta**. The text field **jtfFName** holds the name of the file that is being edited. The text field **jtfFind** holds a string that can be searched for. The buttons **jbtnSave** and **jbtnLoad** cause the file to be saved or loaded, respectively. The **jbtnFind** button activates a search from the top of the file for a string. The **jbntFindNext** button continues a search. The **findIdx** variable holds the index of the point in the file at which a search will begin.

(continued)

3. Begin coding **SimpleTextEditor**'s constructor in the usual way, as shown next:

```
public SimpleTextEditor() {

  // Create a new JFrame container.
  JFrame jfrm = new JFrame("A Simple Text Editor");

  // Specify FlowLayout for the layout manager.
  jfrm.getContentPane().setLayout(new FlowLayout());

  // Give the frame an initial size.
  jfrm.setSize(270, 420);

  // Terminate the program when the user closes the application.
  jfrm.setDefaultCloseOperation(JFrame.EXIT_ON_CLOSE);
```

4. Create the labels for the application. Notice that all specify a preferred size and alignment. This makes it easier to manage the layout.

```
// Create the message label.
jlabMsg = new JLabel();
jlabMsg.setPreferredSize(new Dimension(200, 30));
jlabMsg.setHorizontalAlignment(SwingConstants.CENTER);

// Create an empty label to add space.
JLabel jlabSeparator = new JLabel();
jlabSeparator.setPreferredSize(new Dimension(200, 30));

// Create the Search For and Filename labels.
JLabel jlabFind = new JLabel("Search For:");
jlabFind.setPreferredSize(new Dimension(70, 20));
jlabFind.setHorizontalAlignment(SwingConstants.RIGHT);

JLabel jlabFilename = new JLabel("Filename:");
jlabFilename.setPreferredSize(new Dimension(70, 20));
jlabFilename.setHorizontalAlignment(SwingConstants.RIGHT);
```

5. Create the **JTextArea** that handles the editing.

```
// Create the text field.
jta = new JTextArea();

// Put the text area into a scroll pane.
JScrollPane jscrlp = new JScrollPane(jta);
jscrlp.setPreferredSize(new Dimension(250, 200));
```

Notice that, like most text areas, **jta** is contained within a scroll pane. This makes scrolling automatic and allows the editor to handle any length or width file. Also notice that no wrapping is used. When editing things such as program source files, line wrapping is often more trouble than benefit. However, you might want to add line wrapping as an experiment.

6. Next, create the text field that holds the filename.

```
// Create text field for filename.
jtfFName = new JTextField(15);
```

7. Add the caret listener shown here:

```
// Add a caret listener for the text area. This
// handler displays the number of characters in the
// file. It is updated with each caret change.
// The findIdx variable is also set to the current
// caret location.
jta.addCaretListener(new CaretListener() {
  public void caretUpdate(CaretEvent ce) {
    String str = jta.getText();
    jlabMsg.setText("Current size: " + str.length());
    findIdx = jta.getCaretPosition();
  }
});
```

Each time the caret is moved, the caret event handler displays the current size of the file. It also sets **findIdx** to the current caret location. This enables the Find Next button to find the next match that is after the current location.

8. Create the Save File and Load File buttons and add their listeners. The actual saving and loading of a file is handled by the methods **save( )** and **load( )**, which are described shortly.

```
// Create the Save File and Load File buttons.
jbtnSave = new JButton("Save File");
jbtnLoad = new JButton("Load File");

// Add action listener for the Save File button.
jbtnSave.addActionListener(new ActionListener() {
  public void actionPerformed(ActionEvent le) {
    save();
  }
});

// Add action listener for the Load File button.
jbtnLoad.addActionListener(new ActionListener() {
  public void actionPerformed(ActionEvent le) {
    load();
  }
});
```

(continued)

9. Create the text field that holds a string to be searched for. Also create the Find From Top and Find Next buttons. Then add the button's action listeners, as shown here:

```
// Create the Search For text field.
jtfFind = new JTextField(15);

// Create the Find From Top and Find Next buttons.
jbtnFind = new JButton("Find From Top");
jbtnFindNext = new JButton("Find Next");

// Add action listener for the Find From Top button.
jbtnFind.addActionListener(new ActionListener() {
  public void actionPerformed(ActionEvent le) {
    findIdx = 0;
    find(findIdx);
  }
});

// Add action listener for the Find Next button.
jbtnFindNext.addActionListener(new ActionListener() {
  public void actionPerformed(ActionEvent le) {
    find(findIdx+1);
  }
});
```

Notice that the handlers for both the Find From Top and Find Next buttons call the method **find( )** to actually search for the text that is contained in the Search For text field. When searching from the top, **findIdx** is set to 0 and then **find( )** is called with this value. This causes the search to begin at the top of the file. When searching for the next match, the search proceeds from one character after the current match (or from the current caret location if caret events have intervened). The **find( )** method is described in a moment.

10. Add the components to the content pane and then end the constructor in the usual way. Because there are so many components to add, a reference to the content pane is obtained and stored in the variable **cp**. This approach saves some typing on your part.

```
// Add the components to the content pane.
Container cp = jfrm.getContentPane();
cp.add(jscrlp);
cp.add(jlabFind);
cp.add(jtfFind);
cp.add(jbtnFind);
cp.add(jbtnFindNext);
cp.add(jlabSeparator);
cp.add(jlabFilename);
cp.add(jtfFName);
```

```
cp.add(jbtnSave);
cp.add(jbtnLoad);
cp.add(jlabMsg);

// Display the frame.
jfrm.setVisible(true);
}
```

11. Code the **save( )** method as shown next. This is the method that saves the file.

```
// Save the file.
void save() {
  FileWriter fw;

  // Get the filename from the text field.
  String fname = jtfFName.getText();

  // Make sure that there is actually a filename present.
  if(fname.length() == 0) {
    jlabMsg.setText("No filename present.");
    return;
  }

  // Save the file.
  try {
    fw = new FileWriter(fname);
    jta.write(fw);
    fw.close();
  } catch(IOException exc) {
    jlabMsg.setText("Error opening or writing file.");
    return;
  }

  jlabMsg.setText("File written successfully.");
}
```

The operation of the **save( )** method is straightforward. First, it obtains the name of the file from the **jtfFName** text field. It then confirms that the filename is not empty (as it will be if the user failed to enter one). Next, it opens the file and writes the contents to it by calling **write( )** on **jta** (the text area). Recall that **JTextComponent** defines the **write( )** method, which writes the contents of a text area to the specified stream automatically.

12. Add the **load( )** method, shown next:

```
// Load the file.
void load() {
  FileReader fw;
```

(continued)

```
// Get the filename from the text field.
String fname = jtfFName.getText();

// Make sure that there is actually a filename present.
if(fname.length() == 0) {
  jlabMsg.setText("No filename present.");
  return;
}

// Load the file.
try {
  fw = new FileReader(fname);
  jta.read(fw, null);
  fw.close();
} catch(IOException exc) {
  jlabMsg.setText("Error opening or reading file.");
  return;
}

// Reset find index when a new file is loaded.
findIdx = 0;

jlabMsg.setText("File loaded successfully.");
}
```

This method works much like **save( )** except that it loads the file specified in **jtfFName**. To do this, it opens the file for input and then reads the file using the **read( )** method defined by **JTextComponent**. This method reads the contents of the specified stream into the text area, replacing any preexisting contents. Notice that **findIdx** is set to 0. Because a new file is loaded, its old value will be invalid.

13. Create the **find( )** method, which searches for the string contained in the **jtfFind** text field:

```
// Search the file.
void find(int start) {
  // Get the current text as a string.
  String str = jta.getText();

  // Get the string to find.
  String findStr = jtfFind.getText();

  // Beginning at start, find the first
  // occurrence of the specified string.
```

```
    int idx = str.indexOf(findStr, start);

    // See if there is a match.
    if(idx > -1) {
      // If found, set focus to text area
      // and move caret to the location.
      jta.setCaretPosition(idx);
      findIdx = idx; // update the find index
      jlabMsg.setText("String found.");
    }
    else
      jlabMsg.setText("String not found.");

    // Set the focus to the editor window.
    jta.requestFocusInWindow();
  }
```

First, a string containing the contents of the file is obtained from **jta** and stored in **str**. The string to find is obtained from the **jtfFind** text field and stored in **findStr**. The **indexOf( )** method defined by **String** performs the search. It searches for a character sequence in the invoking string (in this case, **str**) that matches the string referred to by its first argument (in this case, **findStr**). The index at which to start searching is passed in its second argument. It returns –1 if no match is found. Otherwise, it returns the index of the start of the first match. In the program, this index is stored in the local variable **idx**.

If a match is found, the caret position within the text area is set to the start of the match, which is **idx**, and **findIdx** is also set to **idx**. The success or failure of the search is also reported in the message label. Before returning, **find( )** sets input focus to **jta** (which is the text area) by calling **requestFocusInWindow( )**. This method is defined by **Component** and overridden by **JComponent**. It moves input focus to the invoking component. Setting focus to the text area is necessary in order to show the location of the match.

14. Define **main( )** and end the class in the usual way, as shown here:

```
  public static void main(String args[]) {
    // Create the frame on the event dispatching thread.
    SwingUtilities.invokeLater(new Runnable() {
      public void run() {
        new SimpleTextEditor();
      }
    });
  }
}
```

(continued)

15. Here is the entire **SimpleTextEditor** class after all the pieces have been assembled:

```
// Project 6-1: Create a simple text editor using Swing.

import java.io.*;
import java.awt.*;
import java.awt.event.*;
import javax.swing.*;
import javax.swing.event.*;

class SimpleTextEditor {

  JLabel jlabMsg;

  JTextArea jta;

  JTextField jtfFName;
  JTextField jtfFind;

  JButton jbtnSave;
  JButton jbtnLoad;
  JButton jbtnFind;
  JButton jbtnFindNext;

  int findIdx;

  public SimpleTextEditor() {

    // Create a new JFrame container.
    JFrame jfrm = new JFrame("A Simple Text Editor");

    // Specify FlowLayout for the layout manager.
    jfrm.getContentPane().setLayout(new FlowLayout());

    // Give the frame an initial size.
    jfrm.setSize(270, 420);

    // Terminate the program when the user closes the application.
    jfrm.setDefaultCloseOperation(JFrame.EXIT_ON_CLOSE);

    // Create the message label.
    jlabMsg = new JLabel();
    jlabMsg.setPreferredSize(new Dimension(200, 30));
    jlabMsg.setHorizontalAlignment(SwingConstants.CENTER);

    // Create an empty label to add space.
```

```
JLabel jlabSeparator = new JLabel();
jlabSeparator.setPreferredSize(new Dimension(200, 30));

// Create the Search For and Filename labels.
JLabel jlabFind = new JLabel("Search For:");
jlabFind.setPreferredSize(new Dimension(70, 20));
jlabFind.setHorizontalAlignment(SwingConstants.RIGHT);

JLabel jlabFilename = new JLabel("Filename:");
jlabFilename.setPreferredSize(new Dimension(70, 20));
jlabFilename.setHorizontalAlignment(SwingConstants.RIGHT);

// Create the text field.
jta = new JTextArea();

// Put the text area into a scroll pane.
JScrollPane jscrlp = new JScrollPane(jta);
jscrlp.setPreferredSize(new Dimension(250, 200));

// Create text field for filename.
jtfFName = new JTextField(15);

// Add a caret listener for the text area. This
// handler displays the number of characters in the
// file. It is updated with each caret change.
// The findIdx variable is also set to the current
// caret location.
jta.addCaretListener(new CaretListener() {
  public void caretUpdate(CaretEvent ce) {
    String str = jta.getText();
    jlabMsg.setText("Current size: " + str.length());
    findIdx = jta.getCaretPosition();
  }
});

// Create the Save File and Load File buttons.
jbtnSave = new JButton("Save File");
jbtnLoad = new JButton("Load File");

// Add action listener for the Save File button.
jbtnSave.addActionListener(new ActionListener() {
  public void actionPerformed(ActionEvent le) {
    save();
  }
});
```

(continued)

```
// Add action listener for the Load File button.
jbtnLoad.addActionListener(new ActionListener() {
  public void actionPerformed(ActionEvent le) {
    load();
  }
});

// Create the Search For text field.
jtfFind = new JTextField(15);

// Create the Find From Top and Find Next buttons.
jbtnFind = new JButton("Find From Top");
jbtnFindNext = new JButton("Find Next");

// Add action listener for the Find From Top button.
jbtnFind.addActionListener(new ActionListener() {
  public void actionPerformed(ActionEvent le) {
    findIdx = 0;
    find(findIdx);
  }
});

// Add action listener for the Find Next button.
jbtnFindNext.addActionListener(new ActionListener() {
  public void actionPerformed(ActionEvent le) {
    find(findIdx+1);
  }
});

// Add the components to the content pane.
Container cp = jfrm.getContentPane();
cp.add(jscrlp);
cp.add(jlabFind);
cp.add(jtfFind);
cp.add(jbtnFind);
cp.add(jbtnFindNext);
cp.add(jlabSeparator);
cp.add(jlabFilename);
cp.add(jtfFName);
cp.add(jbtnSave);
cp.add(jbtnLoad);
cp.add(jlabMsg);

// Display the frame.
jfrm.setVisible(true);
}
```

```
// Save the file.
void save() {
  FileWriter fw;

  // Get the filename from the text field.
  String fname = jtfFName.getText();

  // Make sure that there is actually a filename present.
  if(fname.length() == 0) {
    jlabMsg.setText("No filename present.");
    return;
  }

  // Save the file.
  try {
    fw = new FileWriter(fname);
    jta.write(fw);
    fw.close();
  } catch(IOException exc) {
    jlabMsg.setText("Error opening or writing file.");
    return;
  }

  jlabMsg.setText("File written successfully.");
}

// Load the file.
void load() {
  FileReader fw;

  // Get the filename from the text field.
  String fname = jtfFName.getText();

  // Make sure that there is actually a filename present.
  if(fname.length() == 0) {
    jlabMsg.setText("No filename present.");
    return;
  }

  // Load the file.
  try {
    fw = new FileReader(fname);
    jta.read(fw, null);
    fw.close();
  } catch(IOException exc) {
    jlabMsg.setText("Error opening or reading file.");
```

(continued)

```
      return;
    }

    // Reset find index when a new file is loaded.
    findIdx = 0;

    jlabMsg.setText("File loaded successfully.");
  }

  // Search the file.
  void find(int start) {
    // Get the current text as a string.
    String str = jta.getText();

    // Get the string to find.
    String findStr = jtfFind.getText();

    // Beginning at start, find the first
    // occurrence of the specified string.
    int idx = str.indexOf(findStr, start);

    // See if there is a match.
    if(idx > -1) {
      // If found, set focus to text area
      // and move caret to the location.
      jta.setCaretPosition(idx);
      findIdx = idx; // update the find index
      jlabMsg.setText("String found.");
    }
    else
      jlabMsg.setText("String not found.");

    // Set the focus to the editor window.
    jta.requestFocusInWindow();
  }

  public static void main(String args[]) {
    // Create the frame on the event dispatching thread.
    SwingUtilities.invokeLater(new Runnable() {
      public void run() {
        new SimpleTextEditor();
      }
    });
  }
}
```

✓

Module 6 Mastery Check

1. What is **JTextComponent**? Can you create an instance of **JTextComponent**?

2. Name the six text component classes defined by Swing.

3. When using **JTextField**, what event is generated when the caret is moved? What event is generated when the user presses ENTER while editing text inside a **JTextField**?

4. To input a password, what text component should be used?

5. What is the main advantage of using **JFormattedTextField** over **JTextField**?

6. Show the mask that could be used to format a telephone number of this form: 1 (555) 555-5555.

7. What are the four **JFormattedTextField** focus-lost policy options and what do they do?

8. What type of event is fired when the value of a formatted text field changes?

9. A **JTextArea** will usually be wrapped in a **JScrollPane**. True or false?

10. What method do you call to cause a text area to wrap text?

11. What method do you call to set the tab size in a text area?

12. Can you cut and paste text within the text components? Can you do these things under program control? If so, what methods are used?

13. Add a replace feature to **SimpleTextEditor** in Project 6-1. To do this, use the string in the Search For field as the string to replace. Add another edit field that contains the replacement. Add a button called Replace that replaces one instance of the string each time it is pressed.

14. Change **SimpleTextEditor** so that it displays the number of lines in the file rather than a count of the characters.

15. In **SimpleTextEditor**, add keyboard mnemonics to the Find From Top and Find Next buttons. Use F for Find From Top and N for Find Next.

16. On your own, add other enhancements to **SimpleTextEditor**. For example, you might try adding a check box that makes the search feature case-insensitive.

Module 7

Working with Menus

This chapter covers one of the most fundamental aspects of the modern GUI environment: the menu. Menus form an integral part of all but the most simple applications because they expose the program's functionality to the user. Because of their importance, Swing provides extensive support for menus. Menus are an area in which Swing's power is readily apparent.

The Swing menuing system supports the following elements:

- The menu bar, which is the main menu for an application.

- The standard menu, which can contain either items to be selected or other menus (submenus).

- The popup menu, which is usually activated by right-clicking the mouse.

- The toolbar, which provides rapid access to program functionality, often paralleling menu items.

- The action, which enables two or more different components to be managed by a single object. Although actions have uses in other areas, it is with menus and toolbars that they are most often applied.

Swing menus also support accelerator keys, which enable menu items to be selected without having to activate the menu, and mnemonics, which allow menu items to be selected by using the keyboard once the menu options are displayed.

**CRITICAL SKILL
7.1** Menu Basics

The Swing menuing system is supported by the classes shown in Table 7-1. Although they may seem a bit confusing at first, Swing menus are very easy to use. Swing allows a high degree of customization, if desired; however, you will normally use the menuing classes as-is because they support all of the most-needed options. For example, you can add images and keyboard shortcuts to a menu easily.

Here is a brief overview of how the classes fit together. To create a main menu for an application, you will first create a **JMenuBar** object. This class is, loosely speaking, a container for menus. To the **JMenuBar** instance, you will add instances of **JMenu**. Each **JMenu** object defines a menu. That is, each **JMenu** object contains one or more selectable items. The items displayed by a **JMenu** are objects of **JMenuItem**. Thus, a **JMenuItem** defines a selection that can be chosen by the user.

In addition to menus that descend from the menu bar, you can also create stand-alone popup menus. To create a popup menu, first create an object of type **JPopupMenu**. Then, add **JMenuItem**s to it. A popup menu is normally activated by clicking the right mouse button when the mouse is over a component for which a popup menu has been defined.

Menu Classes	Description
JMenuBar	An object that holds the top-level menu for the application.
JMenu	A standard menu. A menu consists of one or more **JMenuItems**.
JMenuItem	An object that populates menus.
JCheckBoxMenuItem	A check box menu item.
JRadioButtonMenuItem	A radio button menu item.
JSeparator	A visual separator between menu items.
JPopupMenu	A menu that is typically activated by right-clicking the mouse.

Table 7-1 The Swing Menu Classes

In addition to "standard" menu items, you can also include check boxes and radio buttons in a menu. A check box menu item is created by **JCheckBoxMenuItem**. A radio button menu item is created by **JRadioButtonMenuItem**. Both of these classes extend **JMenuItem**. They can be used in both standard menus and popup menus.

JToolBar creates a stand-alone component that is related to the menu. It is often used to provide fast access to functionality contained within the menus of the application. For example, a toolbar might provide fast access to the formatting commands supported by a word processor.

JSeparator is a convenience class that creates a separator line in a menu.

One key point to understand about Swing menus is that each menu item extends **AbstractButton**. Recall that **AbstractButton** is also the superclass of all of Swing's button components, such as **JButton**. Thus, all menu items are, essentially, buttons. Obviously, they won't actually look like buttons when used in a menu, but they will, in many ways, act like buttons. For example, selecting a menu item generates an action event in the same way that pressing a button does.

Another key point is that **JMenuItem** is a superclass of **JMenu**. This allows the creation of submenus, which are, essentially, menus within menus. To create a submenu, you first create and populate a **JMenu** object and then add it to another **JMenu** object. You will see this process in action in the following section.

Swing's menuing system also defines two important interfaces: **SingleSelectionModel** and **MenuElement**. **SingleSelectionModel** determines the actions of a component that contains multiple elements, but from which one and only one element can be selected at any one time. This model is used by both **JMenuBar** and **JPopupMenu**. There is a default implementation called **DefaultSingleSelectionModel**. The **MenuElement** interface defines that nature of a menu item. It is implemented by all of the menu classes, except for **JSeparator**. In general, you will not need to interact with these interfaces directly unless you are customizing the menu system.

As mentioned previously, when a menu item is selected, an action event is generated. The action command string associated with that action event will, by default, be the name of the selection. Thus, you can determine which item was selected by examining the action command. Of course, you can also use a separate anonymous inner class to handle each menu item's action events. Be aware, however, that menu systems tend to get quite large. Using a separate class to handle events for each menu item can cause a large number of classes to be created, which can lead to runtime inefficiencies.

Menus can also generate other types of events. Each time that a menu is activated, selected, or cancelled, a **MenuEvent** is generated. You can listen for these events via a **MenuListener**. When a menu is responding to a keyboard event, a **MenuKeyEvent** is generated. You can listen for menu key events with a **MenuKeyListener**. Mouse drag actions on a menu cause a **MenuDragMouseEvent**. You can listen for mouse drag events with a **MenuDragMouseListener**. When a popup menu is about to appear or disappear, a **PopupMenuEvent** is generated. You can listen for it with a **PopupMenuListener**. It is important to understand that for most applications you will not need to handle these events. Normally, you need only watch for action events. However, the other events are available to you if you want to take detailed control over the way your menus work.

Progress Check

1. What class creates a top-level menu bar?

2. What class creates a menu item?

3. Can a menu item be a check box or a radio button?

CRITICAL SKILL
7.2

An Overview of JMenuBar, JMenu, and JMenuItem

Before you can create a menu, it's necessary to know something about the three core menu classes: **JMenuBar**, **JMenu**, and **JMenuItem**. These form the minimum set of classes needed to construct a main menu for an application. **JMenu** and **JMenuItem** are also used by popup menus. Thus, these classes form the foundation of the menuing system.

---

1. **JMenuBar**
2. **JMenuItem**
3. Yes

JMenuBar

As mentioned, **JMenuBar** is essentially a container for menus. Like all components, it inherits **JComponent** (which inherits **Container** and **Component**). It has only one constructor, which is the default constructor. Therefore, the menu bar will initially be empty, and you will need to populate it with menus prior to use. Each application has one and only one menu bar.

JMenuBar defines several methods, but often you will only need to use one: **add( )**. The **add( )** method adds a **JMenu** to the menu bar. It is shown here:

JMenu add(JMenu *menu*)

Here, *menu* is a **JMenu** instance that is added to the menu bar. A reference to the menu is returned. Menus are positioned in the bar from left to right, in the order in which they are added. If you want to add a menu at a specific location, then use this version of **add( )**, which is inherited from **Container**:

Component add(Component *menu*, int *idx*)

Here, *menu* is added at the index specified by *idx*. Indexing begins at 0, with 0 being the leftmost menu.

In some cases you might want to remove a menu that is no longer needed. You can do this by calling **remove( )**, which is inherited from **Container**. It has these two forms:

void remove(Component *menu*)

void remove(int *idx*)

Here, *menu* is a reference to the menu to remove and *idx* is the index of the menu to be removed. Indexing begins at 0.

Another method that is sometimes useful is **getMenuCount( )**, shown here:

int getMenuCount( )

It returns the number of elements contained within the menu bar.

JMenuBar defines some other methods that you might find helpful in specialized applications. For example, you can obtain an array of references to the menus in the bar by calling **getSubElements( )**. You can determine if a menu is selected by calling **isSelected( )**.

Once a menu bar has been created and populated, it is added to a **JFrame** by calling **setJMenuBar( )** on the **JFrame** instance. (Menu bars *are not* added to the content pane.) The **setJMenuBar( )** method is shown here:

void setJMenuBar(JMenuBar *mb*)

Here, *mb* is a reference to the menu bar. The menu bar will be displayed in a position determined by the look and feel. Usually, this is at the top of the window.

JMenu

JMenu encapsulates a menu, which is populated with **JMenuItems**. As mentioned, it is derived from **JMenuItem**. This means that one **JMenu** can be a selection in another **JMenu**. This enables one menu to be submenu of another. **JMenu** defines the constructors shown in Table 7-2. In all cases, the menu is empty until menu items are added to it.

JMenu defines many methods. Here are brief descriptions of some of the more commonly used ones. To add an item to the menu, use the **add( )** method, which has a number of forms, including the two shown here:

JMenuItem add(JMenuItem *item*)

JMenuItem add(Component *item*, int *idx*)

Here, *item* is the menu item to add. The first form adds the item to the end of the menu. The second form adds the item at the index specified by *idx*. As expected, indexing starts at 0. Both return a reference to the item added. As a point of interest, you can also use **insert( )** to add menu items to a menu.

You can add a separator (an object of type **JSeparator**) to a menu by calling **addSeparator( )**, shown here:

void addSeparator( )

The separator is added onto the end of the menu. You can insert a separator at a specified index by calling **insertSeparator( )**, shown next:

void insertSeparator(int *idx*)

Here, *idx* specifies the zero-based index at which the separator will be added.

Constructor	Description
JMenu( )	Creates an unnamed menu.
JMenu(String *name*)	Creates a menu that has the title specified by *name*.
JMenu(String *name*, boolean *tearOff*)	Creates a menu that has the title specified by *name*. At the time of this writing, *tearOff* is ignored.
JMenu(Action *action*)	Creates a menu as prescribed by *action*.

Table 7-2 The **JMenu** Constructors

Ask the Expert

Q: I know that JMenu **defines the** addSeparator( ) **and** insertSeparator( ) **methods, which add a separator to a menu. Why is a separate** JSeparator **class needed?**

A: **JSeparator** can be used any place that a visual separator is needed. Be aware, however, that its precise effects depend upon the look and feel.

You can remove an item from a menu by calling **remove( )**, shown here:

void remove(JMenuItem *menu*)

void remove(int *idx*)

Here, *menu* is a reference to the item to remove, and *idx* is the index of the item to remove.

You can obtain the number of items in the menu by calling **getMenuComponentCount( )**, shown here:

int getMenuComponentCount( )

You can get an array of the items in the menu by calling **getMenuComponents( )**, shown next:

Component[ ] getMenuComponents( )

An array containing the components is returned.

JMenuItem

JMenuItem encapsulates an element in a menu. This element can be either a selection linked to some program action, such as Save or Close, or it can cause a submenu to be displayed. As mentioned, **JMenuItem** is derived from **AbstractButton**, and every item in a menu can be thought of as a special kind of button. Therefore, when a menu item is selected, an action event is generated. (This is similar to the way a **JButton** fires an action event when it is pressed.) **JMenuItem** defines the constructors shown in Table 7-3. Notice that you can specify a mnemonic when the menu item is created. This mnemonic enables you to select an item from the menu by pressing the specified key.

Constructor	Description
JMenuItem( )	Creates an unnamed menu item.
JMenuItem(String *name*)	Creates a menu item with the name specified by *name*.
JMenuItem(Icon *image*)	Creates a menu item that displays the image specified by *image*.
JMenuItem(String *name*, Icon *image*)	Creates a menu item with the name specified by *name* and the image specified by *image*.
JMenuItem(String *name*, int *mnem*)	Creates a menu item with the name specified by *name*. It uses the keyboard mnemonic specified by *mnem*.
JMenuItem(Action *action*)	Creates a menu item using the information specified in *action*.

Table 7-3 The **JMenuItem** Constructors

Because menu items inherit **AbstractButton**, you have access to the functionality provided by **AbstractButton**. For example, you can enable/disable a menu item by calling **setEnabled( )**, shown here:

void setEnabled(boolean *enable*)

If *enable* is true, the menu item is enabled. If *enable* is false, the item is disabled and cannot be selected.

Progress Check

1. What method adds an item to a menu?

2. What does **addSeparator( )** do?

3. A menu item cannot be disabled. True or false?

---

1. **add( )**
2. It adds a separator (which visually separates menu items) to a menu.
3. False

CRITICAL SKILL
 7.3 Create a Main Menu

The most commonly used menu is the *main menu*. This is the menu defined by the menu bar, and it is the menu that defines all (or nearly all) of the functionality of an application. Fortunately, Swing makes it very easy to create and manage the main menu. This section shows how to construct a basic main menu. Subsequent sections will show how to add options to it.

Constructing the main menu requires several steps. First, create the **JMenuBar** object that will hold the menus. Next, construct each menu that will be in the menu bar. In general, a menu is constructed by first creating a **JMenu** object and then adding **JMenuItem**s to it. After the menus have been created, add them to the menu bar. The menu bar, itself, must then be added to the frame by calling **setJMenuBar( )**. Finally, for each menu item, you must add an action listener that handles the action event fired when the menu item is selected.

The best way to understand the process of creating and managing menus is to work through an example. Here is a program that creates a simple menu bar that contains three menus. The first is a standard File menu that contains Open, Close, Save, and Exit selections. The second menu is called Options, and it contains two submenus called Colors and Priority. The third menu is called Help, and it has one item: About. When a menu item is selected, the name of the selection is displayed in a label in the content pane. Sample output is shown in Figure 7-1.

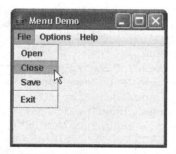

Figure 7-1 Sample output from the **MenuDemo** program

```
// Demonstrate a simple main menu.

import java.awt.*;
import java.awt.event.*;
import javax.swing.*;

class MenuDemo implements ActionListener {

  JLabel jlab;

  MenuDemo() {
    // Create a new JFrame container.
    JFrame jfrm = new JFrame("Menu Demo");

    // Specify FlowLayout for the layout manager.
    jfrm.getContentPane().setLayout(new FlowLayout());

    // Give the frame an initial size.
    jfrm.setSize(220, 200);

    // Terminate the program when the user closes the application.
    jfrm.setDefaultCloseOperation(JFrame.EXIT_ON_CLOSE);

    // Create a label that will display the menu selection.
    jlab = new JLabel();

    // Create the menu bar.
    JMenuBar jmb = new JMenuBar();          ◄──────── Create a menu bar.

    // Create the File menu.
    JMenu jmFile = new JMenu("File");
    JMenuItem jmiOpen = new JMenuItem("Open");
    JMenuItem jmiClose = new JMenuItem("Close");      ├── Create the File menu items.
    JMenuItem jmiSave = new JMenuItem("Save");
    JMenuItem jmiExit = new JMenuItem("Exit");
    jmFile.add(jmiOpen);
    jmFile.add(jmiClose);
    jmFile.add(jmiSave);                    ├── Add the File menu items to the File menu.
    jmFile.addSeparator();
    jmFile.add(jmiExit);
    jmb.add(jmFile);                        ◄──────── Add the File menu to the menu bar.

    // Create the Options menu.
    JMenu jmOptions = new JMenu("Options");  ◄──────── Create the Options menu.

    // Create the Colors submenu.
```

```
JMenu jmColors = new JMenu("Colors");
JMenuItem jmiRed = new JMenuItem("Red");
JMenuItem jmiGreen = new JMenuItem("Green");
JMenuItem jmiBlue = new JMenuItem("Blue");
jmColors.add(jmiRed);
jmColors.add(jmiGreen);
jmColors.add(jmiBlue);
jmOptions.add(jmColors);
```
Create the Colors submenu.

Add Colors submenu to the Options menu.

```
// Create the Priority submenu.
JMenu jmPriority = new JMenu("Priority");
JMenuItem jmiHigh = new JMenuItem("High");
JMenuItem jmiLow = new JMenuItem("Low");
jmPriority.add(jmiHigh);
jmPriority.add(jmiLow);
jmOptions.add(jmPriority);
```
Create the Priority submenu.

Add Priority submenu to the Options menu.

```
// Create the Reset menu item.
JMenuItem jmiReset = new JMenuItem("Reset");
jmOptions.addSeparator();
jmOptions.add(jmiReset);
```
Create the Reset item and add it to the Options menu.

```
// Finally, add the entire Options menu to
// the menu bar.
jmb.add(jmOptions);
```
Add the Options menu to the menu bar.

```
// Create the Help menu.
JMenu jmHelp = new JMenu("Help");
JMenuItem jmiAbout = new JMenuItem("About");
jmHelp.add(jmiAbout);
jmb.add(jmHelp);
```
Create the Help menu and add it to the menu bar.

```
// Add action listeners for the menu items.
jmiOpen.addActionListener(this);
jmiClose.addActionListener(this);
jmiSave.addActionListener(this);
jmiExit.addActionListener(this);
jmiRed.addActionListener(this);
jmiGreen.addActionListener(this);
jmiBlue.addActionListener(this);
jmiHigh.addActionListener(this);
jmiLow.addActionListener(this);
jmiReset.addActionListener(this);
jmiAbout.addActionListener(this);
```
Add the action listeners for the menu items.

```
    // Add the label to the content pane.
    jfrm.getContentPane().add(jlab);

    // Add the menu bar to the frame.
    jfrm.setJMenuBar(jmb);  ◄————————— Add the menu bar to the frame.

    // Display the frame.
    jfrm.setVisible(true);
  }

  // Handle menu item action events.
  public void actionPerformed(ActionEvent ae) {
    // Get the action command from the menu selection.
    String comStr = ae.getActionCommand();

    // If user chooses Exit, then exit the program.
    if(comStr.equals("Exit")) System.exit(0);  ◄———  Exit the program when the
                                                     user chooses Exit from
    // Otherwise, display the selection.              the File menu.
    jlab.setText(comStr + " Selected");
  }

  public static void main(String args[]) {
    // Create the frame on the event dispatching thread.
    SwingUtilities.invokeLater(new Runnable() {
      public void run() {
        new MenuDemo();
      }
    });
  }
}
```

Let's examine in detail how the menus are created, beginning with the **MenuDemo** constructor. It begins with the usual statements. Then, the menu bar is constructed and a reference to it is assigned to **jmb** by this statement:

```
// Create the menu bar.
JMenuBar jmb = new JMenuBar();
```

Next, the File menu **jmFile** and its menu entries are created by this sequence:

```
// Create the File menu.
JMenu jmFile = new JMenu("File");
JMenuItem jmiOpen = new JMenuItem("Open");
JMenuItem jmiClose = new JMenuItem("Close");
```

```
JMenuItem jmiSave = new JMenuItem("Save");
JMenuItem jmiExit = new JMenuItem("Exit");
```

The names Open, Close, Save, and Exit will be shown as selections in the menu. Next, the menu entries are added to the file menu by this sequence:

```
jmFile.add(jmiOpen);
jmFile.add(jmiClose);
jmFile.add(jmiSave);
jmFile.addSeparator();
jmFile.add(jmiExit);
```

Finally, the file menu is added to the menu bar by this line:

```
jmb.add(jmFile);
```

Once the preceding code sequence completes, the menu bar will contain one entry: File. The File menu will contain four selections in this order: Open, Close, Save, and Exit. However, notice that a separator has been added before Exit. This visually separates the Exit menu item from the preceding three selections.

The Options menu is constructed using the same basic process as the File menu. However, the Options menu consists of two submenus, Colors and Priority, and a Reset entry. The submenus are first constructed individually and then added to the Options menu. The Reset item is added last. Then, the Options menu is added to the menu bar. The Help menu is constructed using the same process.

Notice that **MenuDemo** implements the **ActionListener** interface and action events generated by a menu selection are handled by the **actionPerformed( )** method defined by **MenuDemo**. Therefore, the program adds **this** as the action listener for the menu items. Notice that no listeners are added to the Colors or Priority items because they are not actually selections. They simply activate submenus.

Finally, the menu bar is added to the frame by the following line:

```
jfrm.setJMenuBar(jmb);
```

As mentioned, menu bars are not added to the content pane. They are added directly to the **JFrame**.

The **actionPerformed( )** method handles the action events generated by the menu. It obtains the action command string associated with the selection by calling **getActionCommand( )** on the event. It stores a reference to this string in **comStr**. Then it tests the action command against "Exit", as shown here:

```
if(comStr.equals("Exit")) System.exit(0);
```

If the action command is "Exit" then the program terminates by calling **System.exit( )**. This method causes the immediate termination of a program and passes its argument as a status code to the calling process, which is usually the operating system or the browser. By convention, a status code of 0 means normal termination. Anything else indicates that the program terminated abnormally.

At this point, you might want to experiment a bit with the **MenuDemo** program. Try adding another menu or adding additional items to an existing menu. It is important that you understand the basic menu concepts before moving on because you will be evolving the program throughout the remainder of this module.

CRITICAL SKILL
7.4

Add Mnemonics and Accelerators to Menu Items

The menu created in the preceding example is functional, but it is possible to make it better. In real applications, a menu usually includes support for keyboard shortcuts. These come in two forms: mnemonics and accelerators. As it applies to menus, a mnemonic defines a key that lets you select an item from an active menu by typing the key. Thus, a mnemonic allows you to use the keyboard to selected an item from a menu that is already being displayed. An accelerator is a key that lets you select a menu item without having to activate the menu first.

A mnemonic can be specified for both **JMenuItem** and **JMenu** objects. There are two ways to set the mnemonic for **JMenuItem**. First, it can be specified when an object is constructed. (See Table 7-3.) Second, you can set the mnemonic by calling **setMnemonic( )**. To specify a mnemonic for **JMenu**, you must call **setMnemonic( )**. This method is inherited by both classes from **AbstractButton** and is shown here:

void setMnemonic(int *mnem*)

As explained in Module 2 (when buttons were discussed), *mnem* specifies the mnemonic. It should be one of the constants defined in **java.awt.event.KeyEvent**, such as **KeyEvent.VK_F**. (There is another version of **setMnemonic( )** that takes a **char** argument, but it is considered obsolete.) Mnemonics are not case-sensitive, so in the example of **VK_A**, typing either *a* or *A* will work.

By default, the first matching letter in the menu item will be underscored. In instances in which you want to underscore a letter other than the first match, specify the index of the letter as an argument to **setDisplayedMnemonicIndex( )**, which is inherited by both **JMenu** and **JMenuItem** from **AbstractButton**. It is shown here:

void setDisplayedMnemonicIndex(int *idx*)

The index of the letter to underscore is specified by *idx*.

An accelerator can be associated with both **JMenu** and **JMenuItem** objects. It is specified by calling **setAccelerator( )**, shown next:

void setAccelerator(KeyStroke *ks*)

Here, *ks* is the key combination that is pressed to select the menu item. **KeyStroke** is a class that contains several factory methods that construct various types of keystroke accelerators. Here are three examples:

static KeyStroke getKeyStroke(char *ch*)

static KeyStroke getKeyStroke(Character *ch*, int *modifier*)

static KeyStroke getKeyStroke(int *ch*, int *modifier*)

Here, *ch* specifies the accelerator character. In the first version, the character is specified as a **char** value. In the second, it is specified as an object of type **Character**. In the third, it is a value of type **KeyEvent**, previously described. The value of *modifier* must be one or more of the following constants, defined in the **java.awt.event.InputEvent** class:

InputEvent.ALT_MASK	InputEvent.CTRL_MASK
InputEvent.META_MASK	InputEvent.SHIFT_MASK

Therefore, if you pass **VK_A** for the key character and **InputEvent.CTRL_MASK** for the modifier, the accelerator key combination is CTRL-A.

The following sequence adds both mnemonics and accelerators to the File menu created by the **MenuDemo** program in the previous section. Figure 7-2 shows how this menu looks when activated.

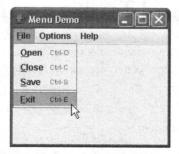

Figure 7-2 The File menu after adding mnemonics and accelerators

```
// Create the File menu with mnemonics and accelerators.
JMenu jmFile = new JMenu("File");
jmFile.setMnemonic(KeyEvent.VK_F);
```
◄——————— The File menu has *F* as its mnemonic.

```
JMenuItem jmiOpen = new JMenuItem("Open",
                              KeyEvent.VK_O);
jmiOpen.setAccelerator(
        KeyStroke.getKeyStroke(KeyEvent.VK_O,
                            InputEvent.CTRL_MASK));

JMenuItem jmiClose = new JMenuItem("Close",
                              KeyEvent.VK_C);
jmiClose.setAccelerator(
        KeyStroke.getKeyStroke(KeyEvent.VK_C,
                            InputEvent.CTRL_MASK));
```

In each case, the mnemonic is the first letter of the item's name. The accelerator is the same letter in combination with the CTRL key.

```
JMenuItem jmiSave = new JMenuItem("Save",
                             KeyEvent.VK_S);
jmiSave.setAccelerator(
        KeyStroke.getKeyStroke(KeyEvent.VK_S,
                            InputEvent.CTRL_MASK));

JMenuItem jmiExit = new JMenuItem("Exit",
                             KeyEvent.VK_E);
jmiExit.setAccelerator(
        KeyStroke.getKeyStroke(KeyEvent.VK_E,
                            InputEvent.CTRL_MASK));
```

After making this change, you can select the File menu by typing ALT-F. Then, you can use the mnemonics O, C, S, or E to select an option. Alternatively, you can select a File menu option directly by pressing CTRL-O, CTRL-C, CTRL-S, or CTRL-E.

CRITICAL SKILL
7.5

Add Images and Tooltips to Menu Items

You can add images to menu items or use images instead of text. The easiest way to add an image is to specify it when the menu item is being constructed. For example, here are **JMenuItem** constructors that allow you to add an icon to the menu item:

JMenuItem(Icon *image*)

JMenuItem(String *name*, Icon *image*)

Ask the Expert

Q: Given that accelerators work both when a menu is displayed and when it is not displayed, why would I want to bother with also defining mnemonics for menu selections?

A: Although accelerators can be used by themselves, for the reason stated in your question, they have one downside: they must be used in conjunction with a modifier key, such as CTRL or ALT. However, by specifying a mnemonic, you give the user the option of selecting an item by simply typing its key (without a modifier), when a menu is displayed. For example, if you make the mnemonic for a Save option the letter *S* and its accelerator CTRL-S, then when the menu is displayed, the user can select Save by simply typing S, without needing to also press the CTRL key. While it may seem like a small issue, it's the way that top-of-the-line applications work. Therefore, to give your programs a professional look and feel, both mnemonics and accelerators are needed.

The first creates a menu item that displays the image specified by *image*. The second creates a menu item with the name specified by *name* and the image specified by *image*. For example, here the About menu item is associated with an image when it is created:

```
ImageIcon icon = new ImageIcon("AboutIcon.gif");
JMenuItem jmiAbout = new JMenuItem("About", icon);
```

After this addition, the icon specified by **icon** will be displayed next to the text "About" when the Help menu is displayed. This is shown in Figure 7-3. You can also add an icon to a menu item after the item has been created by calling **setIcon( )** (which is inherited from **AbstractButton**). You can specify the horizontal alignment of the image relative to the text by calling **setHorizontalTextPosition( )**.

Figure 7-3 The About menu item with the addition of an icon

You can specify a disabled icon, which is shown when the menu item is disabled, by calling **setDisabledIcon( )**. Normally, when a menu item is disabled, the default icon is shown in gray. If a disabled icon is specified, then that icon is displayed when the menu item is disabled. These methods are inherited from **AbstractButton** and work the same for a menu item as they do for a button.

Because all menu items inherit **JComponent**, which supports tooltips, you can add a tooltip to a menu item. To do this, simply call **setToolTipText( )** on the item, specifying the text you want displayed. For example, this creates a tooltip for the About item:

```
jmiAbout.setToolTipText("Info about the MenuDemo program.");
```

Although tooltips are not commonly attached to menu items, this capability shows the power and flexibility that Swing's architecture offers to the GUI designer.

Progress Check

1. Both **setMnemonic( )** and **setAccelerator( )** take objects of type **KeyEvent** as an argument. True or False?

2. What is the mask for the CTRL key?

3. What method sets a menu item's tooltip text?

Project 7-1 Dynamically Add and Remove Menu Items

DynMenuDemo.java

It is possible to change the contents of a menu during the execution of your program. For example, you can add an item when it is needed and remove it when it is no longer needed. You can also change the name of an item at runtime. These capabilities make it possible to create dynamic menus that change as necessary to meet the needs of the user. This project demonstrates the process by walking through the steps needed to add and remove additional colors to the Colors menu of the **MenuDemo** program shown at the start of this module.

The project adds a menu item to the Colors menu called More Colors. When More Colors is selected, it causes the colors Yellow, Purple, and Orange to be added to the menu, and the More Colors menu item is changed to Less Colors. When Less Colors is selected, the

---

1. False, **setAccelerator( )** requires a **KeyStroke** object.

2. **InputEvent.CTRL_MASK**

3. **setToolTipText( )**

colors are removed and Less Colors is changed back to More Colors. Sample output is shown here:

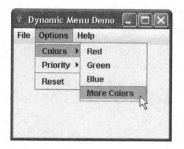
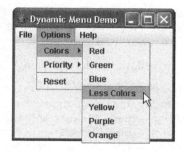

Step by Step

1. Copy the **MenuDemo** program shown at the start of this module into a file called **DynMenuDemo.java**. (If you have been following along, you can use the version of **MenuDemo** that includes the accelerators, mnemonics, and icon. However, for brevity, the code shown here simply uses the original **MenuDemo** program as the starting point.)

2. Change the name of the class from **MenuDemo** to **DynMenuDemo**. Then, add three **JMenuItems** called **jmiYellow**, **jmiPurple**, and **jmiOrange** as instance variables. Also, make the local variable **jmColors** into an instance variable. After these changes, the beginning of the program will look like this:

```java
// Project 7-1: Add and remove menu items dynamically.

import java.awt.*;
import java.awt.event.*;
import javax.swing.*;

class DynMenuDemo implements ActionListener {

  JLabel jlab;

  JMenuItem jmiYellow;
  JMenuItem jmiPurple;
  JMenuItem jmiOrange;

  JMenu jmColors;
```

(continued)

3. Create a menu item called **jmiMoreLess** with the name More Colors and add it to the **jmColors** menu, as shown here:

```
// Create the More/Less Colors Menu item.
JMenuItem jmiMoreLess = new JMenuItem("More Colors");
jmColors.add(jmiMoreLess);
```

4. Create the Yellow, Purple, and Orange color selections like this:

```
// Create the additional colors. These will be
// added or removed on demand.
jmiYellow = new JMenuItem("Yellow");
jmiPurple = new JMenuItem("Purple");
jmiOrange = new JMenuItem("Orange");
```

5. Add listeners for the new menu items as shown next:

```
// Add listeners for the additional
// colors option.
jmiMoreLess.addActionListener(this);
jmiYellow.addActionListener(this);
jmiPurple.addActionListener(this);
jmiOrange.addActionListener(this);
```

6. Change the **actionPerformed( )** method to handle the new selections, as shown here:

```
// Handle menu item action events.
public void actionPerformed(ActionEvent ae) {
  // Get the action command from the menu selection.
  String comStr = ae.getActionCommand();

  // If user chooses Exit, then exit the program.
  if(comStr.equals("Exit"))
    System.exit(0);
  else if(comStr.equals("More Colors")) {
    jmColors.add(jmiYellow);
    jmColors.add(jmiPurple);
    jmColors.add(jmiOrange);
    JMenuItem mi = (JMenuItem) ae.getSource();
    mi.setText("Less Colors");
  } else if(comStr.equals("Less Colors")) {
    jmColors.remove(jmiYellow);
    jmColors.remove(jmiPurple);
    jmColors.remove(jmiOrange);
    JMenuItem mi = (JMenuItem) ae.getSource();
```

```
      mi.setText("More Colors");
   }

   // Otherwise, display the selection.
   jlab.setText(comStr + " Selected");
}
```

Notice that when More Colors is selected, the three new colors are added to the Colors menu and the name of the **jmiMoreLess** menu item is changed to Less Colors. When Less Colors is chosen, the new colors are removed from the menu and the name of **jmiMoreLess** is returned to More Colors. Recall that a menu item can be removed from a menu by calling **remove( )**.

7. After making all of the changes, the program will look like that shown here:

```
// Project 7-1: Add and remove menu items dynamically.

import java.awt.*;
import java.awt.event.*;
import javax.swing.*;

class DynMenuDemo implements ActionListener {

  JLabel jlab;

  JMenuItem jmiYellow;
  JMenuItem jmiPurple;
  JMenuItem jmiOrange;

  JMenu jmColors;

  DynMenuDemo() {
    // Create a new JFrame container.
    JFrame jfrm = new JFrame("Dynamic Menu Demo");

    // Specify FlowLayout for the layout manager.
    jfrm.getContentPane().setLayout(new FlowLayout());

    // Give the frame an initial size.
    jfrm.setSize(220, 200);

    // Terminate the program when the user closes the application.
    jfrm.setDefaultCloseOperation(JFrame.EXIT_ON_CLOSE);
```

(continued)

```
// Create a label that will display the menu selection.
jlab = new JLabel();

// Create the menu bar.
JMenuBar jmb = new JMenuBar();

// Create the File menu.
JMenu jmFile = new JMenu("File");
JMenuItem jmiOpen = new JMenuItem("Open");
JMenuItem jmiClose = new JMenuItem("Close");
JMenuItem jmiSave = new JMenuItem("Save");
JMenuItem jmiExit = new JMenuItem("Exit");
jmFile.add(jmiOpen);
jmFile.add(jmiClose);
jmFile.add(jmiSave);
jmFile.addSeparator();
jmFile.add(jmiExit);
jmb.add(jmFile);

// Create the Options menu.
JMenu jmOptions = new JMenu("Options");

// Create the Colors submenu.
jmColors = new JMenu("Colors");
JMenuItem jmiRed = new JMenuItem("Red");
JMenuItem jmiGreen = new JMenuItem("Green");
JMenuItem jmiBlue = new JMenuItem("Blue");
jmColors.add(jmiRed);
jmColors.add(jmiGreen);
jmColors.add(jmiBlue);

// Create the More/Less Colors Menu item.
JMenuItem jmiMoreLess = new JMenuItem("More Colors");
jmColors.add(jmiMoreLess);

// Add Colors menu to the Options menu.
jmOptions.add(jmColors);

// Create the additional colors. These will be
// added or removed on demand.
jmiYellow = new JMenuItem("Yellow");
jmiPurple = new JMenuItem("Purple");
jmiOrange = new JMenuItem("Orange");
```

```
// Create the Priority submenu.
JMenu jmPriority = new JMenu("Priority");
JMenuItem jmiHigh = new JMenuItem("High");
JMenuItem jmiLow = new JMenuItem("Low");
jmPriority.add(jmiHigh);
jmPriority.add(jmiLow);

// Add the Priority menu to the Options menu.
jmOptions.add(jmPriority);

// Create the Reset menu item.
JMenuItem jmiReset = new JMenuItem("Reset");
jmOptions.addSeparator();
jmOptions.add(jmiReset);

// Finally, add the entire Options menu to
// the menu bar.
jmb.add(jmOptions);

// Create the Help menu.
JMenu jmHelp = new JMenu("Help");
JMenuItem jmiAbout = new JMenuItem("About");
jmHelp.add(jmiAbout);
jmb.add(jmHelp);

// Add action listeners for the menu items.
jmiOpen.addActionListener(this);
jmiClose.addActionListener(this);
jmiSave.addActionListener(this);
jmiExit.addActionListener(this);
jmiRed.addActionListener(this);
jmiGreen.addActionListener(this);
jmiBlue.addActionListener(this);
jmiHigh.addActionListener(this);
jmiLow.addActionListener(this);
jmiReset.addActionListener(this);
jmiAbout.addActionListener(this);

// Add listeners for the additional
// colors option.
jmiMoreLess.addActionListener(this);
jmiYellow.addActionListener(this);
jmiPurple.addActionListener(this);
jmiOrange.addActionListener(this);
```

(continued)

```java
      // Add the label to the content pane.
      jfrm.getContentPane().add(jlab);

      // Add the menu bar to the frame.
      jfrm.setJMenuBar(jmb);

      // Display the frame.
      jfrm.setVisible(true);
    }

    // Handle menu item action events.
    public void actionPerformed(ActionEvent ae) {
      // Get the action command from the menu selection.
      String comStr = ae.getActionCommand();

      // If user chooses Exit, then exit the program.
      if(comStr.equals("Exit"))
        System.exit(0);
      else if(comStr.equals("More Colors")) {
        jmColors.add(jmiYellow);
        jmColors.add(jmiPurple);
        jmColors.add(jmiOrange);
        JMenuItem mi = (JMenuItem) ae.getSource();
        mi.setText("Less Colors");
      } else if(comStr.equals("Less Colors")) {
        jmColors.remove(jmiYellow);
        jmColors.remove(jmiPurple);
        jmColors.remove(jmiOrange);
        JMenuItem mi = (JMenuItem) ae.getSource();
        mi.setText("More Colors");
      }

      // Otherwise, display the selection.
      jlab.setText(comStr + " Selected");
    }

    public static void main(String args[]) {
      // Create the frame on the event dispatching thread.
      SwingUtilities.invokeLater(new Runnable() {
        public void run() {
          new DynMenuDemo();
        }
      });
    }
  }
```

CRITICAL SKILL
7.6 Use JRadioButtonMenuItem and JCheckBoxMenuItem

Although the types of menu items used by the preceding examples are the most common, Swing defines two others: check boxes and radio buttons. These items can streamline a GUI by allowing a menu to provide functionality that would otherwise require additional, stand-alone components. Also, sometimes including check boxes or radio buttons in a menu simply seems the most natural place for a specific set of features. Whatever your reason, Swing makes it easy to use check boxes and radio buttons in menus, and both are examined here.

To add a check box to a menu, create a **JCheckBoxMenuItem**. Its constructors are shown in Table 7-4. **JCheckBoxMenuItemCheck** inherits **JMenuItem**. Check boxes in menus work like stand-alone check boxes. For example, they generate action events and item events when

Constructor	Description
JCheckBoxMenuItem( )	Creates a check box menu item that has neither a name nor an image associated with it.
JCheckBoxMenuItem(String *name*)	Creates a check box menu item that is associated with the name specified by *name*.
JCheckBoxMenuItem(Icon *icon*)	Creates a check box menu item that is associated with the image passed in *icon*.
JCheckBoxMenuItem(String *name*, boolean *state*)	Creates a check box menu item that is associated with the name passed in *name*. If *state* is true, the box is initially checked. Otherwise, it is cleared.
JCheckBoxMenuItem(String *name*, Icon *icon*)	Creates a check box menu item that is associated with the name passed in *name* and the image passed in *icon*.
JCheckBoxMenuItem(String *name*, Icon *icon*, boolean *state*)	Creates a check box that is associated with the name passed in *name* and the image passed in *icon*. If *state* is true, the box is initially checked. Otherwise, it is cleared.
JCheckBoxMenuItem(Action *act*)	Creates a check box menu item whose name, image, and other properties are defined by the object passed in *act*.

Table 7-4 The **JCheckBoxMenuItem** Constructors

their state changes. Check boxes are especially useful in menus when you have options that can be selected and you want to display their selected/deselected status.

A radio button can be added to a menu by creating an object of type **JRadioButtonMenuItem**. Its constructors are shown in Table 7-5. **JRadioButtonMenuItem** inherits **JMenuItem**. It works like a stand-alone radio button, generating item and action events. Like stand-alone radio buttons, menu-based radio buttons must be put into a button group in order for them to exhibit mutually exclusive selection behavior.

To try check box and radio button menu items, first remove the code that creates the Options menu in the **MenuDemo** example program. Then substitute the following code sequence, which uses check boxes for the Colors submenu and radio buttons for the Priority submenu. After making the substitution, the Options menu will look like those shown in Figure 7-4.

Constructor	Description
JRadioButtonMenuItem( )	Creates a radio button menu item that has neither a name nor an image associated with it.
JRadioButtonMenuItem(String *name*)	Creates a radio button menu item that is associated with the name passed in *name*.
JRadioButtonMenuItem(Icon *icon*)	Creates a radio button menu item that is associated with the image passed in *icon*.
JRadioButtonMenuItem(String *name*, boolean *state*)	Creates a radio button menu item that is associated with the name passed in *name*. If *state* is true, the button is initially selected. Otherwise, it is deselected.
JRadioButtonMenuItem(Icon *icon*, boolean *state*)	Creates a radio button menu item that is associated with the image passed in *icon*. If *state* is true, the button is initially selected. Otherwise, it is deselected.
JRadioButtonMenuItem(String *name*, Icon *icon*)	Creates a radio button menu item that is associated with the name passed in *name* and the image passed in *icon*.
JRadioButtonMenuItem(String *name*, Icon *icon*, boolean *state*)	Creates a radio button menu item that is associated with the name passed in *name* and the image passed in *icon*. If *state* is true, the button is initially selected. Otherwise, it is deselected.
JRadioButtonMenuItem(Action *act*)	Creates a check box menu item whose name, image, and other properties are defined by the object passed in *act*.

Table 7-5 The **JRadioButtonMenuItem** Constructors

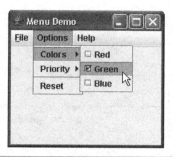 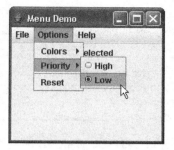

Figure 7-4 The effects of check box and radio button menu items

```
// Create the Options menu.
JMenu jmOptions = new JMenu("Options");

// Create the Colors submenu.
JMenu jmColors = new JMenu("Colors");

// Use check boxes for colors. This allows
// the user to select more than one color.
JCheckBoxMenuItem jmiRed = new JCheckBoxMenuItem("Red");
JCheckBoxMenuItem jmiGreen = new JCheckBoxMenuItem("Green");
JCheckBoxMenuItem jmiBlue = new JCheckBoxMenuItem("Blue");

jmColors.add(jmiRed);
jmColors.add(jmiGreen);
jmColors.add(jmiBlue);
jmOptions.add(jmColors);

// Create the Priority submenu.
JMenu jmPriority = new JMenu("Priority");

// Use radio buttons for the priority setting.
// This lets the menu show which priority is used
// but also ensures that one and only one priority
// can be selected at any one time. Notice that
// the High radio button is initially selected.
JRadioButtonMenuItem jmiHigh =
  new JRadioButtonMenuItem("High", true);
JRadioButtonMenuItem jmiLow =
  new JRadioButtonMenuItem("Low");
```

Use check boxes for the colors.

Use radio buttons for the priorities.

```
jmPriority.add(jmiHigh);
jmPriority.add(jmiLow);
jmOptions.add(jmPriority);

// Create button group for the radio button menu items.
ButtonGroup bg = new ButtonGroup();
bg.add(jmiHigh);
bg.add(jmiLow);
```

Put the Priority radio buttons into a button group.

```
// Create the Reset menu item.
JMenuItem jmiReset = new JMenuItem("Reset");
jmOptions.addSeparator();
jmOptions.add(jmiReset);

// Finally, add the entire Options menu to
// the menu bar.
jmb.add(jmOptions);
```

Progress Check

1. What class creates a check box menu item?

2. When **JRadioButtonMenuItem**s are added to a menu, they are automatically part of a button group. True or false?

Create a Popup Menu

A popular alternative or addition to the menu bar is the popup menu. Typically, a popup menu is activated by clicking the right mouse button when over a component. Popup menus are supported in Swing by the **JPopupMenu** class. The **JPopupMenu** constructors are shown in Table 7-6.

In general, popup menus are constructed like regular menus. First create a **JPopupMenu** object and then add menu items to it. Menu item selections are also handled in the same way: by listening for action events. The main difference between a popup menu and regular menu is the activation process.

---

1. **JCheckBoxMenuItem**
2. False. You must explicitly put radio button menu items in a button group.

Constructor	Description
JPopupMenu( )	Creates a default popup menu.
JPopupMenu(String *name*)	Creates a popup menu that has the title specified by *name*. Whether this title is displayed is subject to the look and feel.

Table 7-6 The **JPopupMenu** Constructors

Activating a popup menu requires three steps:

1. You must register a listener for mouse events.

2. Inside the mouse event handler, you must watch for the popup trigger.

3. When a popup trigger is received, you must show the popup menu by calling **show( )**.

Let's examine each of these steps closely.

A popup menu is normally activated by clicking the right mouse button when the mouse pointer is over a component for which a popup menu is defined. Thus, the *popup trigger* is usually caused by right-clicking the mouse on a popup menu–enabled component. To listen for the popup trigger, your program must implement the **MouseListener** interface and then register the listener by calling the **addMouseListener( )** method. **MouseListener** defines the methods shown here:

void mouseClicked(MouseEvent *me*)

void mouseEntered(MouseEvent *me*)

void mouseExited(MouseEvent *me*)

void mousePressed(MouseEvent *me*)

void mouseReleased(MouseEvent *me*)

Of these, the only two that matter relative to the popup are **mousePressed( )** and **mouseReleased( )** because, depending on the installed look and feel, either of these two events can trigger a popup menu. Because (relative to popup menus) the other three handlers are not important, it is generally easier to use a **MouseAdapater** to implement the **MouseListener** interface and simply override **mousePressed( )** and **mouseReleased( )**.

The **MouseEvent** class defines several methods, but only four are essential to activating a popup menu. They are shown here:

int getX( )

int getY( )

boolean isPopupTrigger( )

Component getComponent( )

The current X,Y location of the mouse relative to the source of the event is found by calling **getX( )** and **getY( )**. These will be used to specify the upper left corner of the popup menu when it is displayed. The **isPopupTrigger( )** method returns true if the mouse event represents a popup trigger and false otherwise. You will use this method to determine when to pop up the menu. To obtain a reference to the component that generated the mouse event, call **getComponent( )**.

To actually display the popup menu, call the **show( )** method defined by **JPopupMenu**. It is shown here:

void show(Component *invoker*, int *upperX*, int *upperY*)

Here, *invoker* is the component relative to which the menu will be displayed. The values of *upperX* and *upperY* define the X,Y location of the upper left corner of the menu, relative to *invoker*. A common way to obtain the invoker is to call **getComponent( )** on the event object passed to the mouse event handler.

Let's put the preceding theory into practice by adding a popup Edit menu to the **MenuDemo** program shown at the start of this module. This menu will have three items called Cut, Copy, and Paste. Begin by adding the following instance variable to **MenuDemo**:

```
JPopupMenu jpu;
```

The **jpu** variable will hold a reference to the popup menu.

Next, add the following code sequence to the **MenuDemo** constructor:

```
// Create an Edit popup menu.
jpu = new JPopupMenu();          ←——————— Create a popup menu.

// Create the popup menu items
JMenuItem jmiCut = new JMenuItem("Cut");
JMenuItem jmiCopy = new JMenuItem("Copy");       ┐—— Create the menu items
JMenuItem jmiPaste = new JMenuItem("Paste");     ┘   for the popup menu.
```

```
// Add the menu items to the popup menu.
jpu.add(jmiCut);
jpu.add(jmiCopy);                      Add the items to the popup menu.
jpu.add(jmiPaste);

// Add a listener for the popup trigger.            Watch for the popup trigger.
jfrm.getContentPane().addMouseListener(new MouseAdapter() {
  public void mousePressed(MouseEvent me) {
    if(me.isPopupTrigger())
      jpu.show(me.getComponent(), me.getX(), me.getY());
  }
  public void mouseReleased(MouseEvent me) {
    if(me.isPopupTrigger())
      jpu.show(me.getComponent(), me.getX(), me.getY());
  }
});
```

This sequence begins by constructing an instance of **JPopupMenu** and storing it in **jpu**. Then, it creates the three menu items, Cut, Copy, and Paste, in the usual way and adds them to **jpu**. This finishes the construction of the popup Edit menu. Popup menus are not added to the menu bar or any other object.

Next, a **MouseListener** is added by creating an anonymous inner class. This class is based on the **MouseAdapter** class, which means that the listener need only override those methods that are relevant to the popup menu: **mousePressed( )** and **mouseReleased( )**. The adapter provides default implementations of the other **MouseListener** methods. Notice that the mouse listener is added to the content pane of **jfrm**. This means that a right-button click inside any part of the content pane will trigger the popup menu.

The **mousePressed( )** and **mouseReleased( )** methods call **isPopupTrigger( )** to determine if the mouse event is a popup trigger event. If it is, the popup menu is displayed by calling **show( )**. The invoker is obtained by calling **getComponent( )** on the mouse event. In this case, the invoker will be the content pane. The X,Y coordinates of the upper left corner are obtained by calling **getX( )** and **getY( )**. This makes the menu pop up with its upper left corner directly under the mouse pointer.

Finally, you will also need to add these action listeners to the program. They handle the action events fired when the user selects an item from the popup menu.

```
jmiCut.addActionListener(this);
jmiCopy.addActionListener(this);
jmiPaste.addActionListener(this);
```

After you have made these additions, the popup menu can be activated by clicking the right mouse button anywhere inside the content pane of the application. Figure 7-5 shows the result.

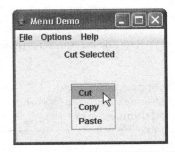

Figure 7-5 A popup Edit menu

Progress Check

1. To use a popup menu, your program must listen for _____ events.

2. What does **isPopupTrigger( )** do?

3. What **JPopupMenu** method do you call to pop up the menu?

Ask the Expert

Q: You used getComponent( ) to obtain the component in whose space the popup menu would be invoked. However, since in your example this will always be the content pane, can you explicitly pass the content pane?

A: Yes. If you make **jfrm** into an instance variable of the **MenuDemo** class (rather than a local variable) so that it's accessible to an inner class, then you can use this call to **show( )** to display the popup menu:

```
jpu.show(jfrm.getContentPane(), me.getX(), me.getY());
```

The advantage of using **getComponent( )** is that the popup menu will automatically pop up relative to the invoking component. Thus, if the **checkPU( )** method was moved outside of the anonymous inner class, it could be used to display any popup menu relative to its invoking object.

---

1. mouse

2. **isPopupTrigger( )** determines if a mouse event is a popup trigger.

3. **show( )**

CRITICAL SKILL

 7.8 Create a Toolbar

A toolbar is a component that can serve as both an alternative and as an adjunct to a menu. A toolbar contains a list of buttons (or other components) that give the user immediate access to various program options. For example, a toolbar might contain buttons that select various font options, such as bold, italic, highlighted, or underlined. These options can be selected without the need to drop through a menu. Typically, toolbar buttons show icons rather than text, although either or both are allowed. Furthermore, tooltips are often associated with icon-based toolbar buttons. Toolbars can be positioned on any side of a window by dragging the toolbar, or they can be dragged out of the window entirely, in which case they become free floating. In Swing, toolbars are instances of the **JToolBar** class. Its constructors are shown in Table 7-7. A toolbar is typically used with a window that uses a border layout. There are two reasons for this. First, it allows the toolbar to be initially positioned along one of the four border positions. Frequently, the top position is used. Second, it allows the toolbar to be dragged to any side of the window.

In addition to dragging the toolbar to different locations within a window, you can also drag it out of the window. Doing so creates an *undocked* toolbar. If you specify a title when you create the toolbar, then that title will be shown when the toolbar is undocked.

You add buttons (or other components) to a toolbar in much the same way that you add them to a menu bar. Simply call **add( )**. The components are shown in the toolbar in the order in which they are added.

Once you have created a toolbar, you *do not* add it to the menu bar (if one exists). Instead, you add it to the window container. As mentioned, you will typically add a toolbar to the top (that is, north) position of a border layout. The component that it will be affecting is added to the center of the border layout. Using this approach causes the program to begin running with the toolbar in the expected location. However, you can drag the toolbar to any of the

Constructor	Description
JToolBar( )	Creates a horizontal toolbar with no title.
JToolBar(String *title*)	Creates a horizontal toolbar with the title specified by *title*. The title will show only when the toolbar is dragged out of its window.
JToolBar(int *how*)	Creates a toolbar that is oriented as specified by *how*. The value of *how* must be either **JToolBar.VERTICAL** or **JToolBar.HORIZONTAL**.
JToolBar(String *title*, int *how*)	Creates a toolbar that has the title specified by *title* and is oriented as specified by *how*. The value of *how* must be either **JToolBar.VERTICAL** or **JToolBar.HORIZONTAL**.

Table 7-7 The Constructors for **JToolBar**

other four positions. In all cases, the component being affected remains in the center. Of course, you can also drag the toolbar out of the window.

To illustrate the toolbar, we will add one to the **MenuDemo** program that we have been working with. The toolbar will support three debugging options: set a breakpoint, clear a breakpoint, and resume program execution. Three steps are needed to add the toolbar.

First, remove this line from the program:

```
jfrm.getContentPane().setLayout(new FlowLayout());
```

By removing this line, the **JFrame** will automatically use border layout.

Second, since **BorderLayout** is being used, change the line that adds the label **jlab** to the frame, as shown next:

```
jfrm.getContentPane().add(jlab, BorderLayout.CENTER);
```

This line explicitly adds **jlab** to the center of the border layout. (Explicitly specifying the center position is technically not necessary because, by default, components are added to the center when a border layout is used. However, explicitly specifying the center makes it clear to anyone reading the code that a border layout is being used and that **jlab** goes in the center.)

Next, add the following code, which creates the Debug toolbar:

```
// Create a Debug toolbar.
JToolBar jtb = new JToolBar("Debug");          ◄──────── Create a toolbar.

// Load the images.
ImageIcon set = new ImageIcon("setBP.gif");
ImageIcon clear = new ImageIcon("clearBP.gif");        ─── Load images for the
ImageIcon resume = new ImageIcon("resume.gif");            toolbar buttons.

// Create the toolbar buttons.
JButton jbtnSet = new JButton(set);
jbtnSet.setActionCommand("Set Breakpoint");
jbtnSet.setToolTipText("Set Breakpoint");

JButton jbtnClear = new JButton(clear);
jbtnClear.setActionCommand("Clear Breakpoint");        ─── Using the images, construct the
jbtnClear.setToolTipText("Clear Breakpoint");              buttons that will be shown in
                                                           the toolbar. Also, set the action
JButton jbtnResume = new JButton(resume);                  command and tooltip text.
jbtnResume.setActionCommand("Resume");
jbtnResume.setToolTipText("Resume");
```

```
// Add the buttons to the toolbar.
jtb.add(jbtnSet);   ┐
jtb.add(jbtnClear);  ├──────── Add the buttons to the toolbar.
jtb.add(jbtnResume); ┘
```

Add the toolbar to the north
side of the content pane.

```
// Add the toolbar to the north position of
// the content pane.
jfrm.getContentPane().add(jtb, BorderLayout.NORTH);  ◄┐
```

Let's look at this code closely. First, a **JToolBar** is created and given the title "Debug."
Then, a set of **ImageIcon** objects are created that hold the images for the toolbar buttons.
Next, three toolbar buttons are created. Notice that each has an image, but no text. Also, each
is explicitly given an action command and a tooltip. The action commands are set because the
buttons are not given names when they are constructed. Tooltips are especially useful when
applied to icon-based toolbar components because sometimes it's hard to design images that
are intuitive to all users. The buttons are then added to the toolbar, and the toolbar is added to
the north side of the border layout of the frame.

Finally, add the action listeners for the toolbar, as shown here:

```
// Add the toolbar action listeners.
jbtnSet.addActionListener(this);
jbtnClear.addActionListener(this);
jbtnResume.addActionListener(this);
```

Each time the user presses a toolbar button, an action event is fired and it is handled in the
same way as the other menu-related events. Figure 7-6 shows the toolbar in action.

Figure 7-6 The Debug toolbar in action

Some Toolbar Options

JToolBar supports several useful options. For example, you can add a separator to a toolbar by calling the **addSeparator( )** method. It has two forms and both are shown here:

void addSeparator( )

void addSeparator(Dimension *dim*)

The first adds a separator whose size is defined by the look and feel. The second lets you specify the size.

You can prevent the toolbar from being moved by calling **setFloatable( )**, shown next:

void setFloatable(boolean *canFloat*)

Here, if *canFloat* is true, the toolbar can be moved. If *canFloat* is false, the toolbar is fixed. The default state is floatable.

You can specify the rollover action by calling **setRollover( )**, shown here:

void setRollover(boolean *on*)

If *on* is true, then the toolbar buttons will change their visual state when rolled over by the mouse. If *on* is false, the rollover effect is disabled. The rollover property can be ignored by a look and feel.

Progress Check

1. A toolbar should never duplicate functionality found in a menu. True or false?

2. The frame that holds a toolbar will normally use what type of layout manager?

3. How do you prevent a toolbar from being dragged to a new location?

---

1. False, toolbars often duplicate functionality found in a menu.
2. **BorderLayout**, with the toolbar being located on the **NORTH**
3. Call **setFloatable(false)**.

CRITICAL SKILL

7.9 Use Actions

It is quite common for a toolbar and a menu item to contain items in common. For example, the same functions provided by the Debug toolbar in the preceding example might also be offered through a menu selection. In such a case, selecting an option (such as setting a breakpoint) causes the same action to occur, independently of whether the menu or the toolbar was used. Also, both the toolbar button and the menu item would (most likely) use the same icon. Furthermore, when a toolbar button is disabled, the corresponding menu item would also need to be disabled. Such a situation would normally lead to a fair amount of duplicated, interdependent code, which is less than optimal. Fortunately, Swing provides a solution: the *action*.

An action is an instance of the **Action** interface. **Action** extends the **ActionListener** interface and provides a means of combining state information with the **actionPerformed( )** event handler. This combination allows one action to manage two or more components. For example, an action lets you centralize the control and handling of a toolbar button and a menu item. Instead of having to duplicate code, your program need only create an action that automatically handles both components.

An action encapsulates the following properties:

- The accelerator key
- The mnemonic key
- The name
- The icon
- The tooltip text
- A long description
- The action command string
- The enabled/disabled status

These properties define the state information of an action.

As mentioned, **Action** extends **ActionListener**. Thus, an action must also provide an implementation of the **actionPerformed( )** method. This handler will process the action events generated by the objects linked to the action.

In addition to the inherited **actionPerformed( )** method, **Action** defines several methods of its own. They are shown in Table 7-8. Notice the methods **putValue( )** and **getValue( )**.

Method	Description
void addPropertyChangeListener(PropertyChangeListerner *pcl*)	Adds the property change listener specified by *pcl*.
Object getValue(String *key*)	Returns a reference to the property specified by *key*.
boolean isEnabled( )	Returns true if the action is enabled and false otherwise.
void putValue(String *key*, Object *val*)	Assigns *val* to the property specified by *key*.
void removePropertyChangeListener(PropertyChangeListener *pcl*)	Removes the property change listener specified by *pcl*.
void setEnabled(boolean *enabled*)	If *enabled* is true, the action is enabled. If *enabled* is false, the action is disabled.

Table 7-8 The Methods Defined by **Action**

These methods set or get the value of the various properties associated with an action. They operate by specifying a *key* that represents the desired property. The key values are shown in Table 7-9. For example, to set the mnemonic to the letter X, use this call to **putValue( )**:

```
actionOb.putValue(MNEMONIC_KEY, new Integer(KeyEvent.VK_X));
```

Action Key	Description
static String ACCELERATOR_KEY	Represents the accelerator property. Accelerators are specified as **KeyStroke** objects.
static String ACTION_COMMAND_KEY	Represents the action command property. An action command is specified as a string.
static String DEFAULT	Not used.
static String LONG_DESCRIPTION	Represents a long description of the action. This description is specified as a string.
static String MNEMONIC_KEY	Represents the mnemonic property. A mnemonic is specified as a **KeyEvent** constant.
static String NAME	Represents the name of the action (which also becomes the name of the button or menu item to which the action is linked). The name is specified as a string.
static String SHORT_DESCRIPTION	Represents the tooltip text associated with the action. The tooltip text is specified as a string.
static String SMALL_ICON	Represents the icon associated with the action. The icon is specified as an object of type **Icon**.

Table 7-9 The Keys Associated with **Action**

The only **Action** property that is not accessible through **putValue( )** and **getValue( )** is the enabled/disabled status. For this, you will use the **setEnabled( )** and **isEnabled( )** methods. Notice that **Action** includes support for **PropertyChangeEvent**. Any class that implements **Action** must throw this event whenever the state of the action properties change.

Although you can implement all of the **Action** interface yourself, you won't usually need to. Instead, Swing provides a partial implementation called **AbstractAction** which you can extend. By extending **AbstractAction**, you need implement only one method: **actionPerformed( )**. The other **Action** methods are provided for you. **AbstractAction** provides the constructors shown in Table 7-10.

Once you have created an action, it can be added to a **JToolBar** and used to construct a **JMenuItem**. To add an action to a **JToolBar**, use this version of **add( )**:

void add(Action *actObj*)

Here, *actObj* is the action that is being added to the toolbar. The properties defined by *actObj* are used to create a toolbar button. To create a menu item from an action, use this constructor:

JMenuItem(Action *actObj*)

Here, *actObj* is the action used to construct a menu item according to its properties.

NOTE

In addition to **JToolBar** and **JMenuItem**, actions are also supported by several other Swing components, such as **JPopupMenu**, **JButton**, **JRadioButton**, and **JCheckBox**. **JRadioButtonMenuItem** and **JCheckBoxMenuItem** also support actions.

To illustrate the benefit of actions, we will use them to manage the Debug toolbar created in the previous section. We will also add a Debug submenu under the Options main menu. The Debug submenu will contain the same selections as the Debug toolbar: Set Breakpoint, Clear Breakpoint, and Resume. The same actions that support these items in the toolbar will also

Constructor	Description
AbstractAction( )	Constructs a default object.
AbstractAction(String *name*)	Constructs an **AbstractAction** that has the name specified by *name*.
AbstractAction(String *name*, Icon *image*)	Constructs an **AbstractAction** that has the name specified by *name* and the icon specified by *image*.

Table 7-10 The Constructors for **AbstractAction**

support these items in the menu. Therefore, instead of having to create duplicate code to handle both the toolbar and menu, both are handled by the actions.

Begin by creating an inner class called **DebugAction** that extends **AbstractAction**, as shown here:

```
// A class to create an action for the Debug menu
// and toolbar.
class DebugAction extends AbstractAction {
  public DebugAction(String name, Icon image, int mnem,
                     int accel, String tTip) {
    super(name, image);
    putValue(ACCELERATOR_KEY,
             KeyStroke.getKeyStroke(accel,
                                    InputEvent.CTRL_MASK));
    putValue(MNEMONIC_KEY, new Integer(mnem));
    putValue(SHORT_DESCRIPTION, tTip);
  }

  // Handle events for both the toolbar and the
  // Debug menu.
  public void actionPerformed(ActionEvent ae) {
    String comStr = ae.getActionCommand();

    jlab.setText(comStr + " Selected");

    // Toggle the enabled status of the
    // Set and Clear Breakpoint options.
    if(comStr.equals("Set Breakpoint")) {
      clearAct.setEnabled(true);
      setAct.setEnabled(false);
    } else if(comStr.equals("Clear Breakpoint")) {
      clearAct.setEnabled(false);
      setAct.setEnabled(true);
    }
  }
}
```

Create an **Action** class that manages toolbar and menu items.

Handle action events for **DebugAction**.

DebugAction extends **AbstractAction**. It creates an action class that will be used to define the properties associated with the Debug menu and toolbar. Its constructor has five parameters that let you specify the following items:

- Name
- Icon
- Mnemonic

- Accelerator

- Tooltip

The first two are passed to **AbstractAction**'s constructor via **super**. The other three properties are set through calls to **putValue( )**.

The **actionPerformed( )** method of **DebugAction** handles events for the action. This means that when an instance of **DebugAction** is used to create a toolbar button and a menu item, events generated by either of those components are handled by the **actionPerformed( )** method in **DebugAction**. Notice that this handler displays the selection in **jlab**. In addition, if the Set Breakpoint option is selected, then the Clear Breakpoint option is enabled and the Set Breakpoint option is disabled. If the Clear Breakpoint option is selected, then the Set Breakpoint option is enabled and the Clear Breakpoint option is disabled. This illustrates how an action can be used to enable or disable a component. When an action is disabled, it is disabled for all uses of that action. In this case, if Set Breakpoint is disabled, then it is disabled both in the toolbar and in the menu.

Next, add these **DebugAction** instance variables to **MenuDemo**:

```
DebugAction setAct;
DebugAction clearAct;
DebugAction resumeAct;
```

Next, create three **ImageIcon**s that represent the Debug options, as shown here:

```
// Load the images for the actions.
ImageIcon setIcon = new ImageIcon("setBP.gif");
ImageIcon clearIcon = new ImageIcon("clearBP.gif");
ImageIcon resumeIcon = new ImageIcon("resume.gif");
```

Now, create the actions that manage the Debug options, as shown here:

```
// Create actions.
setAct =
  new DebugAction("Set Breakpoint",
                  setIcon,
                  KeyEvent.VK_S,
                  KeyEvent.VK_B,
                  "Set a breakpoint.");

clearAct =
  new DebugAction("Clear Breakpoint",
                  clearIcon,
                  KeyEvent.VK_C,
                  KeyEvent.VK_L,
                  "Clear a breakpoint.");
```

Create the actions used by the Debug toolbar and menu.

```
resumeAct =
  new DebugAction("Resume",
                  resumeIcon,
                  KeyEvent.VK_R,
                  KeyEvent.VK_R,
                  "Resume execution after breakpoint.");

// Initially disable the Clear Breakpoint option.
clearAct.setEnabled(false);  ◄──────── Initially, disable the Clear Breakpoint option.
```

Notice that the accelerator for Set Breakpoint is *B* and the accelerator for Clear Breakpoint is *L*. The reason these keys are used rather than *S* and *C* is that these keys are already allocated by the File menu for Save and Close. However, they can still be used as mnemonics because each mnemonic is localized to its own menu. Also notice that the action that represents Clear Breakpoint is initially disabled. It will be enabled only after a breakpoint has been set.

Next, use the actions to create buttons for the toolbar and then add those buttons to the toolbar, as shown here:

```
// Create the toolbar buttons by using the actions.
JButton jbtnSet = new JButton(setAct);
JButton jbtnClear = new JButton(clearAct);     ─── Create the toolbar buttons
JButton jbtnResume = new JButton(resumeAct);        using the actions.

// Create a Debug toolbar.
JToolBar jtb = new JToolBar("Breakpoints");

// Add the buttons to the toolbar.
jtb.add(jbtnSet);
jtb.add(jbtnClear);
jtb.add(jbtnResume);

// Add the toolbar to the north position of
// the content pane.
jfrm.getContentPane().add(jtb, BorderLayout.NORTH);
```

Finally, create the Debug menu, as shown next:

```
// Now, create a Debug menu that goes under the Options
// menu bar item. Use the actions to create the items.
JMenu jmDebug = new JMenu("Debug");
JMenuItem jmiSetBP = new JMenuItem(setAct);
JMenuItem jmiClearBP = new JMenuItem(clearAct);   ─── Create the Debug menu
JMenuItem jmiResume = new JMenuItem(resumeAct);        items using the actions.
```

```
jmDebug.add(jmiSetBP);
jmDebug.add(jmiClearBP);
jmDebug.add(jmiResume);
jmOptions.add(jmDebug);
```

After making these changes and additions, the actions that you created will be used to manage both the Debug menu and the toolbar. Thus, changing a property in the action (such as disabling it) will affect all uses of that action. The program will now look as shown in Figure 7-7.

Progress Check

1. In what type of circumstance is an action used?

2. What class defines a partial implementation of the **Action** interface?

3. If you disable an action, will all components based on that action also be disabled?

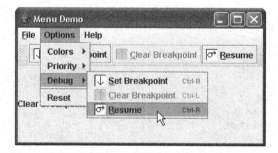

Figure 7-7   Using actions to manage the Debug toolbar and menu

---

1. An action should be used when two or more components access the same functionality, such as when a menu item and a toolbar button both do the same thing.

2. **AbstractAction**

3. Yes

Put the Entire MenuDemo Program Together

Throughout the course of this discussion you have been making many changes and additions to the **MenuDemo** program shown at the start of the module. Before concluding, it will be helpful to assemble all the pieces. Doing so not only eliminates any ambiguity about the way the pieces fit together, but it gives you a complete menu demonstration program that you can experiment with.

The following version of **MenuDemo** includes all of the additions and enhancements described in this module. For clarity, the program has been reorganized, with separate methods being used to construct the various menus and toolbar. Notice that several of the menu-related variables, such as **jmb**, **jmFile**, and **jtb**, have been made into instance variables.

```java
// The complete MenuDemo program.

import java.awt.*;
import java.awt.event.*;
import javax.swing.*;

class MenuDemo implements ActionListener {

  JLabel jlab;

  JMenuBar jmb;

  JToolBar jtb;

  JPopupMenu jpu;

  DebugAction setAct;
  DebugAction clearAct;
  DebugAction resumeAct;

  MenuDemo() {
    // Create a new JFrame container.
    JFrame jfrm = new JFrame("Complete Menu Demo");

    // Use default border layout.

    // Give the frame an initial size.
    jfrm.setSize(360, 200);

    // Terminate the program when the user closes the application.
    jfrm.setDefaultCloseOperation(JFrame.EXIT_ON_CLOSE);
```

```java
// Create a label that will display the menu selection.
jlab = new JLabel();

// Create the menu bar.
jmb = new JMenuBar();

// Create the File menu.
makeFileMenu();

// Construct the Debug actions.
makeActions();

// Create the toolbar.
makeToolBar();

// Create the Options menu.
makeOptionsMenu();

// Create the Help menu.
makeHelpMenu();

// Create the Edit popup menu.
makeEditPUMenu();

// Add a listener for the popup trigger.
jfrm.getContentPane().addMouseListener(new MouseAdapter() {
  public void mousePressed(MouseEvent me) {
    if(me.isPopupTrigger())
      jpu.show(me.getComponent(), me.getX(), me.getY());
  }
  public void mouseReleased(MouseEvent me) {
    if(me.isPopupTrigger())
      jpu.show(me.getComponent(), me.getX(), me.getY());
  }
});

// Add the label to the center of the content pane.
jfrm.getContentPane().add(jlab, SwingConstants.CENTER);

// Add the toolbar to the north position of
// the content pane.
jfrm.getContentPane().add(jtb, BorderLayout.NORTH);

// Add the menu bar to the frame.
jfrm.setJMenuBar(jmb);
```

```java
      // Display the frame.
      jfrm.setVisible(true);
    }

    // Handle menu item action events.
    // This does NOT handle events generated
    // by the Debug options.
    public void actionPerformed(ActionEvent ae) {
      // Get the action command from the menu selection.
      String comStr = ae.getActionCommand();

      // If user chooses Exit, then exit the program.
      if(comStr.equals("Exit")) System.exit(0);

      // Otherwise, display the selection.
      jlab.setText(comStr + " Selected");
    }

    // An action class for the Debug menu
    // and toolbar.
    class DebugAction extends AbstractAction {
      public DebugAction(String name, Icon image, int mnem,
                         int accel, String tTip) {
        super(name, image);
        putValue(ACCELERATOR_KEY,
                 KeyStroke.getKeyStroke(accel,
                                        InputEvent.CTRL_MASK));
        putValue(MNEMONIC_KEY, new Integer(mnem));
        putValue(SHORT_DESCRIPTION, tTip);
      }

      // Handle events for both the toolbar and the
      // Debug menu.
      public void actionPerformed(ActionEvent ae) {
        String comStr = ae.getActionCommand();

        jlab.setText(comStr + " Selected");

        // Toggle the enabled status of the
        // Set and Clear Breakpoint options.
        if(comStr.equals("Set Breakpoint")) {
          clearAct.setEnabled(true);
          setAct.setEnabled(false);
        } else if(comStr.equals("Clear Breakpoint")) {
          clearAct.setEnabled(false);
          setAct.setEnabled(true);
```

```java
      }
    }
  }

  // Create the File menu with mnemonics and accelerators.
  void makeFileMenu() {
    JMenu jmFile = new JMenu("File");
    jmFile.setMnemonic(KeyEvent.VK_F);

    JMenuItem jmiOpen = new JMenuItem("Open",
                                     KeyEvent.VK_O);
    jmiOpen.setAccelerator(
           KeyStroke.getKeyStroke(KeyEvent.VK_O,
                                  InputEvent.CTRL_MASK));

    JMenuItem jmiClose = new JMenuItem("Close",
                                     KeyEvent.VK_C);
    jmiClose.setAccelerator(
           KeyStroke.getKeyStroke(KeyEvent.VK_C,
                                  InputEvent.CTRL_MASK));

    JMenuItem jmiSave = new JMenuItem("Save",
                                     KeyEvent.VK_S);
    jmiSave.setAccelerator(
           KeyStroke.getKeyStroke(KeyEvent.VK_S,
                                  InputEvent.CTRL_MASK));

    JMenuItem jmiExit = new JMenuItem("Exit",
                                     KeyEvent.VK_E);
    jmiExit.setAccelerator(
           KeyStroke.getKeyStroke(KeyEvent.VK_E,
                                  InputEvent.CTRL_MASK));

    jmFile.add(jmiOpen);
    jmFile.add(jmiClose);
    jmFile.add(jmiSave);
    jmFile.addSeparator();
    jmFile.add(jmiExit);
    jmb.add(jmFile);

    // Add the action listeners for the File menu.
    jmiOpen.addActionListener(this);
    jmiClose.addActionListener(this);
    jmiSave.addActionListener(this);
    jmiExit.addActionListener(this);
  }
```

```java
// Create the Options menu.
void makeOptionsMenu() {
  JMenu jmOptions = new JMenu("Options");

  // Create the Colors submenu.
  JMenu jmColors = new JMenu("Colors");

  // Use check boxes for colors. This allows
  // the user to select more than one color.
  JCheckBoxMenuItem jmiRed = new JCheckBoxMenuItem("Red");
  JCheckBoxMenuItem jmiGreen = new JCheckBoxMenuItem("Green");
  JCheckBoxMenuItem jmiBlue = new JCheckBoxMenuItem("Blue");

  // Add the items to the Colors menu.
  jmColors.add(jmiRed);
  jmColors.add(jmiGreen);
  jmColors.add(jmiBlue);
  jmOptions.add(jmColors);

  // Create the Priority submenu.
  JMenu jmPriority = new JMenu("Priority");

  // Use radio buttons for the priority setting.
  // This lets the menu show which priority is used
  // but also ensures that one and only one priority
  // can be selected at any one time.  Notice that
  // the High radio button is initially selected.
  JRadioButtonMenuItem jmiHigh =
    new JRadioButtonMenuItem("High", true);
  JRadioButtonMenuItem jmiLow =
    new JRadioButtonMenuItem("Low");

  // Add the items to the Priority menu.
  jmPriority.add(jmiHigh);
  jmPriority.add(jmiLow);
  jmOptions.add(jmPriority);

  // Create a button group for the radio button
  // menu items.
  ButtonGroup bg = new ButtonGroup();
  bg.add(jmiHigh);
  bg.add(jmiLow);

  // Now, create a Debug submenu that goes under
  // the Options menu bar item. Use actions to
  // create the items.
```

```
JMenu jmDebug = new JMenu("Debug");
JMenuItem jmiSetBP = new JMenuItem(setAct);
JMenuItem jmiClearBP = new JMenuItem(clearAct);
JMenuItem jmiResume = new JMenuItem(resumeAct);

// Add the items to the Debug menu.
jmDebug.add(jmiSetBP);
jmDebug.add(jmiClearBP);
jmDebug.add(jmiResume);
jmOptions.add(jmDebug);

// Create the Reset menu item.
JMenuItem jmiReset = new JMenuItem("Reset");
jmOptions.addSeparator();
jmOptions.add(jmiReset);

// Finally, add the entire Options menu to
// the menu bar.
jmb.add(jmOptions);

// Add the action listeners for the Options menu,
// except for those supported by the Debug menu.
jmiRed.addActionListener(this);
jmiGreen.addActionListener(this);
jmiBlue.addActionListener(this);
jmiHigh.addActionListener(this);
jmiLow.addActionListener(this);
jmiReset.addActionListener(this);
}

// Create the Help menu.
void makeHelpMenu() {
  JMenu jmHelp = new JMenu("Help");

  // Add an icon to the About menu item.
  ImageIcon icon = new ImageIcon("AboutIcon.gif");

  JMenuItem jmiAbout = new JMenuItem("About", icon);
  jmiAbout.setToolTipText("Info about the MenuDemo program.");
  jmHelp.add(jmiAbout);
  jmb.add(jmHelp);

  // Add action listener for About.
  jmiAbout.addActionListener(this);
}
```

```java
// Construct the actions needed by the Debug menu
// and toolbar.
void makeActions() {
  // Load the images for the actions.
  ImageIcon setIcon = new ImageIcon("setBP.gif");
  ImageIcon clearIcon = new ImageIcon("clearBP.gif");
  ImageIcon resumeIcon = new ImageIcon("resume.gif");

  // Create actions.
  setAct =
    new DebugAction("Set Breakpoint",
                    setIcon,
                    KeyEvent.VK_S,
                    KeyEvent.VK_B,
                    "Set a breakpoint.");

  clearAct =
    new DebugAction("Clear Breakpoint",
                    clearIcon,
                    KeyEvent.VK_C,
                    KeyEvent.VK_L,
                    "Clear a breakpoint.");

  resumeAct =
    new DebugAction("Resume",
                    resumeIcon,
                    KeyEvent.VK_R,
                    KeyEvent.VK_R,
                    "Resume execution after breakpoint.");

  // Initially disable the Clear Breakpoint option.
  clearAct.setEnabled(false);
}

// Create the Debug toolbar.
void makeToolBar() {
  // Create the toolbar buttons by using the actions.
  JButton jbtnSet = new JButton(setAct);
  JButton jbtnClear = new JButton(clearAct);
  JButton jbtnResume = new JButton(resumeAct);

  // Create the Debug toolbar.
  jtb = new JToolBar("Breakpoints");

  // Add the buttons to the toolbar.
  jtb.add(jbtnSet);
```

```
    jtb.add(jbtnClear);
    jtb.add(jbtnResume);
  }

  // Create the Edit popup menu.
  void makeEditPUMenu() {
    jpu = new JPopupMenu();

    // Create the popup menu items
    JMenuItem jmiCut = new JMenuItem("Cut");
    JMenuItem jmiCopy = new JMenuItem("Copy");
    JMenuItem jmiPaste = new JMenuItem("Paste");

    // Add the menu items to the popup menu.
    jpu.add(jmiCut);
    jpu.add(jmiCopy);
    jpu.add(jmiPaste);

    // Add the Edit popup menu action listeners.
    jmiCut.addActionListener(this);
    jmiCopy.addActionListener(this);
    jmiPaste.addActionListener(this);
  }

  public static void main(String args[]) {
    // Create the frame on the event dispatching thread.
    SwingUtilities.invokeLater(new Runnable() {
      public void run() {
        new MenuDemo();
      }
    });
  }
}
```

✓ Module 7 Mastery Check

1. What are the core Swing menu classes?

2. What class creates a menu? What class creates a popup menu? To create a main menu bar, what class is used?

3. What event is generated when a menu item is selected?

4. Images are not allowed in menus. True or false?

5. What method adds a menu bar to a window?

6. What method adds a mnemonic to a menu item?

7. Can an icon be used as a menu item? If so, does it prevent the use of a name?

8. What class creates a radio button menu item?

9. Although check box menu items are permitted, their use is discouraged because they make a menu look strange. True or false?

10. A popup menu is usually triggered by _____-_____ the mouse.

11. What methods defined by **MouseListener** must be overridden when listening for a popup trigger? What **MouseEvent** method must be called to determine if a popup trigger has been received?

12. What method is called to determine the source of a popup trigger?

13. A toolbar is an instance of what class?

14. Can a toolbar be added to the menu bar?

15. What interface defines an action?

16. List the properties that an action defines.

17. What does **System.exit( )** do?

18. On your own, add mnemonics and accelerators to the rest of the menu items in the final version of the **MenuDemo** program.

19. On your own, add a View menu to the menu bar of the final version of the **MenuDemo** program. Have it contain these selections: Full Screen, Normal, and Thumbnail. Also add this functionality to the toolbar. Use actions to manage the selections.

Module 8

Tables and Trees

This chapter examines two of Swing's most sophisticated components: **JTable** and **JTree**. **JTable** lets you display and manage data in a tabular, two-dimensional format. **JTree** lets you structure data as a tree. Both are powerful, feature-rich controls that greatly enhance the appearance and usability of any application. Both are also very large topics because each supports many options and customizations, and it is not possible to discuss all their features in this book. Instead, this module focuses on the basic techniques that will be applicable to nearly all applications.

JTable Fundamentals

JTable is perhaps the single most powerful component in the Swing library. It creates, displays, and manages tables of information. Tables are especially important to enterprise applications because they are often used to display database entries. Of course, any type of data that benefits from a tabular format can be presented in a table. For example, a table offers a convenient way to display a list of e-mail messages, name and address information, or order status, to name just a few. Whatever the use, tables are an important part of many Swing GUIs.

Like the other Swing components, **JTable** is packaged inside **javax.swing**. However, many of its support classes and interfaces are found in **javax.swing.table**. A separate package is used because of the large number of interfaces and classes that are related to tables. Don't be intimidated by this fact. As you will see, simple tables are quite easily constructed and managed, and are not much harder to use than any other Swing component. Of course, the more sophisticated the table, the more hands-on control and customization that will be required. Fortunately, most common customizations can still be handled without substantial effort.

At its core, **JTable** is conceptually simple. It is a component that consists of one or more columns of information. At the top of each column is a heading. In addition to describing the data in a column, the heading also provides the mechanism by which the user can change the size of a column, change the location of a column within the table, and display a tooltip, if desired.

The information within the table is contained in *cells*. Each cell has associated with it a *cell renderer*, which determines how the information is displayed, and a *cell editor*, which determines how the user edits the information. **JTable** supplies default cell renderers and editors that are suitable for many applications. However, it is possible to specify your own custom renderers and editors, if desired.

JTable does not provide any scrolling capabilities. Instead, a table is normally wrapped in a **JScrollPane**. This also causes the column header to be automatically displayed. If you don't wrap a **JTable** in a **JScrollPane**, then you must explicitly display both the table and header. (See "Ask the Expert" at the end of this section.)

After putting the table inside a scroll pane you will normally want to set the preferred size of the table's *scrollable viewport*. The scrollable viewport defines a region within the table in which the data is displayed and scrolled. It does not include the column headers. If you don't set this size, a default value will be used, and it will most likely not be suitable for your application. To set the scrollable viewport size, use **setPreferredScrollableViewportSize( )**, shown here:

setPreferredScrollableViewportSize(Dimension *dim*)

Here, *dim* specifies the desired size of the scrollable area.

JTable relies on three models. The first is the table model, which is defined by the **TableModel** interface. This model defines those things related to displaying data in a two-dimensional format. The second is the table column model, which is represented by **TableColumnModel**. **JTable** is defined in terms of columns, and it is **TableColumnModel** that specifies the characteristics of a column. These two models are packaged in **javax.swing.table**.

The third model determines how items are selected, and it is specified by the **ListSelectionModel**. You learned about this model in Module 5. It is packaged in **javax.swing**. By default, **JTable** allows the user to select one or more rows. You can change this behavior two ways. First, you can let the user select columns or individual cells. Second, you can restrict the user to a single selection, rather than allowing multiple selections. You will see how these things are accomplished later in this module.

Tables generate a variety of events. The two most important are **ListSelectionEvent**, which is fired when a row, column, or cell in the table is selected, and **TableModelEvent**, which is generated when the data in the table changes. Both events are examined in detail in the next section. A **JTable** can also generate a **TableColumnModelEvent**, when the table column model changes.

JTable supplies the constructors shown in Table 8-1. Although more sophisticated tables will require that you specify one or more models when constructing the table, you won't always need to do so. **JTable** supplies two constructors that automate the process of creating simple tables. The first is

JTable(Object[ ][ ] *data*, Object[ ] *headerNames*)

This constructor automatically creates a table that fits the data specified in *data* and that has the header names specified by *headerNames*. The table will use the default cell renderers and editors, which are suitable for many table applications. The *data* array is two-dimensional, with the first dimension specifying the number of rows in the table and the second dimension specifying the number of elements in each row. For example, the following array would provide data for a seven-row table with nine elements in each row.

```
Object[][]  info = new Object[7][9];
```

In all cases, the length of each row must be equal to the length of *headerNames*. This constructor is the easiest way to create a table from a fixed set of data. If your data is fairly straightforward, then this constructor is often a good choice.

In some cases, especially in cases in which data is being obtained from a collection, it may be easier to pass **Vector**s rather than arrays to **JTable**. When this is the case, use this constructor:

JTable(Vector *data*, Vector *headerNames*)

In this case, data is a **Vector** of **Vector**s. Each **Vector** must contain as many elements as there are header names specified by *headerNames*. Otherwise, it works like the previously described constructor. Even though tables are very powerful, feature-rich components, these two constructors give you an easy way to create one that is suitable for a great many applications.

Let's put the foregoing theory into action. The following program creates a simple table that displays an e-mail list. Understand that this program does not respond to any user interaction. It simply displays the data. (Table events are covered in the following section.) Sample output is shown in Figure 8-1.

Constructor	Description
JTable( )	Creates an empty table that uses the default models.
JTable(Object[][] *data*, Object[] *headerNames*)	Creates a table that contains the data specified by *data* and the column header names specified by *headerNames*. The default selection and column models are used.
JTable(Vector *data*, Vector *headerNames*)	Creates a table that contains the data specified by *data* and the column header name specified by *headerNames*. Here, *data* must be a **Vector** that contains the **Vector**s that contain the cell data. The default selection and column models are used.
JTable(int *rows*, int *cols*)	Creates an empty table that has the number of rows specified by *rows* and the number of columns specified by *cols*. The default table, selection, and column models are used.
JTable(TableModel *tm*)	Creates a table that uses the table model specified by *tm*. The default column and selection models are used.
JTable(TableModel *tm*, TableColumnModel *tcm*)	Creates a table that uses the table model specified by *tm* and the column model specified by *tcm*. The default selection model is used.
JTable(TableModel *tm*, TableColumnModel *tcm*, ListSelectionModel *lsm*)	Creates a table that uses the table model specified by *tm*, the column model specified by *tcm*, and the selection model specified by *lsm*.

Table 8-1 The **JTable** Constructors

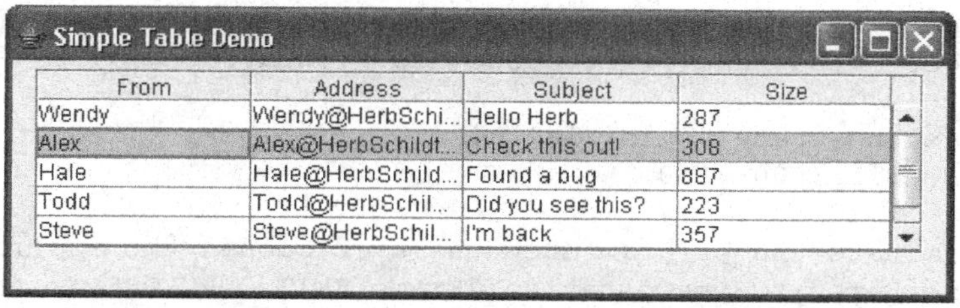

Figure 8-1 The table produced by the **TableDemo** program

```
// Demonstrate a simple table.

import java.awt.*;
import javax.swing.*;
import javax.swing.event.*;
import javax.swing.table.*;

class TableDemo {

  String[] headings = { "From", "Address", "Subject", "Size" };

  Object[][] data = {
       { "Wendy", "Wendy@HerbSchildt.com",
         "Hello Herb", new Integer(287) },
       { "Alex", "Alex@HerbSchildt.com",
         "Check this out!", new Integer(308) },
       { "Hale", "Hale@HerbSchildt.com",
         "Found a bug", new Integer(887) },
       { "Todd", "Todd@HerbSchildt.com",
         "Did you see this?", new Integer(223) },
       { "Steve", "Steve@HerbSchildt.com",
         "I'm back", new Integer(357) },
       { "Ken", "Ken@HerbSchildt.com",
         "Arrival time change", new Integer(512) }
  };

  JTable jtabEmail;

  TableDemo() {
    // Create a new JFrame container.
    JFrame jfrm = new JFrame("Simple Table Demo");
```

This array holds the table headings.

This array holds the table data.

```
    // Specify FlowLayout for the layout manager.
    jfrm.getContentPane().setLayout(new FlowLayout());

    // Give the frame an initial size.
    jfrm.setSize(500, 160);

    // Terminate the program when the user closes the application.
    jfrm.setDefaultCloseOperation(JFrame.EXIT_ON_CLOSE);

    // Create a table that displays the e-mail data.
    jtabEmail = new JTable(data, headings);   ◄──── Create a table that uses the
                                                     headings and data provided
                                                     by the arrays.
    // Wrap the data in a scroll pane.
    JScrollPane jscrlp = new JScrollPane(jtabEmail);  ◄─┐
                                                         Wrap the table in a scroll pane.
    // Set the scrollable viewport size.
    jtabEmail.setPreferredScrollableViewportSize(  ◄──────┐
            new Dimension(450, 80));              Set the dimensions of the scrollable
                                                  portion of the viewport.
    // Add the table to the content pane.
    jfrm.getContentPane().add(jscrlp);

    // Display the frame.
    jfrm.setVisible(true);
  }

  public static void main(String args[]) {
    // Create the frame on the event dispatching thread.
    SwingUtilities.invokeLater(new Runnable() {
      public void run() {
        new TableDemo();
      }
    });
  }
}
```

Although this program is quite short (and does not handle any table-generated events), it still creates a fully functional table. The table allows the widths of the columns to be adjusted, and it allows the position of the columns relative to each other to be changed. For example, Figure 8-2 shows the same table after the width of the Address column has been reduced and the columns have been rearranged. Also, the cells can be edited.

Let's look closely at how the table is constructed. First, notice that two arrays are created and initialized. The first, called **heading**, is an array of strings that define the headings used by the table. Because this array is four elements long, the table will have four columns. The second array, **data**, is a two-dimensional array of **Object** that contains the data that will be

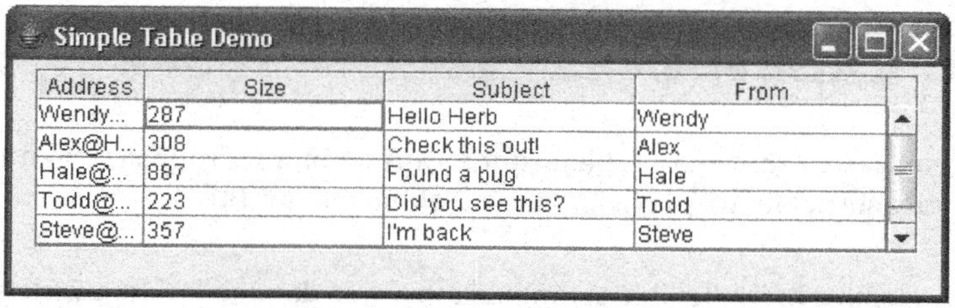

Figure 8-2 The e-mail table after changing the width of the Address column and rearranging the columns

displayed in the table. Each row in the array translates into a row of data in the table. As mentioned, each row must contain exactly the same number of elements as there are headings.

The table is constructed by passing **data** and **heading** to the following **JTable** constructor:

JTable(Object[ ][ ] *data*, Object[ ] *headerNames*)

It constructs a table that automatically has an appropriate table model. It uses the default column and selection model and the default cell renderers and editors. It is important to understand that all cell data is rendered in its default string format. As a result, this constructor is best suited for relatively simple tables that don't have special formatting needs.

After the table has been created, it is wrapped in a scroll pane and then its preferred scrollable viewport size is set. Thus, given the arrays containing the data and headers, it takes only three steps to actually create a usable table! This is remarkable given the amount of functionality supplied by **JTable**. As you will see over the next few sections, you can expend a substantially greater amount of effort customizing a table, but the basic creation process is still reasonably easy.

Progress Check

1. **JTable** relies on three models. What are they?

2. Does a **JTable** automatically provide scrolling for table data?

3. Each cell in a table has associated with it a cell _____ and a cell _____.

---

1. **TableModel**, **ListSelectionModel**, and **TableColumnModel**
2. No, you must wrap **JTable** in **JScrollpane** if scrolling is needed.
3. Each cell in a table has associated with it a cell renderer and a cell editor.

Ask the Expert

Q: Earlier you stated that if a JTable **is not wrapped in a** JScrollpane, **then the headers are not automatically displayed. Can you elaborate on this?**

A: **JTable** is an amazingly flexible component that was designed to fit a variety of needs. Although you will usually want to wrap a table in a scroll pane, it is not necessary. When you add **JTable** by itself to the content pane, it is displayed without any column headers. To display the headers, you must explicitly add them to the content pane. This gives you the flexibility to use a table that does not include a header, which might be appropriate for small tables in which the meaning of the columns is obvious. For example, here is the way that the e-mail table looks when not wrapped in a scroll pane:

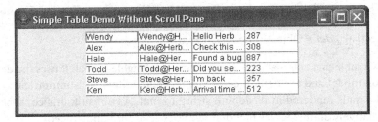

To add the header, you must first obtain it from the table by calling **getTableHeader( )**, shown here:

JTableHeader getTableHeader( )

It returns a reference to the header. **JTableHeader** is the component that manages table headers.

When not wrapping a table in a scroll pane, you will usually put the table and the header into a container that uses border layout. The table is placed in the center and the header is placed in the north position. However, there is no requirement that you do this, and separating the header from the table opens some very interesting possibilities. For example, you can put the header at the *bottom* of the table. To try this, start with the **TableDemo** program shown at the start of this module and then remove the lines that wrap **jtabEmail** in a scroll pane. Next, add this line.

```
JTableHeader jth = jtabEmail.getTableHeader();
```

Then, add the table and the header to the content pane, like this:

```
// Add the table and header to the content pane.
jfrm.getContentPane().add(jtabEmail);
jfrm.getContentPane().add(jth);
```

After making these changes, the table will look like this:

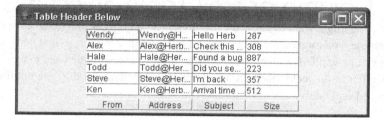

You might want to experiment with other alternatives and arrangements. **JTable** gives you many options.

CRITICAL SKILL
8.2

Change the Table Selection Mode

As the preceding program shows, by default a **JTable** allows the user to select one or more rows. However, you might want restrict a user to selecting precisely one row. To accomplish this you must change the *selection mode* by calling **setSelectionMode( )**, which is defined by **JTable.** It is shown here:

void setSelectionMode(int *mode*)

Here, *mode* specifies the selection mode. It must be one of these values defined by **ListSelectionModel**:

SINGLE_SELECTION	One row, column, or cell can be selected.
SINGLE_INTERVAL_SELECTION	A single range of rows, columns, or cells can be selected.
MULTIPLE_INTERVAL_SELECTION	Multiple ranges of rows, columns, or cells can be selected. This is the default.

Keep in mind that when you set another mode, the new mode affects both row and column selections.

To see the effect of setting the selection mode to **SINGLE_SELECTION**, try adding this line to the **TableDemo** program:

```
jtabEmail.setSelectionMode(ListSelectionModel.SINGLE_SELECTION);
```

After making this change, you will be able to select only one row at a time.

Allow Column or Cell Table Selections

In some cases, you might want to allow the user to select columns or individual cells rather than rows. For example, you might want to allow the user to select a column so that a transformation of some type can be applied to all entries in the column. The technique used to enable column selection is similar to the technique used to enable cell selection, but they are not the same, so each is examined separately.

Enable Column Selection

Enabling column selection is a two-step process. First, pass **true** to **setColumnSelectionAllowed( )**, which is shown here:

void setColumnSelectionAllowed(boolean *enabled*)

When *enabled* is true, column selection is enabled. When it is false, column selection is disabled. Second, turn off row selection by passing false to **setRowSelectionAllowed( )**, which is shown next:

void setRowSelectionAllowed(boolean *enabled*)

When *enabled* is true, row selection is enabled. When it is false, row selection is disabled. After these two calls, when you click on the table, a column rather than a row will be selected. To try this, add these lines to the preceding program:

```
jtabEmail.setColumnSelectionAllowed(true);
jtabEmail.setRowSelectionAllowed(false);
```

After making this change, you can select columns, as shown in Figure 8-3.

Enable Cell Selection

The are two different ways to enable individual cell selection. First, you can enable both column selection and row selection. Because row selection is on by default, this means that

Simple Table Demo			
From	Address	Subject	Size
Wendy	Wendy@HerbSchi...	Hello Herb	287
Alex	Alex@HerbSchildt...	Check this out!	308
Hale	Hale@HerbSchild...	Found a bug	887
Todd	Todd@HerbSchil...	Did you see this?	223
Steve	Steve@HerbSchil...	I'm back	357

Figure 8-3 Selecting a column in a table

if you simply turn on column selection, then both will be enabled. This condition causes cell selection to be turned on.

The second way to enable cell selection is to call **setCellSelectionEnabled( )**, shown here:

void setCellSelectionEnabled(boolean *enabled*)

If *enabled* is true, cell selection is enabled. If *enabled* is false, then cell selection is disabled. This method translates into calls to **setRowSelectionAllowed( )** and **setColumnSelectionAllowed( )** with *enabled* passed as an argument. Thus, you need to be a bit careful when using this method to turn off cell selection. It will result in both row and column selection also being turned off, which means that nothing can be selected! Therefore, the best way to turn off cell selection is to turn off *either* row or column selection.

To try cell selection, remove the two previously added lines shown earlier and then add this line to the program:

```
jtabEmail.setCellSelectionEnabled(true);
```

After making this change, you will be able to select cells, as shown in Figure 8-4.

Progress Check

1. What **JTable** method is called to change the selection mode?

2. What method is used to enable column selections?

3. Cell selection is allowed when both row and column selection modes are enabled. True or False?

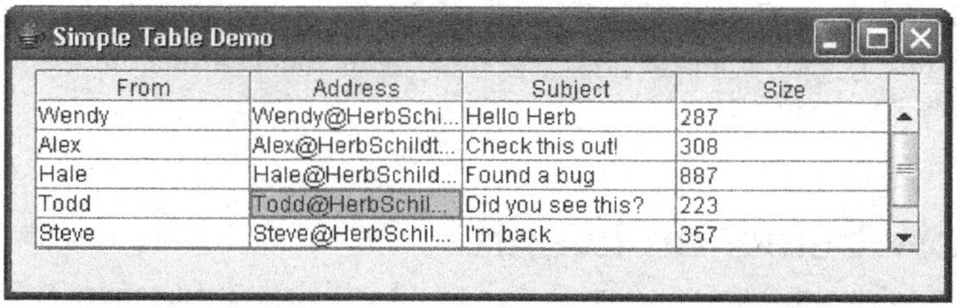

Figure 8-4 Selecting cells in a table

1. **setSelectionMode( )**
2. **setColumnSelectionAllowed( )**
3. True

Handle Table Selection Events

So far, the examples have been using tables to simply display data. They have been ignoring the events that the tables have generated. A **JTable** can generate several different events. The two most fundamental to a table's operation are **ListSelectionEvent** and **TableModelEvent**. The first event is generated when the user selects something in the table. The second is fired when that table changes in some way. This section explains how to handle selection events. The next section describes table model events.

There are three possible types of table selections: row, column, and cell. By default, **JTable** allows you to select one or more complete rows, but you can change this behavior to allow one or more columns or one or more individual cells to be selected. Although the general way in which each of these events is handled is similar, they differ in their specifics. Therefore, each is described separately. We will begin with a general overview of table selection events that applies to all situations.

Table Selection Basics

When a row, column, or cell is selected within a table, a **ListSelectionEvent** is fired. To handle this event, you must register a **ListSelectionListener**. You are already familiar with **ListSelectionEvent** and **ListSelectionListener** because they were used in Module 5 to handle selections from a **JList**. Both **ListSelectionEvent** and **ListSelectionListener** are packaged in **javax.swing.event**.

Recall from Module 5 that **ListSelectionListener** specifies only one method, called **valueChanged( )**, which is shown here:

void valueChanged(ListSelectionEvent *le*)

Here, *le* is a reference to the object that generated the event. **ListSelectionEvent** does provide some methods of its own, but often you will interrogate the **JTable** object or its models to determine what has occurred.

Handle Row Selection Events

To handle row selection events, you must register a **ListSelectionListener**. This listener is *not* added to the **JTable** instance. Instead, it is added to the list selection model. You obtain a reference to this model by calling **getSelectionModel( )** on the **JTable** instance. It is shown here:

ListSelectionModel getSelectionModel( )

ListSelectionModel defines several methods that let you determine the state of the model. Much of its functionality is available directly in **JTable**. However, there is one method defined by **ListSelectionModel** that is useful: **getValueIsAdjusting( )**. It returns true if the selection process is still taking place and false when it is over. (**getValueIsAdjusting( )** works just like it does in **JList**, **JScrollBar**, and **JSlider**, described earlier in this book.)

Once a **ListSelectionEvent** has been retrieved, you can determine what row has been selected by calling **getSelectedRow( )** or **getSelectedRows( )** on the table. They are shown here:

int getSelectedRow( )

int [ ] getSelectedRows( )

The **getSelectedRow( )** method returns the index of the first row selected, which will be the only row selected if single selection mode is being used. If no row has been selected, then –1 is returned. When multiple selection is enabled (which it is by default), then call **getSelectedRows( )** to obtain a list of the indices of all selected rows. If no rows are selected, the array returned will have a length of zero. If only one row is selected, then the array will be exactly one element long. Thus, you can use **getSelectedRows( )** even when you are using a single selection mode.

The following program demonstrates handling table selection events. It reworks the first example so that the indices of the rows selected by the user are displayed in a label. Sample output is shown in Figure 8-5.

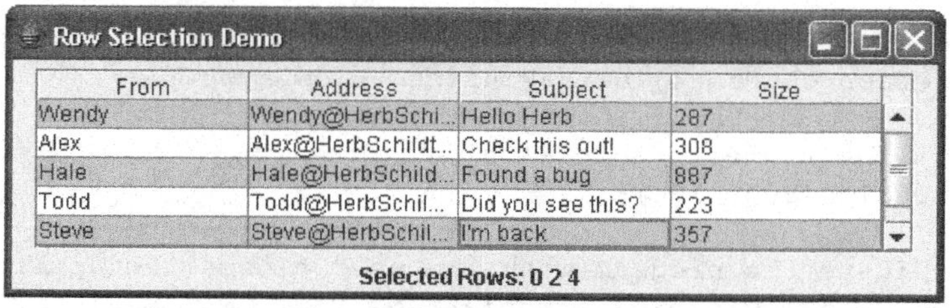

Figure 8-5 Sample output from the row selection event demo

```java
// Handle table row selections.

import java.awt.*;
import javax.swing.*;
import javax.swing.event.*;
import javax.swing.table.*;

class RowSelDemo {

  String[] headings = { "From", "Address", "Subject", "Size" };

  Object[][] data = {
        { "Wendy", "Wendy@HerbSchildt.com",
          "Hello Herb", new Integer(287) },
        { "Alex", "Alex@HerbSchildt.com",
          "Check this out!", new Integer(308) },
        { "Hale", "Hale@HerbSchildt.com",
          "Found a bug", new Integer(887) },
        { "Todd", "Todd@HerbSchildt.com",
          "Did you see this?", new Integer(223) },
        { "Steve", "Steve@HerbSchildt.com",
          "I'm back", new Integer(357) },
        { "Ken", "Ken@HerbSchildt.com",
          "Arrival time change", new Integer(512) }
  };

  JTable jtabEmail;

  JLabel jlab;

  RowSelDemo() {
    // Create a new JFrame container.
    JFrame jfrm = new JFrame("Row Selection Demo");

    // Specify FlowLayout for the layout manager.
    jfrm.getContentPane().setLayout(new FlowLayout());

    // Give the frame an initial size.
    jfrm.setSize(500, 160);

    // Terminate the program when the user closes the application.
    jfrm.setDefaultCloseOperation(JFrame.EXIT_ON_CLOSE);
```

```
// Create a label that will display the table selection.
jlab = new JLabel();

// Create a table that displays the e-mail data.
jtabEmail = new JTable(data, headings);

// Wrap the data in a scroll pane.
JScrollPane jscrlp = new JScrollPane(jtabEmail);

// Set the viewport size.
jtabEmail.setPreferredScrollableViewportSize(
        new Dimension(450, 80));

// Get the list selection model for row selections.
ListSelectionModel lsmRow = jtabEmail.getSelectionModel();

// Listen for row selection events.
lsmRow.addListSelectionListener(new ListSelectionListener() {
  public void valueChanged(ListSelectionEvent le) {
    String str = "Selected Rows: ";

    // Get a list of all selected rows.
    int[] rows = jtabEmail.getSelectedRows();

    // Create a string that contains the indices.
    for(int i=0; i < rows.length; i++)
      str += rows[i] + " ";

    // Display the indices of the selected rows.
    jlab.setText(str);
  }
});

// Add the table and label to the content pane.
jfrm.getContentPane().add(jscrlp);
jfrm.getContentPane().add(jlab);

// Display the frame.
jfrm.setVisible(true);
}
```

Row selection events are listened for on the list selection model used by the table.

Add a listener to the list selection model. This listener will respond to row selection events.

Obtain the indices of all selected rows.

```
public static void main(String args[]) {
  // Create the frame on the event dispatching thread.
  SwingUtilities.invokeLater(new Runnable() {
    public void run() {
      new RowSelDemo();
    }
  });
}
}
```

This program makes three additions to the previous one. First, the label **jlab** is added. This label will display the selected row or rows. Second, the program obtains a reference to the list selection model by using this statement:

```
ListSelectionModel lsmRow = jtabEmail.getSelectionModel();
```

It then adds a list selection listener to the model and handles list selection events with an anonymous inner class. Inside **valueChanged( )**, the indices of selected rows are obtained by calling **getSelectedRows( )** on the table. If only one row is selected, then the array returned will contain only one element. The indices are then displayed.

Handle Column Selection Events

As with row selection events, to handle column selection events, you must register a **ListSelectionListener**. However, this listener is *not* registered with the list selection model provided by **JTable**. Instead, it must be registered with the list selection model used by the table's column model. (Recall that the model for each column is specified by its implementation of **TableColumnModel**.) You obtain a reference to this model by calling **getColumnModel( )** on the **JTable** instance. It is shown here:

TableColumnModel getColumnModel( )

Using the reference returned, you can obtain a reference to the **ListSelectionModel** used by the columns. Therefore, assuming a **JTable** called **jtable**, you will use a sequence like this to obtain the list selection model for a column:

```
TableColumnModel tcm = jtable.getColumnModel();
ListSelectionModel lsmCol = tcm.getSelectionModel();
```

Once a **ListSelectionEvent** has been received, you can determine what column has been selected by calling **getSelectedColumn( )** or **getSelectedColumns( )** on the **JTable**. They are shown here:

int getSelectedColumn( )

int [ ] getSelectedColumns( )

The **getSelectedColumn( )** method returns the index of the first column selected, which will be the only column selected if single selection mode is being used. If no column has been selected, then –1 is returned. When multiple selection is enabled (which it is by default), then call **getSelectedColumns( )** to obtain a list of the indices of all selected columns. If no columns are selected, the array returned will have a length of zero. If only one column is selected, then the array will be exactly one element long. Thus, you can use **getSelectedColumns( )** even when you are using a single selection mode. One fact to keep firmly in mind is that the indices returned by these methods are relative to the view (in other words, the column positions displayed on the screen). Because the columns can be repositioned by the user, these indices might differ from that of the table model, which is fixed.

Here is a reworked version of the preceding program that allows column (rather than row) selection. Notice how it handles the selection events. Sample output is shown in Figure 8-6.

```
// Handle table column selections.

import java.awt.*;
import javax.swing.*;
import javax.swing.event.*;
import javax.swing.table.*;

class ColSelDemo {

  String[] headings = { "From", "Address", "Subject", "Size" };

  Object[][] data = {
        { "Wendy", "Wendy@HerbSchildt.com",
          "Hello Herb", new Integer(287) },
        { "Alex", "Alex@HerbSchildt.com",
          "Check this out!", new Integer(308) },
        { "Hale", "Hale@HerbSchildt.com",
          "Found a bug", new Integer(887) },
        { "Todd", "Todd@HerbSchildt.com",
          "Did you see this?", new Integer(223) },
        { "Steve", "Steve@HerbSchildt.com",
```

```
                    "I'm back", new Integer(357) },
            { "Ken", "Ken@HerbSchildt.com",
                "Arrival time change", new Integer(512) }
  };

  JTable jtabEmail;

  JLabel jlab;

  ColSelDemo() {
    // Create a new JFrame container.
    JFrame jfrm = new JFrame("Column Selection Demo");

    // Specify FlowLayout for the layout manager.
    jfrm.getContentPane().setLayout(new FlowLayout());

    // Give the frame an initial size.
    jfrm.setSize(500, 160);

    // Terminate the program when the user closes the application.
    jfrm.setDefaultCloseOperation(JFrame.EXIT_ON_CLOSE);

    // Create a label that will display the table selection.
    jlab = new JLabel();

    // Create a table that displays the e-mail data.
    jtabEmail = new JTable(data, headings);

    // Wrap the data in a scroll pane.
    JScrollPane jscrlp = new JScrollPane(jtabEmail);

    // Set the viewport size.
    jtabEmail.setPreferredScrollableViewportSize(
            new Dimension(450, 80));

    // Allow column selection.
    jtabEmail.setColumnSelectionAllowed(true);
    jtabEmail.setRowSelectionAllowed(false);

    // Get the list selection model for the column model.
    TableColumnModel tcm = jtabEmail.getColumnModel();
    ListSelectionModel lsmCol = tcm.getSelectionModel();

    // Listen for column selection events.
```

Turn on column selection.
Turn off row selection.

Column selection events are listened for on the list selection model used by the column model.

```
lsmCol.addListSelectionListener(new ListSelectionListener() {
  public void valueChanged(ListSelectionEvent le) {
    String str = "Selected Columns: ";

    // Get a list of all selected columns.
    int[] cols = jtabEmail.getSelectedColumns();

    // Create a string that contains the indices.
    for(int i=0; i < cols.length; i++)
      str += cols[i] + " ";

    // Display the indices of the selected columns.
    jlab.setText(str);
  }
});

// Add the table and label to the content pane.
jfrm.getContentPane().add(jscrlp);
jfrm.getContentPane().add(jlab);

// Display the frame.
jfrm.setVisible(true);
}

public static void main(String args[]) {
  // Create the frame on the event dispatching thread.
  SwingUtilities.invokeLater(new Runnable() {
    public void run() {
      new ColSelDemo();
    }
  });
}
}
```

Add a listener for column selection events.

Get the indices of all selected columns.

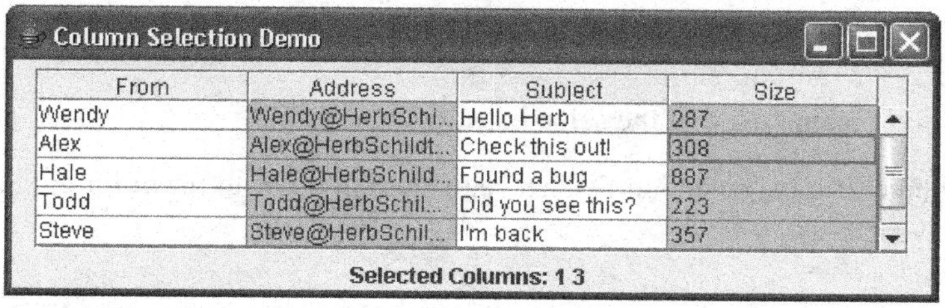

Figure 8-6 Sample output from the column selection event program

Before moving on it is important to mention that given the screen index of a column, you can obtain the column's model index. This is often useful because the model index of the column will not change. Here is the procedure to follow. First, obtain a reference to the table's column model by calling **getColumnModel( )**. Second, retrieve a reference to the desired column by calling **getColumn( )** on the column model. The **getColumn( )** method is shown here:

TableColumn getColumn(int *idx*)

Here, *idx* specifies the zero-based index, such as one obtained by calling **getSelectedColumns( )**, of the column you want to obtain. **TableColumn** is the class that encapsulates a column. It defines several methods. The one used to obtain the model index is **getModelIndex( )**. It is shown here:

int getModelIndex( )

It returns the index of the column relative to the model. Therefore, using the preceding program, the following sequence gets the model index of the column with a current screen index of 1:

```
jtabEmail.getColumnModel().getColumn(1).getModelIndex();
```

Handle Cell Selections

When cell selection is enabled, you will determine which cell has been selected by obtaining both the column index and the row index when a **ListSelectionEvent** is received. You will also need to register selection listeners on both the row selection model and the column selection model, as described the preceding sections.

Progress Check

1. Is a row selection listener registered with the **JTable** instance?

2. What method obtains a list of the selected rows?

3. On what object is a list selection listener registered in order to listen for column selection events?

---

1. No. It is registered with the **ListSelectionModel** used by the table.

2. **getSelectedRows( )**

3. To listen for column selection events, a listener must be registered with the **ListSelectionModel** used by the **TableColumnModel**.

Ask the Expert

Q: Are the methods getSelectedRow( ), getSelectedRows( ), getSelectedColumn( ), and getSelectedColumns( ) **available at any time or only when one of their related events occurs?**

A: The various **getSelected**X methods can be called at any time to determine if a row, column, or cell is selected in the table. For example, when a row is selected, **getSelectedColumn( )** will return the column in which the keyboard or mouse event occurred that selected the row. Furthermore, when cell selection is enabled, both row and column indices can be obtained by either the row selection listener or the column selection listener.

CRITICAL SKILL
8.5
Handle Table Model Events

You can listen for changes to the table's data (such as when the user changes the value of a cell) by registering a **TableModelListener** with the table model. The table model is obtained by calling **getModel( )** on the **JTable** instance. It is shown here:

TableModel getModel( )

TableModel defines the **addTableModelListener( )** method, which you use to add a listener for **TableModelEvent**s. It is shown here:

void addTableModelListener(TableModelListener *tml*)

TableModelListener defines only one method, **tableChanged( )**. It is shown next:

void tableChanged(TableModelEvent *tme*)

This method is called whenever the table model changes, which includes changes to the data, changes to the headers, and insertions or deletions of columns.

    TableModelEvent defines the methods shown in Table 8-2. The methods **getFirstRow( )**, **getLastRow( )**, and **getColumn( )** return the index of the row (or rows) and column that have been changed. This same information can be obtained by calling methods defined by **JTable** (as previously described), but sometimes it is more convenient to obtain it from the event object. However, you need to be careful because **getColumn( )** returns the column index as maintained by the table model. If the user rearranges the columns, then it will differ from the column index returned by a method such as **JTable**'s **getSelectedColumn( )**, which reflects the position of the columns in the current view. Therefore, don't mix the two indices.

Also notice **getType( )**. It returns a value that indicates what type of change has taken place. The possible return values defined by **TableModelEvent** are shown here:

DELETE	A row or column has been removed.
INSERT	A row or column has been added.
UPDATE	Cell data has changed.

Often, if cell data has been changed, your application will need to update the underlying data source to reflect this change. Thus, if your table allows cell editing, watching for **UPDATE** table model events is especially important.

When data inside a cell changes, you can obtain the new value by calling **getValueAt( )** on the model instance. It is shown next:

Object getValueAt(int *row*, int *column*)

Here, *row* and *column* specify the coordinates of the cell that changed. As a point of interest, you can set the data under program control by calling **setValueAt( )**, which is shown here:

void setValueAt(Object *val*, int *row*, int *column*)

It sets the value of the cell located at *row* and *column* to the *val*. For both methods, the values of *row* and *column* are relative to the model, not the view.

The following program shows how to handle table model events. For comparison, it also handles row selection events. Handling both events lets you clearly see when each type of event is generated. When you select a row, a selection event is fired and the row index is displayed. If you change the value in the cell, a table model event is generated. In this case, the row and column index of the cell is displayed, along with the updated data. Figure 8-7 shows sample output.

Method	Description
int getColumn( )	Returns the zero-based index of the column in which the event occurred. A return value of **TableModelEvent.ALL_COLUMNS** means that all columns within the selected row were affected.
int getFirstRow( )	Returns the zero-based index of the first row in which the event occurred. If the header changed, the return value is **TableModelEvent.HEADER_ROW**.
int getLastRow( )	Returns the zero-based index of the last row in which the event occurred.
int getType( )	Returns a value that indicates what type of change occurred. It will be one of these values: **TableModelEvent.DELETE**, **TableModelEvent.INSERT**, or **TableModelEvent.UPDATE**.

Table 8-2 The Methods Defined by **TableModelEvent**

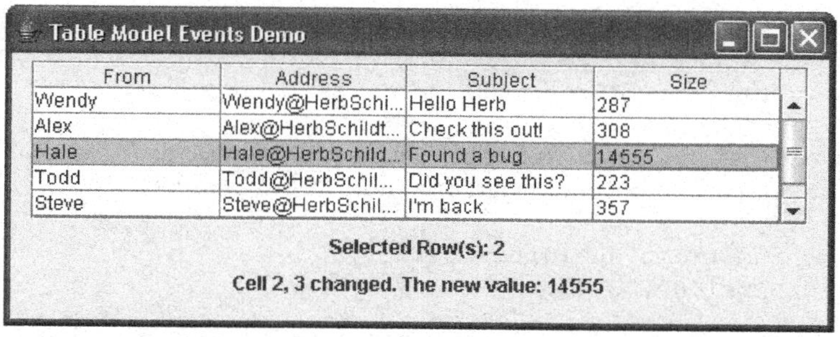

Figure 8-7 Sample output from the **TabModEventDemo** program

```java
// Handle changes to the data.

import java.awt.*;
import javax.swing.*;
import javax.swing.event.*;
import javax.swing.table.*;

class TabModEventDemo {

  String[] headings = { "From", "Address", "Subject", "Size" };

  Object[][] data = {
        { "Wendy", "Wendy@HerbSchildt.com",
          "Hello Herb", new Integer(287) },
        { "Alex", "Alex@HerbSchildt.com",
          "Check this out!", new Integer(308) },
        { "Hale", "Hale@HerbSchildt.com",
          "Found a bug", new Integer(887) },
        { "Todd", "Todd@HerbSchildt.com",
          "Did you see this?", new Integer(223) },
        { "Steve", "Steve@HerbSchildt.com",
          "I'm back", new Integer(357) },
        { "Ken", "Ken@HerbSchildt.com",
          "Arrival time change", new Integer(512) }
  };

  JTable jtabEmail;

  JLabel jlab;
  JLabel jlab2;

  TableModel tm;
```

```
TabModEventDemo() {
  // Create a new JFrame container.
  JFrame jfrm = new JFrame("Table Model Events Demo");

  // Specify FlowLayout for the layout manager.
  jfrm.getContentPane().setLayout(new FlowLayout());

  // Give the frame an initial size.
  jfrm.setSize(500, 200);

  // Terminate the program when the user closes the application.
  jfrm.setDefaultCloseOperation(JFrame.EXIT_ON_CLOSE);

  // Create a label that will display the table selection.
  jlab = new JLabel();
  jlab.setPreferredSize(new Dimension(400, 20));
  jlab.setHorizontalAlignment(SwingConstants.CENTER);

  // Create a label that will display the changes to the data.
  jlab2 = new JLabel();

  // Create a table that displays the e-mail data.
  jtabEmail = new JTable(data, headings);

  // Wrap the data in a scroll pane.
  JScrollPane jscrlp = new JScrollPane(jtabEmail);

  // Set the viewport size.
  jtabEmail.setPreferredScrollableViewportSize(
            new Dimension(450, 80));

  // Get the list selection model.
  ListSelectionModel listSelMod = jtabEmail.getSelectionModel();

  // Listen for row selection events.
  listSelMod.addListSelectionListener(new ListSelectionListener() {
    public void valueChanged(ListSelectionEvent le) {
      String str = "Selected Row(s): ";

      // Get a list of all selected rows.
      int[] rows = jtabEmail.getSelectedRows();

      // Create a string that contains the indices.
      for(int i=0; i < rows.length; i++)
        str += rows[i] + " ";
```

```
      // Display the indices of the selected rows.
      jlab.setText(str);
    }
  });

  // Get the table model.
  tm = jtabEmail.getModel();  ◄──────── Obtain the table model.

  // Add a table model listener.
  tm.addTableModelListener(new TableModelListener() {  ◄─── Listen for changes
    public void tableChanged(TableModelEvent tme) {             to the table model.
      if(tme.getType() == TableModelEvent.UPDATE) {
        jlab2.setText("Cell " + tme.getFirstRow() + ", " +
                    tme.getColumn() + " changed." +
                    " The new value: " +
                    tm.getValueAt(tme.getFirstRow(),
                                  tme.getColumn())));
      }
    }
  });
```

Display the location of the
change and the new value.

```
  // Add the table and label to the content pane.
  jfrm.getContentPane().add(jscrlp);
  jfrm.getContentPane().add(jlab);
  jfrm.getContentPane().add(jlab2);

  // Display the frame.
  jfrm.setVisible(true);
}

public static void main(String args[]) {
  // Create the frame on the event dispatching thread.
  SwingUtilities.invokeLater(new Runnable() {
    public void run() {
      new TabModEventDemo();
    }
  });
}
}
```

Let's look closely at the portions of this program that handles model change events. First, notice that the program includes a **TableModel** field called **tm**. Later in the program, a reference to the table model is obtained by calling **getModel( )** on the **jtabEmail** (the **JTable** instance) and stored in **tm**, as shown here:

```
tm = jtabEmail.getModel();
```

Next, a table model listener is registered on **tm**.

In the table model listener, pay special attention to the **tableChanged( )** event handler. This method is called whenever the table model changes. In this program, it is called whenever a cell has its data changed by the user. (The program does not insert or delete columns, nor does it change the header.) It uses the methods **getFirstRow( )** and **getColumn( )** to obtain the coordinates of the cell that changed. It also uses these coordinates to obtain the updated data from the column model. To do this, it calls **getValueAt( )** on the table model (**tm**), passing the values obtained from **getFirstRow( )** and **getColumn( )**. This ensures that no matter how the user rearranges the table, the data from the proper cell is obtained because the table model column indices do not change.

Notice that **tableChanged( )** first confirms that the event involves a change to cell data by calling **getType( )** and checking its return value against **UPDATE**. This step is not technically necessary in this program because **UPDATE** is the only type of model event that the program will generate, but it is included to illustrate the technique.

Progress Check

1. What event encapsulates changes to a table's data?

2. Is a table model event listener registered with the table directly?

3. What are the three values that can be returned by **TableModelEvent**'s method **getType( )**?

CRITICAL SKILL
8.6 # Change Table Resize Modes

JTable supports several *resizing modes*, which control the way that columns widths are changed when the user adjusts the size of a column by dragging its header border. By default, when you change the width of a column, all subsequent columns (that is, all columns to the right of the one being changed) are adjusted in width so that the overall width of the table is unchanged. Any columns prior to the one being changed are left as-is. However, this default behavior is just one of five different resize modes from which you can select.

---

1. **TableModelEvent**

2. No, the table model event listener is registered with the table model.

3. **INSERT**, **DELETE**, and **UPDATE**

To change the resize mode, use the **setAutoResizeMode( )** method, shown here:

void setAutoResizeMode(int *how*)

Here, *how* must be one of five constants defined by **JTable**. They are shown in Table 8-3. You should experiment a bit with these modes to make sure you understand their effects. There is one mode, however, that warrants a bit more discussion: **AUTO_RESIZE_OFF**.

When you turn auto-resizing off by specifying **AUTO_RESIZE_OFF**, no automatic sizing takes place when a column is adjusted. Instead, if a column width adjustment results in the table exceeding the size of the scrollable viewport, then a horizontal scroll bar is added that lets the user scroll the table left and right. Furthermore, no attempt is made to fill the scrollable viewport area when a column width adjustment causes the width of the table to drop below the width of the scrollable viewport area. This results in a blank area in the table being created. Finally, when the table is first created, the columns are not necessarily sized to fill the table width. Thus, if you turn auto-resize off, you may need to specify the columns widths manually.

To see the effects of turning off auto-resizing, add this line to the previous example program:

```
jtabEmail.setAutoResizeMode(JTable.AUTO_RESIZE_OFF);
```

Figure 8-8 shows the effect after the columns have been resized. Notice that a horizontal scroll bar has been added to allow the hidden parts of the table to be scrolled into view.

Resize Mode	Description
AUTO_RESIZE_ALL_COLUMNS	The width of all columns are adjusted when the width of one column is changed.
AUTO_RESIZE_LAST_COLUMN	The width of only the rightmost column is adjusted when a column is changed.
AUTO_RESIZE_NEXT_COLUMN	The width of only the next column is adjusted when a column is changed.
AUTO_RESIZE_OFF	No column adjustments are made. Instead, the table width is changed. If the table is wrapped in a scroll pane and the table width is expanded beyond the bounds of the viewport, then the viewport remains the same size and a horizontal scroll bar is added that allows the table to be scrolled left and right to bring the other columns into view.
AUTO_RESIZE_SUBSEQUENT_COLUMNS	The widths of all columns to the right of the column being changed are adjusted. This is the default setting.

Figure 8-3 The **JTable** Resize Modes

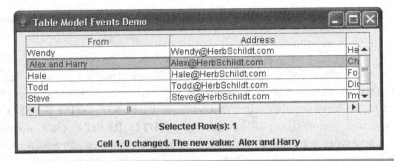

Figure 8-8 The effect of auto-resizing being turned off

Ask the Expert

Q: Can I set the size of a column under program control? Can I obtain the current width of a column during runtime?

A: Yes to both questions! To specify the width of a column involves three steps. First, obtain a reference to the table's column model by calling **getColumnModel( )**. Second, retrieve a reference to the desired column by calling **getColumn( )** on the column model. As explained earlier, **getColumn( )** has this general form:

TableColumn getColumn(int *idx*)

The value of *idx* specifies the zero-based view index of the column you want to obtain. **TableColumn** includes several column size–related methods. The one used to set the width is **setPreferredWidth( )**. It is shown here:

void setPreferredWidth(int *w*)

Here, *w* is the preferred width. Therefore, the third step is to set the column width by calling **setPreferredWidth( )** on the column.

To put these steps into action, try adding these lines to one of the previous programs:

```
TableColumnModel tcm = jtabEmail.getColumnModel();
TableColumn tc = tcm.getColumn(1);
tc.setPreferredWidth(200);
```

After these statements execute, the second column (which is the column specified by index 1) will have a width of 200.

In addition to setting the preferred width, you can also set the minimum and maximum allowable width of a column by calling **setMinWidth( )** and **setMaxWidth( )**, shown here:

void setMinWidth(int *w*)

void setMaxWidth(int *w*)

Here, *w* specifies the desired width.

You can obtain the current width of a column by calling **getWidth( )**. It is shown here:

int getWidth( )

It returns the current width of the column, which will change each time the column is resized.

You can obtain a column's preferred width and its minimum and maximum allowed widths by using these methods:

int getPreferredWidth( )

int getMinWidth( )

int getMaxWidth( )

Each returns the indicated value.

Progress Check

1. What is the default resizing mode?

2. If the resize mode is set to **AUTO_RESIZE_OFF**, what happens when the table width exceeds the width of the enclosing scroll pane?

---

1. **AUTO_RESIZE_SUBSEQUENT_COLUMNS**
2. A horizontal scroll bar is displayed that allows the user to scroll the window.

CRITICAL SKILL
8.7 Implement a Custom Table Model

All of the previous table examples have operated on data that was stored in an array. While this is perfectly fine for some types of applications, it is inappropriate for others. For example, if the data in the table depends on a computation or is obtained from some source external to the program (a database, for example), then having to store the values in an array is both cumbersome and potentially inefficient. However, Swing offers a solution: you can create your own table model that allows you to specify how the data in a table is obtained. This enables you to handle cases easily in which the data is dynamically obtained or computed.

To create a table model, you will create an instance of the **TableModel** interface. It defines the methods shown in Table 8-4. Although it is perfectly acceptable to implement all of the **TableModel** methods on your own, it is often easier to extend the **AbstractTableModel** class.

AbstractTableModel provides default implementations of all but the following methods: **getValueAt( )**, **getRowCount( )**, and **getColumnCount( )**. However, if you want to use something other than the default column header names (which are A through Z), then you must also override **getColumnName( )**.

The following program shows how easy it is to implement a simple custom table model. It creates a model called **NumInfoModel** that displays a list of integers (beginning at 2) in the first column. The second column reports if the value in the first column is prime. The next column displays the square of the value, and the final column displays the square root of the value. All values are computed dynamically and (except for the header names) no arrays are used to hold the table information. Sample output is shown in Figure 8-9.

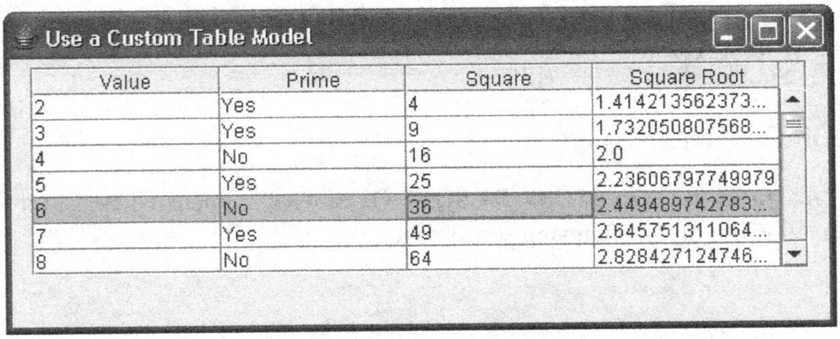

Figure 8-9 Sample output from the custom table model program

Method	Description
void addTableModelListener(TableModelListener *tml*)	Adds *tml* as a listener for table model events.
Class<?> getColumnClass(int *idx*)	Returns the data type of the information in the column specified by *idx*.
int getColumnCount( )	Returns the column count.
String getColumnName(int *idx*)	Returns the name of the column specified by *idx*.
int getRowCount( )	Returns the row count.
Object getValueAt(int *rIdx*, int *cIdx*)	Returns the value at the row and column coordinates specified by *rIdx* and *cIdx*.
boolean isCellEditable(int *rIdx*, int *cIdx*)	If the cell at the coordinate specified by *rIdx* and *cIdx* can be edited, true is returned. Otherwise, false is returned.
void removeTableModelListener(TableModelListener *tml*)	Removes *tml* as a listener for table model events.
void setValueAt(Object *v*, int *rIdx*, int *cIdx*)	Stores *v* as the value at the row and column coordinates specified by *rIdx* and *cIdx*.

Table 8-4 The Methods Defined by **TableModel**

```
// Implement a custom table model.
// The model displays the integers 2 to N in column 1.
// In the subsequent three columns, it indicates if
// the value in column 1 is prime and shows its
// square and its square root.

import java.awt.*;
import javax.swing.*;
import javax.swing.table.*;

// Create a model that provides the numeric data.
class NumInfoModel extends AbstractTableModel {     ◄──────  Define a custom table
  int numRows;                                                model that generates
                                                              its data dynamically.

  String colNames[] = { "Value", "Prime",
                        "Square", "Square Root" };  ◄──────  This array holds
                                                              the header names.
  NumInfoModel(int len) {
```

```
      super();
      numRows = len;
    }

    public int getRowCount() { return numRows; }
    public int getColumnCount() { return 4; }

    // Return the name of the column as specified
    // by the colNames array.
    public String getColumnName(int c) {
      return colNames[c];                   ◄──────── Return the header string given the column index.
    }

    // For column 0, return the row number + 2.
    // For column 1, return "Yes" if column 1 is prime.
    // For column 2, return the square of column 1.
    // For column 3, return the square root of column 1.
    public Object getValueAt(int r, int c) { ◄──────  Compute and return
                                                       the proper data
                                                       for a given row
      if(c==0) return new Integer(r+2);                and column.
      else if(c==1) {
        if(isPrime(r+2)) return "Yes";
        else return "No";
      }
      else if(c==2) return new Integer((r+2) * (r+2));
      else return new Double(Math.sqrt(r+2));
    }

    // Return true if v is prime.
    boolean isPrime(int v) {
      int i;

      for(i=2; i <= v/i; i++)
        if((v%i) == 0) return false;

      return true;
    }
  }

class NumInfoTable {

  JTable jtabNumInfo;

  NumInfoTable() {
    // Create a new JFrame container.
    JFrame jfrm = new JFrame("Use a Custom Table Model");
```

```
      // Specify FlowLayout for the layout manager.
      jfrm.getContentPane().setLayout(new FlowLayout());

      // Give the frame an initial size.
      jfrm.setSize(500, 200);

      // Terminate the program when the user closes the application.
      jfrm.setDefaultCloseOperation(JFrame.EXIT_ON_CLOSE);

      // Create a table that uses NumInfoModel to
      // display information on the values 2 through 100.
      jtabNumInfo = new JTable(new NumInfoModel(99));   ◄─── Construct a table that
                                                             uses the custom model.
      // Wrap the data in a scroll pane.
      JScrollPane jscrlp = new JScrollPane(jtabNumInfo);

      // Set the viewport size.
      jtabNumInfo.setPreferredScrollableViewportSize(
              new Dimension(450, 110));

      // Add the table to the content pane.
      jfrm.getContentPane().add(jscrlp);

      // Display the frame.
      jfrm.setVisible(true);
   }

   public static void main(String args[]) {
      // Create the frame on the event dispatching thread.
      SwingUtilities.invokeLater(new Runnable() {
        public void run() {
          new NumInfoTable();
        }
      });
   }
}
```

This program includes several new, important techniques, so let's examine it closely. First, notice that the package **javax.swing.table** is included. As explained earlier, this is the package in which all of the **JTable** support interfaces and classes are stored. It is needed because it contains **AbstractTableModel**.

The first class defined by the program is **NumInfoModel**, which extends **AbstractTableModel**. **NumInfoModel** defines two fields. The first is **numRows**, which holds the number of rows in the model. As you will see, the model's constructor allows you to create a table of any number of rows. The number specified is stored in **numRows**. The second is **colNames**, which is an array of strings that holds the column header names.

Next, **NumInfoModel** declares its constructor. It requires that the user pass in the number of rows of information desired. It first calls **AbstractTableModel**'s constructor via **super( )** and then sets **numRows** to the value passed in **len**.

NumInfoModel then overrides **getRowCount( )** (which returns the value of **numRows**) and **getColumnCount( )** (which always returns 4). The reason that **getColumnCount( )** always returns 4 is because (in this case) the number of columns will not change. Next, **NumInfoModel** overrides **getColumnName( )**, which returns the column name given its index. In this case, it simply returns the corresponding name from the **colNames** array.

Of most interest is the override of **getValueAt( )**. It computes and returns the values for all four columns. For the first column, it simply returns the row number plus 2. For the second column, it calls the method **isPrime( )** to determine if the value in the first column is prime. If it is prime, it returns "Yes"; otherwise it returns "No." For the third and fourth columns, the method returns the square and the square root of the value in first column. Therefore, for all four columns, all values are computed dynamically, and none come from an array. You could easily apply the same basic technique if you wanted to create a table that contained data that was obtained from a database; a network data source, such as real-time weather data; or from a file.

Finally, the program creates the **NumInfoTable** class to demonstrate **NumInfoModel**. It works like the previous examples, except that it creates a **JTable** by passing it an instance of **NumInfoModel**, as shown here:

```
jtabNumInfo = new JTable(new NumInfoModel(99));
```

Thus, instead of constructing a table from an array or a vector, the table is constructed from the specified model.

The preceding example does not allow the user to edit a cell. In cases in which you want the user to edit a cell, you will need to override **isCellEditable( )** and **setValueAt( )**. The return value from **isCellEditable( )** determines whether a cell can or cannot be edited by the user. The default implementation of **isCellEditable( )** provided by **AbstractTableModel** returns false, which prevents a cell from being edited. Thus, you must override **isCellEditable( )** to enable a cell to be edited. However, overriding **isCellEditable( )** to return true is only half the solution because the default implementation of **setValueAt( )** does nothing. Thus, even if **isCellEditable( )** returns true for a specific cell, that value won't be reflected in the model unless **setValueAt( )** is overridden so that it handles the updated data. **setValueAt( )** must also fire a **TableModelEvent** to inform listeners that the data in the cell has changed. An easy way to do this is to call the **fireTableCellUpdated( )** method, which is defined by

AbstractTableModel. (The answer to Mastery Check question 16 shows an example of this process in action. See the Appendix.)

One last point: notice that the values in the Square Root column are displayed with a large number of fractional values. This is the output produced by the default cell renderer. To reduce the number of decimal places shown (or otherwise change the format of data displayed in a table), you will need to create a custom cell renderer.

CRITICAL SKILL
8.8 # Some Table Options

This module has only scratched the surface of the features available in **JTable**. Here are a few of its other capabilities.

One option that you will find very useful is **JTable**'s ability to print a table. This is accomplished by calling **print( )**. This method has several forms and was added by JDK 5. Its simplest form is shown here:

boolean print( ) throws java.awt.print.PrinterException

It returns true if the table is printed and false if the user cancels printing. This method causes the standard Print dialog to be displayed. For example, to print the e-mail table used earlier in this chapter, you can use the following code sequence:

```
try {
  jtabEmail.print();
} catch (java.awt.print.PrinterException exc) { // ... }
```

You might want to try adding this code to one of the previous examples just to prove that it *really is* that easy to print a table!

You can control a couple of properties related to the grid. First, you can set the grid color by calling **setGridColor( )**. Second, you can control whether the grid lines are shown at all by calling **setShowGrid( )**. By default, the grid lines are shown. If you pass false to this method, the grid lines are not shown. Alternatively, you can control the display of the horizontal and vertical grid lines independently by calling **setShowVerticalLines( )** and **setShowHorizontalLines( )**.

You can add a column to a table by calling **addColumn( )**. You can remove a column by calling **removeColumn( )**. You can move a column be calling **moveColumn( )**.

One of the most important options enables you to set the cell renderer. As mentioned earlier, a cell renderer is a component that controls how the contents of a cell are displayed. If you don't specify a cell renderer explicitly, a default renderer is used, which simply calls **toString( )** on each object in a cell. While this is fine for simple tables, it is inadequate for more sophisticated uses. For example, when displaying monetary values you will normally want to show those values in the money format of the current locale. A cell renderer is an object of a class that implements the **TableCellRenderer** interface. To set the cell renderer, call **setDefaultRenderer( )**. Once you have specified a renderer, then the cells in the table will be rendered by that component automatically. (See Project 8-1 for an example of implementing a cell renderer.)

Another important customization is to define your own cell editor. A cell editor is the component invoked when the user edits the data within a cell. Often the default editors are sufficient, but in some cases you will want to define your own. A cell editor is an object of a class that implements the **TableCellEditor** interface. To set the cell editor, call **setDefaultEditor( )**. Once you have specified an editor, it will be invoked automatically when the user edits a cell. Creating a custom cell editor is beyond the scope of this book, but it is something that you will want to explore on your own as you advance in your study of Swing.

Progress Check

1. What interface must you implement to create a custom table model?
2. When extending **AbstractTableModel**, what methods must you implement on your own?
3. What method added by JDK 5 will print a table?

Project 8-1   Create a Custom Cell Renderer

CellRendererDemo.java   The previous table examples have used the default cell renderer to format data for display. This is perfectly acceptable for many applications, especially those that display only strings or integers. However, if you want to format floating-point values, display currency, or format date and time, then you will need to create a custom cell renderer for your table. For example, in the **NumInfoTable** custom model example, the square roots were displayed using the default renderer. This resulted in 16 fractional digits being shown—more than would normally be desirable. By creating a custom cell renderer, you can control the number of fractional digits displayed precisely.

---

1. **TableModel**
2. **getValueAt( )**, **getRowCount( )**, and **getColumnCount( )**
3. **print( )**

Creating a custom cell renderer is actually quite easy. As explained, a cell renderer is an instance of the **TableCellRenderer** interface. It defines only one method, shown here:

Component getTableCellRendererComponent(JTable *jtab*, Object *val*,
                                  boolean *selected*,
                                  boolean *focus*,
                                  int *r*, int *c*);

Here, *jtab* is a reference to the table that generated the call. The object to be rendered is passed in *val*. If *selected* is true, then the cell must be rendered as selected. If *focus* is true, then the cell must be rendered as being the focus of input. The row and column coordinates of the cell are passed in *r* and *c*. The method returns a **Component** that will render the value.

Although you can implement **TableCellRenderer** on your own, it is usually easier to start with the renderer created by **DefaultTableCellRenderer**, customizing it as needed. **DefaultTableCellRenderer** is the default renderer for **JTable**. It inherits **JLabel**. Thus, it uses **JLabel** as the component that renders the values. This means that you have access to all of **JLabel**'s properties and methods. For example, to render a value after you have formatted it, simply call **setText( )** on the component supplied by **DefaultTableCellRenderer**.

To use a custom renderer, you must set the default renderer on the **JTable** object by calling **setDefaultRenderer( )**, shown here:

void setDefaultRenderer(Class<?> *cl*, TableCellRenderer *tcr*)

Here, *cl* is the class type of the data that the custom renderer will render. For example, to set the renderer for **double**s, you would pass **Double.class**. The renderer is passed in *tcr*. Therefore, after a call to **setDefaultRenderer( )**, when the table needs to render the specified type, the custom renderer is used automatically.

In this project, you will create a custom cell renderer that is used by the **NumInfoTable** class so that the Square Root column displays just four 4 fractional digits rather than the 16 shown by default. After the custom cell renderer has been installed, the table will look like the one shown here:

Use a Custom Cell Renderer				
Value	Prime	Square	Square Root	
2	Yes	4	1.4142	▲
3	Yes	9	1.7321	≡
4	No	16	2.0000	
5	Yes	25	2.2361	
6	No	36	2.4495	
7	Yes	49	2.6458	
8	No	64	2.8284	▼

(continued)

Step by Step

1. Copy the **NumInfoTable** program shown earlier in this module into a file called **CellRendererDemo.java**.

2. To format the **double** values displayed in the Square Root column, we will use the **NumberFormat** formatter. The **NumberFormat** class is packaged in **java.text**, so begin by adding this import statement to the program.

```
import java.text.*;
```

3. Begin creating the custom renderer class, which is called **MyRenderer**, as shown here:

```
// A simple renderer that uses four decimal places for double
// values.
class MyRenderer extends DefaultTableCellRenderer {
```

Notice that **MyRenderer** extends **DefaultTableCellRenderer**. By leveraging off the default implementation, **MyRenderer** does not have to completely implement a renderer on its own.

4. Begin overriding **getTableCellRendererComponent( )** as shown next:

```
// Override getTableCellRendererComponent().
public Component getTableCellRendererComponent(
                 JTable jtab, Object v,
                 boolean selected, boolean focus,
                 int r, int c) {

  // Get the default component so it can be customized.
  JLabel rendComp =
         (JLabel) super.getTableCellRendererComponent(
                      jtab, v, selected, focus, r, c);
```

The important thing to notice here is that the superclass version of **getTableCellRendererComponent( )** is called and a reference to the object returned is stored in **rendComp**. Recall that the **DefaultTableCellRenderer** is a subclass of **JLabel**. This means that the component returned by **getTableCellRendererComponent( )** is a **JLabel**.

5. Create a formatter that will format **double** values such that four fractional digits are displayed. To do this, first obtain a **NumberFormat** object. Then, set the maximum and minimum number of fractional digits to four. This is shown here:

```
// Obtain a formatter.
NumberFormat nf = NumberFormat.getNumberInstance();
```

```
// Display four decimal places.
nf.setMaximumFractionDigits(4);
nf.setMinimumFractionDigits(4);
```

6. Format the value using the formatter and assign the resulting string to **rendComp**, as shown here:

```
// Set the text in the label to the formatted value.
rendComp.setText(nf.format(v));
```

Because **rendComp** is a **JLabel**, this sets the text that will be displayed. Thus, the value is now displayed using four decimal places.

7. Finish **MyRenderer** by returning **rendComp**:

```
    // Return the customized renderer.
    return rendComp;
  }
}
```

8. Inside **NumInfoModel**, you must override the **getColumnClass( )** method, as shown here:

```
// This returns the Double class for the square root column.
// Returns Object for the others.
public Class getColumnClass(int c) {
  if(c==3) return Double.class;
  else return Object.class;
}
```

This method returns the **Object** class for all columns except for Square Root. For that column it returns **Double**. The cell rendering mechanism uses the value returned by **getColumnClass( )** to choose an appropriate renderer for the data in a column. In this case, it means that the values in the fourth column will be formatted as **Double** values rather than **Object** values (assuming that a **Double** renderer is available).

9. Once a **JTable** has been created using the **NumInfoModel**, you must set its default renderer for **Double** values. This is done by calling the **setDefaultRenderer( )**.

```
// Add a custom cell renderer.
jtabNumInfo.setDefaultRenderer(Double.class, new MyRenderer());
```

After this call, the table referred to by **jtabNumInfo** will render all **double** values by using the **MyRenderer**.

(continued)

10. Here is the complete, reworked version of the program that uses the custom cell renderer:

```java
// Project 8-1: Add a custom cell renderer to the
// NumInfoModel. The renderer will display the square
// roots to be displayed with four fractional digits.

import java.awt.*;
import javax.swing.*;
import javax.swing.table.*;
import java.text.*;

// A simple renderer that uses four decimal places for double values.
class MyRenderer extends DefaultTableCellRenderer {

  // Override getTableCellRendererComponent().
  public Component getTableCellRendererComponent(
                    JTable jtab, Object v,
                    boolean selected, boolean focus,
                    int r, int c) {

    // Get the default component so it can be customized.
    JLabel rendComp =
            (JLabel) super.getTableCellRendererComponent(
                            jtab, v, selected, focus, r, c);

    // Obtain a formatter.
    NumberFormat nf = NumberFormat.getNumberInstance();

    // Display four decimal places.
    nf.setMaximumFractionDigits(4);
    nf.setMinimumFractionDigits(4);

    // Set the text in the label to the formatted value.
    rendComp.setText(nf.format(v));

    // Return the customized renderer.
    return rendComp;
  }
}

// Create a model that provides the numeric data.
class NumInfoModel extends AbstractTableModel {
  int numRows;

  String colNames[] = { "Value", "Prime",
                        "Square", "Square Root" };
```

```java
NumInfoModel(int len) {
  super();
  numRows = len;
}

public int getRowCount() { return numRows; }
public int getColumnCount() { return 4; }

// Return the name of the column as specified
// by the colNames array.
public String getColumnName(int c) {
  return colNames[c];
}

// For column 0, return the row number + 2.
// For column 1, return "Yes" if column 1 is prime.
// For column 2, return the square of column 1.
// For column 3, return the square root of column 1.
public Object getValueAt(int r, int c) {

  if(c==0) return new Integer(r+2);
  else if(c==1) {
    if(isPrime(r+2)) return "Yes";
    else return "No";
  }
  else if(c==2) return new Integer((r+2) * (r+2));
  else return new Double(Math.sqrt(r+2));
}

// Return true if v is prime.
boolean isPrime(int v) {
  int i;

  for(i=2; i <= v/i; i++)
    if((v%i) == 0) return false;

  return true;
}

// This returns the Double class for the square root column.
// Returns Object for the others.
public Class getColumnClass(int c) {
  if(c==3) return Double.class;
  else return Object.class;
}
}
```

(continued)

```java
class CellRendererDemo {

  JTable jtabNumInfo;

  CellRendererDemo() {
    // Create a new JFrame container.
    JFrame jfrm = new JFrame("Use a Custom Cell Renderer");

    // Specify FlowLayout for the layout manager.
    jfrm.getContentPane().setLayout(new FlowLayout());

    // Give the frame an initial size.
    jfrm.setSize(500, 200);

    // Terminate the program when the user closes the application.
    jfrm.setDefaultCloseOperation(JFrame.EXIT_ON_CLOSE);

    // Create a table that uses NumInfoModel to
    // display information on the values 2 through 100.
    jtabNumInfo = new JTable(new NumInfoModel(99));

    // Add a custom cell renderer for double values.
    jtabNumInfo.setDefaultRenderer(Double.class, new MyRenderer());

    // Wrap the data in a scroll pane.
    JScrollPane jscrlp = new JScrollPane(jtabNumInfo);

    // Set the viewport size.
    jtabNumInfo.setPreferredScrollableViewportSize(
            new Dimension(450, 110));

    // Add the table to the content pane.
    jfrm.getContentPane().add(jscrlp);

    // Display the frame.
    jfrm.setVisible(true);
  }

  public static void main(String args[]) {
    // Create the frame on the event dispatching thread.
    SwingUtilities.invokeLater(new Runnable() {
      public void run() {
        new CellRendererDemo();
      }
    });
  }
}
```

JTree Fundamentals

JTree is one of the most interesting components in the Swing GUI library. It presents a hierarchical view of data in a tree-like format. In this context, the term *hierarchical* means some items are subordinate to others. For example, a tree is commonly used to display the contents of a file system. In this case, the individual files are subordinate to the directory that contains them. In the tree, branches can be expanded or collapsed on demand, by the user. This allows the tree to present hierarchical data in a compact, yet expandable form.

Like the other Swing components, **JTree** is packaged inside **javax.swing**. However, many of its support classes and interfaces are found in **javax.swing.tree**. A separate package is used because a large number of interfaces and classes are related to trees. Like tables, trees support many customization options. Fortunately, you will often find that the default tree style and capabilities are suitable. Therefore, even though trees support a sophisticated structure, they are still quite easy to work with.

JTree supports a conceptually simple tree-based data structure. A tree begins with a single *root node* that indicates the start of the tree. Under the root are one or more *child nodes*. There are two types of child nodes: *leaf nodes* (also called *terminal nodes*), which have no children, and *branch nodes*, which form the root nodes of *subtrees*. A subtree is simply a tree that is part of a larger tree. The sequence of nodes that leads from the root to a specific node is called a *path*.

Each node has associated with it a *cell renderer,* which determines how the information is displayed, and a *cell editor,* which determines how the user edits the information. (This is similar to the way that **JTable** works.) **JTree** supplies default cell renderers and editors that are suitable for many (perhaps most) applications. However, it is possible to specify your own custom renderers and editors, if desired.

JTree does not provide any scrolling capabilities. Instead, it is wrapped in a **JScrollPane** when scrolling is desired. Because a tree is normally used to contain and display a large number of selections, a scroll pane is almost always needed. Although a fully collapsed tree might be quite small, its expanded form may be quite large.

JTree relies on two models. The first is the tree model, which is defined by the **TreeModel** interface. This model defines those things related to displaying data in a tree format. Swing provides a default implementation of this model called **DefaultTreeModel**. Both **TreeModel** and **DefaultTreeModel** are packaged in **javax.swing.tree**.

The second model determines how items are selected, and it is specified by the **TreeSelectionModel**. It is also packaged in **javax.swing.tree**. Trees support these three selection modes, defined by **TreeSelectionModel**:

CONTIGUOUS_TREE_SELECTION

DISCONTIGUOUS_TREE_SELECTION

SINGLE_TREE_SELECTION

Contiguous selection allows multiple nodes to be selected, but they must be part of the same path. Discontiguous selection allows multiple nodes to be selected, even if they are not part of the same path. (This is the default selection mode.) Single selection allows only one node to be selected at any one time. You can change the selection mode by calling **setSelectionMode( )** on the tree selection model, passing in the new node. Swing provides a default implementation of **TreeSelectionModel** called **DefaultTreeSelectionModel**.

    JTree can generate a variety of events, but three relate directly to trees: **TreeSelectionEvent**, **TreeExpansionEvent**, and **TreeModelEvent**. These are described in the following section.

    JTree defines the constructors shown in Table 8-5. Perhaps the most commonly used constructor is

JTree(TreeNode *tn*)

Here, *tn* is the root node of a tree. Although you can build the tree dynamically, typically the tree is fully constructed before it is passed to **JTree( )**. This is the constructor that we will use to demonstrate **JTree**.

Constructor	Description
JTree( )	Constructs a tree that contains sample data.
JTree(TreeNode *tn*)	Constructs a tree that has *tn* as its root.
JTree(TreeNode *tn*, boolean *checkLeaf*)	Constructs a tree that has *tn* as its root. If *checkLeaf* is true, then only nodes that disallow children are considered leaf nodes. Otherwise, if a node has no children, it is automatically considered a leaf node.
JTree(Hashtable<?, ?> *ht*)	Constructs a tree from the hash table specified by *ht*. Recall that a hash table stores key/value pairs. Each key in *ht* specifies a child node under the top-level root. If the value is an array, then those values become child nodes under the key node.
JTree(Vector<?> *v*)	Constructs a tree from the vector specified by *v*. Each individual element in *v* specifies a child node of the top-level root. If an element in *v* is a vector, then its members are child nodes under a subtree.
JTree(Object *obj*[ ])	Constructs a tree from the array specified by *obj*. Each individual element in *obj* specifies a child node of the top-level root. If an element in *obj* is an array, then its members are child nodes under a subtree.
JTree(TreeModel *tm*)	Constructs a tree from the model specified by *tm*.

Table 8-5 The Constructors for **JTree**

The **TreeNode** interface declares methods that encapsulate information about a tree node. For example, it is possible to obtain a reference to the parent node or an enumeration of the child nodes. You can also determine if a node is a leaf. The **MutableTreeNode** interface extends **TreeNode**. It defines a node that can have its data changed, or have child nodes added or removed.

There is a default implementation of **MutableTreeMode** called **DefaultMutableTreeNode**. This class can be used to construct nodes that are suitable for a wide variety of applications, and we will use it to construct nodes for the sample tree applications that follow. It has three constructors. The one we will use is shown here:

DefaultMutableTreeNode(Object *obj*)

Here, *obj* is the object to be enclosed in this tree node.

In order to create a hierarchy of tree nodes, one node is added to another. This is accomplished by calling the **add( )** method of **DefaultMutableTreeNode**. It is shown here:

void add(MutableTreeNode *child*)

Here, *child* is a mutable tree node that will be added as a child of the invoking node. Thus, to build a tree, you will create a root node and then add subordinate nodes to it.

The following example shows how to build a tree. The tree contains a hierarchy that describes food. The root is labeled Food. Under it are two direct descendent nodes: Fruit and Vegetables. Under Fruit are two descendent nodes: Apples and Pears. Under Apples, Pears, and Vegetables are various leaf nodes, such as Winesap and Corn. Sample output is shown in Figure 8-10.

Figure 8-10 Sample output from the **TreeDemo** program

```
// Demonstrate a tree.
//
// This program shows how to construct and
// display a tree. It does not handle tree events.

import java.awt.*;
import javax.swing.*;
import javax.swing.tree.*;

class TreeDemo {

  TreeDemo() {
    // Create a new JFrame container.
    JFrame jfrm = new JFrame("Tree Demo");

    // Use the default border layout manager.

    // Give the frame an initial size.
    jfrm.setSize(200, 200);

    // Terminate the program when the user closes the application.
    jfrm.setDefaultCloseOperation(JFrame.EXIT_ON_CLOSE);

    // Begin creating the tree by defining the
    // structure and relationship of its nodes.

    // First, create the root node of the tree.
    DefaultMutableTreeNode root =
                new DefaultMutableTreeNode("Food");

    // Next, create two subtrees. One contains
    // fruit, the other vegetables.

    // Create the root of the Fruit subtree.
    DefaultMutableTreeNode fruit =
                new DefaultMutableTreeNode("Fruit");
    root.add(fruit); // add the Fruit node to the tree.

    // The Fruit subtree has two subtrees of its own.
    // The first is Apples. The second is Pears.

    // Create an Apples subtree.
    DefaultMutableTreeNode apples =
                new DefaultMutableTreeNode("Apples");
    fruit.add(apples); // add the Apples node to Fruit

    // Populate the Apples subtree by adding
```

Create the root of the tree.

Create the Fruit node and make it a child of the root.

Create the Apples node and make it a child of Fruit.

```
   // apple varieties to the Apples subtree.
   apples.add(new DefaultMutableTreeNode("Jonathan"));
   apples.add(new DefaultMutableTreeNode("Winesap"));
```

Add leaf nodes to Apples. This completes the Apples subtree.

```
   // Create a Pears subtree.
   DefaultMutableTreeNode pears =
                  new DefaultMutableTreeNode("Pears");
   fruit.add(pears); // add the Pears node to fruit

   // Populate the Pears subtree by adding
   // pear varieties to the Pears subtree.
   pears.add(new DefaultMutableTreeNode("Bartlett"));
```

Create the Pears subtree.

```
   // Create the root of the Vegetables subtree.
   DefaultMutableTreeNode veg =
                  new DefaultMutableTreeNode("Vegetables");
   root.add(veg); // add the Vegetable node to the tree

   // Populate Vegetables.
   veg.add(new DefaultMutableTreeNode("Beans"));
   veg.add(new DefaultMutableTreeNode("Corn"));
   veg.add(new DefaultMutableTreeNode("Potatoes"));
   veg.add(new DefaultMutableTreeNode("Rice"));
```

Create the Vegetables subtree.

```
   // Now, create a JTree that uses the structure
   // defined by the preceding statements.
   JTree jtree = new JTree(root);
```

Construct a **JTree** using the tree just created.

```
   // Finally, wrap the tree in a scroll pane.
   JScrollPane jscrlp = new JScrollPane(jtree);
```

Wrap the tree in a scroll pane.

```
   // Add the tree and label to the content pane.
   jfrm.getContentPane().add(jscrlp, BorderLayout.CENTER);

   // Display the frame.
   jfrm.setVisible(true);
  }

  public static void main(String args[]) {
    // Create the frame on the event dispatching thread.
    SwingUtilities.invokeLater(new Runnable() {
      public void run() {
        new TreeDemo();
      }
    });
  }
}
```

Ask the Expert

Q: **Does** JTree **support cell renderers and cell editors similar to the way** JTable **supports these items?**

A: Yes. The situation is very similar. Of course, **JTree** uses cell renderers and editors that are specific to trees. For a tree, the cell renderer must be an object that implements the **TreeCellRenderer** interface. The tree cell editor must be an object that implements the **TreeCellEditor** interface. When you create a tree as shown in this chapter, a default cell renderer and editor are provided. They are **DefaultTreeCellRenderer** and **DefaultTreeCellEditor**, respectively. One last point: By default, trees are not editable. To enable a cell to be edited, you must call **setEditable(true)** on the tree.

Let's look closely at how the tree is created. First, a root node called **root** is constructed, and it is assigned the string "Food." Next, the **fruit** node is created, assigned the string "Fruit," and added to **root**. The **fruit** node forms the root of a subtree that contains various types of fruit. Then to **fruit** is added a node called **apples** that represents apples. This node forms the root of the subtree under **fruit** that contains apples. To **apples** are added leaf nodes that represent specific types of apples. This same process is repeated for pears. After both the **apples** and **pears** subtrees have been constructed, the **fruit** node has two child nodes, both of which are root nodes of their own subtrees. Next, a node called **veg** is constructed and added to **root**. It becomes the root of the Vegetables subtree. To **veg** are added leaves that represent beans, corn, potatoes, and rice.

At this point, the entire tree has been constructed and the **JTree** can be created by the following line:

```
JTree jtree = new JTree(root);
```

Here, **root** is passed to the **JTree** constructor. This means that **jtree** will display the tree that descends from **root**. Next, **jtree** is wrapped in a scroll pane, and the scroll pane is added to the center of the content pane. (Notice that the default border layout is used by this example.)

Progress Check

1. What two models does **JTree** rely on?

2. What is **TreeNode**?

3. To add a child to a node, what method is called?

CRITICAL SKILL
8.10 # Handle Tree Events

There are three events that are directly related to trees: **TreeSelectionEvent**, **TreeExpansionEvent**, and **TreeModelEvent**. A **TreeSelectionEvent** is fired when a node is selected or deselected. A **TreeExpansionEvent** is fired when the tree is expanded or collapsed, or when a tree will be expanding or collapsing. A **TreeModelEvent** is fired when the data or the structure of the tree changes. Each is examined here.

TreeSelectionEvent

To listen for a **TreeSelectionEvent**, you must implement the **TreeSelectionListener** interface and register the listener with the **JTree** instance. **TreeSelectionListener** defines the following method:

void valueChanged(TreeSelectionEvent *tse*)

Here, *tse* is the selection event.

   TreeSelectionEvent defines several methods. One of particular interest is **getPath( )**, shown here:

TreePath getPath( )

The path that leads to the selection is returned as a **TreePath** object.

---

1. **TreeModel** and **TreeSelectionModel**
2. **TreeNode** is the interface that encapsulates a node in a tree.
3. **add( )**

TreePath is a class packaged in **javax.swing.tree**. It encapsulates a path that leads from the root of the tree to the node selected. **TreePath** defines several methods. Two are of special interest:

Object[ ] getPath( )

Object getLastPathComponent( )

The **getPath( )** method returns an array of objects that represent all nodes in the path. The **getLastPathComponent( )** returns a reference to the last node in the path.

TreeExpansionEvent

To listen for a **TreeExpansionEvent**, you must implement the **TreeExpansionListener** interface and register the listener with the **JTree** instance. **TreeExpansionListener** defines the following two methods:

void treeCollapsed(TreeExpansionEvent *tee*)

void treeExpanded(TreeExpansionEvent *tee*)

Here, *tee* is the tree expansion event. The first method is called when a subtree is hidden, and the second method is called when a subtree becomes visible. However, **JTree** allows you to listen for two types of tree expansion notifications. First, you can be notified *just before* an expansion event by registering a **TreeWillExpandListener**. Second, you can be notified after the expansion event by registering a **TreeExpansionListener**. Usually, you will register a **TreeExpansionListener**, but Swing gives you the choice.

TreeExpansionEvent defines only one method, **getPath( )**, which is shown here:

TreePath getPath( )

This method returns a **TreePath** object that contains the path to the node that was or will be expanded or collapsed.

TreeModelEvent

To listen for a **TreeModelEvent**, you must implement the **TreeModelListener** interface and register the listener with the tree model. **TreeModelEvent** defines the following methods:

void treeNodesChanged(TreeModelEvent *tme*)

void treeStructureChanged(TreeModelEvent *tme*)

void treeNodesInserted(TreeModelEvent *tme*)

void treeNodesRemoved(TreeModelEvent *tme*)

Here, *tme* is the tree model event. The names imply the type of model event that has occurred.
   TreeModelEvent defines several methods. One of special interest is **getTreePath( )**,
shown here:

TreePath getTreePath( )

This method returns the path to the parent of the node at which point the change occurred.
   As mentioned, a tree model listener must be registered with the tree model, not with the
JTree instance. The tree model is obtained by calling **getModel( )** on the **JTree** instance. It
is shown here:

TreeModel getModel( )

A Tree Event Demonstration Program

The following program reworks the previous example so that it handles all three **JTree** events:
TreeSelectionEvent, **TreeExpansionEvent**, and **TreeModelEvent**. Each time one of these
events occurs, a message describing the event is displayed in a label. Sample output is shown
in Figure 8-11.

Figure 8-11 Sample output from the **TreeEventDemo** program

```
// Demonstrate tree events.

import java.awt.*;
import javax.swing.*;
import javax.swing.event.*;
import javax.swing.tree.*;

class TreeEventDemo {

  JLabel jlab;

  TreeEventDemo() {
    // Create a new JFrame container.
    JFrame jfrm = new JFrame("Tree Event Demo");

    // Use the default border layout manager.

    // Give the frame an initial size.
    jfrm.setSize(200, 200);

    // Terminate the program when the user closes the application.
    jfrm.setDefaultCloseOperation(JFrame.EXIT_ON_CLOSE);

    // Create a label that will display the tree selection.
    jlab = new JLabel();

    // Begin creating the tree by defining the
    // structure and relationship of its nodes.

    // First, create the root node of the tree.
    DefaultMutableTreeNode root =
                    new DefaultMutableTreeNode("Food");

    // Next, create two subtrees. One contains
    // fruit. The other vegetables.

    // Create the root of the Fruit subtree.
    DefaultMutableTreeNode fruit =
                    new DefaultMutableTreeNode("Fruit");
    root.add(fruit); // add the Fruit node to the tree.

    // The Fruit subtree has two subtrees of its own.
    // The first is Apples, the second is Pears.

    // Create an Apples subtree.
    DefaultMutableTreeNode apples =
```

```
                    new DefaultMutableTreeNode("Apples");
fruit.add(apples); // add the Apples node to Fruit

// Populate the Apples subtree by adding
// apple varieties to the Apples subtree.
apples.add(new DefaultMutableTreeNode("Jonathan"));
apples.add(new DefaultMutableTreeNode("Winesap"));

// Create a Pears subtree.
DefaultMutableTreeNode pears =
                    new DefaultMutableTreeNode("Pears");
fruit.add(pears); // add the Pears node to fruit

// Populate the Pears subtree by adding
// pear varieties to the Pears subtree.
pears.add(new DefaultMutableTreeNode("Bartlett"));

// Create the root of the Vegetables subtree.
DefaultMutableTreeNode veg =
                    new DefaultMutableTreeNode("Vegetables");
root.add(veg); // add the Vegetable node to the tree

// Populate Vegetables.
veg.add(new DefaultMutableTreeNode("Beans"));
veg.add(new DefaultMutableTreeNode("Corn"));
veg.add(new DefaultMutableTreeNode("Potatoes"));
veg.add(new DefaultMutableTreeNode("Rice"));

// Now, create a JTree that uses the structure
// defined by the preceding statements.
JTree jtree = new JTree(root);

// Allow the tree to be edited so that model
// events can be generated.
jtree.setEditable(true);

// Set the tree selection mode to single selection.
TreeSelectionModel tsm = jtree.getSelectionModel();
tsm.setSelectionMode(TreeSelectionModel.SINGLE_TREE_SELECTION);

// Finally, wrap the tree in a scroll pane.
JScrollPane jscrlp = new JScrollPane(jtree);

// Listen for tree expansion events.
jtree.addTreeExpansionListener(new TreeExpansionListener() {
  public void treeExpanded(TreeExpansionEvent tse) {
```

Set the tree to single selection mode.

Listen for expansion events.

```
          // Get the path to the expansion point.
          TreePath tp = tse.getPath();

          // Display the node
          jlab.setText("Expansion: " +
                       tp.getLastPathComponent());
      }

      public void treeCollapsed (TreeExpansionEvent tse) {
        // Get the path to the expansion point.
        TreePath tp = tse.getPath();

        // Display the node
        jlab.setText("Collapse: " +
                     tp.getLastPathComponent());
      }
    });
```

Listen for selection events.

```
    // Listen for tree selection events.
    jtree.addTreeSelectionListener(new TreeSelectionListener() {
      public void valueChanged(TreeSelectionEvent tse) {
        // Get the path to the selection.
        TreePath tp = tse.getPath();

        // Display the selected node.
        jlab.setText("Selection event: " +
                     tp.getLastPathComponent());
      }
    });
```

Listen for model events.

```
    // Listen for tree model events. Notice that the
    // listener is registered with the tree model.
    jtree.getModel().addTreeModelListener(new TreeModelListener() {
      public void treeNodesChanged(TreeModelEvent tse) {
        // Get the path to the change.
        TreePath tp = tse.getTreePath();

        // Display the path.
        jlab.setText("Model change path: " + tp);
      }

      // Empty implementations of the remaining TreeModelEvent
      // methods. Implement these if your application
      // needs to handle these actions.
      public void treeNodesInserted(TreeModelEvent tse) {}
      public void treeNodesRemoved(TreeModelEvent tse) {}
```

```
      public void treeStructureChanged(TreeModelEvent tse) {}
    });

    // Add the tree and label to the content pane.
    jfrm.getContentPane().add(jscrlp, BorderLayout.CENTER);
    jfrm.getContentPane().add(jlab, BorderLayout.SOUTH);

    // Display the frame.
    jfrm.setVisible(true);
  }

  public static void main(String args[]) {
    // Create the frame on the event dispatching thread.
    SwingUtilities.invokeLater(new Runnable() {
      public void run() {
        new TreeEventDemo();
      }
    });
  }
}
```

This program uses the same tree structure as the previous one and the way that the tree is constructed has not changed. However, in order to handle tree events, the event handlers have been included and several other additions have been made. Let's look closely at the changes. First, notice that a label called **jlab** has been included that will be used to display information about the events. This label is added to the south position of the content pane.

In order to generate model events, the tree has been made editable by calling **setEditable(true)** on **jtree**. By default, trees are not editable. The **setEditable( )** method is shown here:

void setEditable(boolean *canEdit*)

If *canEdit* is true, the tree nodes can be edited. If *canEdit* is false, the contents of the nodes cannot be edited.

By default, a tree allows multiple nodes to be selected. The program changes this to single selection mode. This is done with the following sequence:

```
TreeSelectionModel tsm = jtree.getSelectionModel();
tsm.setSelectionMode(TreeSelectionModel.SINGLE_TREE_SELECTION);
```

As explained, the selection mode is controlled by the selection model. Therefore, a reference to the selection model is obtained and then **setSelectionMode( )** is called to set the selection mode.

Next, the three event handlers are added. The **TreeExpansionListener** implements the **treeExpanded( )** and **treeCollapsed( )** methods and reports expansion and collapse events by displaying the node at which the expansion or collapse occurred. The **TreeSelectionListener** implements the **valueChanged( )** method, which displays the node that has been selected. The **TreeModelListener** implements **treeNodesChanged( )** so that it displays the path to the node that changed. This handler will be called when you edit a node, for example. The remaining three methods defined by **TreeModelListener** are given empty implementations because they are not needed by the program.

CRITICAL SKILL
8.11
Some Tree Options

Like tables, trees support a wide range of options. For example, you can define a custom tree model. You can also define custom cell renderers and editors. (See the preceding "Ask the Expert.") However, often the default tree (with the default model, cell renderers, and cell editors) is exactly what you want, so you might not have reason to change these items.

A method in **JTree** that you might find useful on occasion is **setRootVisible( )**, shown next. It determines if the root node is displayed.

void setRootVisible(boolean *visible*)

If *visible* is true, the root is displayed. Otherwise, it is not shown. Not showing the root is helpful in cases in which displaying the root adds no useful information. By not showing the root, the tree can be displayed in a smaller area.

A small, but sometimes beneficial customization is to turn on or off the root handles. Depending on the look and feel, a root node may or may not have *handles* associated with it. (A handle is a small icon that indicates whether a branch is expanded or collapsed.) You can turn on or off the root handles by calling **setShowsRootHandles( )**, shown here:

void setShowsRootHandles(boolean *on*)

If *on* is true, the root handles are shown. Otherwise, they are not shown.

Several interesting options are available through **DefaultMutableTreeNode**. Following is a sampling. You can change the contents of a node by calling **setUserObject( )**, shown here:

void setUserObject(Object *obj*)

Here, *obj* becomes the new object associated with the invoking node.

You can remove a node by calling **remove( )** on the parent node. One form is shown here:

void remove(MutableTreeNode *node*)

Here, *node* must be a child of the invoking node.

You can determine if a node is a leaf by calling **isLeaf( )**, shown here:

boolean isLeaf( )

It returns true if the invoking node is a terminal node (one without any child nodes). It returns false otherwise.

You can obtain enumerations of various traversals of the nodes of a tree by using the following methods defined by **DefaultMutableTreeNode**:

Enumeration breadthFirstEnumeration( )

Enumeration depthFirstEnumeration( )

Enumeration postorderEnumeration( )

Enumeration preorderEnumeration( )

Each returns the specified enumeration. Beginning at the root, a breadth first traversal visits all nodes on the same level before advancing to the next level. A depth first traversal (which is the same as a postorder traversal) first visits the leaves and then the root of each subtree. A preorder traversal visits the root followed by the leaves of each subtree.

Progress Check

1. When a node is expanded, a _____ is fired.

2. What event is generated when the data in a node changes?

3. What is **TreePath**?

4. What method returns a preorder traversal of a tree?

---

1. **TreeExpansionEvent**

2. **TreeModelEvent**

3. **TreePath** is a class that encapsulates the nodes that lead from the root to a specific node.

4. **preorderEnumeration( )**

Project 8-2 Enumerate a Tree

TreeEnum.java This project shows how to enumerate the Food tree used by the tree examples in this module. It will use a preorder traversal, but the same basic technique can be used to obtain and display any other tree traversal.

Step by Step

1. Copy the **TreeDemo** program into a file called **TreeEnum.java**.

2. Add the following **import** statement.

```
import java.util.*;
```

This package is needed because it contains the **Enumeration** class.

3. After the entire tree has been constructed, add the following lines of code.

```
Enumeration preorder = root.preorderEnumeration();
while(preorder.hasMoreElements())
   System.out.println(preorder.nextElement());
```

This sequence obtains a preorder traversal of the nodes in the tree, beginning at the root node. For simplicity, it displays the nodes on the console, but you can easily change it to display the nodes in a label or a text field. The output is shown here:

```
Food
Fruit
Apples
Jonathan
Winesap
Pears
Bartlett
Vegetables
Beans
Corn
Potatoes
Rice
```

4. As this project shows, it is quite easy to obtain a list of all nodes in a tree. On your own, try displaying the other traversals. Make sure that you understand how each sequence is ordered and why they differ.

Module 8 Mastery Check

1. **JTable** relies on several support classes and interfaces. What package are they stored in?

2. What method sets the scrollable viewport size in a table?

3. What is the name of the model that defines a table?

4. If a **JTable** is not wrapped in a scroll pane, its header will not be shown unless you explicitly request it. True or false?

5. To listen for column selection events on a table, you must register a **ListSelectionListener** with what object?

6. To listen for table model events, you must register a _____.

7. Relative to **TableModel**, what does **setValueAt( )** do?

8. What **JTable** method changes the auto-resizing mode?

9. To implement a custom table model, what class will you normally extend?

10. What interface defines the form of a cell renderer for a table?

11. **JTree** can be used to display only balanced, binary trees. True or False?

12. What is a leaf node?

13. To construct a tree from objects of type **DefaultMutableTreeNode**, what procedure is followed?

14. When the data in a tree changes, what type of event is fired?

15. To obtain an enumeration that contains a postorder traversal of a tree, what method is called?

16. Create a program that displays a table that computes the tip for a meal. In the first column, display the cost of the meal in increments of 1. Have the next three columns compute the tip using the percentages: 10, 15, and 20. In the final column, allow the user to entered a suggested tip. Use a custom cell renderer to display the values in money format. Allow the

number of rows to be specified when the table is constructed. When you are done, your table should look like the one shown here:

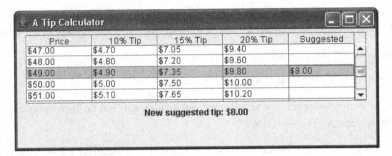

17. Show the statement you must add to the **TreeDemo** program to cause the root node to be hidden.

18. Adapt the enumeration code in Project 8-2 so that it reports whether each node in the traversal is a leaf or has child nodes.

19. On your own and using the **TreeDemo** program as a guide, create a program that uses a tree to organize a display of your collection of books. Organize each book under an appropriate category. For example, this book will be a leaf in the following path: Programming | Java | Swing.

Module 9

Dialogs

413

Although the individual controls provided by Swing, such as text fields, buttons, and lists, form the foundation of any GUI, there will be times when you need to link two or more of these controls together as a unit in order to handle more sophisticated input operations. For example, if your program needs a username and password before allowing access to a network, you will want to request both of these items as a single logical and visual unit. The way that this is accomplished is by creating a *dialog*.

A dialog is a separate window that requests some form of response from the user. It will contain at least a message and a button, but much more sophisticated dialogs are both possible and commonplace. Dialogs are also commonly referred to as *dialog boxes* or *dialog windows*.

A dialog provides a means by which your program can achieve two important goals. First, a dialog gives you a way to organize the components necessary for complex input situations that go beyond what the basic components can handle individually. For example, a word processor would use a dialog to allow the user to select a type font, point size, and style. Such a dialog would be a composite of several individual components that, when combined, define a typeface. Second, a dialog gives your program a way to request input from the user that is necessary before the program proceeds. For example, you might use a dialog to prompt the user for a password and then wait until the password is entered. Whatever the use, dialogs are an important part of many Swing applications.

Swing provides extensive support for dialogs. The main dialog class is **JDialog**, but you won't often use it directly. Instead, many dialog situations can be handled by using **JOptionPane**, which provides a wide variety of built-in dialog styles. Swing also provides two important predefined dialogs called **JFileChooser** and **JColorChooser**. They handle two common, yet somewhat difficult tasks. This chapter examines all of these classes, but the main emphasis is on **JOptionPane**.

CRITICAL SKILL
9.1 JOptionPane

In the modern GUI programming environment, there are two basic ways that dialogs are used. First, there are the larger, more complicated dialogs that link several input components. An example is a dialog that enables a user to configure a modem connection. Such a dialog contains components that allow the user to specify the modem speed and protocol, enable hardware flow control, specify an initialization command, and so on. To create a sophisticated dialog such as this requires the use of **JDialog**, which is discussed later in this module.

The second type of dialog is much simpler. This is a dialog that prompts the user and then waits for a response. Perhaps the most common example is the "Exit? Yes/No" dialog that simply confirms if you really want to exit a program. Because these relatively simple dialogs form such an important part of Java programming, Swing provides extensive built-in support for them through the **JOptionPane** class.

JOptionPane is an easy-to-use dialog class that provides solutions to many common dialog-based problems. **JOptionPane** supports the four basic types of dialogs listed here:

- Message

- Confirmation

- Input

- Option

A message dialog displays a message and then waits until the user presses the OK button. This dialog provides an easy and effective way to ensure that the user is aware of some piece of information. For example, you could use a message dialog to tell the user that a network connection has been lost by displaying "Connection Lost" inside the dialog.

A confirmation dialog asks the user a Yes/No question and waits for a response. This dialog is used in cases in which a course of action needs to be confirmed. For example, a confirmation dialog that displays the message "Exit without saving changes?" could be used to ensure that the user *does* actually want to exit a program without saving the changes.

An input dialog allows the user to enter a string or select an item from a list. The advantage of this dialog is that it allows the user to respond by entering a string of their own choosing. Thus, it goes beyond a simple Yes/No response. You might use this type of dialog to obtain the URL of some resource, for example.

An option dialog lets you specify a list of options from which the user will choose. Thus, it enables you to create a dialog that supplies options that are not available with the other dialogs.

Somewhat surprisingly, **JOptionPane** is not derived from **JDialog**. Instead, **JOptionPane** is a container for the components that will be used by the dialog. However, it does *use* **JDialog**. **JOptionPane** constructs a **JDialog** object automatically and adds itself to that object. It then handles the details of displaying the dialog, obtaining the response, and closing the dialog. In essence, **JOptionPane** provides a streamlined way to create and manage simple dialogs.

All dialogs created by **JOptionPane** are *modal*. A modal dialog is executed on the invoking thread. As a result, it demands a response before the program will continue. You cannot refocus input to another part of the application without first closing the dialog. Thus, from a user's point of view a modal dialog stops the program until the user responds. Although modal dialogs are the most common, you can also create *non-modal* (also called *modeless*) dialogs. A non-modal dialog runs in its own thread and *does not* prevent other parts of the program from being used. Thus, the rest of the program remains active and input can be refocused to other windows. However, you cannot create a non-modal dialog using **JOptionPane**. (Non-modal dialogs are easily created by **JDialog**, however, as described later in this module.)

Although you can create a **JOptionPane** by using one of its constructors, you normally won't do so. Instead, you will usually use one of its **show** factory methods. These methods automatically construct a dialog in one of the four styles and then return the user's response. For example, to create a simple message dialog, you can use the **showMessageDialog( )** method. It creates a dialog that displays a message and then waits until the user clicks the OK button. As you will see, the factory methods make **JOptionPane** extraordinarily easy to use.

JOptionPane supports two basic categories of **show** methods. The first creates a dialog that uses **JDialog** to hold the dialog. This is the type of **JOptionPane** that you will normally create, and it is the only type described in this book. The second category uses a **JInternalFrame** to hold the dialog. This type of dialog is much less common and the topic of internal frames is beyond the scope of this book.

JOptionPane defines the following four factory methods that create standard, **JDialog**-based dialogs: **showConfirmDialog( )**, **showInputDialog( )**, **showMessageDialog( )**, and **showOptionDialog( )**. Each creates the type of dialog implied by its name. All are static methods. The first three have several overloaded forms. The remainder of this discussion examines each style of dialog separately.

NOTE

As a point of interest, the **show** factory methods that use internal frames use the same names as those just described, except that they add **Internal** to the name of the corresponding noninternal frame method. For example, the internal frame version of **showMessageDialog( )** is called **showInternalMessageDialog( )**.

Progress Check

1. What are the four types of dialogs that can be created by **JOptionPane**?

2. What is the difference between modal and non-modal dialogs?

3. Is **JOptionPane** derived from **JDialog**?

1. Message, confirmation, input, and option

2. A modal dialog executes on the invoking thread, thus suspending other program activity. A non-modal dialog executes on its own thread, thus allowing the rest of the program to remain active.

3. No

CRITICAL SKILL
9.2 # showMessageDialog( )

The **showMessageDialog( )** method creates the simplest dialog that can be constructed. It displays a message and then waits until the user presses the OK button. Despite this simplicity, **showMessageDialog( )** still has three forms. Its simplest version is shown here:

```
static void showMessageDialog(Component parent, Object msg)
    throws HeadlessException
```

Here, *parent* specifies the component relative to which the dialog is displayed. If you pass null for this argument, then the dialog is usually displayed in the center of the screen. The message to display is passed in *msg*. Technically, this does not have to be a string. For example, you could pass a **JLabel**. However, for simple dialogs, a string is typically used. When the dialog is displayed, an OK button is included. The dialog waits until the user presses OK. Therefore, the call to **showMessageDialog( )** will not return until the user either presses OK or closes the dialog by clicking the close box. (As mentioned, all dialogs created by the **show** methods are modal. This means that the calling thread waits until the call returns.) Because there is only one option for the user (the OK button), there is no need to return a response and the return type is **void**.

Notice that **showMessageDialog( )** can throw a **HeadlessException**. This exception is thrown if you attempt to show a dialog in a noninteractive environment, such as one in which no screen, mouse, or keyboard is attached. Because the use of Swing usually implies an interactive, graphical environment, it is not always necessary to handle this exception. However, if you are writing code that might run in an environment that does not support a complete GUI interface, then you will need to watch for a **HeadlessException** and provide an appropriate alternative if the dialog cannot be displayed.

Before going on, it will be useful to see this simplest of dialogs in action. The following program uses **showMessageDialog( )** to display a dialog that tells the user that disk space is low. Sample output is shown in Figure 9-1.

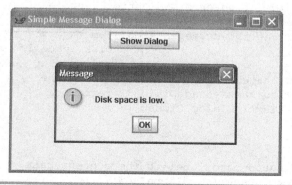

Figure 9-1 Sample output from the **MsgDialogDemo** program

```
// A very simple JOptionPane demonstration.

import java.awt.*;
import java.awt.event.*;
import javax.swing.*;

class MsgDialogDemo {

  JLabel jlab;
  JButton jbtnShow;
  JFrame jfrm;

  MsgDialogDemo() {
    // Create a new JFrame container.
    jfrm = new JFrame("Simple Message Dialog");

    // Specify FlowLayout for the layout manager.
    jfrm.getContentPane().setLayout(new FlowLayout());

    // Give the frame an initial size.
    jfrm.setSize(400, 250);

    // Terminate the program when the user closes the application.
    jfrm.setDefaultCloseOperation(JFrame.EXIT_ON_CLOSE);

    // Create a label that will show when the dialog returns.
    jlab = new JLabel();

    // Create a button that will display the dialog.
    jbtnShow = new JButton("Show Dialog");

    // Add action listener for the button.
    jbtnShow.addActionListener(new ActionListener() {
      public void actionPerformed(ActionEvent le) {
        // Create a dialog that shows a message.
        JOptionPane.showMessageDialog(jfrm,
                              "Disk space is low.");

        // This statement won't execute until the
        // call to showMessageDialog() returns.
        jlab.setText("Dialog Closed");
      }
    });

    // Add the button and label to the content pane.
    jfrm.getContentPane().add(jbtnShow);
    jfrm.getContentPane().add(jlab);
```

Create a message dialog.

```
    // Display the frame.
    jfrm.setVisible(true);
  }

  public static void main(String args[]) {
    // Create the frame on the event dispatching thread.
    SwingUtilities.invokeLater(new Runnable() {
      public void run() {
        new MsgDialogDemo();
      }
    });
  }
}
```

Here is how the program works. The main window contains a button called Show Dialog. When this button is pressed, the action listener linked to the button displays the dialog by calling **showMessageDialog( )**. The parent of the dialog is the **jfrm**, which is the main window of the program. The message to display is "Disk space is low." When the call to **showMessageDialog( )** executes, the dialog is displayed. At that point, the dialog has input focus and, because the dialog is modal, focus cannot be redirected to the main window. Therefore, the main window is inactive until the dialog is closed, either by the user clicking the OK button or clicking the close box in the dialog window. When the dialog is closed, the call to **showMessageDialog( )** returns and the text in **jlab** is set to indicate this fact.

There are two other forms of **showMessageDialog( )** that let you more precisely configure various aspects of the dialog. The first is shown here:

static void showMessageDialog(Component *parent*, Object *msg*,
                    String *title*, int *msgT*)
                    throws HeadlessException

The first two parameters are the same as the version of the method shown earlier. The *title* parameter lets you specify a title for the dialog. By default, the title is Message, as shown in Figure 9-1, but it is usually better to specify a title that fits the message that you are displaying precisely. The *msgT* parameter indicates the nature of the message. It must be one of the following values defined by **JOptionPane**:

ERROR_MESSAGE	Indicates that an error message is displayed. The standard error icon is used.
INFORMATION_MESSAGE	Indicates that an informational message is displayed. The standard information icon is used. This is the default message type.
PLAIN_MESSAGE	Indicates a "plain" message, which is one in which no icon is displayed.

QUESTION_MESSAGE	Indicates that a question message is displayed. The question mark icon is used.
WARNING_MESSAGE	Indicates that a warning message is displayed. The standard warning icon is used.

Like many other aspects of Swing, the precise effect of the *msgT* parameter is determined by the look and feel.

To see the benefits of specifying a title and a message type, substitute the following call to **showMessageDialog( )** in the preceding example:

```
JOptionPane.showMessageDialog(jfrm,
                              "Disk space is low.",
                              "Warning",
                              JOptionPane.WARNING_MESSAGE);
```

After doing so, the dialog will look like the one shown in Figure 9-2.

By default, a message dialog displays a standard system icon. You can specify one of your own by using this version of **showMessageDialog( )**:

static void showMessageDialog(Component *parent*, Object *msg*,
                     String *title*, int *msgT*, Icon *image*)
                        throws HeadlessException

Here, the icon to display is passed in *image*. Keep in mind, however, that if your message falls into one of the predefined categories, then it is probably best to use the standard icon rather than a custom one because the standard icon will be the most easily recognized.

To see the effects of supplying your own icon, create an image file called **myIcon.gif** and then substitute the following call to **showMessageDialog( )** into the preceding program:

```
JOptionPane.showMessageDialog(jfrm,
                              "Disk space is low.",
                              "Warning",
                              JOptionPane.WARNING_MESSAGE,
                              new ImageIcon("myIcon.gif"));
```

After making this change, the dialog will look like the one shown in Figure 9-3.

Figure 9-2 A message dialog that specifies a title and a message type

Figure 9-3 Use a custom icon in a dialog.

Progress Check

1. What type of response does **showMessageDialog( )** request?

2. What is the constant that indicates a warning message?

3. Must the message displayed by **showMessageDialog( )** be a string?

CRITICAL SKILL
9.3 showConfirmDialog( )

Another very common dialog type is one that requests a simple Yes/No response from the user. In Swing, this is called a confirmation dialog, and it is created by calling **showConfirmDialog( )**. There are several versions of this method. The simplest one is shown here:

static int showConfirmDialog(Component *parent*, Object *msg*)
                    throws HeadlessException

Here, *parent* specifies the component relative to which the dialog is displayed. If you pass null for this argument, then the dialog is usually displayed in the center of the screen. The message to display is passed in *msg*. This can be any type of object, but normally a string is used. The dialog automatically contains three buttons called Yes, No, and Cancel. The title of the dialog is Select an Option.

---

1. OK
2. **WARNING_MESSAGE**
3. No, it can be any type of object.

The method returns an integer value that indicates the user's choice (that is, which button was pressed). The return value will be one of these constants defined by **JOptionPane**:

CANCEL_OPTION	Returned if the user clicks Cancel
CLOSED_OPTION	Returned if the user closed the dialog without making a choice
NO_OPTION	Returned if the user clicks No
YES_OPTION	Returned if the user clicks Yes

Notice **CLOSED_OPTION**. This value is returned when the user closes the dialog (by clicking on the close box) instead of pressing one of the buttons. In most applications and in most environments, you should handle a **CLOSED_OPTION** response as if it were a **NO_OPTION** response. A **CLOSED_OPTION** should never be interpreted as a **YES_OPTION**.

The following program creates a simple confirmation dialog and shows how to handle the responses. Figure 9-4 shows the dialog.

```java
// Use a simple confirmation dialog.

import java.awt.*;
import java.awt.event.*;
import javax.swing.*;

class ConfirmDialogDemo {

  JLabel jlab;
  JButton jbtnShow;
  JFrame jfrm;

  ConfirmDialogDemo() {
    // Create a new JFrame container.
    jfrm = new JFrame("A Confirmation Dialog");

    // Specify FlowLayout for the layout manager.
    jfrm.getContentPane().setLayout(new FlowLayout());

    // Give the frame an initial size.
    jfrm.setSize(400, 250);

    // Terminate the program when the user closes the application.
    jfrm.setDefaultCloseOperation(JFrame.EXIT_ON_CLOSE);

    // Create a label that will show the user's response.
    jlab = new JLabel();
```

```
   // Create button that will display the dialog.
   jbtnShow = new JButton("Show Dialog");

   // Add action listener for the button.
   jbtnShow.addActionListener(new ActionListener() {
     public void actionPerformed(ActionEvent le) {
       // Create a confirmation dialog.
       int response = JOptionPane.showConfirmDialog(        ◄─── Create a confirmation
                         jfrm,                                    dialog.
                         "Remove unused files?");

       // Show the response.
       switch(response) {  ◄──────────────────────────  Check the user's response
         case JOptionPane.YES_OPTION:                    and respond appropriately.
           jlab.setText("You answered Yes.");
           break;
         case JOptionPane.NO_OPTION:
           jlab.setText("You answered No.");
           break;
         case JOptionPane.CANCEL_OPTION:
           jlab.setText("Cancel pressed.");
           break;
         case JOptionPane.CLOSED_OPTION:
           jlab.setText("Dialog closed without response.");
           break;
       }
     }
   });

   // Add the button and label to the content pane.
   jfrm.getContentPane().add(jbtnShow);
   jfrm.getContentPane().add(jlab);

   // Display the frame.
   jfrm.setVisible(true);
 }

 public static void main(String args[]) {
   // Create the frame on the event dispatching thread.
   SwingUtilities.invokeLater(new Runnable() {
     public void run() {
       new ConfirmDialogDemo();
     }
   });
 }
}
```

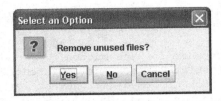

Figure 9-4 The dialog from the **ConfirmDialogDemo** program

As you can see, the code for handling the response from the user is straightforward. Because all dialogs created with **JOptionPane**'s **show** methods are modal, the call to **showConfirmDialog( )** will not return until the user either chooses an option or closes the dialog window by clicking on its close box. The response is returned by **showConfirmDialog( )** and is assigned to a variable called **response**. This variable controls a **switch** statement that displays the user's choice.

Although the preceding form of **showConfirmDialog( )** is quite easy to use, it's not suitable for most applications because it always uses the title Select an Option. However, a more descriptive title for the dialog, such as "Disk Space Is Low," would be better. Fortunately, it is easy to change the title and other aspects of the dialog by using one of the following overloaded versions of **showConfirmDialog( )**:

static int showConfirmDialog(Component *parent*, Object *msg*,
                String *title*, int *optT*)
                       throws HeadlessException

static int showConfirmDialog(Component *parent*, Object *msg*,
                String *title*, int *optT*, int *msgT*)
                       throws HeadlessException

static int showConfirmDialog(Component *parent*, Object *msg*,
                String *title*, int *optT*, int *msgT*,
                Icon *image*)
                       throws HeadlessException

Here, *parent* and *msg* are the same as described earlier. The title of the dialog is specified by *title*. The options (i.e., the buttons) from which the user can choose are specified by *optT*. It must be one of the following constants defined by **JOptionPane**:

YES_NO_OPTION	The dialog includes buttons for Yes and No.
YES_NO_CANCEL_OPTION	The dialog includes buttons for Yes, No, and Cancel.

By default, Yes, No, and Cancel are supplied. However, Cancel is not appropriate in all cases. In situations in which only a Yes or No response is meaningful, pass **YES_NO_OPTION** to the *optT* parameter.

The general type of dialog displayed is passed in *msgT*. It must be one of the following constants described earlier:

ERROR_MESSAGE	INFORMATION_MESSAGE	PLAIN_MESSAGE
QUESTION_MESSAGE	WARNING_MESSAGE	

The default message type is **QUESTION_MESSAGE**.

The icon displayed within the dialog is specified by *image*. By default, a question mark is used.

The dialog displayed by the preceding example can be easily improved by adding a title and removing the Cancel button, as shown in this version of the **ActionListener** from the previous example:

```
jbtnShow.addActionListener(new ActionListener() {
  public void actionPerformed(ActionEvent le) {
    // Create a dialog that shows a message.
    int response = JOptionPane.showConfirmDialog(
                   jfrm,
                   "Remove unused files?",    ← This is the prompt.
                   "Disk Space Is Low",       ← This is the title.
                   JOptionPane.YES_NO_OPTION); ← Display only a Yes
                                                 and No option.

    switch(response) {
      case JOptionPane.YES_OPTION:
        jlab.setText("You answered Yes.");
        break;
      case JOptionPane.NO_OPTION:
        jlab.setText("You answered No.");
        break;
      case JOptionPane.CLOSED_OPTION:
        jlab.setText("Dialog closed without response.");
        break;
    }
  }
});
```

After substituting the code, the dialog will look like the one shown in Figure 9-5. Notice that the title is now "Disk Space Is Low" and that the Cancel button has been removed.

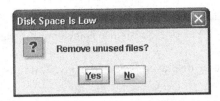

Figure 9-5 The improved confirmation dialog

Progress Check

1. By default, **showConfirmDialog( )** requests a Yes/No/Cancel response. True or False?

2. What effect does passing **YES_NO_OPTION** to the *optT* parameter of **showConfirmDialog( )** have?

CRITICAL SKILL
9.4 showInputDialog( )

Although a Yes/No response is adequate for some simple dialogs, often other, more flexible input is required. To handle these cases, **JOptionPane** provides two other types of dialogs. One is created by **showOptionDialog( )**, which is described in the next section. The other is **showInputDialog( )**, and it is described here.

    showInputDialog( ) supports several different forms. The simplest displays a text field into which the user can enter a string. This version is shown here:

static String showInputdialog(Object *msg*) throws HeadlessException

Here, the message to display is passed in *msg*. The dialog uses the default frame and is centered on the screen. The method returns the string entered by the user. The dialog displays buttons labeled OK and Cancel. Pressing OK causes the string to be returned. Pressing Cancel (or clicking the close button on the window) causes the dialog to discard any string entered by the user and return null. Pressing OK when no string has been entered causes a zero-length string to be returned.

    Here is an example that demonstrates the simplest form of **showInputDialog( )**. It simply prompts for a name. The dialog is shown in Figure 9-6.

---

1. True
2. It causes just the Yes and No options to be displayed.

Figure 9-6 The dialog displayed by the **InputDialogDemo** program

```java
// A simple input dialog.

import java.awt.*;
import java.awt.event.*;
import javax.swing.*;

class InputDialogDemo {

  JLabel jlab;

  JButton jbtnShow;

  JFrame jfrm;

  InputDialogDemo() {
    // Create a new JFrame container.
    jfrm = new JFrame("A Simple Input Dialog");

    // Specify FlowLayout for the layout manager.
    jfrm.getContentPane().setLayout(new FlowLayout());

    // Give the frame an initial size.
    jfrm.setSize(400, 250);

    // Terminate the program when the user closes the application.
    jfrm.setDefaultCloseOperation(JFrame.EXIT_ON_CLOSE);

    // Create a label that shows the response.
    jlab = new JLabel();

    // Create a button that will display the dialog.
    jbtnShow = new JButton("Show Dialog");
```

```
      // Add action listener for the button.
      jbtnShow.addActionListener(new ActionListener() {
        public void actionPerformed(ActionEvent le) {
          // Create a dialog that inputs a string.
          String response = JOptionPane.showInputDialog(
                            "Enter Name");

          // If the response is null, then the dialog
          // was cancelled or closed. If response is a
          // zero-length string, then no input was entered.
          // Otherwise, response contains a string entered
          // by the user.
          if(response == null)
            jlab.setText("Dialog cancelled or closed");
          else if(response.length() == 0)
            jlab.setText("No string entered");
          else
            jlab.setText("Hi there " + response);
        }
      });

      // Add the button and label to the content pane.
      jfrm.getContentPane().add(jbtnShow);
      jfrm.getContentPane().add(jlab);

      // Display the frame.
      jfrm.setVisible(true);
  }

  public static void main(String args[]) {
    // Create the frame on the event dispatching thread.
    SwingUtilities.invokeLater(new Runnable() {
      public void run() {
        new InputDialogDemo();
      }
    });
  }
}
```

Create an input dialog that reads a string.

A null response means that the dialog was cancelled or closed.

Although the input dialog created by the preceding program is fully functional, it is quite limited. For example, it always uses the title "Input," it positions the dialog in the center of the screen rather than within the application window, and it does not let you give an initial value to the text field. Fortunately, all of these deficiencies are easy to rectify by using one of the overloaded forms of **showInputDialog( )**, shown here:

static String showInputDialog(Object *msg*, Object *initVal*)
                             throws HeadlessException

static String showInputDialog(Component *parent*, Object *msg*)
                             throws HeadlessException

static String showInputDialog(Component *parent*, Object *msg*, Object *initVal*)
                             throws HeadlessException

static String showInputDialog(Component *parent*, Object *msg*, String *title*,
                   int *msgT*) throws HeadlessException

Here, *parent* specifies the component relative to which the dialog is displayed. The initial value to put into the text field is passed via *initVal*. The value passed in *title* specifies the title. The type of dialog is passed in *msgT*. It must be one of the following constants described earlier:

ERROR_MESSAGE	INFORMATION_MESSAGE	PLAIN_MESSAGE
QUESTION_MESSAGE	WARNING_MESSAGE	

The default message type is **QUESTION_MESSAGE**.

For example, the following call to **showInputDialog( )** creates a dialog that will be positioned relative to the main window and initialized to the name "Bob Smith."

```
String response = JOptionPane.showInputDialog(
                  jfrm,
                  "Enter Name",
                  "Bob Smith");
```

To see the effect of this change, substitute this call to **showInputDialog( )** into the preceding program. After making this change, the dialog window will look like the one shown in Figure 9-7.

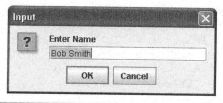

Figure 9-7 An input dialog that has been initialized

There is one more form of **showInputDialog( )** that lets you specify a list of possible selections from which the user can choose and the icon that is displayed. This form is shown here:

static Object showInputDialog(Component *parent*, Object *msg*,
                     String *title*, int *msgT*, Icon *image*,
                     Object[ ] *vals*, Object *initVal*)
                     throws HeadlessException

Here, *parent, title,* and *msgT* are as just described. The icon to be displayed is passed in *image*. If *image* is null, then the standard icon associated with the specified message type is displayed. A list of selections is passed in *vals*. These selections are displayed in a list. However, if *vals* is null, then a text field is displayed into which the user can enter a value. The initial value displayed is passed in *initVal*.

The dialog created by this version of **showInputDialog( )** is especially useful when you want to limit the user to a range of choices. To see this type of input dialog in action, substitute the following action listener for the one shown in the example program. After making this change, the dialog will look like the one shown in Figure 9-8.

```
jbtnShow.addActionListener(new ActionListener() {
  public void actionPerformed(ActionEvent le) {
    String[] names = { "Tom Jones", "Bob Smith",
                       "Mary Doe", "Nancy Oliver" };

    // Create a dialog that lets the user
    // choose from a list of names.
    String response =
            (String) JOptionPane.showInputDialog(
                jfrm,
                "Choose User",
                "Select User Name",
                JOptionPane.QUESTION_MESSAGE,
                null,
                names,
                "Bob Smith");
```

This creates an input dialog that displays a list of strings.

```
    if(response == null)
      jlab.setText("Dialog cancelled or closed");
    else if(response.length() == 0)
      jlab.setText("No string entered");
    else
      jlab.setText("Hi there " + response);
  }
});
```

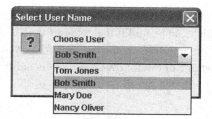

Figure 9-8 An input dialog that lets the user choose from a list

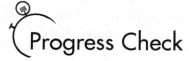

Progress Check

1. What two types of input are supported by **showInputDialog( )**?

2. When using **showInputDialog( )** can you initialize the response?

CRITICAL SKILL
9.5 showOptionDialog( )

Although the dialogs created by **showMessageDialog( )**, **showConfirmDialog( )**, and **showInputDialog( )** satisfy many common dialog needs, there are situations for which they are not appropriate. For this reason **JOptionPane** supplies one more **show** method: **showOptionDialog( )**. This method creates a dialog that contains the elements that you specify. Thus, using **showOptionDialog( )** you can create a dialog tailored more precisely to your needs.

The **showOptionDialog( )** method is shown here:

static int showOptionDialog(Component *parent*, Object *msg*, String *title*,
                            int *optT*, int *msgT*, Icon *image*,
                            Object[ ] *options*, Object *initVal*)
                            throws HeadlessException

1. Depending upon what you request, **showInputDialog( )** can have the user enter a string or select an item from a list.
2. Yes

You are already familiar with most of the parameters. The *parent, msg,* and *title* specify the parent of the dialog (which can be null if the default frame is used), the prompt displayed, and the title of the dialog. The options (i.e., the buttons) from which the user can choose are specified by *optT.* It must be one of the following constants defined by **JOptionPane** and described earlier:

YES_NO_OPTION

YES_NO_CANCEL_OPTION

Understand, however, that the *optT* parameter is used only if the *options* parameter is null. Otherwise, it is ignored. In this case, some programmers use the constant **DEFAULT_OPTION** as a placeholder. The general type of dialog displayed is passed in *msgT.* It must be one of the following constants, also described earlier:

ERROR_MESSAGE	INFORMATION_MESSAGE	PLAIN_MESSAGE
QUESTION_MESSAGE	WARNING_MESSAGE	

The icon displayed within the dialog is specified by *image.* To use the standard icon, simply pass null to this parameter. The initial value displayed is passed through *initVal.*

The one new parameter is *options.* It is an array of **Object** that contains the options that will be displayed in the dialog. Typically, you will pass an array of strings. In this case, each string becomes the label of a button. When you press a button, the dialog ends and the index of the string is returned. You can also pass an array of icons or an array that contains a mix of strings or icons. When an icon is passed, it is automatically embedded in an icon-based button. Other types of objects can be passed. (See "Ask the Expert" at the end of this section.)

Here is an example that uses **showOptionDialog( )** to let the user choose how to connect to the network. The dialog is shown in Figure 9-9.

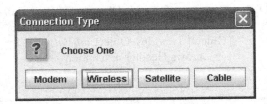

Figure 9-9 The dialog displayed by the **OptionDialogDemo** program

```java
// Demonstrate an option dialog.

import java.awt.*;
import java.awt.event.*;
import javax.swing.*;

class OptionDialogDemo {

  JLabel jlab;
  JButton jbtnShow;
  JFrame jfrm;

  OptionDialogDemo() {
    // Create a new JFrame container.
    jfrm = new JFrame("A Simple Option Dialog");

    // Specify FlowLayout for the layout manager.
    jfrm.getContentPane().setLayout(new FlowLayout());

    // Give the frame an initial size.
    jfrm.setSize(400, 250);

    // Terminate the program when the user closes the application.
    jfrm.setDefaultCloseOperation(JFrame.EXIT_ON_CLOSE);

    // Create a label that will show the selection.
    jlab = new JLabel();

    // Create a button that will display the dialog.
    jbtnShow = new JButton("Show Dialog");

    // Add action listener for the button.
    jbtnShow.addActionListener(new ActionListener() {
      public void actionPerformed(ActionEvent le) {

        // Define the connection options.
        String[] connectOpts = { "Modem", "Wireless",
                                 "Satellite", "Cable" };

        // Create a dialog that lets the user
        // choose how to connect to the network.
        int response = JOptionPane.showOptionDialog(
                            jfrm,
                            "Choose One",
                            "Connection Type",
```

These are the options that will be displayed.

Create an option dialog that displays a list of connection options. Each option is displayed in its own button.

```
                                 JOptionPane.DEFAULT_OPTION,
                                 JOptionPane.QUESTION_MESSAGE,
                                 null,
                                 connectOpts,
                                 "Wireless");

      // Display the choice.
      switch(response) {  ◄──────────────────
        case 0:
          jlab.setText("Connect via modem.");
          break;
        case 1:
          jlab.setText("Connect via wireless.");
          break;
        case 2:
          jlab.setText("Connect via satellite.");
          break;
        case 3:
          jlab.setText("Connect via cable.");
          break;
        case JOptionPane.CLOSED_OPTION:
          jlab.setText("Dialog cancelled.");
          break;
      }
    }
  });

  // Add the button and label to the content pane.
  jfrm.getContentPane().add(jbtnShow);
  jfrm.getContentPane().add(jlab);

  // Display the frame.
  jfrm.setVisible(true);
}

public static void main(String args[]) {
  // Create the frame on the event dispatching thread.
  SwingUtilities.invokeLater(new Runnable() {
    public void run() {
      new OptionDialogDemo();
    }
  });
}
}
```

The response contains the index of the option that was clicked.

Ask the Expert

Q: **When using** showOptionDialog( ) **can I pass something other than strings or icons to the** *options* **parameter?**

A: Yes. You can pass any type of object, including other Swing components. If you pass an array of components, the components are added to the dialog. Thus, it is possible to construct a dialog that contains a text field, two check boxes, and an OK button by passing references to these components. If you pass another type of object, a button is created that contains the results of calling **toString( )** on the object.

Unfortunately, because of the layout limitations inherent in **showOptionDialog( )**, you will usually pass either strings or icons. Other components often produce unsatisfying results. For example, if you use the following sequence to construct a dialog:

```
Object[] ops = { new JLabel("Name"),
                 new JTextField(10),
                 new JLabel("Phone Number"),
                 new JTextField(10),
                 "OK", "Cancel" };

int response = JOptionPane.showOptionDialog(
                 jfrm,
                 "Enter Info",
                 "Get Name and Telephone",
                 JOptionPane.OK_CANCEL_OPTION,
                 JOptionPane.QUESTION_MESSAGE,
                 null,
                 ops,
                 "Cancel");
```

It will produce the following output:

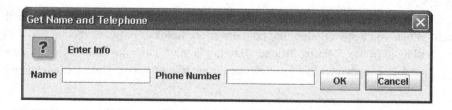

As you can see, the layout is less than optimal.

Looking closely at how the **actionPerfomed( )** handler activates the dialog, first notice the **String** array **names**, which specifies the names of the various connection methods. This name, along with the other information, is passed to **showOptionDialog( )**. When the dialog is created, the names are used as the labels for buttons. When one of these buttons is pressed, an integer corresponding to the index of the name within the array is returned. Therefore, pressing Modem returns 0, pressing Wireless returns 1, and so on.

When specifying options, it is important to remember one point: they override the standard options. Therefore, if you specify a "Cancel" option, the value returned when it is selected will be its index in the array, not **CANCEL_OPTION**. The only standard option that you will be able to check for is **CLOSED_OPTION** because it is generated when the user clicks the window's close box.

Although **showOptionDialog( )** does offer a significant amount of flexibility in determining what a dialog contains, its use is a bit more limited than you might at first think. The reason is that you don't have any real control over the layout of the dialog. In general, all **show** dialogs, including the ones created by **showOptionDialog( )**, use the same pattern. They all have a title, a single-line message, an icon to the left of the message, and a single line of choices. Input dialogs add a text field or list. There is no way to change this layout.

Progress Check

1. **showOptionDialog( )** is very limited because its options cannot be changed. True or false?

2. Why is **showOptionDialog( )** not as useful as one might hope?

CRITICAL SKILL
9.6 JDialog

Although **JOptionPane** offers the easiest way to display a dialog, it is not applicable to all situations. When you need a dialog that contains more fields or requires special handling, then you will need to use **JDialog** instead. **JDialog** is the Swing class that creates a dialog. **JDialog** is a top-level container that is *not* derived from **JComponent**. Thus, it is a heavyweight

---

1. False

2. The reason that **showOptionDialog( )** is not as useful as one might hope is because its basic format is fixed and you have no control over the layout of the options.

component. As explained earlier, **JDialog** is the class that **JOptionPane** uses to construct dialogs. Thus, the dialogs created by **JOptionPane** are instances of **JDialog**.

In general, you create and manage a **JDialog** much like you create a **JFrame**. For example, you add components to the content pane of the **JDialog** just like you add them to a **JFrame**. You can set the layout manager and specify the window size. You use **setVisible( )** to show or hide the window. You can also specify a menu bar. **JDialog** inherits several AWT classes: **Container**, **Component**, **Window**, and **Dialog**. Thus, it has all of the functionality offered by the AWT.

JDialog allows you to construct either a modal or non-modal dialog. As explained previously, a modal dialog is executed on the invoking thread and it causes the application to pause until the dialog is closed. A non-modal dialog executes in its own thread, which means that the application remains active. The ability to create a non-modal dialog is one of the reasons why you might need to create a **JDialog** rather than using one of the **JOptionPane** methods. As you will see, it is easy to construct either style of dialog.

JDialog defines many constructors, which are shown in Table 9-1. The reason that there are so many is because the owner of a **JDialog** can be either a frame or another dialog. Thus, two parallel sets of constructors are needed for the two different owners.

Here are the steps that you will follow to create and display a dialog created by **JDialog**:

1. Create a **JDialog** object.

2. Specify the dialog's layout manager, size, and possibly a default close policy.

3. Add components to the dialog's content pane.

4. Show the dialog by calling **setVisible(true)** on it.

To remove a dialog from the screen use either **setVisible(false)** or **dispose( )**, which is inherited from **Window**. Use **setVisible(false)** when you will be reusing the dialog frequently within the same application. Use **dispose( )** when the dialog is unlikely to be displayed again. Calling **dispose( )** frees all resources associated with the dialog. Calling **setVisible(false)** simply removes the dialog from view.

The following program shows how to create a simple modal dialog by using **JDialog**. The dialog, which has the title Direction, allows the user to choose a direction. It displays two buttons. One is called Up and the other called Down. When a button is pressed, the dialog is closed. The main application window contains two buttons and a label. The label displays the current direction. The button called Show Dialog displays the Direction dialog. The button called Reset Direction resets the direction displayed in the label. Sample output is shown in Figure 9-10.

Constructor	Description
JDialog( )	Creates a non-modal dialog whose owner is a shared, hidden window. It has no title.
JDialog(Frame *parent*)	Creates a non-modal dialog whose owner is specified by *parent*. It has no title.
JDialog(Frame *parent*, String *title*)	Creates a non-modal dialog whose owner is specified by *parent*. It has the title specified by *title*.
JDialog(Frame *parent*, boolean *isModal*)	Creates a dialog whose owner is specified by *parent*. If *isModal* is true, the dialog is modal. If *isModal* is false, the dialog is non-modal. The dialog has no title.
JDialog(Frame *parent*, String *title*, boolean *isModal*)	Creates a dialog whose owner is specified by *parent*. If *isModal* is true, the dialog is modal. If *isModal* is false, the dialog is non-modal. The dialog has the title specified by *title*.
JDialog(Frame *parent*, String *title*, boolean *isModal*, GraphicsConfiguration *graphConfig*)	Creates a dialog whose owner is specified by *parent*. If *isModal* is true, the dialog is modal. If *isModal* is false, the dialog is non-modal. The dialog has the title specified by *title*. The **GraphicsConfiguration** specified by *graphConfig* is used.
JDialog(Dialog *parent*)	Creates a non-modal dialog whose owner is specified by *parent*. It has no title.
JDialog(Dialog *parent*, String *title*)	Creates a non-modal dialog whose owner is specified by *parent*. It has the title specified by *title*.
JDialog(Dialog *parent*, boolean *isModal*)	Creates a dialog whose owner is specified by *parent*. If *isModal* is true, the dialog is modal. If *isModal* is false, the dialog is non-modal. The dialog has no title.
JDialog(Dialog *parent*, String *title*, boolean *isModal*)	Creates a dialog whose owner is specified by *parent*. If *isModal* is true, the dialog is modal. If *isModal* is false, the dialog is non-modal. The dialog has the title specified by *title*.
JDialog(Dialog *parent*, String *title*, boolean *isModal*, GraphicsConfiguration *graphConfig*)	Creates a dialog whose owner is specified by *parent*. If *isModal* is true, the dialog is modal. If *isModal* is false, the dialog is non-modal. The dialog has the title specified by *title*. The **GraphicsConfiguration** specified by *graphConfig* is used.

Table 9-1 The **JDialog** Constructors

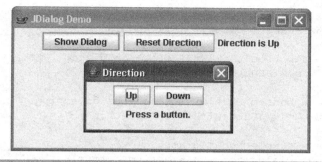

Figure 9-10 Sample output from the **JDialogDemo** program

```java
// Demonstrate a simple JDialog.

import java.awt.*;
import java.awt.event.*;
import javax.swing.*;

class JDialogDemo {

  JLabel jlab;

  JButton jbtnShow;
  JButton jbtnReset;

  // These buttons are contained within the dialog.
  JButton jbtnUp;
  JButton jbtnDown;

  JDialog jdlg;

  JDialogDemo() {
    // Create a new JFrame container.
    JFrame jfrm = new JFrame("JDialog Demo");

    // Specify FlowLayout for the layout manager.
    jfrm.getContentPane().setLayout(new FlowLayout());

    // Give the frame an initial size.
    jfrm.setSize(400, 200);

    // Terminate the program when the user closes the application.
    jfrm.setDefaultCloseOperation(JFrame.EXIT_ON_CLOSE);
```

```
// Create a label that shows the direction.
jlab = new JLabel("Direction is pending.");

// Create a button that will show the dialog.
jbtnShow = new JButton("Show Dialog");

// Create a button that will reset the direction.
jbtnReset = new JButton("Reset Direction");

// Create a simple modal dialog.
jdlg = new JDialog(jfrm, "Direction", true);
jdlg.setSize(200, 100);
jdlg.getContentPane().setLayout(new FlowLayout());

// Create buttons used by the dialog.
jbtnUp = new JButton("Up");
jbtnDown = new JButton("Down");

// Add buttons to the dialog.
jdlg.getContentPane().add(jbtnUp);
jdlg.getContentPane().add(jbtnDown);

// Add a label to the dialog.
jdlg.getContentPane().add(new JLabel("Press a button."));

// Show the dialog when the Show Dialog button is pressed.
jbtnShow.addActionListener(new ActionListener() {
  public void actionPerformed(ActionEvent le) {
    jdlg.setVisible(true);
  }
});

// Reset the direction when the Reset Direction
// button is pressed.
jbtnReset.addActionListener(new ActionListener() {
  public void actionPerformed(ActionEvent le) {
    jlab.setText("Direction is Pending.");
  }
});

// Respond to the Up button in the dialog.
jbtnUp.addActionListener(new ActionListener() {
  public void actionPerformed(ActionEvent le) {
    jlab.setText("Direction is Up");
```

Create and set up a modal dialog.

Add buttons and a label to the dialog.

Show the dialog when the user requests it.

```
        // Hide the dialog after the user selects
        // a direction.
        jdlg.setVisible(false);
    }
});

    // Respond to the Down button in the dialog.
    jbtnDown.addActionListener(new ActionListener() {
      public void actionPerformed(ActionEvent le) {
        jlab.setText("Direction is Down");

        // Hide the dialog after the user selects
        // a direction.
        jdlg.setVisible(false);
      }
    });

    // Add the Show Dialog button and label to the content pane.
    jfrm.getContentPane().add(jbtnShow);
    jfrm.getContentPane().add(jbtnReset);
    jfrm.getContentPane().add(jlab);

    // Display the frame.
    jfrm.setVisible(true);
  }

  public static void main(String args[]) {
    // Create the frame on the event dispatching thread.
    SwingUtilities.invokeLater(new Runnable() {
      public void run() {
        new JDialogDemo();
      }
    });
  }
}
```

Hide the dialog after the user selects a direction.

There are several important things in this program. To begin, notice how the following sequence constructs a modal **JDialog**:

```
// Create a simple modal dialog.
jdlg = new JDialog(jfrm, "Direction", true);
jdlg.setSize(200, 100);
jdlg.getContentPane().setLayout(new FlowLayout());
```

First, a dialog called **jdlg** is created that has Direction as its title, that is owned by the main window of the application, **jfrm**, and that is modal because **true** is passed as the third parameter to the **JDialog** constructor. Then, its size is set and it is given a flow layout manager. At this point, the dialog is fully constructed, but does not contain any components and is not visible.

Next, two buttons and one label are created and added to **jdlg**:

```
// Create buttons used by the dialog.
jbtnUp = new JButton("Up");
jbtnDown = new JButton("Down");

// Add buttons to the dialog.
jdlg.getContentPane().add(jbtnUp);
jdlg.getContentPane().add(jbtnDown);

// Add a label to the dialog.
jdlg.getContentPane().add(new JLabel("Press a button."));
```

As you can see, components are added to the dialog in the same way as they are added to the main window. After this sequence executes, the dialog is fully formed, but is not visible. It won't be made visible until the Show Dialog button (displayed in the main window) is pressed. To display the dialog, the Show Dialog button handler simply calls **setVisible(true)** on **jdlg**.

Next, notice the handlers for the Up and Down buttons that are contained within **jdlg**. Each simply sets the text in **jlab** and then calls **setVisible(false)**, which causes the dialog to be removed from the screen. Using **setVisible(false)** is the most efficient way to hide a dialog that will be needed later.

CRITICAL SKILL
9.7 # Create a Non-Modal Dialog

Using **JDialog**, it is quite easy to create a non-modal dialog: use one of the two-parameter constructors (which automatically create a non-modal dialog), or explicitly pass **false** to one of the three-parameter constructors. The advantage of a non-modal dialog is that the rest of the application remains active. Of course, this is only useful when the rest of the application is not dependent upon the user input requested by the dialog. For example, a photo touch-up application might have a dialog that allows you to select various touch-up filters. In this case, a non-modal dialog would be the best choice because it would let the user change filters interactively without having to constantly close and then re-open the dialog. In general, most dialogs will be modal, but in cases in which a non-modal dialog can be used, they tend to be *very useful*.

Ask the Expert

Q: In Module 1 you pointed out that beginning with JDK 5 it was no longer necessary to call getContentPane( ) to add a component to a JFrame. Is this also true when adding components to a JDialog?

A: Yes. Beginning with JDK 5, you can add a component to **JDialog** by calling **add( )** directly on the **JDialog** instance. The component will be automatically added to the content pane. Therefore, if you are using JDK 5 or later, the following sequence can be used to add the components to **jdlg** in the **JDialogDemo** program:

```
// Add buttons to the dialog.
jdlg.add(jbtnUp);
jdlg.add(jbtnDown);

// Add a label to the dialog.
jdlg.add(new JLabel("Press a button."));
```

This book will continue to use explicit calls to **getContentPane( )** so that the code works for all versions of Java and to make it clear that the components are being added to the content pane. Of course, you are free to remove the calls if you are using JDK 5 or later.

To see the effects of a non-modal dialog, we will rework the preceding program so that the Direction dialog is non-modal. Before we begin, run the **JDialogDemo** program and activate the Direction dialog. Then, try to click the Reset Direction button in the main window. As you will see, because the Direction dialog is modal, you cannot access the Reset Direction button while the dialog is active. By making the Direction dialog non-modal, both windows will be active and you will be able to reset the direction at any time.

To make the Direction dialog modal requires very few changes. First, change the call to the **JDialog** constructor by removing the third argument, as shown here:

```
jdlg = new JDialog(jfrm, "Direction");
```

This form of the constructor automatically creates a non-modal dialog.

Next, remove the calls to **setVisible(false)** that are inside the event handlers for the Up and Down buttons. In other words, these two handlers should now look like this:

```
// Respond to the Up button in the dialog.
jbtnUp.addActionListener(new ActionListener() {
  public void actionPerformed(ActionEvent le) {
```

```
      jlab.setText("Direction is Up");
    }
});

// Respond to the Down button in the dialog.
jbtnDown.addActionListener(new ActionListener() {
  public void actionPerformed(ActionEvent le) {
    jlab.setText("Direction is Down");
  }
});
```

After making these changes, the Direction dialog will remain on the screen until you click its close box. Thus, you will be able to make repeated direction changes. You will also be able to press the Reset Direction button in the main window without closing the Direction dialog.

Progress Check

1. Is **JDialog** derived from **JComponent**?

2. Components in a **JDialog** must be added to the content pane. True or false?

3. What does **dispose( )** do?

4. A non-modal dialog runs in its own _____.

9.8 Select Files with JFileChooser

One of the most common uses for a dialog is also one of the more complicated and tedious to implement: allowing the user to select a file. Thankfully, Swing provides a built-in dialog that handles this somewhat difficult task for you. This dialog is called a *file chooser* and is an instance of **JFileChooser**.

JFileChooser offers two important benefits. The first is consistency. Choosing a file is a common activity. **JFileChooser** ensures that all file selection dialogs will look and feel the same. Thus, once users know how to use one file chooser, they can use them all. This is true

---

1. No

2. True

3. The **dispose( )** method removes a window from the screen, releasing all of its resources in the process.

4. Thread

even between programs written by different programmers. **JFileChooser** provides a standard mechanism that users understand.

The second **JFileChooser** benefit is efficiency. Although conceptually simple, implementing a file selection dialog requires a significant programming effort. By providing a built-in, standard implementation, Swing prevents programmers from having to duplicate this effort over and over again. Therefore, except for some specialized applications, if you need a dialog that lets the user choose a file, you should use **JFileChooser**. It prevents wasted effort.

JFileChooser is derived from **JComponent**. It specifies several constructors of which three are commonly used. They are shown in Table 9-2. It supplies many methods and supports several options. We won't look at all of them here, but once you understand the basic operation of **JFileChooser**, it can be easily tailored to meet your specific needs.

After you have created a **JFileChooser**, it is displayed by calling one of the following methods:

int showOpenDialog(Component *parent*) throws HeadlessException

int showSaveDialog(Component *parent*) throws HeadlessException

int showDialog(Component *parent*, String *name*) throws HeadlessException

In each, *parent* is the component relative to which the file chooser is positioned. If *parent* is null, then the file chooser is centered on the desktop. The **showOpenDialog( )** method displays the standard Open dialog. The **showSaveDialog( )** displays the standard Save dialog. The only difference between the two is the title and the name on the button that signifies that a file has been chosen. For **showOpenDialog( )**, this button is called Open. For **showSaveDialog( )**, this button is called Save. To specify your own title and button name, call **showDialog( )** with the desired name. This still creates a standard file chooser, only the title and button name are different. For example, if you want a file chooser that selects a file for deletion, then you would pass "Delete" to *name*.

Constructor	Description
JFileChooser( )	Creates a file chooser that initially displays the default directory.
JFileChooser(File *dir*)	Creates a file chooser that initially displays the directory specified by *dir*. If *dir* is null, the default directory is used.
JFileChooser(String *dir*)	Creates a file chooser that initially displays the directory specified by *dir*. If *dir* is null, the default directory is used.

Table 9-2 Three Commonly Used **JFileChooser** Constructors

Each of the methods returns an integer that indicates the outcome of the file selection process. It will be one of these values defined by **JFileChooser**:

APPROVE_OPTION	The user selected a file.
CANCEL_OPTION	The user cancelled the selection process by clicking the Cancel button or by clicking the close box.
ERROR_OPTION	An error was encountered.

Keep in mind that the user can enter any filename. It does not have to exist or even be a valid filename. Therefore, just because one of the **show** methods returns **APPROVE_OPTION** does not mean that the file will be valid.

Once a file has been chosen, you can obtain that file by calling **getSelectedFile( )** on the **JFileChooser** instance. It is shown here:

File getSelectedFile( )

It returns a **File** object that represents the selected file. (Remember, this file has not been opened.)

The **File** class encapsulates information about a file. **File** is packaged in **java.io** and it contains several useful methods. For example, to obtain the name of the file, call **getName( )** on the **File** object. It is shown here:

String getName( )

The name is returned as a string. You can determine if the specified file exists by calling **exists( )**, shown next:

boolean exists( )

If the file exists, true is returned. Otherwise, false is returned.

Depending on what options you specify, it is possible for the file chooser to allow you to select both files and directories. (Directories are really just special types of files.) You can determine if the **File** object returned by **getSelectedFile( )** is actually a file by calling **isFile( )** or is a directory by calling **isDirectory( )**. These methods are shown here:

boolean isFile( )

boolean isDirectory( )

Each returns true if the object is of the indicated type and false otherwise. **File** contains many other methods that you will find useful. If you are not familiar with it, it is a class that you will want to explore further.

The following program demonstrates **JFileChooser**. It displays an Open dialog initialized to the default directory. The file chooser dialog is shown in Figure 9-11.

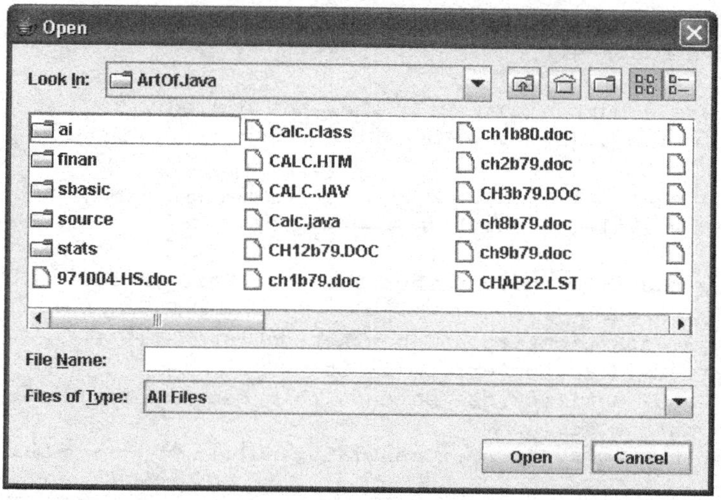

Figure 9-11 The dialog displayed by the **FileChooserDemo** program

```java
// Demonstrate JFileChooser.

import java.awt.*;
import java.awt.event.*;
import javax.swing.*;

class FileChooserDemo {

  JLabel jlab;
  JButton jbtnShow;
  JFileChooser jfc;

  FileChooserDemo() {
    // Create a new JFrame container.
    JFrame jfrm = new JFrame("JFileChooser Demo");

    // Specify FlowLayout for the layout manager.
    jfrm.getContentPane().setLayout(new FlowLayout());

    // Give the frame an initial size.
    jfrm.setSize(400, 200);

    // Terminate the program when the user closes the application.
    jfrm.setDefaultCloseOperation(JFrame.EXIT_ON_CLOSE);
```

```
    // Create a label that will show the selected file.
    jlab = new JLabel();

    // Create a button that will show the dialog.
    jbtnShow = new JButton("Show File Chooser");

    // Create the file chooser.
    jfc = new JFileChooser(); ◄
```

Create a file chooser that starts at the default directory.

```
    // Show the file chooser when the Show File Chooser button
    // is pressed.
    jbtnShow.addActionListener(new ActionListener() {
      public void actionPerformed(ActionEvent le) {
        // Pass null for the parent. This centers the dialog
        // on the screen.
        int result = jfc.showOpenDialog(null); ◄————— Display the file chooser.

        if(result == JFileChooser.APPROVE_OPTION) ◄————— If a file has been selected,
          jlab.setText("Selected file is: " +                display its name.
                       jfc.getSelectedFile().getName());
        else
          jlab.setText("No file selected.");
      }
    });

    // Add the Show File Chooser button and label to the
    // content pane.
    jfrm.getContentPane().add(jbtnShow);
    jfrm.getContentPane().add(jlab);

    // Display the frame.
    jfrm.setVisible(true);
  }

  public static void main(String args[]) {
    // Create the frame on the event dispatching thread.
    SwingUtilities.invokeLater(new Runnable() {
      public void run() {
        new FileChooserDemo();
      }
    });
  }
}
```

The operation of the program is straightforward. When the program begins, a **JFileChooser** called **jfc** is created. Notice that no initial directory is specified, so the file chooser uses the default directory. When the Show File Chooser button is pressed, the

actionPerformed( ) handler displays the file chooser dialog by calling **showOpenDialog( )**. When the method returns, if the return value is **APPROVE_OPTION**, then the name of the selected file is displayed in **jlab**. Otherwise, a message indicating that no file was selected is displayed. One other point: by constructing the file chooser outside of the **actionPerformed( )** handler, it can be used repeatedly without having to be reconstructed each time.

Before moving on, try calling **showSaveDialog( )** instead of **showOpenDialog( )**. As you will see, the only difference is the name.

Add a File Filter

By default, **JFileChooser** displays all nonhidden files in the selected directory. The user can change this behavior by specifying a filename that includes wildcard characters. You can also change this behavior under program control by using a custom file filter. A file filter is an object that extends the **FileFilter** abstract class defined in the **javax.swing.filechooser** package.

Before continuing, it is necessary to mention an important point. Be careful when importing **javax.swing.filechooser.FileFilter**. Java also includes an interface called **FileFilter** that is packaged in **java.io**. When creating a file-chooser file filter, you often need to import both packages (**java.io** and **javax.swing.filechooser**). To avoid a name conflict, you should import the file chooser version of **FileFilter** using its fully qualified name, shown here:

```
import javax.swing.filechooser.FileFilter;
```

This approach avoids the name conflict between the two packages.

The **FileFilter** class defines the two methods shown here:

abstract boolean accept(File *file*)

abstract String getDescription( )

Both must be implemented by your custom file filter. The **accept( )** method must return true to accept the file passed via *file*. In other words, if you want the file to be displayed in the file list, return true. To prevent the file from being displayed, return false. The **getDescription( )** method must return a string that describes the filter. It is displayed in the Files of Type list in the file chooser.

One important point: When you create a custom file filter, directories are not automatically displayed. If you want directories to be displayed, you must explicitly accept them within the **accept( )** method.

To enable a file chooser to use your file filter, you must call **setFileFilter( )** on the **JFileChooser** instance. This method is shown here:

void setFileFilter(FileFilter *ff*)

Here, *ff* is the file filter that you want the file chooser to use.

The following program implements a simple file filter. It displays Java source files. These are files that end in **.java**. It also displays directories, which enable the user to navigate the file system. The effects of the file filter are shown in Figure 9-12.

```java
// Demonstrate a custom file filter.

import java.io.*;
import java.awt.*;
import java.awt.event.*;
import javax.swing.*;
import javax.swing.filechooser.FileFilter;

// A custom file filter that displays
// Java source files and directories.
class JavaFileFilter extends FileFilter {
  public boolean accept(File file) {
    // Return true if the file is a Java source file
    // or if it is a directory.
    if(file.getName().endsWith(".java")) return true;
    if(file.isDirectory()) return true;

    // Otherwise, return false.
    return false;
  }

  public String getDescription() {
    return "Java Source Code Files";
  }
}

class FileFilterDemo {

  JLabel jlab;
  JButton jbtnShow;
  JFileChooser jfc;

  FileFilterDemo() {
    // Create a new JFrame container.
    JFrame jfrm = new JFrame("File Filter Demo");

    // Specify FlowLayout for the layout manager.
    jfrm.getContentPane().setLayout(new FlowLayout());

    // Give the frame an initial size.
    jfrm.setSize(400, 200);

    // Terminate the program when the user closes the application.
```

Create a custom file filter that displays only **.java** files and directories.

```
    jfrm.setDefaultCloseOperation(JFrame.EXIT_ON_CLOSE);

    // Create a label that will show the selected file.
    jlab = new JLabel();

    // Create a button that will show the dialog.
    jbtnShow = new JButton("Show File Chooser");

    // Create the file chooser.
    jfc = new JFileChooser();

    // Set the file filter.
    jfc.setFileFilter(new JavaFileFilter());  ◄──────── Select the file filter for use.

    // Show the file chooser when the Show File Chooser button
    // is pressed.
    jbtnShow.addActionListener(new ActionListener() {
      public void actionPerformed(ActionEvent le) {
        // Pass null for the parent. This centers the dialog
        // on the screen.
        int result = jfc.showOpenDialog(null);

        if(result == JFileChooser.APPROVE_OPTION)
          jlab.setText("Selected file is: " +
                        jfc.getSelectedFile().getName());
        else
          jlab.setText("No file selected.");
      }
    });

    // Add the Show File Chooser button and label to the
    // content pane.
    jfrm.getContentPane().add(jbtnShow);
    jfrm.getContentPane().add(jlab);

    // Display the frame.
    jfrm.setVisible(true);
  }

  public static void main(String args[]) {
    // Create the frame on the event dispatching thread.
    SwingUtilities.invokeLater(new Runnable() {
      public void run() {
        new FileFilterDemo();
      }
    });
  }
}
```

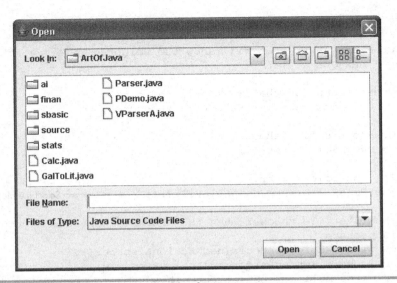

Figure 9-12 The dialog displayed by the **FileFilterDemo** program

The program builds on the previous version. First, it defines a custom file filter class called **JavaFileFilter**. This filter accepts those files that are either directories or Java source files. Notice how this determination is made by the **accept( )** method by use of the following sequence:

```
if(file.getName().endsWith(".java")) return true;
if(file.isDirectory()) return true;

// Otherwise, return false.
return false;
```

If the file has the extension **.java**, then it is accepted. This test is easily accomplished by use of the **endsWith( )** method defined by the **String** class. If the filename ends with **.java**, then **accept( )** returns true. Otherwise, **isDirectory( )** is called to determine if the file is a directory. If it is, **accept( )** returns true. In all other cases, **accept( )** returns false. This means that only **.java** files and directories are displayed.

In order for the file filter to be in effect, it must be set. This is done by calling **setFileFilter( )** on **jfc** immediately after it is created. Before moving on, you might want to experiment a bit by creating some file filters of your own design.

CRITICAL SKILL
9.10 # Some File Chooser Options

JFileChooser supports several options. We will examine a few of the most commonly used. One of the more important options determines whether the user can select only files, only directories, or both. By default, **JFileChooser** allows the user to select only files. To confirm this, try using the preceding example to select a directory. As you will see, this isn't allowed. To allow a directory to be selected, call **setFileSelectionMode( )**, shown here:

void setFileSelectionMode(int *fsm*)

Here, *fsm* specifies the selection mode, which must be one of these constants defined by **JFileChooser**:

FILES_ONLY

DIRECTORIES_ONLY

FILES_AND_DIRECTORIES

Each specifies the mode indicated by its name.

You can obtain the current directory by calling **getCurrentDirectory( )**. It is shown here:

File getCurrentDirectory( )

The returned **File** object encapsulates the current directory. You can obtain the full path name by calling the **getPath( )** method defined by **File** on the returned object.

You can allow the user to select more than one file by calling **setMultiSelectionEnabled( )**, shown here:

void setMultiSelectionEnabled(boolean *on*)

If *on* is true, then multiple file selection is allowed. If *on* is false, then only single files can be selected. By default, only single file selection is allowed.

When using multiple selection mode, you can obtain a list of the selected files by calling **getSelectedFiles( )**, shown here:

File[ ] getSelectedFiles( )

It returns an array of **File** objects that contains the selected files (or directories).

By default, hidden files are not displayed by the file chooser. To change this, call **setFileHidingEnabled( )**, shown here:

void setFileHidingEnabled(boolean *on*)

If *on* is true, then hidden files are not displayed. If *on* is false, then hidden files are shown in the file window.

    JFileChooser is supported by three classes in the **javax.swing.filechooser** package. The first is **FileFilter** described earlier. The other two are **FileView** and **FileSystemView**. The **FileView** class defines how the file view looks in the file chooser's window. The **FileSystemView** encapsulates information about the file system. It provides a portable way to obtain information about files, partitions, drives, and so on. Unless you are creating a highly specialized file chooser, you normally won't need to use either of these classes directly.

Progress Check

1. What method displays the Open file chooser?

2. As it relates to **JFileChooser**, what class do you extend to create a file filter?

3. What method enables multiple file selection?

Project 9-1 Create a File-Comparison Program

`CompareFiles.java`

This projects shows a real-world application of two of Swing's dialog classes: **JOptionPane** and **JFileChooser**. It implements a file-comparison utility. The program first obtains the names of the files to compare from the user. It then compares the two files and reports if their contents are the same or different. Here is the way that the main window looks:

---

1. **showOpenDialog( )**
2. **FileFilter**
3. **setMultiSelectionEnabled( )**

The names of the files to compare can be entered in one of two ways. First, the names can be manually typed into the text field. Second, the user can browse for a file by using the standard file chooser dialog. In this case, the full path and name of the file is copied into the corresponding text field after it has been selected. Once the files have been specified, they are compared when the user presses the Compare Files button. The results are displayed in a message dialog, such as the one shown here:

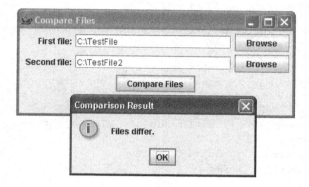

Step by Step

1. Create a file called **CompareFiles.java** and add the following comment and **import** statements.

```
// Project 9-1: A file-comparison program.
//
// This project uses JOptionPane and JFileChooser.

import java.io.*;
import java.util.*;
import java.awt.*;
import java.awt.event.*;
import javax.swing.*;
```

2. Begin the **CompareFiles** class by adding the fields shown here:

```
class CompareFiles {

    JLabel jlabFirst;
    JLabel jlabSecond;

    JButton jbtnGetFirst;
    JButton jbtnGetSecond;
    JButton jbtnCompare;
```

(continued)

```
JTextField jtfFirst;
JTextField jtfSecond;

JFileChooser jfc;
```

The text fields **jtfFirst** and **jtfSecond** will hold the names of the files to be compared. The user can enter names into these fields directly. They are also set if the user selects the files via the file chooser.

3. Begin coding the **CompareFiles** constructor in the familiar way, as shown next:

```
CompareFiles() {
  // Create a new JFrame container.
  JFrame jfrm = new JFrame("Compare Files");

  // Specify FlowLayout for the layout manager.
  jfrm.getContentPane().setLayout(new FlowLayout());

  // Give the frame an initial size.
  jfrm.setSize(400, 160);

  // Terminate the program when the user closes the application.
  jfrm.setDefaultCloseOperation(JFrame.EXIT_ON_CLOSE);
```

4. Create the labels that describe the two text fields and then create the text fields themselves, as shown here:

```
// Create labels for the text fields.
jlabFirst = new JLabel("First file:");
jlabFirst.setPreferredSize(new Dimension(70, 20));
jlabFirst.setHorizontalAlignment(SwingConstants.RIGHT);

jlabSecond = new JLabel("Second file:");
jlabSecond.setPreferredSize(new Dimension(70, 20));
jlabSecond.setHorizontalAlignment(SwingConstants.RIGHT);

// Create the text fields that will hold the filenames.
jtfFirst = new JTextField(20);
jtfSecond = new JTextField(20);
```

Notice that the same dimensions and alignment are specified for the two labels. Also notice that the size of each text field is the same. This allows the components to line up when displayed in the window.

5. Construct the two Browse buttons and the Compare Files button:

```
// Create the Browse buttons.
jbtnGetFirst = new JButton("Browse");
```

```
jbtnGetSecond = new JButton("Browse");

// Create the button that begins the file comparison.
jbtnCompare = new JButton("Compare Files");
```

6. Create the file chooser, specifying the default directory as shown next:

```
// Create the file chooser that will be used
// to select files when the user clicks a
// Browse button.
jfc = new JFileChooser();
```

7. Add the following action listeners for the two Browse buttons:

```
// Browse for the first file.
jbtnGetFirst.addActionListener(new ActionListener() {
  public void actionPerformed(ActionEvent le) {

    int result = jfc.showDialog(null, "Select");

    if(result == JFileChooser.APPROVE_OPTION) {
      File f = jfc.getSelectedFile();
      jtfFirst.setText(f.getPath());
    }
  }
});

// Browse for the second file.
jbtnGetSecond.addActionListener(new ActionListener() {
  public void actionPerformed(ActionEvent le) {

    int result = jfc.showDialog(null, "Select");

    if(result == JFileChooser.APPROVE_OPTION) {
      File f = jfc.getSelectedFile();
      jtfSecond.setText(f.getPath());
    }
  }
});
```

Each **actionPerformed( )** method activates the file chooser, using the name "Select" as the name of the dialog. If the user selects a file, then the full path name of the file is copied into the corresponding text field. This approach ensures that the filename in the text field always matches the one chosen by the dialog. Therefore, the contents of each text field always displays the name of a file to compare.

(continued)

8. Add the action listener for the Compare Files button, shown next. When this button is pressed, the two files displayed within the text fields are compared for equality.

```
// Compare the files.
jbtnCompare.addActionListener(new ActionListener() {
  public void actionPerformed(ActionEvent le) {

    // First, confirm that the user entered
    // both filenames.
    if(jtfFirst.getText().length() == 0 ||
              jtfSecond.getText().length() == 0) {
      JOptionPane.showMessageDialog(null,
                "Please specify the files to compare.",
                "Filename Not Specified",
                JOptionPane.WARNING_MESSAGE);
      return;
    }

    // Next, create File objects from the filenames.
    File f1 = new File(jtfFirst.getText());
    File f2 = new File(jtfSecond.getText());

    // Confirm that both files exist.
    if(!f1.exists()) {
      JOptionPane.showMessageDialog(null,
                "The first file does not exist.",
                "File Not Found",
                JOptionPane.WARNING_MESSAGE);
      return;
    }
    if(!f2.exists()) {
      JOptionPane.showMessageDialog(null,
                "The second file does not exist.",
                "File Not Found",
                JOptionPane.WARNING_MESSAGE);
      return;
    }

    // Compare the files.
    if(compare(f1, f2))
      JOptionPane.showMessageDialog(null,
                "Files compare equal.",
                "Comparison Result",
                JOptionPane.INFORMATION_MESSAGE);
    else
```

```
JOptionPane.showMessageDialog(null,
          "Files differ.",
          "Comparison Result",
          JOptionPane.INFORMATION_MESSAGE);
  }
});
```

This handler first verifies that each text field contains a string. If this is not the case, then a message dialog is displayed that reminds the user to enter the filenames. Next, two **File** objects are created that encapsulate the filenames. Understand that creating a **File** object does not open a file. It simply creates an object that represents a file. Next, a check is made to ensure that both files actually exist. If this is not the case, then a message dialog is displayed that reports this fact.

Assuming that the files exist, the **compare( )** method is called to compare the files. The **compare( )** method returns true if the files are equal. The outcome is reported in a message dialog.

One other point: There is no need to handle events generated by the text fields. This is why there are no listeners for those events. Instead, the program simply retrieves the filenames from the text field when the user presses the Compare Files buttons.

9. Finish the **CompareFiles** constructor by adding the components to the content pane and then displaying the window, as shown next:

```
// Add the components to the content pane.
jfrm.getContentPane().add(jlabFirst);
jfrm.getContentPane().add(jtfFirst);
jfrm.getContentPane().add(jbtnGetFirst);
jfrm.getContentPane().add(jlabSecond);
jfrm.getContentPane().add(jtfSecond);
jfrm.getContentPane().add(jbtnGetSecond);
jfrm.getContentPane().add(jbtnCompare);

// Display the frame.
jfrm.setVisible(true);
}
```

10. Add the **compare( )** method shown here:

```
// Compare two files.
boolean compare(File fileA, File fileB) {

  // If the file lengths differ, the files differ.
  if(fileA.length() != fileB.length()) return false;
```

(continued)

```
FileInputStream f1, f2;
int i, j;
byte buf1[] = new byte[1024];
byte buf2[] = new byte[1024];

try {
  f1 = new FileInputStream(fileA);
  f2 = new FileInputStream(fileB);

  do {
    // This version of read() returns the number of
    // bytes read or -1 when the end of the file
    // is reached.
    i = f1.read(buf1, 0, 1024);
    j = f2.read(buf2, 0, 1024);

    // If the buffers are not equal, then
    // the files differ. In that case,
    // close the files and return false.
    if(!Arrays.equals(buf1, buf2)) {
      f1.close();
      f2.close();
      return false;
    }
  } while(i != -1 && j != -1);

  f1.close();
  f2.close();
} catch(IOException exc) {
  JOptionPane.showMessageDialog(null, exc,
                "File Error!",
                JOptionPane.WARNING_MESSAGE);
  return false; // return false on error
}

// The files are equal, so return true.
return true;
}
```

The **compare( )** method is passed two **File** objects. It first checks if the length of the two files is the same. If it isn't, then **compare( )** returns false because, obviously, two files cannot be the same if their lengths differ. Next, it opens the two files and repeatedly reads and compares blocks of bytes from each file. The process ends when either a mismatch is found, in which case false is returned, or when the end of the files is reached. Recall that the version of **read( )** being used returns –1 when the end of the file is encountered. If no mismatch is found, **compare( )** returns true.

As a point of interest, the files are read 1,024 bytes at a time in the interest of efficiency. It is much faster to read a block of 1,024 bytes as a unit, rather than reading one byte, 1,024 times. The value 1,024 is somewhat arbitrary, although file buffers are often multiples of 256, and 1,024 seems a good compromise between too small or too large a buffer. However, you might want to try experimenting with the buffer size a bit, especially when comparing very large or very small files, to see what works best for you.

11. Finish the program in the usual way:

```
public static void main(String args[]) {
  // Create the frame on the event dispatching thread.
  SwingUtilities.invokeLater(new Runnable() {
    public void run() {
      new CompareFiles();
    }
  });
}
}
```

12. The entire file-comparison program is shown here.

```
// Project 9-1: A file-comparison program.
//
// This project uses JOptionPane and JFileChooser.

import java.io.*;
import java.util.*;
import java.awt.*;
import java.awt.event.*;
import javax.swing.*;

class CompareFiles {

  JLabel jlabFirst;
  JLabel jlabSecond;

  JButton jbtnGetFirst;
  JButton jbtnGetSecond;
  JButton jbtnCompare;

  JTextField jtfFirst;
  JTextField jtfSecond;

  JFileChooser jfc;

  CompareFiles() {
```

(continued)

```java
// Create a new JFrame container.
JFrame jfrm = new JFrame("Compare Files");

// Specify FlowLayout for the layout manager.
jfrm.getContentPane().setLayout(new FlowLayout());

// Give the frame an initial size.
jfrm.setSize(400, 160);

// Terminate the program when the user closes the application.
jfrm.setDefaultCloseOperation(JFrame.EXIT_ON_CLOSE);

// Create labels for the text fields.
jlabFirst = new JLabel("First file:");
jlabFirst.setPreferredSize(new Dimension(70, 20));
jlabFirst.setHorizontalAlignment(SwingConstants.RIGHT);

jlabSecond = new JLabel("Second file:");
jlabSecond.setPreferredSize(new Dimension(70, 20));
jlabSecond.setHorizontalAlignment(SwingConstants.RIGHT);

// Create the text fields that will hold the filenames.
jtfFirst = new JTextField(20);
jtfSecond = new JTextField(20);

// Create the browse buttons.
jbtnGetFirst = new JButton("Browse");
jbtnGetSecond = new JButton("Browse");

// Create the button that begins the file comparison.
jbtnCompare = new JButton("Compare Files");

// Create the file chooser that will be used
// to select files when the user clicks a
// Browse button.
jfc = new JFileChooser();

// Browse for the first file.
jbtnGetFirst.addActionListener(new ActionListener() {
  public void actionPerformed(ActionEvent le) {

    int result = jfc.showDialog(null, "Select");

    if(result == JFileChooser.APPROVE_OPTION) {
      File f = jfc.getSelectedFile();
```

```
          jtfFirst.setText(f.getPath());
      }
    }
});

// Browse for the second file.
jbtnGetSecond.addActionListener(new ActionListener() {
  public void actionPerformed(ActionEvent le) {

    int result = jfc.showDialog(null, "Select");

    if(result == JFileChooser.APPROVE_OPTION) {
      File f = jfc.getSelectedFile();
      jtfSecond.setText(f.getPath());
    }
  }
});

// Compare the files.
jbtnCompare.addActionListener(new ActionListener() {
  public void actionPerformed(ActionEvent le) {

    // First, confirm that the user entered
    // both filenames.
    if(jtfFirst.getText().length() == 0 ||
               jtfSecond.getText().length() == 0) {
      JOptionPane.showMessageDialog(null,
                 "Please specify the files to compare.",
                 "Filename Not Specified",
                 JOptionPane.WARNING_MESSAGE);
      return;
    }

    // Next, create File objects from the filenames.
    File f1 = new File(jtfFirst.getText());
    File f2 = new File(jtfSecond.getText());

    // Confirm that both files exist.
    if(!f1.exists()) {
      JOptionPane.showMessageDialog(null,
                 "The first file does not exist.",
                 "File Not Found",
                 JOptionPane.WARNING_MESSAGE);
      return;
    }
```

(continued)

```
        if(!f2.exists()) {
          JOptionPane.showMessageDialog(null,
                      "The second file does not exist.",
                      "File Not Found",
                      JOptionPane.WARNING_MESSAGE);
          return;
        }

        // Compare the files.
        if(compare(f1, f2))
           JOptionPane.showMessageDialog(null,
                       "Files compare equal.",
                       "Comparison Result",
                       JOptionPane.INFORMATION_MESSAGE);
        else
          JOptionPane.showMessageDialog(null,
                      "Files differ.",
                      "Comparison Result",
                      JOptionPane.INFORMATION_MESSAGE);
      }
    });

    // Add the components to the content pane.
    jfrm.getContentPane().add(jlabFirst);
    jfrm.getContentPane().add(jtfFirst);
    jfrm.getContentPane().add(jbtnGetFirst);
    jfrm.getContentPane().add(jlabSecond);
    jfrm.getContentPane().add(jtfSecond);
    jfrm.getContentPane().add(jbtnGetSecond);
    jfrm.getContentPane().add(jbtnCompare);

    // Display the frame.
    jfrm.setVisible(true);
  }

  // Compare two files.
  boolean compare(File fileA, File fileB) {

    // If the file lengths differ, the files differ.
    if(fileA.length() != fileB.length()) return false;

    FileInputStream f1, f2;
    int i, j;
    byte buf1[] = new byte[1024];
    byte buf2[] = new byte[1024];
```

```
     try {
       f1 = new FileInputStream(fileA);
       f2 = new FileInputStream(fileB);

       do {
         // This version of read() returns the number of
         // bytes read or -1 when the end of the file
         // is reached.
         i = f1.read(buf1, 0, 1024);
         j = f2.read(buf2, 0, 1024);

         // If the buffers are not equal, then
         // the files differ. In that case,
         // close the files and return false.
         if(!Arrays.equals(buf1, buf2)) {
           f1.close();
           f2.close();
           return false;
         }
       } while(i != -1 && j != -1);

       f1.close();
       f2.close();
     } catch(IOException exc) {
       JOptionPane.showMessageDialog(null, exc,
                          "File Error!",
                          JOptionPane.WARNING_MESSAGE);
       return false; // return false on error
     }

     // The files are equal, so return true.
     return true;
   }

   public static void main(String args[]) {
     // Create the frame on the event dispatching thread.
     SwingUtilities.invokeLater(new Runnable() {
       public void run() {
         new CompareFiles();
       }
     });
   }
 }
```

CRITICAL SKILL
9.11 # Select Colors with JColorChooser

Swing's second built-in dialog is **JColorChooser**. It allows the user to select a color from a palette. Although choosing a color is far less common than choosing a file, **JColorChooser** is still an important component because it supplies what would otherwise be a very difficult dialog to create on your own. Because **JColorChooser** is used less frequently than **JFileChooser**, we will examine only its easiest-to-use form. Fortunately, this is also the form that you will usually want.

JColorChooser is derived from **JComponent**. It defines three constructors, but you won't often use them. Instead, you will usually create a color chooser by using the static method **showDialog( )**. It creates a modal color chooser dialog and displays it on the screen. The color selected by the user is returned. Here is its general form:

static Color showDialog(Component *parent*, String *title*, Color *initClr*)
            throws HeadlessException

Here, *parent* specifies the component relative to which the dialog is displayed. If you pass null for this argument, then the dialog is usually displayed in the center of the screen. The title of the color chooser is specified by *title*. Often the title will be something like "Choose Color," but more descriptive titles should be used when possible. The initial color selected in the chooser is passed via *initClr*. The method returns the color selected by the user. It returns null if the user cancels or closes the dialog.

The following program demonstrates **JColorChooser**. It displays the color chooser shown in Figure 9-13.

```
// Demonstrate JColorChooser.

import java.awt.*;
import java.awt.event.*;
import javax.swing.*;

class ColorChooserDemo {

  JLabel jlab;
  JButton jbtnShow;

  ColorChooserDemo() {
    // Create a new JFrame container.
    JFrame jfrm = new JFrame("Color Chooser Demo");

    // Specify FlowLayout for the layout manager.
    jfrm.getContentPane().setLayout(new FlowLayout());
```

```
   // Give the frame an initial size.
   jfrm.setSize(400, 200);

   // Terminate the program when the user closes the application.
   jfrm.setDefaultCloseOperation(JFrame.EXIT_ON_CLOSE);

   // Create a label that will show the color chosen.
   jlab = new JLabel();

   // Create a button that will show the dialog.
   jbtnShow = new JButton("Show Color Chooser");

   // Show the color chooser when the Show Color Chooser button
   // is pressed.
   jbtnShow.addActionListener(new ActionListener() {
     public void actionPerformed(ActionEvent le) {
       // Pass null for the parent. This centers the
       // dialog on the screen. The initial color is red.
       Color color = JColorChooser.showDialog(null,
                                   "Choose Color",
                                   Color.RED);

       if(color != null)
         jlab.setText("Selected color is " +
                     color.toString());
       else
         jlab.setText("Color selection was cancelled.");
     }
   });

   // Add the Show Color Chooser button and label to the
   // content pane.
   jfrm.getContentPane().add(jbtnShow);
   jfrm.getContentPane().add(jlab);

   // Display the frame.
   jfrm.setVisible(true);
 }

 public static void main(String args[]) {
   // Create the frame on the event dispatching thread.
   SwingUtilities.invokeLater(new Runnable() {
     public void run() {
       new ColorChooserDemo();
     }
   });
 }
}
```

If a color is chosen, display its name.

Create a color chooser that is initialized to red.

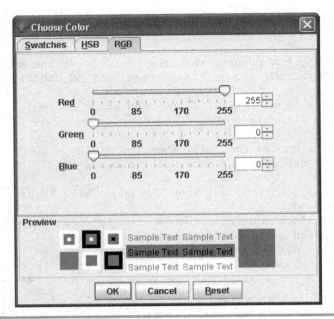

Figure 9-13 The **JColorChooser** dialog

The operation of the program is easy to understand. When the user presses the Show Color Chooser button, the color chooser dialog is displayed by the following call to **showDialog( )**, which is inside the **actionPerformed( )** handler for the button:

```
Color color = JColorChooser.showDialog(null,
                                    "Choose Color",
                                    Color.RED);
```

The parent is null, which causes the color chooser to be centered on the desktop. The title is Choose Color and the initial color is red.

The **showDialog( )** method returns the color selected by the user or null if no selection is made. The outcome is displayed in **jlab** using the following sequence:

```
if(color != null)
  jlab.setText("Selected color is " +
            color.toString());
else
  jlab.setText("Color selection was cancelled.");
```

Of course, in a real program you would normally use the selection to set the color of some component attribute, such as background or text color. As this example illustrates, despite the complexity of the task that it handles, **JColorChooser** is surprisingly easy to work with.

✓

Module 9 Mastery Check

1. A dialog is a composite of two or more components that prompts the user and waits for a response. True or False?

2. What are the four dialog classes provided by Swing? Which two are for general purpose use?

3. What **JOptionPane** method creates an input dialog? Which one creates a message dialog?

4. What **JOptionPane** method would you normally use to create a dialog that confirms that the user wants to save changes to a document? Show what the call would look like.

5. When using a confirmation dialog, what return type indicates that the user clicked the Yes button?

6. What option type is used to show only the Yes and No buttons in a confirmation dialog?

7. If you want to request a string response from the user, what **JOptionPane** method do you call?

8. Must the message parameter to any of **JOptionPane**'s **show** methods be a string? Explain.

9. **JDialog** is a top-level container. True or False?

10. What are the four steps needed to create and display a **JDialog**-based dialog?

11. Can **JDialog** create a non-modal dialog?

12. Explain the difference between **setVisible(false)** and **dispose( )** as it relates to dialogs.

13. What **JFileChooser** method creates a Save file chooser? Which one creates a file chooser that uses your own title?

14. What two methods must be overridden when implementing a **FileFilter** for **JFileChooser**?

15. Can a file chooser be used to select a directory? If so, how is the option enabled?

16. What type of value is returned by **JColorChooser**'s **showDialog( )** method?

17. Module 7 described menus. In that module, the examples included a File menu that always had an Exit entry. The action event handler that processed menu selections handled the Exit entry, as shown here:

```
// Handle menu item action events.
public void actionPerformed(ActionEvent ae) {
  // Get the action command from the menu selection.
  String comStr = ae.getActionCommand();

  // If user chooses Exit, then exit the program.
  if(comStr.equals("Exit")) System.exit(0);
  .
  .
  .
```

Change this code so that it activates a dialog that confirms the user really wants to exit before terminating the program.

18. On your own, experiment with the programs in this module, trying different options and observing the results.

Module 10

Threading, Applets, Painting, and Layouts

471

The preceding nine modules have discussed Swing components, such as **JButton**, **JMenu**, and **JTable**. Because Swing is defined by its components, they comprise a majority of the topics covered in this book. However, there are several other aspects of Swing that warrant examination, and they are discussed in this final module. Although these features do not produce visual controls, they do affect how your Swing programs are organized, the way that they run, and their overall look and feel. Specifically, this module discusses multithreading, the **Timer** class, Swing-based applets, basic painting techniques, and two layout managers. After you complete this chapter, you will be able to begin writing your own Swing-based applications. You will also be ready to continue your study of Swing into those areas in which you are especially interested.

Multithreading in Swing

Multithreading is that aspect of Java that enables different parts of a program to execute concurrently. It gives you the ability to write very efficient programs that make maximum use of the CPU by using otherwise idle time. Multithreading also prevents the entire application from pausing when some part of it is performing a time-consuming task. It is this second reason that makes multithreading especially important to a Swing application. In Swing, time-consuming operations must be executed in their own thread to prevent the application (including its user interface) from becoming sluggish or unresponsive. Therefore, multithreading is part of many Swing programs.

As all Java programmers know, every Java program has at least one thread (the main thread), but other threads can be added, as needed. In general, you will use additional threads within a Swing program in the same way that you use them in any other type of Java program. Thus, what you already know about creating and managing threads also applies to Swing. However, there is a very important, additional threading issue that relates specifically to Swing, and it is the subject of this section.

NOTE

This book assumes that you have a basic working knowledge of threads and multithreading. This includes an understanding of the **Thread** class and the **Runnable** interface. It is not possible to include a comprehensive review of threading in this book. If you need to enhance your understanding of threads, I recommend my book *Java: The Complete Reference*, which is published by McGraw-Hill.

In Module 1, you learned that any code that interacts with a visual component (including its model) must be executed on the event-dispatching thread. Observing this important rule avoids problems, such as two different threads trying to update the same component at the same time. This rule is why **invokeLater( )** is called within **main( )** by all of the programs in this book to construct and display the GUI at program start-up. It causes the GUI to be created on the event-dispatching thread.

It is important to emphasize that this same rule applies *any time* you need to update, change, interrogate, or alter any component. If a piece of code affects a component, it *must be executed* from the event-dispatching thread. Because event handlers are automatically executed on the event-dispatching thread, the code within an event handler can freely affect the GUI. However, code that is executing on another thread cannot. This brings up a potential problem: often code in another thread needs to update a component. For example, consider a program that displays in a **JLabel** the outside temperature, which is updated once every minute. To do this, a separate thread must be used to monitor the temperature. However, this thread cannot be used to update the label because it is not the event-dispatching thread. The problem: How does the thread that monitors the temperature update the label? Or more generally, how does any other thread update a component in the GUI?

The answer is by using either the **invokeLater( )** or the **invokeAndWait( )** methods defined by **SwingUtilities** in much the same way as you have been using **invokeLater( )** to construct and display the GUI. These methods were introduced in Module 1, but let's review them now. They are shown again here, for your convenience:

static void invokeLater(Runnable *obj*)

static void invokeAndWait(Runnable *obj*)
    throws InterruptedException, InvocationTargetException

Here, *obj* is a **Runnable** object that will have its **run( )** method called by the event-dispatching thread. Inside **run( )** put the code that interacts with a Swing component. Thus, when you need to update a component, put the code inside a **Runnable** object and pass that object to either **invokeLater( )** or **invokeAndWait( )**. This causes the code to execute on the event-dispatching thread, which means that the component can be safely changed.

The difference between the two methods is that **invokeLater( )** returns immediately, but **invokeAndWait( )** waits until **obj.run( )** returns. You will normally want to use **invokeLater( )**. However, when constructing the initial GUI for an applet, you will want to use **invokeAndWait( )**. (Creating a Swing applet is described a bit later in this module.) For simplicity, the rest of this discussion refers to **invokeLater( )** but the general principles also apply to **invokeAndWait( )**.

Here is an example that illustrates the proper way to handle a separate thread that continuously updates the GUI. It is an improved version of the **StopWatch** class first created in Project 1-1. This version displays the elapsed time while the stopwatch is running. It does this by creating a separate thread that updates the elapsed time label ten times a second. Notice its use of **invokeLater( )** inside the second thread. Sample output is shown in Figure 10-1.

Figure 10-1 Sample output from the **ThreadStopWatch** program

```java
// An improved version of the StopWatch class
// from Project 1-1. This version uses a separate
// thread to display the elapsed time when the
// stopwatch is running.

import java.awt.*;
import java.awt.event.*;
import javax.swing.*;
import java.util.Calendar;

class ThreadStopWatch {

  JLabel jlab; // display the elapsed time

  JButton jbtnStart; // start the stopwatch
  JButton jbtnStop;  // stop the stopwatch

  long start; // holds the start time in milliseconds

  boolean running=false; // true when stopwatch is running

  Thread thrd; // reference to the timing thread

  ThreadStopWatch() {

    // Create a new JFrame container.
    JFrame jfrm = new JFrame("Thread-based Stopwatch");

    // Specify FlowLayout for the layout manager.
    jfrm.getContentPane().setLayout(new FlowLayout());

    // Give the frame an initial size.
    jfrm.setSize(230, 90);

    // Terminate the program when the user closes the application.
    jfrm.setDefaultCloseOperation(JFrame.EXIT_ON_CLOSE);
```

This will refer to the thread that updates the time display as the stopwatch runs.

```
// Create the elapsed-time label.
jlab = new JLabel("Press Start to begin timing.");

// Make the Start and Stop buttons.
jbtnStart = new JButton("Start");
jbtnStop = new JButton("Stop");

// Initially disable the Stop button.
jbtnStop.setEnabled(false);

// Create the Runnable instance that will
// become the second thread.
Runnable myThread = new Runnable() {
  // This method will run in the separate thread.
  public void run() {
    try {
      // Report elapsed time every tenth of a second.
      for(; ; ) {
        // Pause for a tenth of a second.
        Thread.sleep(100);

        // Invoke updateTime() on the event dispatching thread.
        SwingUtilities.invokeLater(new Runnable() {
          public void run() {
            updateTime();
          }
        });
      }
    } catch(InterruptedException exc) {
      System.out.println("Call to sleep was interrupted.");
      System.exit(1);
    }
  }
};

// Create a new thread.
thrd = new Thread(myThread);

// Start the thread.
thrd.start();

// Add the action listeners for the Start and
// Stop buttons.
jbtnStart.addActionListener(new ActionListener() {
  public void actionPerformed(ActionEvent ae) {
```

Create a **Runnable** object that will execute in its own thread.

Pause for a tenth of a second.

Update the time displayed. This invokes **updateTime( )** on the event-dispatching thread.

Create the thread.

Start the thread.

```
      // Store start time.
      start = Calendar.getInstance().getTimeInMillis();

      // Reverse the state of the buttons.
      jbtnStop.setEnabled(true);
      jbtnStart.setEnabled(false);

      // Start the stopwatch.
      running = true;
    }
  });

  jbtnStop.addActionListener(new ActionListener() {
    public void actionPerformed(ActionEvent ae) {
      long stop = Calendar.getInstance().getTimeInMillis();

      // Compute the elapsed time.
      jlab.setText("Elapsed time is "
          + (double) (stop - start)/1000);

      // Reverse the state of the buttons.
      jbtnStart.setEnabled(true);
      jbtnStop.setEnabled(false);

      // Stop the stopwatch.
      running = false;
    }
  });

  // Add the buttons and label to the content pane.
  jfrm.getContentPane().add(jbtnStart);
  jfrm.getContentPane().add(jbtnStop);
  jfrm.getContentPane().add(jlab);

  // Display the frame.
  jfrm.setVisible(true);
}

// Update the elapsed time display.
void updateTime() {                          ◄——————— This method gets executed on
  if(!running) return;                                 the event-dispatching thread.

  long temp = Calendar.getInstance().getTimeInMillis();
  jlab.setText("Elapsed time is " +
               (double) (temp - start)/1000);
}
```

```
public static void main(String args[]) {
  // Create the frame on the event dispatching thread.
  SwingUtilities.invokeLater(new Runnable() {
    public void run() {
      new ThreadStopWatch();
    }
  });
}
}
```

Let's look closely at how this program works. First, notice the fields **running** and **thrd**. The **running** variable is initially set to false. When the stopwatch is running, it is set to true. When **running** is true, the elapsed time is displayed. The **thrd** field will hold a reference to the thread that updates the time.

Next, notice how the second thread of execution is created. First, a **Runnable** object called **myThread** is created by the following code:

```
// Create the Runnable instance that will
// become the second thread.
Runnable myThread = new Runnable() {
  // This method will run in the separate thread.
  public void run() {
    try {
      // Report elapsed time every tenth of a second.
      for(; ; ) {
        // Pause for a tenth of a second.
        Thread.sleep(100);

        // Invoke updateTime() on the event dispatching thread.
        SwingUtilities.invokeLater(new Runnable() {
          public void run() {
            updateTime();
          }
        });
      }
    } catch(InterruptedException exc) {
      System.out.println("Call to sleep was interrupted.");
      System.exit(1);
    }
  }
};
```

The **Runnable** interface defines only one method: **run( )**. This method is executed in a separate thread of execution. In essence, when the thread starts running, it calls **run( )**.

Inside **run( )**, an infinite loop is established that simply sleeps for a tenth of a second and then calls **invokeLater( )**. Remember, the code within the loop is executing in its own thread, not the event-dispatching thread. (If it were executing in the event-dispatching thread, the window would become unresponsive because the loop would prevent the other parts of the program from executing.)

Now, notice the argument to **invokeLater( )**. It is called with a **Runnable** whose **run( )** method calls the **updateTime( )** method. The **updateTime( )** method is shown here:

```
// Update the elapsed time display.
void updateTime() {
  if(!running) return;

  long temp = Calendar.getInstance().getTimeInMillis();
  jlab.setText("Elapsed time is " +
               (double) (temp - start)/1000);
}
```

The code first tests the value of **running**. If it is false, then the method returns immediately because the stopwatch is not currently being used. Otherwise, **updateTime( )** obtains the current time, subtracts the start time from it, and then updates **jlab** with the current elapsed time. Because **updateTime( )** changes the contents of the label, it must be executed on the event-dispatching thread. This is accomplished by calling **invokeLater( )** with a **Runnable** argument that calls **updateTime( )**. Thus, **updateTime( )** executes on the event-dispatching thread, and it can safely update the time shown in **jlab**.

After the declaration of **myThread**, a new thread is created that uses **myThread** and is then started by the following code:

```
// Create a new thread.
thrd = new Thread(myThread);

// Start the thread.
thrd.start();
```

At this point, the new thread is executing. However, it isn't being used for anything because the stopwatch has not yet been started.

When the user clicks the Start button, the current system time is obtained and stored in the **start** variable. The Start button is disabled, the Stop button is enabled, and **running** is set to true. When the Stop button is pressed, the current system time is obtained. The difference between the current time and the start time is displayed in **jlab**. Then, the enabled state of the buttons is reversed and **running** is set to false.

As this program shows, the key to using threads safely in Swing is to make sure that any code that interacts with a Swing component is executed on the event-dispatching thread. If you are not sure which thread is executing a piece of code, you can call **isEventDispatchThread( )** defined by **SwingUtilities**.

Use Timer

The preceding stopwatch example showed how a separate thread of execution can be used in conjunction with **invokeLater( )** to interact with a Swing component. As you will see, it is actually a bit more complicated than it needs to be. In some cases, you don't really need to create a separate thread explicitly. Instead, what you need is a *timer* that generates an event at periodic intervals. For example, to scroll a banner, you can use a timer to redraw the banner repeatedly in order to achieve an animated appearance. (See Project 10-1.)

The timer class defined by Swing is called **Timer**. It is packaged in **javax.swing**. It must not be confused with the **Timer** class packaged in **java.util**. You will need to specify explicitly which timer you are using when importing both packages into the same program.

Swing's **Timer** automatically fires an action event that will be received by the specified listener. Because this is an event, it will automatically be executed on the event-dispatching thread. Therefore, the **actionPerformed( )** method defined by the **ActionListener** registered with the timer will be executed on the event-dispatching thread as normal. There is no need to use **invokeLater( )** or **invokeAndWait( )**. Thus, to use **Timer**, you will simply create a **Timer** instance, specifying the action listener that will receive the event.

Timer defines only one constructor, shown here:

Timer(int *period*, ActionListener *al*)

Here, *period* specifies the length of time between events. In other words, *period* specifies the timing interval. The action listener that will receive the events is specified by *al*. You can specify additional action listeners that will be notified when the timer goes off by calling **addActionListener( )** on the timer.

To start the timer, call **start( )**. To stop the timer, call **stop( )**. These methods are shown here:

void start( )

void stop( )

By default, the timer continues to fire events at the specified interval. You can cause the timer to fire only one event by calling **setRepeats( )**, shown here:

void setRepeats(booleran *repeats*)

Here, if *repeats* is true, the time repeats. If it is false, the time stops after one interval.

As mentioned, the thread-based stopwatch program shown in the previous section is actually more complicated than it needs to be. Instead of explicitly creating a separate thread, a timer can be used. This approach is shown by the following version of the program.

```java
// This version of the stopwatch uses the Timer class.

import java.awt.*;
import java.awt.event.*;
import javax.swing.*;
import java.util.Calendar;

class TimerStopWatch {

  JLabel jlab; // display the elapsed time

  JButton jbtnStart; // start the stopwatch
  JButton jbtnStop;  // stop the stopwatch

  long start; // holds the start time in milliseconds

  Timer swTimer; // the timer for the stopwatch

  TimerStopWatch() {

    // Create a new JFrame container.
    JFrame jfrm = new JFrame("Timer-based Stopwatch");

    // Specify FlowLayout for the layout manager.
    jfrm.getContentPane().setLayout(new FlowLayout());

    // Give the frame an initial size.
    jfrm.setSize(230, 90);

    // Terminate the program when the user closes the application.
    jfrm.setDefaultCloseOperation(JFrame.EXIT_ON_CLOSE);

    // Create the elapsed-time label.
    jlab = new JLabel("Press Start to begin timing.");

    // Make the Start and Stop buttons.
    jbtnStart = new JButton("Start");
    jbtnStop = new JButton("Stop");
    jbtnStop.setEnabled(false);
```

Use a **Timer** to update the time display. *(annotation pointing to the `Timer swTimer;` line)*

```
// This action listener is called when the timer
// goes off.
ActionListener timerAL = new ActionListener() {
  public void actionPerformed(ActionEvent ae) {
    updateTime();
  }
};
```

This listener is notified when the timer goes off.

```
// Create a timer that goes off every tenth of a second.
swTimer = new Timer(100, timerAL);
```

Create the timer. Notice that **timerAL** is specified to handle the action events generated by the timer.

```
// Add the action listeners for the start and
// stop buttons.
jbtnStart.addActionListener(new ActionListener() {
  public void actionPerformed(ActionEvent ae) {

    // Store start time.
    start = Calendar.getInstance().getTimeInMillis();

    // Reverse the state of the buttons.
    jbtnStop.setEnabled(true);
    jbtnStart.setEnabled(false);

    // Start the stopwatch.
    swTimer.start();
  }
});

jbtnStop.addActionListener(new ActionListener() {
  public void actionPerformed(ActionEvent ae) {
    long stop = Calendar.getInstance().getTimeInMillis();

    // Compute the elapsed time.
    jlab.setText("Elapsed time is "
        + (double) (stop - start)/1000);

    // Reverse the state of the buttons.
    jbtnStart.setEnabled(true);
    jbtnStop.setEnabled(false);

    // Stop the stopwatch.
    swTimer.stop();
  }
});
```

```
    // Add the buttons and label to the content pane.
    jfrm.getContentPane().add(jbtnStart);
    jfrm.getContentPane().add(jbtnStop);
    jfrm.getContentPane().add(jlab);

    // Display the frame.
    jfrm.setVisible(true);
  }

  // Update the elapsed time display. Notice
  // that the running variable is no longer
  // needed.
  void updateTime() {
    long temp = Calendar.getInstance().getTimeInMillis();
    jlab.setText("Elapsed time is " +
                  (double) (temp - start)/1000);
  }

  public static void main(String args[]) {
    // Create the frame on the event dispatching thread.
    SwingUtilities.invokeLater(new Runnable() {
      public void run() {
        new TimerStopWatch();
      }
    });
  }
}
```

As you can see, the program is substantially shorter because it does not contain the code that creates a thread. It also does not need to use the **running** variable. The use of **Timer** greatly simplifies the task. Notice how little code is required to use the timer. First, it is created by this single line:

```
swTimer = new Timer(100, timerAL);
```

This constructs a timer that goes off once every tenth of a second. Here, **timerAL** specifies the action listener that will receive the action events generated by the timer. It is shown next:

```
ActionListener timerAL = new ActionListener() {
  public void actionPerformed(ActionEvent ae) {
    updateTime();
  }
};
```

The **actionPerformed( )** method simply calls **updateTime( )**. Because this code is already executing on the event-dispatching thread, there is no need for **invokeLater( )**.

The timer is started when the user clicks the Start button. It is stopped when Stop is clicked. As you will see when you try the program, the timer can be repeatedly started and stopped. There is no restriction in this regard.

In general, when you need to use a separate thread whose sole purpose is to keep the GUI updated, using **javax.swing.Timer** is a better choice than manually creating your own thread. However, if you will be using a separate thread to perform other duties, then you have no choice but to create one explicitly.

Progress Check

1. Why must Swing components only be interacted with via the event-dispatching thread?

2. What does **invokeLater( )** do?

3. What method starts a **Timer**?

Create Swing Applets

All of the preceding examples in this book are stand-alone Java applications that run on the desktop. However, such applications are not the only kind of Java program. Two others are *applets* and *servlets*. Applets are small programs that are intended to be downloaded from the Internet and run within a browser. Servlets are small programs that execute on the server. Of the two, the applet is the one that relates most to Swing, and it is the subject of this section. Although Swing-based applets are similar to AWT-based applets, some special rules do apply.

The topic of applets is quite substantial, and it is beyond the scope of this book to discuss all of the issues surrounding them or their use. (For in-depth coverage of applets see my book *Java: The Complete Reference,* published by McGraw-Hill.) However, we will review the basic applet architecture and then examine those issues specific to Swing.

---

1. It avoids conflicts between threads, such as two different threads trying to update the same component at the same time.

2. It causes a **Runnable** object to be executed on the event-dispatching thread. It returns immediately rather than waiting for the thread to end.

3. **start( )**

CRITICAL SKILL
10.3 # Applet Basics

All applets are based on the **Applet** class. However, to create a Swing-based applet, you will use **JApplet**, which inherits **Applet**. **JApplet** is a top-level container and is *not* derived from **JComponent**. Because **JApplet** is a top-level Swing container, it includes the various panes described in Module 1. This means that all components are added to its content pane, in the same way that you have been adding components to **JFrame**'s content pane. Furthermore, all interaction with Swing components must take place on the event-dispatching thread, as described by the previous section.

Applets are not executed directly on the desktop. Instead, they are executed within a Java-enabled browser or by a special program called an *applet viewer*. The JDK supplies a standard applet viewer called **appletviewer**. During development, it is easier to test applets by using an applet viewer than it is to load them into a browser. However, for final testing, a browser should be used.

Applets are designed to be embedded in HTML. Currently, Sun recommends that this be done using the APPLET tag and that is the approach used by this book.

CRITICAL SKILL
10.4 # The Applet Skeleton

All applets (whether or not they use Swing) are based on the same skeleton and have the same lifecycle, and all Swing-based applets extend **JApplet**. Applets override a set of methods that provide the basic mechanism by which the browser or applet viewer interfaces to the applet and controls its execution. These methods are **init( )**, **start( )**, **stop( )**, and **destroy( )**. They are defined by **Applet** (and inherited by **JApplet**) and they define the lifecycle of the applet. Default implementations for all of these methods are provided. Therefore, applets do not need to override those methods they do not use. However, only very simple applets will not need to override all of them. These methods can be assembled into the skeleton shown here:

```
// An Swing-based applet skeleton.

import javax.swing.*;

/*
This HTML can be used to launch the applet:

<applet code="AppletSkel" width=300 height=100>
</applet>

*/

public class AppletSkel extends JApplet {
```

```
  // Called first.
  public void init() {
     // Initialize the applet and construct the GUI.
  }

  // Called second, after init(). Also called
  // whenever the applet is restarted.
  public void start() {
     // Start or resume execution.
  }

  // Called when the applet is stopped.
  public void stop() {
     // Suspend execution.
  }

  // Called when applet is terminated. This is
  // the last method executed.
  public void destroy() {
     // Perform shutdown activities.
  }
}
```

The applet lifecycle methods

Although this skeleton does not do anything, it can be compiled and run. You compile an applet just like any other Java program. For example, this line compiles **AppletSkel**:

```
javac AppletSkel.java
```

However, to run the applet, you will need to create an HTML file that contains the APPLET tag. The comment at the top of the skeleton shows HTML that will execute the applet. If you put this code into a file called **AppletSkel.html**, then you can run the applet by loading it into your browser or by using **appletviewer**, as shown here:

```
appletviewer AppletSkel.html
```

When run with the applet viewer, the skeleton generates the window shown in Figure 10-2.

Before moving on, it is important to understand the order in which the applet lifecycle methods are called. When an applet begins, the following methods are called in the sequence indicated:

1. init( )

2. start( )

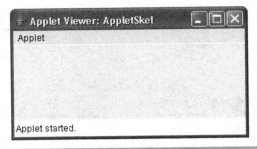

Figure 10-2 The window produced by **AppletSkel** when run using **appletviewer**

When an applet is terminated, the following sequence of method calls takes place:

1. stop( )

2. destroy( )

Let's look more closely at these methods.

The **init( )** method is the first method to be called. This is where you should initialize the applet. This method is called only once during the runtime of your applet. The **init( )** method must also construct the GUI, but it can't do so directly. Instead, it must use **invokeAndWait( )**, as described in the next section.

The **start( )** method is called after **init( )**. It is also called to restart an applet after it has been stopped. Whereas **init( )** is called once—the first time an applet is loaded—**start( )** is called each time an applet's HTML document is displayed onscreen. So, if a user leaves a web page and comes back, the applet resumes execution at **start( )**.

Ask the Expert

Q: The applications throughout this book call invokeLater( ) to construct the GUI. Why does an applet use invokeAndWait( )?

A: Applets must use **invokeAndWait( )** because the **init( )** method must not return until the entire initialization process has been completed. In essence, the **start( )** method cannot be called until after initialization, which means that the GUI must be fully constructed.

The **stop( )** method is called when a browser leaves the HTML document containing the applet—when it goes to another page, for example. When **stop( )** is called, the applet is probably running. You should use **stop( )** to suspend threads that don't need to run when the applet is not visible. You can restart them when **start( )** is called if the user returns to the page.

The **destroy( )** method is called when the environment determines that your applet needs to be completely removed from memory. At this point, you should free up any resources the applet may be using. The **stop( )** method is always called before **destroy( )**.

CRITICAL SKILL
10.5 # Construct an Applet GUI

Although the preceding applet skeleton is functional, it doesn't do anything. It also doesn't contain any components. Like a Swing application, an applet must interact with its components using the event-dispatching thread. This means that you cannot use the **init( )** method itself to build the initial GUI. Instead, inside **init( )** you will call **invokeAndWait( )** to specify a **Runnable** object whose **run( )** method will be executed on the event-dispatching thread. Using this approach, the skeletal form of the **init( )** method is shown here:

```
// Called first.
public void init() {
  try {
    SwingUtilities.invokeAndWait(new Runnable () {
      public void run() {
        guiInit(); // a method that initializes the Swing components
      }
    });
  } catch(Exception exc) {
    System.out.println("Can't create because of "+ exc);
  }
}
```

A Swing-based applet must create its GUI on the event-dispatching thread.

Inside **run( )**, a method called **guiInit( )** is called. This is a method that you provide that sets up and initializes the Swing components. Of course, the name of the method is arbitrary.

A Simple Swing Applet

Putting together all of the pieces, here is a very simple Swing-based applet that displays two buttons. Each time a button is clicked, a message is displayed that states which button was clicked. Sample output of the applet being executed by **appletviewer** is shown in Figure 10-3.

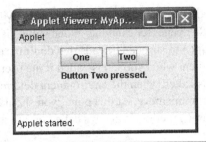

Figure 10-3 Sample output from the **MyApplet** applet

```java
// A simple Swing-based applet

import javax.swing.*;
import java.awt.*;
import java.awt.event.*;

/*
This HTML can be used to launch the applet:

<object code="MyApplet" width=240 height=100>
</object>

*/

public class MyApplet extends JApplet {
  JButton jbtnOne;
  JButton jbtnTwo;

  JLabel jlab;

  // Called first.
  public void init() {
    try {
      SwingUtilities.invokeAndWait(new Runnable () {
        public void run() {
          guiInit(); // initialize the GUI
        }
      });
    } catch(Exception exc) {
      System.out.println("Can't create because of "+ exc);
    }
  }
```

```java
// Called second, after init(). Also called
// whenever the applet is restarted.
public void start() {
  // Not used by this applet.
}

// Called when the applet is stopped.
public void stop() {
  // Not used by this applet.
}

// Called when applet is terminated. This is
// the last method executed.
public void destroy() {
  // Not used by this applet.
}

// Set up and initialize the GUI.
private void guiInit() {
  // Set the applet to use flow layout.
  setLayout(new FlowLayout());

  // Create two buttons and a label.
  jbtnOne = new JButton("One");
  jbtnTwo = new JButton("Two");

  jlab = new JLabel("Press a button.");

  // Add action listeners for the buttons.
  jbtnOne.addActionListener(new ActionListener() {
    public void actionPerformed(ActionEvent le) {
      jlab.setText("Button One pressed.");
    }
  });

  jbtnTwo.addActionListener(new ActionListener() {
    public void actionPerformed(ActionEvent le) {
      jlab.setText("Button Two pressed.");
    }
  });

  // Add the components to the applet's content pane.
  getContentPane().add(jbtnOne);
  getContentPane().add(jbtnTwo);
  getContentPane().add(jlab);
}
}
```

There are two important things about this applet. First, the **init( )** method initializes the Swing GUI by setting up a call to **guiInit( )**. This is accomplished through the use of **invokeAndWait( )**. Inside **guiInit( )**, two buttons and a label are created. Then, an action listener is added to each button. They simply set the text in the label to indicate which button was pressed. Although this example is quite simple, this same general approach must be used when building any Swing GUI that will be used by an applet.

The second point of interest in the applet is the fact that neither **start( )**, **stop( )**, nor **destroy( )** is used by the applet. This is not uncommon for simple applets. In such cases, there is actually no reason to specify empty implementations because **Applet** provides default implementations for you. Therefore, if you don't need to use one of the applet lifecycle methods, you don't need to override it.

Progress Check

1. What class is used to create a Swing-based applet?

2. What are the four applet lifecycle methods?

3. What method do you call to construct the GUI when a Swing-based applet initializes?

Project 10-1 Scroll Text in an Applet

ScrollText.java This project demonstrates both Swing-based applets and Swing timers. It uses a timer to scroll a text message within a **JLabel**. As you will see, the code to accomplish this is surprisingly short and to the point because Swing's **Timer** class makes the process extremely easy to code. Sample output from the applet is shown here:

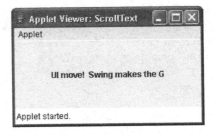

---

1. **JApplet**
2. **init( )**, **start( )**, **stop( )**, and **destroy( )**
3. **invokeAndWait( )**

Step by Step

1. Create a file called **ScrollText.java** and add the following comments and **import** statements:

```
// Project 10-1: A Swing-based applet that scrolls
// text through a label.

import javax.swing.*;
import java.awt.*;
import java.awt.event.*;

/*
This HTML can be used to launch the applet:

<object code="ScrollText" width=240 height=100>
</object>

*/
```

2. Begin creating the **ScrollText** class as shown here:

```
public class ScrollText extends JApplet {

  JLabel jlab;

  String msg = " Swing makes the GUI move! ";

  ActionListener scroller;

  Timer stTimer; // this timer controls the scroll rate
```

Because **ScrollText** is a Swing-based applet, it extends **JApplet**. It then declares a label that will be used to display the scrolling message, the message that will be scrolled, an action listener that will perform the scrolling, and a timer that controls the rate of scroll.

3. Add the **init( )** method shown next:

```
// Initialize the applet.
public void init() {
  try {
    SwingUtilities.invokeAndWait(new Runnable () {
      public void run() {
        guiInit();
      }
    });
  } catch(Exception exc) {
    System.out.println("Can't create because of "+ exc);
```

(continued)

```
  }
}
```

This method simply invokes **guiInit( )** on the event-dispatching thread as described earlier.

4. Add the **start( )**, **stop( )**, and **destroy( )** methods, shown here:

```
// Start the timer when the applet is started.
public void start() {
  stTimer.start();
}

// Stop the timer when the applet is stopped.
public void stop() {
  stTimer.stop();
}

// Stop the timer when the applet is destroyed.
public void destroy() {
  stTimer.stop();
}
```

Although very short, these methods perform important functions. Each time the applet is displayed in a page, the timer is started. Each time the browser stops the applet, the timer is stopped. The timer is also stopped when the applet is destroyed.

5. Finish the applet with the **guiInit( )** method shown here:

```
// Initialize the timer GUI.
private void guiInit() {

  // Create the label that will scroll the message.
  jlab = new JLabel(msg);
  jlab.setHorizontalAlignment(SwingConstants.CENTER);

  // Create the action listener for the timer.
  scroller = new ActionListener() {
    public void actionPerformed(ActionEvent ae) {
      // Left-scroll the message one character.
      char ch = msg.charAt(0);
      msg = msg.substring(1, msg.length());
      msg += ch;
      jlab.setText(msg);
    }
  };

  // Create the timer.
  stTimer = new Timer(200, scroller);
```

```
      // Add the label to the applet content pane.
      getContentPane().add(jlab);
   }
}
```

This method creates the label in which the text is scrolled. The text is aligned in the center. This is done to make the scrolling text more visually appealing. It is not technically necessary. Next, an action listener is created that scrolls the text left one character each time it is called. This listener is then passed to the **Timer** constructor when the timer is created. The timing period is one fifth of a second, but you might want to experiment with the delay period. Obviously, the shorter the period, the faster the scroll. Finally, the label is added to the content pane.

6. The entire **ScrollText** applet is shown here:

```
// Project 10-1: A Swing-based applet that scrolls
// text through a label.

import javax.swing.*;
import java.awt.*;
import java.awt.event.*;

/*
This HTML can be used to launch the applet:

<object code="ScrollText" width=240 height=100>
</object>

*/

public class ScrollText extends JApplet {

  JLabel jlab;

  String msg = " Swing makes the GUI move! ";

  ActionListener scroller;

  Timer stTimer; // this timer controls the scroll rate

  // Initialize the applet.
  public void init() {
    try {
      SwingUtilities.invokeAndWait(new Runnable () {
        public void run() {
          guiInit();
```

(continued)

```
        }
      });
    } catch(Exception exc) {
      System.out.println("Can't create because of "+ exc);
    }
  }

  // Start the timer when the applet is started.
  public void start() {
    stTimer.start();
  }

  // Stop the timer when the applet is stopped.
  public void stop() {
    stTimer.stop();
  }

  // Stop the timer when the applet is destroyed.
  public void destroy() {
    stTimer.stop();
  }

  // Initialize the timer GUI.
  private void guiInit() {

    // Create the label that will scroll the message.
    jlab = new JLabel(msg);
    jlab.setHorizontalAlignment(SwingConstants.CENTER);

    // Create the action listener for the timer.
    scroller = new ActionListener() {
      public void actionPerformed(ActionEvent ae) {
        // Left-scroll the message one character.
        char ch = msg.charAt(0);
        msg = msg.substring(1, msg.length());
        msg += ch;
        jlab.setText(msg);
      }
    };

    // Create the timer.
    stTimer = new Timer(200, scroller);

    // Add the label to the applet content pane.
    getContentPane().add(jlab);
  }
}
```

Painting

The main focus of this book is on the Swing component set and the techniques required to use them. However, there is another part of Swing that lets you create your own visual output by writing directly into the display area of a frame, panel, or one of Swing's other components, such as **JLabel**. Although many (perhaps most) uses of Swing will *not* involve drawing directly to the surface of a component, it is available for those applications that need this capability. To write output directly to the surface of a component involves one or more drawing methods, such as **drawLine( )** or **drawRect( )**, and requires that you take some manual control over the painting process. Although it is far beyond the scope of this book to describe either of these topics in detail, this section will cover the basic techniques that you will use to manually paint output.

Painting Fundamentals

The first thing to understand about painting in Swing is that it is a somewhat complicated process. In fact, Swing has an entire subsystem dedicated to managing painting, which is built on the original AWT-based approach. Before examining the specifics of Swing-based painting, it is useful to understand the mechanism that underlies it.

To begin, recall that **JComponent** inherits the AWT class **Component**. This class defines a method called **paint( )**. This method is called when the component needs to be displayed on the screen. For the most part, **paint( )** is not called by your program. (In fact, only in extremely rare cases should it ever be called by your program.) Rather, **paint( )** is called by the runtime system whenever a component must be rendered. This situation can occur for several reasons. For example, the window in which the component is displayed can be overwritten by another window and then uncovered. Or, the window might be minimized and then restored. The **paint( )** method is also called when a program begins running. When writing AWT-based code, an application will override **paint( )** when it needs to write output directly to the surface of the component.

Although Swing's lightweight components do inherit the **paint( )** method from **Component**, you will not override it to paint directly to the surface of a component. The reason is that Swing uses a bit more sophisticated approach to painting that involves three distinct methods: **paintComponent( )**, **paintBorder( )**, and **paintChildren( )**. These methods paint the indicated portion of a component and divide the painting process into its three distinct, logical actions. In a lightweight component, the original AWT method **paint( )** simply executes calls to these methods, in the order just shown.

To paint to the surface of a Swing component, you will create a subclass of the component and then override its **paintComponent( )** method. This is the method that paints the interior of the component. You will not normally override the other two painting methods. When overriding

paintComponent( ), the first thing you must do is called **super.paintComponent( )**, so that the superclass portion of the painting process takes place. (The only time this is not required is when you are taking complete manual control over how a component is displayed.) After that, write the output that you want to display.

The **paintComponent( )** method is shown here:

protected void paintComponent(Graphics g)

The parameter g is the graphics context to which output is written.

The Graphics Context

In Java, each component has associated with it a *graphics context*. This context is encapsulated by the **Graphics** class and it maintains various pieces of information about the display environment, such as the drawing color and font. As just described, this context is passed to the various paint methods, such as **paintComponent( )**. When you paint to a component, you will do so through this context, using methods that it provides.

Graphics defines many methods that write output to the component. Here are three examples:

void drawLine(int *startX*, int *startY*, int *endX*, int *endY*)

void drawRect(int *left*, int *top*, int *width*, int *height*)

void drawString(String *str*, int *left*, int *top*)

The **drawLine( )** method draws a line in the current drawing color that begins at *startX,startY* and ends at *endX,endY*. **drawRect( )** draws a rectangle in the current drawing color that begins at *left,top* and is *width* wide and *height* tall. **drawString( )** writes the string specified by *str* with the baseline of the string starting at the location specified by *left,top*.

For all components, the origin of the display area is located at the upper-left corner and has the coordinates 0,0. Furthermore, all display locations are relative to this origin. All coordinates are specified in terms of pixels. Therefore, if you write output at location 12,14, the output is written 12 pixels right and 14 pixels down from the upper left corner.

Compute the Paintable Area

When drawing to the surface of a component, you must be careful to restrict your output to the area that is inside the border. Although Swing automatically clips any output that will exceed the boundaries of a component, it is still possible to paint into the border, which will then get overwritten when the border is drawn. To avoid this, you must compute the *paintable area* of the component. This is the area defined by the current size of the component minus the space used by the border. Therefore, before you paint to a component, you must obtain the width of the border and then adjust your drawing accordingly.

To obtain the border width, call **getInsets( )**, shown here:

Insets getInsets( )

This method is defined by **Container** and overridden by **JComponent**. It returns an **Insets** object that contains the dimensions of the border. The inset values can be obtained by using these fields:

int top;

int bottom;

int left;

int right;

These values are then used to compute the drawing area given the width and the height of the component. You can obtain the width and height of the component by calling **getWidth( )** and **getHeight( )** on the component. They are shown here:

int getWidth( )

int getHeight( )

By subtracting the value of the insets, you can compute the overall width and height of the component.

CRITICAL SKILL
10.9 Request Painting

As just explained, normally a component is painted only when its **paint( )** method is called, which, in the case of a Swing component, causes calls to **paintComponent( )**, **paintBorder( )**, and **paintChildren( )**. This raises an important question: How can the program itself cause a component to be updated when its contents change? For example, if a program plots data in a bar graph and that data changes, how does the program cause the graph to be redrawn? The answer: your program calls **repaint( )**.

The **repaint( )** method is defined by **Component**. Calling it causes the system to call **paint( )** as soon as it is possible to do so. Since painting is a time-consuming operation, this mechanism allows the runtime system to momentarily defer painting until some higher-priority task has finished, for example. Of course, in Swing the call to **paint( )** results in a call to **paintComponent( )**. Therefore, to output to the surface of a component, your program will store the output until **paintComponent( )** is called. Inside the overridden **paintComponent( )**, you will draw the stored output.

There are several forms of **repaint( )** that give you substantial control over the painting process. However, this module uses only its simplest form, shown here:

void repaint( )

This version causes the entire component to be redrawn.

A Paint Example

Here is a program that puts into action the preceding discussion. It creates a class called **PaintPanel** that extends **JPanel**. The program then uses an object of that class to display a bar graph that plots randomly generated data. In addition to the bar graph, the program includes two buttons. One allows you to display a different set of values. The other lets you change the size of the border around the graph. Sample output is shown in Figure 10-4.

Figure 10-4 Sample output from the **PaintPanel** program

Ask the Expert

Q: Other than the graphics context passed to methods such as paintComponent( ), is it possible to obtain the graphics context for a component in any other way?

A: Yes, the graphics context is returned by the **getGraphics( )** method defined by **Component**. As explained, normally an application will not display output except when **paintComponent( )** is called. However, it is possible, in very specialized circumstances, for a program to display output at other times. To do this, it obtains the graphics context by calling **getGraphics( )** and then uses it to output to the surface of the component.

```
// Paint lines to a panel.

import java.awt.*;
import java.awt.event.*;
import javax.swing.*;
import java.util.*;

// This class extends JPanel. It overrides
// the paintComponent() method so that random
// data is plotted in the panel.
class PaintPanel extends JPanel {            PaintPanel extends JPanel.
  Insets ins; // holds the panel's insets

  Random rand; // used to generate random numbers

  PaintPanel(int w, int h) {

    // Ensure that the panel is opaque.
    setOpaque(true);

    // Use a red line border.
    setBorder(
      BorderFactory.createLineBorder(Color.RED, 1));

    // Set the preferred dimension as specified.
    setPreferredSize(new Dimension(w, h));

    rand = new Random();
  }
```

```
    // Override the paintComponent() method.
    protected void paintComponent(Graphics g) {
      // Always call the superclass method first.
      super.paintComponent(g);

      // Get the height and width of the component.
      int height = getHeight();
      int width = getWidth();

        // Get the insets.
      ins = getInsets();

      // Fill the panel by plotting random data
      // in the form of a bar graph.
      for(int i=ins.left+5; i <= width-ins.right-5; i += 4) {
        // Obtain a random number between 0 and
        // the maximum height of the drawing area.
        int h = rand.nextInt(height-ins.bottom);

        // If generated value is within or too close to
        // the border, change it to just outside the border.
        if(h <= ins.top) h = ins.top+1;

        // Draw a line that represents the data.
        g.drawLine(i, height-ins.bottom, i, h);
      }
    }

  // Change the border size.
  public void changeBorderSize(int size) {
    setBorder(
      BorderFactory.createLineBorder(Color.RED, size));
  }
}

// Demonstrate painting directly onto a panel.
class PaintDemo {

  JButton jbtnMore;
  JButton jbtnSize;
  JLabel jlab;
  PaintPanel pp;

  boolean big; // use to toggle size of panel

  PaintDemo() {
```

Override **paintComponent( )** to paint to the surface of the component.

Remember to call the superclass implementation.

Draw the graph of random data.

```
// Create a new JFrame container.
JFrame jfrm = new JFrame("Painting Demo");

// Specify FlowLayout for the layout manager.
jfrm.getContentPane().setLayout(new FlowLayout());

// Give the frame an initial size.
jfrm.setSize(240, 260);

// Terminate the program when the user closes the application.
jfrm.setDefaultCloseOperation(JFrame.EXIT_ON_CLOSE);

// Create the panel that will be painted.
pp = new PaintPanel(100, 100);

// Make the buttons.
jbtnMore = new JButton("Show More Data");
jbtnSize = new JButton("Change Border Size");

// Describe the graph.
jlab = new JLabel("Bar Graph of Random Data");

// Repaint the panel when the Show More Data button
// is clicked.
jbtnMore.addActionListener(new ActionListener() {
  public void actionPerformed(ActionEvent ae) {
    pp.repaint();
  }
});
```

Request that the panel be painted.

```
// Set the border size of the panel when the
// Change Border Size button is clicked.
// Changing the border size automatically
// results in a repaint.
jbtnSize.addActionListener(new ActionListener() {
  public void actionPerformed(ActionEvent ae) {
    if(!big) pp.changeBorderSize(5);
    else pp.changeBorderSize(1);
    big = !big;
  }
});
```

Change the border size of the graph.

```
// Add the buttons, label, and panel to the content pane.
jfrm.getContentPane().add(jlab);
jfrm.getContentPane().add(pp);
```

```
      jfrm.getContentPane().add(jbtnMore);
      jfrm.getContentPane().add(jbtnSize);

      big = false;

      // Display the frame.
      jfrm.setVisible(true);
    }

    public static void main(String args[]) {
      // Create the frame on the event dispatching thread.
      SwingUtilities.invokeLater(new Runnable() {
        public void run() {
          new PaintDemo();
        }
      });
    }
  }
```

Let's examine this program closely. The **PaintPanel** class extends **JPanel** and overrides the **paintComponent( )** method. This enables **PaintPanel** to write directly to the surface of the component when painting takes place. The **PaintPanel** constructor takes two parameters that specify the preferred width and height of the panel. The constructor also specifies a 1-pixel wide, red border.

Inside the override of **paintComponent( ),** notice that it first calls **super.paintComponent( ).** As explained, this is necessary to ensure that the component is properly drawn. Next the width and height of the panel are obtained along with the insets. These values are used to restrict the height and position of the graph bars to within the drawing area of the panel. The drawing area is the overall width and height of a component less the border width. The computations are designed to work with differently sized **PaintPanel**s and borders.

The **changeBorderSize( )** method changes the border size of the panel. Because **paintComponent( )** automatically displays data that fills the current size of the drawing area of the panel, the border width can be changed without any problems.

The **PaintDemo** class demonstrates **PaintPanel**. It creates a **PaintPanel** called **pp** with the dimensions 100 by 100. It also creates two buttons called **jbtnMore** and **jbtnSize**. When the **jbtnMore** is clicked, **repaint( )** is called on **pp**. This results in **PaintPanel**'s **paintComponent( )** being called. Thus, each time **jbtnMore** is pressed, new randomly generated data is displayed. When **jbtnSize** is clicked, the width of the border is toggled between 1 and 5. Because **paintComponent( )** computes the boundaries of the drawing area dynamically, the border can be set to any arbitrary value.

Ask the Expert

Q: I was looking through the API documentation for JComponent **and noticed a method called** revalidate( ). **What does it do?**

A: The **revalidate( )** method causes the layout manager to review the layout for the component and adjust as needed. Normally you don't need to call this method because any change to the visual aspects of the component causes a *revalidation* automatically. However, there are a few cases in which you might need to call it directly. One occurs when you change the preferred size of the component after it has been displayed. Changing the preferred size does not cause an automatic revalidation, so if you want the effects of a change in preferred size to be seen immediately, you will need to call **revalidate( )**.

One last point: as the preceding discussion has shown, many of the classes and methods that are used to draw directly into the display area of a component are supplied by the AWT, not by Swing. If you will be creating Swing applications that do a substantial amount of manually produced output, you will need to be fully versed in the AWT. It is an important part of Java.

Progress Check

1. To write output directly into the drawing area of a Swing component, what method must you override?

2. What method obtains the width of the current border?

3. How do you cause the **paint( )** method to be called?

Two Versatile Layout Managers

The preceding modules have used three layout managers: **BorderLayout**, **FlowLayout**, and **GridLayout**. As explained in Module 1, Java defines several more. Some are a bit specialized,

---

1. **paintComponent( )**
2. **getInsets( )**
3. To cause **paint( )** to be called, call **repaint( )**.

such as **CardLayout** and **SpringLayout**. However, two are quite versatile and they are frequently used in Swing programming. They are **GridBagLayout** and **BoxLayout**. This section presents an overview of both.

GridBagLayout

Although layouts such as **FlowLayout** and **BorderLayout** are very useful and are perfectly acceptable for some applications, many Swing programs will require that you take more control over how the components are arranged within a window. A good way to do this is to use a grid-bag layout, which is specified by the **GridBagLayout** class. What makes the grid bag useful is that you can specify the relative placement of components by indicating their positions within cells inside a grid. The key to the grid bag is that each component can be a different size, and each row in the grid can have a different number of columns. This is why the layout is called a *grid bag*. It's a collection of small grids joined together. **GridBagLayout** is packaged in **java.awt**.

The location and size of each component in a grid bag is determined by a set of constraints that are linked to it. The constraints are contained in an object of type **GridBagConstraints**. Constraints include the height and width of a cell, and the placement of a component, its alignment, and its anchor point within the cell.

The general procedure for using a grid bag is to first create a new **GridBagLayout** object and make it the current layout manager. Then, set the constraints that apply to each component. Finally, add the components to the layout manager. Although **GridBagLayout** is a bit more complicated than the other layout managers, it is still quite easy to use once you understand how it works.

GridBagLayout defines only one constructor, which is shown here:

GridBagLayout( )

GridBagLayout defines several methods, of which many are protected and not for general use. There is one method, however, that you must use: **setConstraints( )**. This method sets the constraints that apply to a component that will be put into the grid bag. It is shown here:

void setConstraints(Component *comp*, GridBagConstraints *cons*)

Here, *comp* is the component for which the constraints specified by *cons* apply.

The key to successfully using **GridBagLayout** is the proper setting of the constraints, which are stored in a **GridBagConstraints** object. **GridBagConstraints** defines several fields that you can set to govern the size, placement, and spacing of a component. These are shown in Table 10-1. Several are described in greater detail in the following discussion.

Field	Purpose
int anchor	Specifies the location of a component within a cell. The default is **GridBagConstraints.CENTER**.
int fill	Specifies how a component is resized if the component is smaller than its cell. Valid values are **GridBagConstraints.NONE** (the default), **GridBagConstraints.HORIZONTAL**, **GridBagConstraints.VERTICAL**, or **GridBagConstraints.BOTH**
int gridheight	Specifies the height of a component in terms of cells. The default is 1.
int gridwidth	Specifies the width of a component in terms of cells. The default is 1.
int gridx	Specifies the X coordinate of the cell to which the component will be added. The default value is **GridBagConstraints.RELATIVE**.
int gridy	Specifies the Y coordinate of the cell to which the component will be added. The default value is **GridBagConstraints.RELATIVE**.
Insets insets	Specifies the insets. Default insets are all 0.
int ipadx	Specifies extra horizontal space that surrounds a component within a cell. The default is 0.
int ipady	Specifies extra vertical space that surrounds a component within a cell. The default is 0.
double weightx	Specifies a weight value that determines the horizontal spacing between cells, and between cells and the edges of the container. The default value is 0.0. The greater the weight, the more space that is allocated. If all values are 0.0, extra space is distributed evenly around the edges of the container.
double weighty	Specifies a weight value that determines the vertical spacing between cells, and between cells and the edges of the container. The default value is 0.0. The greater the weight, the more space that is allocated. If all values are 0.0, extra space is distributed evenly around the edges of the container.

Table 10-1 Constraint Fields Defined by **GridBagConstraints**

GridBagConstraints also defines several static fields that contain standard constraint values, such as **GridBagConstraints.CENTER** and **GridBagConstraints.VERTICAL**.

When a component is smaller than its cell, you can use the **anchor** field to specify where within the cell the component's top-left corner will be located. There are two types of values that you can give to **anchor**. The first are absolute:

GridBagConstraints.CENTER	GridBagConstraints.EAST
GridBagConstraints.NORTH	GridBagConstraints.NORTHEAST

GridBagConstraints.NORTHWEST	GridBagConstraints.SOUTH
GridBagConstraints.SOUTHEAST	GridBagConstraints.SOUTHWEST
GridBagConstraints.WEST	

As their names imply, these values cause the component to be placed at the specific locations.

The second type of values that can be given to **anchor** is relative, which means the values are relative to the container's orientation, which might differ between languages. The relative values are shown here:

GridBagConstraints.FIRST_LINE_END	GridBagConstraints.FIRST_LINE_START
GridBagConstraints.LAST_LINE_END	GridBagConstraints.LAST_LINE_START
GridBagConstraints.LINE_END	GridBagConstraints.LINE_START
GridBagConstraints.PAGE_END	GridBagConstraints.PAGE_START

Their names describe the placement.

The **weightx** and **weighty** fields are both quite important, and quite confusing at first glance. In general, their values determine how much of the extra space within a container is allocated to each row and column. By default, both these values are 0. When all values within a row or a column are 0, extra space is distributed evenly between the edges of the container and components. By increasing the weight, you increase that row's or column's allocation of space proportional to the other rows or columns. The best way to understand how these values work is to experiment with them a bit.

The **gridwidth** variable lets you specify the width of a cell in terms of cell units. The default is 1. To specify that a component uses the remaining space in a row, use **GridBagConstraints.REMAINDER**. To specify that a component uses up to the next to last cell in a row, use **GridBagConstraints.RELATIVE**. The **gridheight** constraint works the same way, but in the vertical direction.

You can specify a padding value that will be used to increase the minimum size of a component. To pad horizontally, assign a value to **ipadx**. To pad vertically, assign a value to **ipady**.

Here is an example that uses **GridBagLayout** that demonstrates several of the points just discussed. Sample output is shown in Figure 10-5.

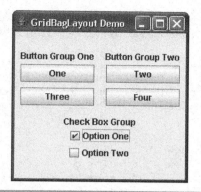

Figure 10-5 Sample output from the **GBDemo** program

```java
// Demonstrate GridBagLayout.

import java.awt.*;
import javax.swing.*;

class GBDemo {

  GBDemo() {

    // Create a new JFrame container.
    JFrame jfrm = new JFrame("GridBagLayout Demo");

    // Create the grid bag.
    GridBagLayout gbag = new GridBagLayout();
    GridBagConstraints gbc = new GridBagConstraints();

    // Set the grid bag as the layout manager for the
    // the content pane.
    jfrm.getContentPane().setLayout(gbag);

    // Give the frame an initial size.
    jfrm.setSize(240, 240);
```

Create an empty **GridBagLayout** and **GridBagConstraints**.

Make the grid bag the layout manager for the frame.

```
// Terminate the program when the user closes the application.
jfrm.bsetDefaultCloseOperation(JFrame.EXIT_ON_CLOSE);

// Make the labels.
JLabel jlabOne = new JLabel("Button Group One");
JLabel jlabTwo = new JLabel("Button Group Two");
JLabel jlabThree = new JLabel("Check Box Group");

// Make the buttons.
JButton jbtnOne = new JButton("One");
JButton jbtnTwo = new JButton("Two");
JButton jbtnThree = new JButton("Three");
JButton jbtnFour = new JButton("Four");

Dimension btnDim = new Dimension(100, 25);
jbtnOne.setPreferredSize(btnDim);
jbtnTwo.setPreferredSize(btnDim);
jbtnThree.setPreferredSize(btnDim);
jbtnFour.setPreferredSize(btnDim);

// Make the check boxes.
JCheckBox jcbOne = new JCheckBox("Option One");
JCheckBox jcbTwo = new JCheckBox("Option Two");

// Define the grid bag.

// By using a weightx of 1.0, the components divide the
// horizontal space. However, because weighty uses its
// default value of 0.0, the components remain centered
// in the vertical space.
gbc.weightx = 1.0;    ◄──────────  Set weightx to 1.0 so that the
                                   horizontal space is evenly distributed.

// Define the grid location for each component.

// Put the button labels in locations 0,0 and 1,0.──┐
gbc.gridx = 0;
gbc.gridy = 0;                                        ├── Define the grid-bag
gbag.setConstraints(jlabOne, gbc); ──────────────────┘   locations and
                                                         constraints for
gbc.gridx = 1;                                           jlabOne. The other
gbc.gridy = 0;                                           components are
gbag.setConstraints(jlabTwo, gbc);                       specified in similar
                                                         fashion.

// Add some space around the buttons.
gbc.insets = new Insets(4, 4, 4, 4);  ◄──────────────    Add some space
                                                         between the buttons.
```

```
// Put the buttons at locations 0,1 and 1,1, and so on.
gbc.gridx = 0;
gbc.gridy = 1;
gbag.setConstraints(jbtnOne, gbc);

gbc.gridx = 1;
gbc.gridy = 1;
gbag.setConstraints(jbtnTwo, gbc);

gbc.gridx = 0;
gbc.gridy = 2;
gbag.setConstraints(jbtnThree, gbc);

gbc.gridx = 1;
gbc.gridy = 2;
gbag.setConstraints(jbtnFour, gbc);

// Have the last label and the two check boxes
// use the remaining space.
gbc.gridwidth = GridBagConstraints.REMAINDER;          ◄——— Center the check
                                                                box group.
// Use an inset of 10 from the top for the label.
gbc.insets = new Insets(10, 0, 0, 0);          ◄——————— Add a 10-pixel gap between
gbc.gridx = 0;                                            the label and check boxes.
gbc.gridy = 3;
gbag.setConstraints(jlabThree, gbc);

// No insets for the check boxes.
gbc.insets = new Insets(0, 0, 0, 0);          ◄——————— No extra space needed
gbc.gridx = 0;                                           by the check boxes.
gbc.gridy = 4;
gbag.setConstraints(jcbOne, gbc);

gbc.gridx = 0;
gbc.gridy = 5;
gbag.setConstraints(jcbTwo, gbc);

// Add everything to the content pane.
jfrm.getContentPane().add(jlabOne);
jfrm.getContentPane().add(jlabTwo);
jfrm.getContentPane().add(jbtnOne);
jfrm.getContentPane().add(jbtnTwo);
jfrm.getContentPane().add(jbtnThree);
jfrm.getContentPane().add(jbtnFour);
jfrm.getContentPane().add(jlabThree);
jfrm.getContentPane().add(jcbOne);
```

```
      jfrm.getContentPane().add(jcbTwo);

      // Display the frame.
      jfrm.setVisible(true);
  }

  public static void main(String args[]) {
      // Create the frame on the event dispatching thread.
      SwingUtilities.invokeLater(new Runnable() {
        public void run() {
          new GBDemo();
        }
      });
  }
}
```

This layout uses a grid bag to create three visual groupings of components. The first two consist of a label that is positioned over two buttons. Thus, two columns of buttons are created. The third is a label over two check boxes. These items are centered under the buttons. If you resize the window, you will see that the relative positions of the components remain the same. This is the major benefit of grid layout. It lets you specify relative positions that don't change even though the size of the window changes.

There are several things of interest in the program. First, notice that **weightx** is given a value of 1.0. By default, **weightx** is 0.0 and all extra space is put around the edges of the container, causing the components to be tightly centered left-to-right. There is nothing wrong with this approach, but by specifying a value other than 0.0, the components will be positioned to better fill the horizontal space when the container changes its size. However, for the sake of illustration, **weighty** remains at its default value of 0.0. This means that the components will always remain centered top-to-bottom. You should experiment with both of these properties and observe the results.

Next, the labels over the buttons are positioned at the top of the grid and then the insets for the buttons are set to 4. This ensures that there is a bit of space between the buttons. Before the check box label and check boxes are added, the **gridwidth** is set to **REMAINDER**. This enables those components to occupy all of the remaining room in the row. Because the components are centered within a cell by default, this means that the third label and the check boxes will be centered within the remaining space.

GridBagLayout is a powerful layout manager. It is worth taking some time to experiment with and explore. Once you understand what the various settings and properties do, you can easily use **GridBagLayout** to position components with a high degree of precision and confidence.

Progress Check

1. What two classes work together when using a grid-bag layout?

2. What **GridBagConstraints** fields determine the grid location of a component?

3. What do **weightx** and **weighty** do?

CRITICAL SKILL
10.11 BoxLayout

As useful as **GridBagLayout** is (and it *is* very useful) it is somewhat complicated to work with and often involves several steps to set up properly. Often, all you want is the ability to create a group of components that are laid out either vertically or horizontally as a unit. To handle these types of situations, Swing adds a layout manager called **BoxLayout**. It is packaged in **javax.swing**.

BoxLayout gives you an easy way to create groups of components that are organized into boxes. Usually, you won't use **BoxLayout** as the layout manager for the content pane itself (although you can). Instead, you will normally create one or more panels that use **BoxLayout**. Add the components to the panels, and then add the panels to the content pane. In this way, you can easily create groups of components that lay out as a unit. Although you can implement this approach manually by first creating a **JPanel**, setting its layout manager to **BoxLayout**, adding the components to the panel, and then adding the panel to content pane, Swing offers a more convenient approach. The **Box** class can be used to create a container that uses **BoxLayout** automatically. **Box** also includes some utility methods that simplify the positioning of components within the box. Because most uses of **BoxLayout** use the **Box** class, that is the approach described here.

It is possible to create a **Box** two ways. First, you can use its constructor, which is shown here.

Box(int *orientation*)

Here, *orientation* determines the orientation of the box, and it must be one of these values (which are defined by **BoxLayout**).

---

1. **GridBayLayout** and **GridBagConstraints**

2. **gridx** and **gridy**

3. **weightx** and **weighty** determine how space is distributed throughout the container.

X_AXIS	Lay out components left to right.
Y_AXIS	Lay out components top to bottom.
LINE_AXIS	Lay out components in the order consistent with the locale.
PAGE_AXIS	Lay out components in the order consistent with the locale.

Although there is nothing wrong with creating a **Box** using its constructor, you usually won't because **Box** provides factory methods that are easier to use.

Box defines the following factory methods that construct a **Box**:

static Box createHorizontalBox( )

static Box createVerticalBox( )

The first creates a horizontal box in which components are positioned left to right. The second creates a vertical box in which components are positioned top to bottom. Thus, these two methods create a container that uses a **BoxLayout** of the specified type.

Once you have a **Box**, you simply add components to it. The components are displayed in the order in which they are added. Remember, the box is either vertical or horizontal. Therefore, the components are either in a vertical line or a horizontal line.

By default, the components are positioned immediately next to each other. To add space between the components, you can insert an object created by the **createRigidArea( )** method, shown here:

static Component createRigidArea(Dimension *dim*)

Here, *dim* specifies the size of the space that is created. A component of the specified size is returned. After the component has been created, it is added to the box at the point at which the space is desired.

The component created by **createRigidArea( )** is called a *rigid area* because its size is fixed and will not be adjusted if the size of the box changes. **Box** supplies other methods that create other space-related options; however, rigid areas are commonly used. (See "Ask the Expert" at the end of this section.) One thing to understand is that **createRigidArea( )** returns a **Component**. Recall that a component can be added only once to a layout. Therefore, you will need to create a new rigid area for each place in which you want to add space.

The following program demonstrates **BoxLayout** via the **Box** class. It reworks the grid layout example by putting each of the component groups into their own separate boxes. The advantage of this approach is that it keeps the components in each group together, but lets the position of each box move when the frame size is changed. Another advantage is that the code for the boxes is shorter than for the grid layout. Sample output is shown in Figure 10-6.

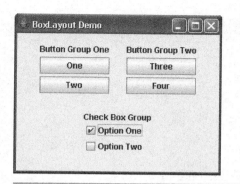
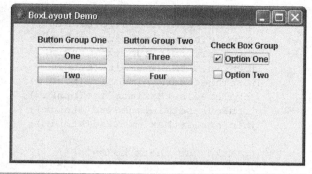

Figure 10-6 Sample output from the **BoxDemo** program

```
// Demonstrate BoxLayout and the Box class.

import java.awt.*;
import javax.swing.*;

class BoxDemo {

  BoxDemo() {

    // Create a new JFrame container.
    JFrame jfrm = new JFrame("BoxLayout Demo");

    // *** Use FlowLayout for the content pane. ***
    jfrm.getContentPane().setLayout(new FlowLayout());

    // Give the frame an initial size.
    jfrm.setSize(300, 240);

    // Terminate the program when the user closes the application.
    jfrm.setDefaultCloseOperation(JFrame.EXIT_ON_CLOSE);

    // Make the labels.
    JLabel jlabOne = new JLabel("Button Group One");
    JLabel jlabTwo = new JLabel("Button Group Two");
    JLabel jlabThree = new JLabel("Check Box Group");

    // Make the buttons.
    JButton jbtnOne = new JButton("One");
    JButton jbtnTwo = new JButton("Two");
    JButton jbtnThree = new JButton("Three");
    JButton jbtnFour = new JButton("Four");
    Dimension btnDim = new Dimension(100, 25);
```

Use a flow layout for
the content pane.

```
// Set minimum and maximum sizes for the buttons.
jbtnOne.setMinimumSize(btnDim);
jbtnOne.setMaximumSize(btnDim);
jbtnTwo.setMinimumSize(btnDim);
jbtnTwo.setMaximumSize(btnDim);
jbtnThree.setMinimumSize(btnDim);
jbtnThree.setMaximumSize(btnDim);
jbtnFour.setMinimumSize(btnDim);
jbtnFour.setMaximumSize(btnDim);

// Make the check boxes.
JCheckBox jcbOne = new JCheckBox("Option One");
JCheckBox jcbTwo = new JCheckBox("Option Two");

// Create three vertical boxes.
Box box1 = Box.createVerticalBox();
Box box2 = Box.createVerticalBox();            Create three Box containers.
Box box3 = Box.createVerticalBox();

// Create invisible borders around the boxes.
box1.setBorder(
      BorderFactory.createEmptyBorder(10, 10, 10, 10));
box2.setBorder(                                             Give all
      BorderFactory.createEmptyBorder(10, 10, 10, 10));     three boxes
box3.setBorder(                                             an invisible
      BorderFactory.createEmptyBorder(10, 10, 10, 10));     border.

// Add the components to the boxes.
box1.add(jlabOne);
box1.add(Box.createRigidArea(new Dimension(0, 4)));
box1.add(jbtnOne);
box1.add(Box.createRigidArea(new Dimension(0, 4)));
box1.add(jbtnTwo);
                                                       Add button
                                                       groups to box1
box2.add(jlabTwo);                                     and box2.
box2.add(Box.createRigidArea(new Dimension(0, 4)));    Notice the use
box2.add(jbtnThree);                                   of rigid areas.
box2.add(Box.createRigidArea(new Dimension(0, 4)));
box2.add(jbtnFour);

box3.add(jlabThree);
box3.add(jcbOne);              Add the check box group to box3.
box3.add(jcbTwo);

// Add the boxes to the content pane.
jfrm.getContentPane().add(box1);
jfrm.getContentPane().add(box2);
jfrm.getContentPane().add(box3);
```

```
      // Display the frame.
      jfrm.setVisible(true);
   }

   public static void main(String args[]) {
      // Create the frame on the event dispatching thread.
      SwingUtilities.invokeLater(new Runnable() {
         public void run() {
            new BoxDemo();
         }
      });
   }
}
```

The operation of the program is easy to understand. After creating all of the components, the program creates three **Box** objects. Next, it gives each box an invisible border that is 10-pixels wide. This is not necessary, but it does provide an easy way to ensure some visual space between the three boxes. Next, it adds the component groups to the boxes. Notice the use of the rigid areas. They provide a small amount of space between the label and the buttons. No rigid areas are needed in the check box group because the visual space between the check boxes is sufficient as-is.

As the foregoing example shows, often **BoxLayout** can be used in place of **GridBagLayout**. When this is the case, the code is shorter, there is less overhead, and the layout is easier to configure. Using a box layout also allows groups of related components to be treated as a unit visually, but still lets the position of the entire box be freely moved by the container's layout manager when the user changes the size or shape of the window. For these reasons, box layouts should used when possible, reserving a grid bag for those circumstances in which it is truly needed.

Progress Check

1. **BoxLayout** can be used to arrange components in either _____ or _____ rows.

2. What class creates a container that uses box layout automatically?

3. What method creates a fixed-space component that is used to add space between components in a box layout?

---

1. horizontal or vertical
2. **Box**
3. **createRigidArea( )**

Ask the Expert

Q: What other types of spacing objects are available from the Box class?

A: In addition to rigid areas, **Box** provides *glue* and *struts*. As it relates to boxes, glue is badly misnamed! It is actually used to specify a point of *expansion* between two components. It ensures that extra space is put at the point of the glue rather than being put on the end. The methods that create glue are: **createGlue( )**, **createHorizontalGlue( )**, and **createVerticalGlue( )**.

A strut is an object that has one fixed dimension and one variable dimension. There are two kinds of struts: horizontal and vertical. For a horizontal strut, the width is fixed, but the height is adjustable. For the vertical strut, the height is fixed, but the width is adjustable. Struts are created using the **createHorizontalStrut( )** and **createVerticalStrut( )** methods.

What's Next?

Congratulations! If you have read and worked through the preceding 10 modules, then you have acquired a firm foundation in the fundamentals of Swing programming. You can now begin to apply your knowledge to real-world applications. Of course, there are still many aspects of Swing left to learn, but you have a solid foundation upon which to build your knowledge and expertise.

Here are a few of the topics that you will want to learn more about:

- **JInternalPane**
- **JDesktopPane**
- **JLayeredPane**
- **JTextPane**
- Accessibility
- Undo with text components
- Creating a custom component

You will also want to study the properties, fields, and methods available in each Swing component closely. This book focused on those aspects of the components that are most widely used. However, you may find some of their other features helpful in your applications. You may also want to learn about how the Drag and Drop feature is used with a Swing application. Finally, for those who want to be involved at the highest levels of Swing programming, you will need to learn how to create your own look and feel.

As stated at the start of this book, Swing is a large, sophisticated framework. It is worth the time and effort necessary to master it. The visual interface shapes the user's first impression of your program. As we all know, first impressions often become lasting impressions. Mastery of Swing will help ensure that your first impressions are good ones.

Module 10 Mastery Check

1. Any code that affects a Swing component must be executed on the _____ _____ thread.

2. When using **javax.swing.Timer**, what event is generated when the timer goes off?

3. What methods start and stop **javax.swing.Timer**?

4. What are the four applet lifecycle methods? When are they called?

5. What method must an applet use to create its GUI?

6. Can your program paint directly onto the surface of a component?

7. What three paint methods are called when a Swing component must display itself?

8. What method is called to request that a component redisplay its contents?

9. What methods obtain the current width and height of a component?

10. **GridBagLayout** is so named because it is a _____ of small _____ joined together.

11. Each component in a grid-bag layout is associated with a set of constraints encapsulated by what class?

12. Why is **BoxLayout** sometimes a more efficient alternative to **GridBagLayout**?

13. In a horizontal **Box**, can there be more than one row of components?

14. Rework the bar graph painting example so that the color of the border cycles through red, green, and blue at one-second intervals. Also, have the border's size vary from 1 to 5 pixels, with an interval of one-fifth second between changes. Use the **javax.swing.Timer** class.

15. Rework the applet in Project 10-1 so that the direction of scroll reverses at periodic intervals. For example, have the text scroll left for a while, and then right for a while, and so on. The precise timing is up to you, but the answer shown in the Appendix reverses scroll direction every 20 seconds.

16. On your own, continue to experiment with Swing's components, containers, and features. It is a rich framework that requires serious study to master.

Appendix

Answers to Mastery Checks

Module 1: Swing Fundamentals

1. **Most AWT components translate into native peers. Why is this a problem and how does Swing fix it?**

   Native peers are problematic because their use may cause a component to look or act differently on different platforms. Because they use native resources, the appearance of a native peer is not easily changed. They also have limitations, such as being opaque and rectangular.

2. **Most Swing components are written in 100 percent Java code. True or False?**

   True

3. **What are the four top-level, heavyweight containers?**

   JFrame, **JApplet**, **JDialog**, and **JWindow**

4. **What is the most commonly used top-level container for an application?**

   JFrame

5. **JFrame contains several panes. To what pane are components added?**

   Components are added to the content pane.

6. **An event listener must _____ with a source in order to receive event notifications.**

   register

7. **To receive an action event, a class must implement what interface?**

   ActionListener

8. **When using a** JButton **or a** JTextField**, what method must be called to set the action command?**

   setActionCommand( )

9. **Name three layout managers.**

   Here are a few of the layout managers: **FlowLayout**, **BorderLayout**, **GridLayout**, **GridBagLayout**, **BoxLayout**, and **SpringLayout**.

10. **The stopwatch example in Project 1-1 uses two buttons, one to start the stopwatch and the other to stop it. However, it is possible to use only one button, which alternates between starting and stopping the stopwatch. One way to do this is to reset the text within the button after each press, alternating between Start and Stop. Because, by default, this text is also the action command associated with the button, you can use the same button for two different purposes. Your job is to rewrite Project 1-1 so that it implements this approach.**

    To solve this problem, you will use another JButton **method:** setText( ). **This method sets the text in a button. It is shown here:**

    void setText(String *msg*)

Here, *msg* specifies the text that will be shown inside the button. This method lets you set the text inside a button during the execution of a program.

Here is one solution:

```
// A version of the stopwatch for Project 1-1 that
// uses a single push button.

import java.awt.*;
import java.awt.event.*;
import javax.swing.*;
import java.util.*;

class StopWatch implements ActionListener {

  JLabel jlab;
  long start; // holds the start time in milliseconds
  JButton jbtnStartStop; // a start or stop button

  StopWatch() {

    // Create a new JFrame container.
    JFrame jfrm = new JFrame("A Simple Stopwatch");

    // Specify FlowLayout for the layout manager.
    jfrm.getContentPane().setLayout(new FlowLayout());

    // Give the frame an initial size.
    jfrm.setSize(230, 90);

    // Terminate the program when the user closes the application.
    jfrm.setDefaultCloseOperation(JFrame.EXIT_ON_CLOSE);

    // Make one button.
    jbtnStartStop = new JButton("Start");

    // Add action listeners.
    jbtnStartStop.addActionListener(this);

    // Add the buttons to the content pane.
    jfrm.getContentPane().add(jbtnStartStop);

    // Create a text-based label.
    jlab = new JLabel("Press Start to begin timing.");

    // Add the label to the frame.
    jfrm.getContentPane().add(jlab);
```

```java
      // Display the frame.
      jfrm.setVisible(true);
    }

    // Handle button events.
    public void actionPerformed(ActionEvent ae) {
      Calendar cal = Calendar.getInstance(); // get the current system time

      if(ae.getActionCommand().equals("Start")) {
        // Store start time.
        start = cal.getTimeInMillis();
        jlab.setText("Stopwatch is Running...");
        jbtnStartStop.setText("Stop");
      }
      else {
        // Compute the elapsed time.
        jlab.setText("Elapsed time is "
             + (double) (cal.getTimeInMillis() - start)/1000);
        jbtnStartStop.setText("Start");
      }
    }

    public static void main(String args[]) {

      // Create the frame on the event dispatching thread.
      SwingUtilities.invokeLater(new Runnable() {
        public void run() {
          new StopWatch();
        }
      });
    }
  }
```

11. **If you are using JDK 5 or later, rewrite the code for Project 1-2 so that the explicit calls to** getContentPane( ) **are not used.**

   Here is a version of Project 1-2 that avoids calls to **getContentPane( )**:

```java
   // A version of Project 1-2 that does not use getContentPane().

   import java.awt.*;
   import java.awt.event.*;
   import javax.swing.*;

   class Coder implements ActionListener {
```

```
JTextField jtfPlaintext;
JTextField jtfCiphertext;

Coder() {

  // Create a new JFrame container.
  JFrame jfrm = new JFrame("A Simple Code Machine");

  // Specify FlowLayout for the layout manager.
  jfrm.setLayout(new FlowLayout());

  // Give the frame an initial size.
  jfrm.setSize(340, 120);

  // Terminate the program when the user closes the application.
  jfrm.setDefaultCloseOperation(JFrame.EXIT_ON_CLOSE);

  // Create two labels.
  JLabel jlabPlaintext = new JLabel("   Plain Text: ");
  JLabel jlabCiphertext = new JLabel("Cipher Text: ");

  // Create two text field instances.
  jtfPlaintext = new JTextField(20);
  jtfCiphertext = new JTextField(20);

  // Set the action commands for the text fields.
  jtfPlaintext.setActionCommand("Encode");
  jtfCiphertext.setActionCommand("Decode");

  // Add action listeners for the text fields.
  jtfPlaintext.addActionListener(this);
  jtfCiphertext.addActionListener(this);

  // Add the text fields and labels to the content pane.
  jfrm.add(jlabPlaintext);
  jfrm.add(jtfPlaintext);
  jfrm.add(jlabCiphertext);
  jfrm.add(jtfCiphertext);

  // Create push button instances.
  JButton jbtnEncode = new JButton("Encode");
  JButton jbtnDecode = new JButton("Decode");
  JButton jbtnReset =  new JButton("Reset");
```

```
   // Add action listeners for the buttons.
   jbtnEncode.addActionListener(this);
   jbtnDecode.addActionListener(this);
   jbtnReset.addActionListener(this);

   // Add the buttons to the content pane.
   jfrm.add(jbtnEncode);
   jfrm.add(jbtnDecode);
   jfrm.add(jbtnReset);

   // Display the frame.
   jfrm.setVisible(true);
 }

 // Handle action events.
 public void actionPerformed(ActionEvent ae) {

   // If action command is "Encode" then encode the string.
   if(ae.getActionCommand().equals("Encode")) {

     // Obtain the plain text and put it into a StringBuilder.
     StringBuilder str = new StringBuilder(jtfPlaintext.getText());

     // Add 1 to each character.
     for(int i=0; i<str.length(); i++)
       str.setCharAt(i, (char)(str.charAt(i) + 1));

     // Set the coded text into the Cipher Text field.
     jtfCiphertext.setText(str.toString());

   }

   // If action command is "Decode" then decode the string.
   else if(ae.getActionCommand().equals("Decode")) {

     // Obtain the cipher text and put it into a StringBuilder.
     StringBuilder str = new StringBuilder(jtfCiphertext.getText());

     // Subtract 1 from each character.
     for(int i=0; i<str.length(); i++)
       str.setCharAt(i, (char)(str.charAt(i) - 1));

     // Set the decoded text into the Plain Text field.
     jtfPlaintext.setText(str.toString());
   }
```

```
    // Otherwise, must be "Reset" command.
    else {
      jtfPlaintext.setText("");
      jtfCiphertext.setText("");
    }
  }

  public static void main(String args[]) {

    // Create the frame on the event dispatching thread.
    SwingUtilities.invokeLater(new Runnable() {
      public void run() {
        new Coder();
      }
    });
  }
}
```

Module 2: Labels, Buttons, and Borders

1. **What method sets a component's border?**

setBorder( )

2. **By default, the contents of a label are centered vertically and aligned horizontally on the _____ edge.**

leading

3. **In a label, what method sets the vertical position of the text relative to the icon?**

setVerticalTextPosition( )

4. **Why is** ImageIcon **useful?**

ImageIcon is a class that implements the **Icon** interface. Among other capabilities, it can load an image from a file.

5. **By default, when a component is disabled, it is shown in gray. True or False?**

True

6. **What is a keyboard mnemonic?**

A keyboard mnemonic is a key that when pressed in conjunction with the ALT key causes input focus to jump to the component linked to the mnemonic.

7. **Name the four types of buttons provided by Swing.**

JButton, **JToggleButton**, **JCheckBox**, and **JRadioButton**

8. **What method must be provided in order to implement the** ItemListener **interface?**

   itemStateChanged( )

9. JToggleButton **is the superclass for what other two-state buttons?**

   JCheckBox and **JRadioButton**

10. **What is** setDefaultButton( ) **used for?**

    The **setDefaultButton( )** method sets the button that will be activated when the user presses ENTER on the keyboard.

11. **To what object must radio buttons be added in order for their mutually exclusive behavior to be exhibited?**

    Radio buttons must be added to a **ButtonGroup** instance in order for them to act in a mutually exclusive manner.

12. **Extra Challenge: Rework and improve the** StopWatch **program in Project 1-1 from Module 1 in the following ways:**

    - **Instead of using the** Calendar **class and** getTimeInMillis( ) **to obtain the current system time, use the timestamp provided when an action event is generated. Recall that this timestamp is available through** getWhen( )**.**
    - **Disable the Stop button until the Start button is pressed. Then, disable the Start button until the Stop button is pressed.**
    - **Add a check box that controls whether a log of elapsed times is displayed. If it is checked, have the times added to the log. When the box is cleared, have the log erased. Only store and display the last three times. When the log is full (contains three entries), have an old time drop off the end of the list each time a new time is added.**

    Here is one solution:

```
// An improved version of Project 1-1.

import java.awt.*;
import java.awt.event.*;
import javax.swing.*;

class StopWatch {

  JLabel jlab;
  JLabel jlabLog;
  JCheckBox jcbKeepLog;

  JButton jbtnStart;
  JButton jbtnStop;

  long start; // holds the start time in milliseconds
```

```
String[] etstr; // holds elapsed time strings

static final int LOGMAX = 3; // maximum log entries

StopWatch() {

  // Initialize etstr to null strings.
  etstr = new String[LOGMAX];
  for(int i=0; i<LOGMAX; i++) etstr[i] = "";

  // Create a new JFrame container.
  JFrame jfrm = new JFrame("Improved Stopwatch");

  // Specify FlowLayout for the layout manager.
  jfrm.getContentPane().setLayout(new FlowLayout());

  // Give the frame an initial size.
  jfrm.setSize(230, 170);

  // Terminate the program when the user closes the application.
  jfrm.setDefaultCloseOperation(JFrame.EXIT_ON_CLOSE);

  // Make start and stop buttons.
  jbtnStart = new JButton("Start");
  jbtnStop = new JButton("Stop");

  // Disable the stop button.
  jbtnStop.setEnabled(false);

  // Create the Keep Time Log check box.
  jcbKeepLog = new JCheckBox("Keep Time Log");

  // Create Log label.
  jlabLog = new JLabel("<html>-Time Log-<br><br><br><br>");

  // Put a border around the time log.
  jlabLog.setBorder(BorderFactory.createLineBorder(Color.BLUE));

  // Create a timing label.
  jlab = new JLabel("Press Start to begin timing.");

  // Add action listener for the Start button.
  jbtnStart.addActionListener(new ActionListener() {
    public void actionPerformed(ActionEvent ae) {
```

```
          // Store start time.
          start = ae.getWhen();

          jlab.setText("Stopwatch is Running...");
          jbtnStop.setEnabled(true);
          jbtnStart.setEnabled(false);
        }
      });

      // Add action listener for the Stop button.
      jbtnStop.addActionListener(new ActionListener() {
        public void actionPerformed(ActionEvent ae) {
          String logstr = "<html>-Time Log-<br>";
          double t;

          // Compute the elapsed time.
          t = (double) (ae.getWhen()-start)/1000;
          jlab.setText("Elapsed time is " + t);

          jbtnStop.setEnabled(false);
          jbtnStart.setEnabled(true);

          if(jcbKeepLog.isSelected()) {
            // Move existing time log entries down.
            for(int i = LOGMAX-1; i>0; i-)
              etstr[i] = etstr[i-1];

            // Store the elapsed time.
            etstr[0] = "" + t;

            // Construct time log string.
            for(int i=0; i<LOGMAX; i++)
              logstr += etstr[i]+"<br>";

            // Update the time log label.
            jlabLog.setText(logstr);
          }
        }
      });

      // Add item listener for the time log check box.
      // This clears the log strings when it is deselected.
      jcbKeepLog.addItemListener(new ItemListener() {
        public void itemStateChanged(ItemEvent ie) {
          if(!jcbKeepLog.isSelected()) {
```

```
                // Clear the time log strings.
                for(int i=0; i<LOGMAX; i++)
                  etstr[i] = "";

                // Clear the time log.
                jlabLog.setText("<html>-Time Log-<br><br><br><br>");
            }
          }
        });

        // Add components to the content pane.
        jfrm.getContentPane().add(jbtnStart);
        jfrm.getContentPane().add(jbtnStop);
        jfrm.getContentPane().add(jlab);
        jfrm.getContentPane().add(jcbKeepLog);
        jfrm.getContentPane().add(jlabLog);

        // Display the frame.
        jfrm.setVisible(true);
      }

      public static void main(String args[]) {
        // Create the frame on the event dispatching thread.
        SwingUtilities.invokeLater(new Runnable() {
          public void run() {
            new StopWatch();
          }
        });
      }
    }
```

Module 3: Scroll Bars, Sliders, and Progress Bars

1. Scroll bars, sliders, and progress bars all use the _____ model.

   BoundedRangeModel

2. Describe the relationship between the current value and the minimum, maximum, and extent.

   The current value must be greater than or equal to the minimum and less than or equal to the maximum plus the extent.

3. When the user clicks on the paging area of a scroll bar, the thumb is advanced by the amount specified by the block increment. True or False?

   True

4. To receive scroll bar events, what event listener must your program implement?

AdjustmentListener

5. Explain the difference between the major and minor tick marks in a slider.

For a slider, the major tick marks divide the slider's range by a larger unit, such as 10. The minor tick marks divide the range between the major tick marks. Often the minor tick marks are spaced 1 unit apart.

6. What type of event is generated by a slider?

A slider generates a change event when it is moved by the user.

7. Having a slider display labels is a three-step process. **Describe the steps.**

To display labels on a slider you must first create the labels, such as by calling **createStandardLabels( )**. Second, you must add the labels to the slider by calling **setLabelTable( )**. Third, you must cause the labels to be painted by calling **setPaintLabels(true)**.

8. Do progress bars generate events based on user input?

No

9. Is it possible to create a progress bar that does not have a border? If so, how is this achieved?

Yes, you can create a progress bar without a border by calling **setBorderPainted(false)**.

10. If you want to monitor the state of a progress bar, what event listener must be implemented?

Progress bars generate change events when a property changes. Therefore, you must implement a change listener.

11. Create a program that contains a slider and a scroll bar that are linked together. That is, each time the slider is moved, the scroll bar will move the same amount and vice versa.

Here is one solution:

```
// Link a scroll bar and a slider.

import java.awt.*;
import java.awt.event.*;
import javax.swing.*;
import javax.swing.event.*;

class SBSlider {

  JScrollBar jsb;
  JSlider jsldr;

  SBSlider() {
    // Create a new JFrame container.
    JFrame jfrm = new JFrame("Scroll Bar with Slider");
```

```
      // Specify a flow layout.
      jfrm.getContentPane().setLayout(new FlowLayout());

      // Give the frame an initial size.
      jfrm.setSize(260, 100);

      // Terminate the program when the user closes the application.
      jfrm.setDefaultCloseOperation(JFrame.EXIT_ON_CLOSE);

      // Create a scroll bar and a slider.
      jsb = new JScrollBar(Adjustable.HORIZONTAL, 0, 0, 0, 100);
      jsldr = new JSlider(0, 100, 0);

      // Increase the display size of the scroll bar.
      jsb.setPreferredSize(new Dimension(220, 20));

      // Add adjustment listener for the scroll bar.
      jsb.addAdjustmentListener(new AdjustmentListener() {
        public void adjustmentValueChanged(AdjustmentEvent ae) {
          jsldr.setValue(jsb.getValue());
        }
      });

      // Add change listener for slider.
      jsldr.addChangeListener(new ChangeListener() {
        public void stateChanged(ChangeEvent ce) {
          jsb.setValue(jsldr.getValue());
        }
      });

      // Add components to the content pane.
      jfrm.getContentPane().add(jsb);
      jfrm.getContentPane().add(jsldr);

      // Display the frame.
      jfrm.setVisible(true);
    }

  public static void main(String args[]) {
    // Create the frame on the event dispatching thread.
    SwingUtilities.invokeLater(new Runnable() {
      public void run() {
        new SBSlider();
      }
    });
  }
}
```

12. **Project 2-2 creates a simple phone list. Add a scroll bar to the program that scrolls through the list of names and numbers. To do this, add a label that displays a name and number. Each time the scroll bar is moved, show the next name and number.**

Here is one solution:

```java
// Add a scroll bar to Project 2-2.

import java.awt.*;
import java.awt.event.*;
import javax.swing.*;

class Phonebook {

    JTextField jtfName;
    JTextField jtfNumber;

    JRadioButton jrbExact;
    JRadioButton jrbStartsWith;
    JRadioButton jrbEndsWith;

    JCheckBox jcbIgnoreCase;

    JScrollBar jsb;

    // A short list of names and phone numbers
    String[][] phonelist = {
      {"Jon", "555-8765"},
      {"Jessica", "555-5643"},
      {"Adam", "555-1212" },
      {"Rachel", "555-3435"},
      {"Tom & Jerry", "555-1001"}
    };

    Phonebook() {

        // Create a new JFrame container.
        JFrame jfrm = new JFrame("A Simple Phone List");

        // Specify a GridLayout for the layout manager.
        jfrm.getContentPane().setLayout(new GridLayout(0, 1));

        // Give the frame an initial size.
        jfrm.setSize(240, 220);

        // Terminate the program when the user closes the application.
        jfrm.setDefaultCloseOperation(JFrame.EXIT_ON_CLOSE);
```

```java
// Create labels.
JLabel jlabName = new JLabel("Name");
JLabel jlabNumber = new JLabel("Number");
JLabel jlabOptions = new JLabel("Search Options");

// Create text fields.
jtfName = new JTextField(10);
jtfNumber = new JTextField(10);

// Create check box for Ignore Case.
jcbIgnoreCase = new JCheckBox("Ignore Case");

// Create radio buttons.
jrbExact = new JRadioButton("Exact Match", true);
jrbStartsWith = new JRadioButton("Starts With");
jrbEndsWith = new JRadioButton("Ends With");

// Add radio buttons to button group.
ButtonGroup bg = new ButtonGroup();
bg.add(jrbExact);
bg.add(jrbStartsWith);
bg.add(jrbEndsWith);

// Create scroll bar.
jsb = new JScrollBar(Adjustable.HORIZONTAL, 0, 0, 0, 4);

// Add action listener for the Name text field.
jtfName.addActionListener(new ActionListener() {
  public void actionPerformed(ActionEvent ae) {
    jtfNumber.setText(lookupName(jtfName.getText()));
  }
});

// Add action listener for the Number text field.
jtfNumber.addActionListener(new ActionListener() {
  public void actionPerformed(ActionEvent ae) {
    jtfName.setText(lookupNumber(jtfNumber.getText()));
  }
});

// Handle scroll bar events by scrolling through the
// phone list.
jsb.addAdjustmentListener(new AdjustmentListener() {
  public void adjustmentValueChanged(AdjustmentEvent ae) {
    int i = jsb.getValue();
```

```
          jtfName.setText(phonelist[i][0]);
          jtfNumber.setText(phonelist[i][1]);
      }
    });

    // Add components to the content pane.
    jfrm.getContentPane().add(jlabName);
    jfrm.getContentPane().add(jtfName);
    jfrm.getContentPane().add(jlabNumber);
    jfrm.getContentPane().add(jtfNumber);
    jfrm.getContentPane().add(new JLabel());
    jfrm.getContentPane().add(jlabOptions);
    jfrm.getContentPane().add(jcbIgnoreCase);
    jfrm.getContentPane().add(new JLabel());
    jfrm.getContentPane().add(jrbExact);
    jfrm.getContentPane().add(jrbStartsWith);
    jfrm.getContentPane().add(jrbEndsWith);
    jfrm.getContentPane().add(jsb);

    // Display the frame.
    jfrm.setVisible(true);
  }

  // Look up a name and return the number.
  String lookupName(String n) {
    for(int i=0; i < phonelist.length; i++) {
      if(jrbStartsWith.isSelected()) {
        if(jcbIgnoreCase.isSelected()) {
          if(phonelist[i][0].toLowerCase().startsWith(n.toLowerCase()))
            return phonelist[i][1];
        } else {
          if(phonelist[i][0].startsWith(n))
            return phonelist[i][1];
        }
      }
      else if(jrbEndsWith.isSelected()) {
        if(jcbIgnoreCase.isSelected()) {
          if(phonelist[i][0].toLowerCase().endsWith(n.toLowerCase()))
            return phonelist[i][1];
        } else {
          if(phonelist[i][0].endsWith(n))
            return phonelist[i][1];
        }
      }
```

```
      else {
        if(jcbIgnoreCase.isSelected()) {
          if(phonelist[i][0].toLowerCase().equals(n.toLowerCase()))
            return phonelist[i][1];
        } else {
          if(phonelist[i][0].equals(n))
            return phonelist[i][1];
        }
      }
    }

    return "Not Found";
  }

  // Look up a number and return the name.
  String lookupNumber(String n) {
    for(int i=0; i < phonelist.length; i++) {
      if(phonelist[i][1].equals(n))
        return phonelist[i][0];
    }
    return "Not Found";
  }

  public static void main(String args[]) {
    // Create the frame on the event dispatching thread.
    SwingUtilities.invokeLater(new Runnable() {
      public void run() {
        new Phonebook();
      }
    });
  }
}
```

Module 4: Managing Components with Panels, Panes, and Tooltips

1. **What is double buffering and why is it important?**

Double buffering is a mechanism that is commonly employed to achieve a better user experience when screen refreshes take place. Instead of drawing each component directly on the screen, which can lead to "flicker," the components are rendered to a separate buffer. When the rendering is complete, the buffer is copied to the screen in one fast, uninterrupted operation. In this way, the complete contents of a panel appear instantaneously, rather than slowly and in pieces.

2. **What method do you call to make a JPanel opaque?**

   setOpaque( )

3. **Can you set the content pane of a** JFrame **to a JPanel that your program creates?**

   Yes

4. **Although very powerful,** JScrollPane **can be tricky to use properly. True or False?**

   False. **JScrollPane** is amazingly easy to use despite the fact that it is a very powerful component.

5. **What are the nine parts of** JScrollPane**?**

   The nine parts of a **JScrollPane** are the viewport, vertical scroll bar, horizontal scroll bar, row header, column header, and the four corners.

6. **What method do you call to set a row header in a** JScrollPane**?**

   setRowHeaderView( )

7. **What method is used to add components to a** JTabbedPane**?**

   addTab( )

8. **How do you add a tooltip to a tab in a** JTabbedPane**?**

   Use the form of **addTab( )** that includes a parameter for the tooltip text.

9. **In what two orientations can a** JSplitPane **be shown?**

   Vertically or horizontally

10. **Explain the one-touch-expandable feature of** JSplitPane**. What method is called to turn it on?**

   One-touch-expandable is the feature that creates two small buttons within the divider of a **JSplitPane**. Pressing one of these buttons causes one side of the split pane to be expanded to the full size of the window and the other side to be removed from view. The hidden side can be brought back into view by pressing the other button. To turn on the one-touch-expandable feature, call **setOneTouchExpandable( )**.

11. **Can a tooltip be added to any lightweight Swing control? If so, how?**

   Yes. To do so, call **setToolTipText( )**.

12. **It's best not to use too many tooltips because they clutter the GUI. True or False?**

   False. Tooltips do not clutter the GUI.

13. **Add tooltips to the buttons in the** CustomCPDemo **program shown earlier in this chapter.**

   Here is one solution:

```
// Add tooltips to the second JPanel example.
import java.awt.*;
```

```
import java.awt.event.*;
import javax.swing.*;

// This class creates a panel by extending JPanel.
// It adds no new functionality, but the
// object that it constructs can be used
// anywhere that a JPanel can.
class MyContentPanel extends JPanel {

  JLabel jlab;
  JButton jbtnRed;
  JButton jbtnBlue;

  MyContentPanel() {

    // Ensure that the panel is opaque.
    setOpaque(true);

    // Start with a green, 5-pixel border.
    setBorder(
      BorderFactory.createLineBorder(Color.GREEN, 5));

    // Create a label.
    jlab = new JLabel("Select Border Color");

    // Make two buttons.
    jbtnRed = new JButton("Red");
    jbtnBlue = new JButton("Blue");

    // Add tooltips to the buttons.
    jbtnRed.setToolTipText("Makes the border red.");
    jbtnBlue.setToolTipText("Makes the border blue.");

    // Add action listeners for the buttons.
    jbtnRed.addActionListener(new ActionListener() {
      public void actionPerformed(ActionEvent ae) {
        setBorder(
          BorderFactory.createLineBorder(Color.RED, 5));
      }
    });

    jbtnBlue.addActionListener(new ActionListener() {
      public void actionPerformed(ActionEvent ae) {
        setBorder(
          BorderFactory.createLineBorder(Color.BLUE, 5));
```

```
      }
    });

    // Add the buttons and label to the panel.
    add(jbtnRed);
    add(jbtnBlue);
    add(jlab);

  }
}

// Create a top-level container and use the panel
// created by MyContentPanel as the content pane.
class CustomCPDemo {
  CustomCPDemo() {
    // Create a new JFrame container. Use the default
    // border layout.
    JFrame jfrm = new JFrame("Set the Content Pane");

    // Give the frame an initial size.
    jfrm.setSize(240, 150);

    // Terminate the program when the user closes the application.
    jfrm.setDefaultCloseOperation(JFrame.EXIT_ON_CLOSE);

    // Create an instance of the custom content pane.
    MyContentPanel mcp = new MyContentPanel();

    // Make mcp the content pane.
    jfrm.setContentPane(mcp);

    // Display the frame.
    jfrm.setVisible(true);
  }

  public static void main(String args[]) {
    // Create the frame on the event dispatching thread.
    SwingUtilities.invokeLater(new Runnable() {
      public void run() {
        new CustomCPDemo();
      }
    });
  }
}
```

A

Answers to Mastery Checks

14. **Modify the split pane example so that it contains the scroll pane shown in Project 4-1 on the left side.**

Here is one solution:

```
// Add a scroll pane to a split pane.

import javax.swing.*;
import java.awt.*;

class SplitPaneDemo {

  SplitPaneDemo() {
    // Create a new JFrame container. Use the default
    // border layout.
    JFrame jfrm = new JFrame("Split Pane Demo");

    // Give the frame an initial size.
    jfrm.setSize(380, 150);

    // Terminate the program when the user closes the application.
    jfrm.setDefaultCloseOperation(JFrame.EXIT_ON_CLOSE);

    // Make the right-side label.
    JLabel jlab2 =
      new JLabel(" Right side: ABCDEFGHIJKLMNOPQRSTUVWXYZ");

    // Set the minimum size for the label.

    jlab2.setMinimumSize(new Dimension(90, 30));

    // Now, create the scroll pane.

    // Create a label.
    JLabel jlabOptions = new
      JLabel("Select one or more options: ");

    // Make some check boxes.
    JCheckBox jcbOpt1 = new JCheckBox("Option One");
    JCheckBox jcbOpt2 = new JCheckBox("Option Two");
    JCheckBox jcbOpt3 = new JCheckBox("Option Three");
    JCheckBox jcbOpt4 = new JCheckBox("Option Four");
    JCheckBox jcbOpt5 = new JCheckBox("Option Five");

    // No event handlers needed for this example.
```

```
    // Create a JPanel to hold the Option check boxes.
    JPanel  jpnl = new JPanel();
    jpnl.setLayout(new GridLayout(6, 1));
    jpnl.setOpaque(true);

    // Add checkboxes and label to the JPanel.
    jpnl.add(jlabOptions);
    jpnl.add(jcbOpt1);
    jpnl.add(jcbOpt2);
    jpnl.add(jcbOpt3);
    jpnl.add(jcbOpt4);
    jpnl.add(jcbOpt5);

    // Create a scroll pane that will scroll the panel.
    JScrollPane jscrlp = new JScrollPane(jpnl);
    jscrlp.setMinimumSize(new Dimension(140, 140));

    // Create a split pane.
    JSplitPane jsp =
      new JSplitPane(JSplitPane.HORIZONTAL_SPLIT, true, jscrlp, jlab2);

    // Add the split pane to the content pane.
    jfrm.getContentPane().add(jsp);

    // Display the frame.
    jfrm.setVisible(true);
  }

  public static void main(String args[]) {
    // Create the frame on the event dispatching thread.
    SwingUtilities.invokeLater(new Runnable() {
      public void run() {
        new SplitPaneDemo();
      }
    });
  }
}
```

Module 5: Lists

1. **A JList provides a mechanism by which a user selects one or more items from a list. True or False?**

True

2. **If you want a JList to be scrollable, what must you do?**

You must wrap it in a **JScrollPane.**

3. **What type of event is generated by a** JList **when the user makes a selection? What method is called to obtain the index of the first selected item?**

When the user selects an item in a **JList**, a **ListSelectionEvent** is generated. To obtain the index of the first item selected, call **getSelectedIndex( )**.

4. **What model does** JList **use?**

ListModel

5. **What Swing component provides a pop-up list?**

JComboBox

6. **What method obtains the selected item in a** JComboBox**?**

getSelectedItem( )

7. **What method do you call to create an editable combo box?**

setEditable(true)

8. **Can you add items to a combo box dynamically at runtime? If so, what method do you call?**

Yes, by calling **addItem( )**

9. **Can you display and remove the pop-up list of a combo box under program control? If so, what method do you call?**

Yes, by calling **setPopupVisible( )**

10. **A spinner is supported by what Swing class?**

JSpinner

11. **What spinner method obtains the current value? What method obtains the previous value?**

To obtain a spinner's current value, call **getValue( )**. To obtain the previous value, call **getPrevious( )**.

12. **Can a spinner manage a list of strings?**

Yes, a spinner can manage a list of strings or any other type of data.

13. **Create a program that spins a set of** double **values between the range of 0.0 to 9.9. Set the increment at 0.1.**

Here is one solution:

```
// Spin doubles.

import javax.swing.*;
import javax.swing.event.*;
import java.awt.*;
```

```java
class SpinDoubles {

  JSpinner jspin;
  JLabel jlab;

  SpinDoubles() {
    // Create a new JFrame container.
    JFrame jfrm = new JFrame("Spin Doubles");

    // Specify FlowLayout manager.
    jfrm.getContentPane().setLayout(new FlowLayout());

    // Give the frame an initial size.
    jfrm.setSize(160, 120);

    // Terminate the program when the user closes the application.
    jfrm.setDefaultCloseOperation(JFrame.EXIT_ON_CLOSE);

    // Create a double spinner model.
    SpinnerNumberModel spm =
           new SpinnerNumberModel(0.0, 0.0, 9.9, 0.1);

    // Create a JSpinner using the model.
    jspin = new JSpinner(spm);

    // Set the preferred size of the spinner.
    jspin.setPreferredSize(new Dimension(40, 20));

    // Make a label that displays the selection.
    jlab = new JLabel(" Current value is: 0 ");

    // Add change listener for the spinner.
    jspin.addChangeListener(new ChangeListener() {
      public void stateChanged(ChangeEvent ce) {
        // Get the current value.
        Double val = (Double) jspin.getValue();

        // Report the current value.
        jlab.setText(" Current value is: " + val + " ");
      }
    });

    // Add the spinner and label to the content pane.
    jfrm.getContentPane().add(jspin);
    jfrm.getContentPane().add(jlab);
```

```
      // Display the frame.
      jfrm.setVisible(true);
    }

    public static void main(String args[]) {
      // Create the frame on the event dispatching thread.
      SwingUtilities.invokeLater(new Runnable() {
        public void run() {
          new SpinDoubles();
        }
      });
    }
  }
```

14. **Starting with the** DynamicComboBox **program, add a** JList **component. Each time the user
removes an apple variety from the combo box, have this variety be inserted into the** JList.
Thus, the JList **will contain a record of the varieties removed.**

Here is one solution:

```
// Add elements removed from the combo box
// to a list box.

import javax.swing.*;
import java.awt.*;
import java.awt.event.*;

class DynamicComboBox {

  JComboBox jcbb;
  JLabel jlab;
  JButton jbtnRemove;
  JList jlst;

  // Create an array of apple varieties.
  String apples[] = { "Winesap", "Cortland", "Red Delicious",
                      "Golden Delicious", "Gala", "Fuji",
                      "Granny Smith", "Jonathan" };

  DynamicComboBox() {
    // Create a new JFrame container.
    JFrame jfrm = new JFrame("Dynamic JComboBox");

    // Specify FlowLayout manager.
    jfrm.getContentPane().setLayout(new FlowLayout());
```

```
// Give the frame an initial size.
jfrm.setSize(220, 240);

// Terminate the program when the user closes the application.
jfrm.setDefaultCloseOperation(JFrame.EXIT_ON_CLOSE);

// Create a JComboBox.
jcbb = new JComboBox(apples);

// Make the combo box editable.
jcbb.setEditable(true);

// Make a label that displays the selection.
jlab = new JLabel();

// Make a list box and wrap it in a scroll pane.
jlst = new JList(new DefaultListModel());
JScrollPane jscrlp = new JScrollPane(jlst);

// Set the preferred size of the scroll pane.
jscrlp.setPreferredSize(new Dimension(120, 90));

// Add action listener for the combo box.
// If the user enters a new item, it is added
// to the list.
jcbb.addActionListener(new ActionListener() {
  public void actionPerformed(ActionEvent le) {
    // Get a reference to the item selected.
    String item = (String) jcbb.getSelectedItem();

    // Ignore if nothing is selected.
    if(item==null) return;

    // Display the selected item.
    jlab.setText("Current selection: " + item);

    // Add the item to the list if it's not already in it.
    int i;

    // See if it is in the list.
    for(i=0; i < jcbb.getItemCount(); i++)
      if(item.equals(jcbb.getItemAt(i))) break; // in list

    // If not, then add it.
    if(i==jcbb.getItemCount())
      jcbb.addItem(item);
  }
});
```

```
      // Initially select the first item in the list.
      jcbb.setSelectedIndex(0);

      // Create the Remove Selection button.
      jbtnRemove = new JButton("Remove Selection");

      // Add action listener for the button.
      jbtnRemove.addActionListener(new ActionListener() {
        public void actionPerformed(ActionEvent le) {
          // Get a reference to the item selected.
          String item = (String) jcbb.getSelectedItem();

          // Ignore if nothing is selected.
          if(item==null) return;

          // Remove the item.
          jcbb.removeItem(item);

          // Display the selected item.
          jlab.setText("Removed " + item);

          // Add removed items to the list box.
          DefaultListModel dlm =
                 (DefaultListModel) jlst.getModel();
          dlm.addElement(item);
        }
      });

      // Add the combo box, label, and button to the content pane.
      jfrm.getContentPane().add(jcbb);
      jfrm.getContentPane().add(jlab);
      jfrm.getContentPane().add(jbtnRemove);
      jfrm.getContentPane().add(jscrlp);

      // Display the frame.
      jfrm.setVisible(true);
  }

  public static void main(String args[]) {
    // Create the frame on the event dispatching thread.
    SwingUtilities.invokeLater(new Runnable() {
      public void run() {
        new DynamicComboBox();
      }
    });
  }
}
```

Module 6: Text Components

1. **What is** JTextComponent? **Can you create an instance of** JTextComponent?

   JTextComponent is the class from which all of Swing's text components are derived. You cannot create an instance of **JTextComponent** because it is abstract.

2. **Name the six text component classes defined by Swing.**

   JTextField, **JPasswordField**, **JFormattedTextField**, **JTextArea**, **JEditorPane**, and **JTextPane**

3. **When using** JTextField, **what event is generated when the caret is moved? What event is generated when the user presses** ENTER **while editing text inside a** JTextField?

   When the caret is moved, **JTextField** fires a **CaretEvent**. When the user presses ENTER, an **ActionEvent** is generated.

4. **To input a password, what text component should be used?**

   JPasswordField

5. **What is the main advantage of using** JFormattedTextField **over** JTextField?

   The main advantage offered by **JFormattedTextField** over **JTextField** is that **JFormattedTextField** edits and displays values in a specific format.

6. **Show the mask that could be used to format a telephone number of this form: 1 (555) 555-5555.**

   # (###) ###-####.

7. **What are the four** JFormattedTextField **focus-lost policy options and what do they do?**

   The four **JFormattedTextField** focus-lost policies are

COMMIT	REVERT	COMMIT_OR_REVERT	PERSIST

   COMMIT_OR_REVERT is the default value. It causes a valid entry to become the new value, but an invalid entry causes the value to revert to its previous value. **COMMIT** causes a valid entry to be committed. An invalid entry is retained in the text field, but no change to the value is made. **REVERT** causes the previous value to be obtained and displayed. **PERSIST** maintains the current edit, but no change to the value occurs.

8. **What type of event is fired when the value of a formatted text field changes?**

   PropertyChangeEvent

9. **A** JTextArea **will usually be wrapped in a** JScrollPane. **True or False?**

   True

10. **What method do you call to cause a text area to wrap text?**

setLineWrap( )

11. **What method do you call to set the tab size in a text area?**

setTabSize( )

12. **Can you cut and paste text within the text components? Can you do these things under program control? If so, what methods are used?**

Yes, you can cut and paste text with the text components, and you can do this under program control. The methods that handle cut and paste are **cut( )** and **paste( )**. The **copy( )** method is also available.

13. **Add a replace feature to** SimpleTextEditor **in Project 6-1. To do this, use the string in the Search For field as the string to replace. Add another edit field that contains the replacement. Add a button called Replace that replaces one instance of the string each time it is pressed.**

Here is one solution:

```
// Enhance Project 6-1 to support search and replace.

import java.io.*;
import java.awt.*;
import java.awt.event.*;
import javax.swing.*;
import javax.swing.event.*;

class SimpleTextEditor {

  JLabel jlabMsg;

  JTextArea jta;

  JTextField jtfFName;
  JTextField jtfFind;
  JTextField jtfReplace;

  JButton jbtnSave;
  JButton jbtnLoad;
  JButton jbtnFind;
  JButton jbtnFindNext;
  JButton jbtnReplace;

  int findIdx;

  public SimpleTextEditor() {
```

```java
// Create a new JFrame container.
JFrame jfrm = new JFrame("A Simple Text Editor");

// Specify FlowLayout for the layout manager.
jfrm.getContentPane().setLayout(new FlowLayout());

// Give the frame an initial size.
jfrm.setSize(270, 480);

// Terminate the program when the user closes the application.
jfrm.setDefaultCloseOperation(JFrame.EXIT_ON_CLOSE);

// Create the message label.
jlabMsg = new JLabel();
jlabMsg.setPreferredSize(new Dimension(200, 30));
jlabMsg.setHorizontalAlignment(SwingConstants.CENTER);

// Create an empty label to add space.
JLabel jlabSeparator = new JLabel();
jlabSeparator.setPreferredSize(new Dimension(200, 30));

// Create the Search For and Filename labels.
JLabel jlabFind = new JLabel("Search For:");
jlabFind.setPreferredSize(new Dimension(70, 20));
jlabFind.setHorizontalAlignment(SwingConstants.RIGHT);

JLabel jlabFilename = new JLabel("Filename:");
jlabFilename.setPreferredSize(new Dimension(70, 20));
jlabFilename.setHorizontalAlignment(SwingConstants.RIGHT);

// Create the Replace label.
JLabel jlabReplace = new JLabel("Replace:");
jlabReplace.setPreferredSize(new Dimension(70, 20));
jlabReplace.setHorizontalAlignment(SwingConstants.RIGHT);

// Create the text field.
jta = new JTextArea();

// Put the text area into a scroll pane.
JScrollPane jscrlp = new JScrollPane(jta);
jscrlp.setPreferredSize(new Dimension(250, 200));

// Create text field for filename.
jtfFName = new JTextField(15);

// Add a caret listener for the text area. This
```

```
// handler displays the number of characters in the
// file. It is updated with each caret change.
// The findIdx variable is also set to the current
// caret location.
jta.addCaretListener(new CaretListener() {
  public void caretUpdate(CaretEvent ce) {
    String str = jta.getText();
    jlabMsg.setText("Current size: " + str.length());
    findIdx = jta.getCaretPosition();
  }
});

// Create the Save File and Load File buttons.
jbtnSave = new JButton("Save File");
jbtnLoad = new JButton("Load File");

// Add action listener for the Save File button.
jbtnSave.addActionListener(new ActionListener() {
  public void actionPerformed(ActionEvent le) {
    save();
  }
});

// Add action listener for the Load File button.
jbtnLoad.addActionListener(new ActionListener() {
  public void actionPerformed(ActionEvent le) {
    load();
  }
});

// Create the Search For text field.
jtfFind = new JTextField(15);

// Create the Replace text field.
jtfReplace = new JTextField(15);

// Create the Find From Top and Find Next buttons.
jbtnFind = new JButton("Find From Top");
jbtnFindNext = new JButton("Find Next");

// Add action listener for the Find From Top button.
jbtnFind.addActionListener(new ActionListener() {
  public void actionPerformed(ActionEvent le) {
    findIdx = 0;
    find(findIdx);
  }
});
```

```java
      // Add action listener for the Find Next button.
      jbtnFindNext.addActionListener(new ActionListener() {
        public void actionPerformed(ActionEvent le) {
          find(findIdx+1);
        }
      });

      // Create the Replace button.
      jbtnReplace = new JButton("Replace");

      // Add action listener for the Replace button.
      jbtnReplace.addActionListener(new ActionListener() {
        public void actionPerformed(ActionEvent le) {
          replace(findIdx);
        }
      });

      // Add the components to the content pane.
      Container cp = jfrm.getContentPane();
      cp.add(jscrlp);
      cp.add(jlabFind);
      cp.add(jtfFind);
      cp.add(jlabReplace);
      cp.add(jtfReplace);
      cp.add(jbtnFind);
      cp.add(jbtnFindNext);
      cp.add(jbtnReplace);
      cp.add(jlabSeparator);
      cp.add(jlabFilename);
      cp.add(jtfFName);
      cp.add(jbtnSave);
      cp.add(jbtnLoad);
      cp.add(jlabMsg);

      // Display the frame.
      jfrm.setVisible(true);
    }

    // Save the file.
    void save() {
      FileWriter fw;

      // Get the filename from the text field.
      String fname = jtfFName.getText();
```

```
      // Make sure that there is actually a filename present.
      if(fname.length() == 0) {
        jlabMsg.setText("No filename present.");
        return;
      }

      // Save the file.
      try {
        fw = new FileWriter(fname);
        jta.write(fw);
        fw.close();
      } catch(IOException exc) {
        jlabMsg.setText("Error opening or writing file.");
        return;
      }

      jlabMsg.setText("File written successfully.");
    }

    // Load the file.
    void load() {
      FileReader fw;

      // Get the filename from the text field.
      String fname = jtfFName.getText();

      // Make sure that there is actually a filename present.
      if(fname.length() == 0) {
        jlabMsg.setText("No filename present.");
        return;
      }

      // Load the file.
      try {
        fw = new FileReader(fname);
        jta.read(fw, null);
        fw.close();
      } catch(IOException exc) {
        jlabMsg.setText("Error opening or reading file.");
        return;
      }

      // Reset find index when a new file is loaded.
      findIdx = 0;
```

```
      jlabMsg.setText("File loaded successfully.");
  }

  // Search the file.
  void find(int start) {
    // Get the current text as a string.
    String str = jta.getText();

    // Get the string to find.
    String findStr = jtfFind.getText();

    // Beginning at start, find the first
    // occurrence of the specified string.
    int idx = str.indexOf(findStr, start);

    // See if there is a match.
    if(idx > -1) {
      // If found, set focus to text area
      // and move caret to the location.
      jta.setCaretPosition(idx);
      findIdx = idx; // update the find index
      jlabMsg.setText("String found.");
    }
    else
      jlabMsg.setText("String not found.");

    // Set the focus to the editor window.
    jta.requestFocusInWindow();
  }

  // Replace one string with another.
  void replace(int start) {
    // Get the current text as a string.
    String str = jta.getText();

    // Get the string to replace.
    String findStr = jtfFind.getText();

    // Get the string to substitute.
    String repString = jtfReplace.getText();

    // Beginning at start, find the first
    // occurrence of the specified string.
```

```
      int idx = str.indexOf(findStr, start);

      // See if there is a match.
      if(idx > -1) {
        // If found, set focus to text area
        // and move caret to the location.
        jta.setCaretPosition(idx);
        findIdx = idx; // update the find index

        // Replace the text.
        jta.replaceRange(repString, findIdx,
                         findIdx+findStr.length());

        jlabMsg.setText("String replaced.");
      }
      else
        jlabMsg.setText("String not found.");

      // Set the focus to the editor window.
      jta.requestFocusInWindow();
    }

  public static void main(String args[]) {
    // Create the frame on the event dispatching thread.
    SwingUtilities.invokeLater(new Runnable() {
      public void run() {
        new SimpleTextEditor();
      }
    });
  }
}
```

14. **Change** SimpleTextEditor **so that it displays the number of lines in the file rather than a count of the characters.**

To cause the **SimpleTextEditor** to display the line count rather than the character count, change the caret listener as shown here:

```
jta.addCaretListener(new CaretListener() {
  public void caretUpdate(CaretEvent ce) {
    jlabMsg.setText("Line count: " + jta.getLineCount());
    findIdx = jta.getCaretPosition();
  }
});
```

15. In SimpleTextEditor, add keyboard mnemonics to the Find From Top and Find Next buttons. Use F for Find From Top and N for Find Next.

Here are the statements that you must add:

```
jbtnFind.setMnemonic('F');
jbtnFindNext.setMnemonic('N');
jbtnFindNext.setDisplayedMnemonicIndex(5);
```

Module 7: Working with Menus

1. What are the core Swing menu classes?

JMenu, JMenuItem, and **JMenuBar**

2. What class creates a menu? What class creates a popup menu? To create a main menu bar, what class is used?

JMenu creates a menu. **JPopupMenu** creates a popup menu. **JMenuBar** creates a menu bar.

3. What event is generated when a menu item is selected?

An action event is generated.

4. Images are not allowed in menus. True or False?

False, images are allowed in menus.

5. What method adds a menu bar to a window?

setJMenuBar( )

6. What method adds a mnemonic to a menu item?

setMnemonic( )

7. Can an icon be used as a menu item? If so, does it prevent the use of a name?

Yes, an icon can be used as a menu item. No, it does not prevent the use of a name.

8. What class creates a radio button menu item?

JRadioButtonMenuItem

9. Although check box menu items are permitted, their use is discouraged because they make a menu look strange. True or False?

False, check box menu items are popular, standard menu options.

10. A popup menu is usually triggered by _____-_____ the mouse.

right-clicking

11. What methods defined by MouseListener **must be overridden when listening for a popup trigger? What** MouseEvent **method must be called to determine if a popup trigger has been received?**

The **mousePressed( )** and **mouseReleased( )** methods must be overridden when listening for a popup trigger. The **isPopupTrigger( )** method is called to determine if a popup trigger has been received.

12. What method is called to determine the source of a popup trigger?

getComponent( )

13. A toolbar is an instance of what class?

JToolBar

14. Can a toolbar be added to the menu bar?

No

15. What interface defines an action?

Action

16. List the properties that an action defines.

An action defines these properties:

- The accelerator key
- The mnemonic key
- The name
- The icon
- The tooltip text
- A long description
- The action command string
- The enabled/disabled status

17. What does System.exit( ) **do?**

System.exit( ) terminates the program.

Module 8: Tables and Trees

1. JTable **relies on several support classes and interfaces. What package are they stored in?**

javax.swing.table

2. **What method sets the scrollable viewport size in a table?**

setPreferredScrollableViewportSize( )

3. **What is the name of the model that defines a table?**

TableModel

4. **If a** JTable **is not wrapped in a scroll pane, its header will not be shown unless you explicitly request it. True or False?**

True

5. **To listen for column selection events on a table, you must register a** ListSelectionListener **with what object?**

The table's column model

6. **To listen for table model events, you must register a** _____.

TableModelListener

7. **Relative to** TableModel, **what does** setValueAt( ) **do?**

setValueAt( ) sets the value at a cell, which is specified by its row and column coordinates relative to the model, not the view.

8. **What** JTable **method changes the auto-resizing mode?**

setAutoResizeMode( )

9. **To implement a custom table model, what class will you normally extend?**

AbstractTableModel

10. **What interface defines the form of a cell renderer for a table?**

TableCellRenderer

11. JTree **can be used to display only balanced, binary trees. True or False?**

False. **JTree** can be used to display any type of hierarchical data.

12. **What is a leaf node?**

A leaf node is a node that has no children.

13. **To construct a tree from objects of type** DefaultMutableTreeNode, **what procedure is followed?**

First, create a root node. Then, using the **add( )** method, add child nodes to it. Remember, a child node may be the root of a subtree. Thus, trees of any complexity can be created using this procedure.

14. **When the data in a tree changes, what type of event is fired?**

TreeModelEvent

15. To obtain an enumeration that contains a postorder traversal of a tree, what method is called?

postorderEnumeration( ) (The depthFirstEnumeration( ) method can also be used.)

16. Create a program that displays a table that computes the tip for a meal. In the first column, display the cost of the meal in increments of 1. Have the next three columns compute the tip using the percentages: 10, 15, and 20. In the final column, allow the user to entered a suggested tip. Use a custom cell renderer to display the values in money format. Allow the number of rows to be specified when the table is constructed. When you are done, your table should look like the one shown here:

Here is one solution:

```
// A program that displays tip percentages in
// a table. It uses a custom cell renderer to
// display the values in a money format. It also
// allows you to enter a suggested tip.

import java.awt.*;
import javax.swing.*;
import javax.swing.event.*;
import javax.swing.table.*;
import java.text.*;

// A simple renderer for currency values.
class MoneyRenderer extends DefaultTableCellRenderer {
  public Component getTableCellRendererComponent(
                  JTable jtab, Object v,
                  boolean selected, boolean focus,
                  int r, int c) {

    // Get the default component so we can customize it.
    JLabel rendComp = (JLabel)
                  super.getTableCellRendererComponent(
                    jtab, v, selected, focus, r, c);
```

```
      // Obtain a currency formatter.
      NumberFormat nf = NumberFormat.getCurrencyInstance();

      // If the value is not 0, format the value using
      // the currency format. Otherwise, display nothing.
      if(((Double) v).doubleValue() != 0.0)
        rendComp.setText(nf.format(v));
      else
        rendComp.setText("");

      return rendComp;
    }
  }

// A custom table model for displaying tips.
class TipModel extends AbstractTableModel {
    int numRows;

    String colNames[] = { "Price", "10% Tip",
                          "15% Tip", "20% Tip",
                          "Suggested" };

    // This array holds other tip suggestions entered
    // by the user.
    double[] other;

    // The number of rows to display are passed
    // in len.
    TipModel(int len) {
      super();
      numRows = len;
      other = new double[numRows];
    }

    public int getRowCount() { return numRows; }
    public int getColumnCount() { return 5; }

    public String getColumnName(int c) {
      return colNames[c];
    }

    // This method returns the price in the first column
    // and the amount of the tip in the remaining
    // four columns.
    public Object getValueAt(int r, int c) {
      if(c==0) return new Double(r+1);
```

```
    else if(c>0 & c<4)
      return new Double((r+1) * ((c+1)*0.05));
    else
      return new Double(other[r]);
  }


  // This sets the value in the Suggested column
  // if the user enters a suggested tip. It also fires
  // a table model event to tell the table that the
  // data has changed.
  public void setValueAt(Object v, int r, int c) {
    if(c==4) {
      other[r] = ((Double) v).doubleValue();
      fireTableCellUpdated(r, c);
    }
  }


  // This method returns false except for column
  // 4, which can be edited by the user.
  public boolean isCellEditable(int r, int c) {
    if(c==4) return true;
    return false;
  }


  // This returns the Double class for all columns.
  public Class getColumnClass(int c) {
    return Double.class;
  }
}


// Display a table of tip percentages.
class TipTable {

  JTable jtabTip;
  JLabel jlab;

  TipTable(int size) {
    // Create a new JFrame container.
    JFrame jfrm = new JFrame("A Tip Calculator");

    // Specify FlowLayout for the layout manager.
    jfrm.getContentPane().setLayout(new FlowLayout());

    // Give the frame an initial size.
    jfrm.setSize(500, 200);
```

```java
// Terminate the program when the user closes the application.
jfrm.setDefaultCloseOperation(JFrame.EXIT_ON_CLOSE);

// Create a label that will display the suggested tip.
jlab = new JLabel();

// Create a table that displays the tip data.
jtabTip = new JTable(new TipModel(size));

// Wrap the data in a scroll pane.
JScrollPane jscrlp = new JScrollPane(jtabTip);

// Set the viewport size.
jtabTip.setPreferredScrollableViewportSize(
        new Dimension(450, 80));

// Add a custom cell renderer.
jtabTip.setDefaultRenderer(Double.class, new MoneyRenderer());

// Get the list selection model.
ListSelectionModel lsm = jtabTip.getSelectionModel();
lsm.setSelectionMode(ListSelectionModel.SINGLE_SELECTION);

// Get the table model.
TableModel tm = jtabTip.getModel();

// Add a table model listener.
tm.addTableModelListener(new TableModelListener() {
  // Display the suggested tip.
  public void tableChanged(TableModelEvent tme) {
    if(tme.getType() == TableModelEvent.UPDATE) {
      jlab.setText("New suggested tip: " +
        NumberFormat.getCurrencyInstance().format(
                jtabTip.getModel().getValueAt(
                            tme.getFirstRow(),
                            tme.getColumn())))
                );
    }
  }
});

// Add the table to the content pane.
jfrm.getContentPane().add(jscrlp);
jfrm.getContentPane().add(jlab);
```

```
    // Display the frame.
    jfrm.setVisible(true);
  }

  public static void main(String args[]) {
    // Create the frame on the event dispatching thread.
    SwingUtilities.invokeLater(new Runnable() {
      public void run() {
        new TipTable(100);
      }
    });
  }
}
```

17. **Show the statement you must add to the** TreeDemo **program to cause the root node to be hidden.**

jtree.setRootVisible(false);

18. **Adapt the enumeration code in Project 8-2 so that it reports whether each node in the traversal is a leaf or has child nodes.**

Here is one solution:

```
TreeNode tn;

Enumeration preorder = root.preorderEnumeration();

while(preorder.hasMoreElements()) {
  tn = (TreeNode) preorder.nextElement();
  if(tn.isLeaf()) System.out.println(tn + " is leaf");
  else System.out.println(tn + " has children");
}
```

Module 9: Dialogs

1. **A dialog is a composite of two or more components that prompts the user and waits for a response. True or False?**

True

2. **What are the four dialog classes provided by Swing. Which two are for general purpose use?**

JDialog, JOptionPane, JFileChooser, and **JColorChooser**. The first two are general purpose.

3. **What** JOptionPane **method creates an input dialog? Which one creates a message dialog?**

The **showInputDialog( )** method creates an input dialog. The **showMessageDialog( )** method creates a message dialog.

4. What JOptionPane **method would you normally use to create a dialog that confirms that the user wants to save changes to a document? Show what the call would look like.**

The **JOptionPane** method normally used for this purpose is **showConfirmDialog( )**. Here is an example of how to call it:

showConfirmDialog(null, "Save Changes?");

5. When using a confirmation dialog, what return type indicates that the user clicked the Yes button?

YES_OPTION

6. What option type is used to show only the Yes and No buttons in a confirmation dialog?

YES_NO_OPTION

7. If you want to request a string response from the user, what JOptionPane **method do you call?**

showInputDialog( )

8. Must the message parameter to any of JOptionPane's show **methods be a string? Explain.**

No. The message parameter to any of **JOptionPane**'s show methods can be, but does not have to be, a string. It can be any type of object.

9. JDialog **is a top-level container. True or False?**

True

10. What are the four steps needed to create and display a JDialog-**based dialog?**

1. Create a **JDialog** object.

2. Specify the dialog's layout manager, size, and possibly a default close policy.

3. Add components to the dialog's content pane.

4. Show the dialog by calling **setVisible(true)** on it.

11. Can JDialog **create a non-modal dialog?**

Yes

12. Explain the difference between setVisible(false) **and** dispose( ) **as they relate to dialogs.**

setVisible(false) removes a dialog from the screen. **dispose( )** removes the dialog and also frees its resources.

13. What JFileChooser **method creates a Save file chooser? Which one creates a file chooser that uses your own title?**

The **showSaveDialog( )** method creates a Save file chooser. The **showDialog( )** method lets you specify your own title.

14. **What two methods must be overridden when implementing a** FileFilter **for** JFileChooser?

accept( ) and **getDescription( )**

15. **Can a file chooser be used to select a directory? If so, how is the option enabled?**

Yes. To enable directory selection, call **setFileSelectionMode( )**.

16. **What type of value is returned by** JColorChooser's showDialog( ) **method?**

A reference to type **Color**

17. **Module 7 described menus. In that module, the examples included a File menu that always had an Exit entry. The action event handler that processed menu selections handled the Exit entry, as shown here:**

```
// Handle menu item action events.
public void actionPerformed(ActionEvent ae) {
  // Get the action command from the menu selection.
  String comStr = ae.getActionCommand();

  // If user chooses Exit, then exit the program.
  if(comStr.equals("Exit")) System.exit(0);
  .
  .
  .
```

Change this code so it activates a dialog that confirms that the user really wants to exit before terminating the program.

Substitute the following code to handle the Exit item.

```
// If user chooses Exit, then exit the program.
if(comStr.equals("Exit")) {
  int response = JOptionPane.showConfirmDialog(
                            null,
                            "Exit Now?",
                            "Terminate Program",
                            JOptionPane.YES_NO_OPTION);

  if(response == JOptionPane.YES_OPTION) {
    System.exit(0);
  }
}
```

Module 10: Threading, Applets, Painting, and Layouts

1. **Any code that affects a Swing component must be executed on the _____-_____ thread.**

   event-dispatching

2. **When using** javax.swing.Timer, **what event is generated when the timer goes off?**

   ActionEvent

3. **What methods start and stop** javax.swing.Timer?

   start( ) and **stop( )**

4. **What are the four applet lifecycle methods? When are they called?**

   The four applet lifecycle methods are **init( )**, **start( )**, **stop( )**, and **destroy( )**. The **init( )** method is called first. It initializes the applet. The **start( )** method is called to begin (or resume) execution of the applet. It is called whenever the applet is displayed on a page. The **stop( )** method is called to stop the applet, such as when the browser leaves the page containing the applet. The **destroy( )** method is called when the applet is unloaded from memory.

5. **What method must an applet use to create its GUI?**

   invokeAndWait( )

6. **Can your program paint directly onto the surface of a component?**

   Yes

7. **What three paint methods are called when a Swing component must display itself?**

   paintComponent( ), **paintBorder( )**, and **paintChildren( )**

8. **What method is called to request that a component redisplay its contents?**

   repaint( )

9. **What methods obtain the current width and height of a component?**

   getWidth( ) and **getHeight( )**

10. GridBagLayout **is so named because it is a _____ of small _____ joined together.**

    collection, grids

11. **Each component in a grid-bag layout is associated with a set of constraints encapsulated by what class?**

    GridBagConstraints

12. Why is BoxLayout **sometimes a more efficient alternative to** GridBagLayout**?**

BoxLayout requires fewer program statements, has less overhead, and is easier to configure.

13. In a horizontal Box**, can there be more than one row of components?**

No. There can be only one row of components.

14. Rework the bar graph painting example so that the color of the border cycles through red, green, and blue at one-second intervals. Also, have the border's size vary from 1 to 5 pixels, with an interval of one-fifth second between changes. Use the javax.swing.Timer **class.**

Here is one solution:

```java
// Answer to Question 14.

import java.awt.*;
import java.awt.event.*;
import javax.swing.*;
import java.util.Random;

// This class extends JPanel. It overrides
// the paintComponent() method so that random
// data is plotted in the panel.
class PaintPanel extends JPanel {
  Insets ins; // holds the panel's insets

  Random rand; // used to generate random numbers

  PaintPanel(int w, int h) {

    // Ensure that the panel is opaque.
    setOpaque(true);

    // Start with a red line border.
    setBorder(
      BorderFactory.createLineBorder(Color.RED, 1));

    // Set the preferred dimension as specified.
    setPreferredSize(new Dimension(w, h));

    rand = new Random();
  }

  // Override the paintComponent() method.
  protected void paintComponent(Graphics g) {
    // Always call the superclass method first.
```

```
    super.paintComponent(g);

    // Get the height and width of the component.
    int height = getHeight();
    int width = getHeight();

      // Get the insets.
    ins = getInsets();

    // Fill the panel by plotting random data
    // in the form of a bar graph.
    for(int i=ins.left+5; i <= width-ins.right-5; i += 4) {
      // Obtain a random number between 0 and
      // the maximum height of the drawing area.
      int h = rand.nextInt(height-ins.bottom);

      // If generated value is within or too close to
      // the border, change it to just outside the border.
      if(h <= ins.top) h = ins.top+1;

      // Draw a line that represents the data.
      g.drawLine(i, height-ins.bottom, i, h);
    }
  }

  // Change the border size and color.
  public void changeBorder(Color color, int size) {
    setBorder(
      BorderFactory.createLineBorder(color, size));
  }
}

// Demonstrate painting directly onto a panel.
class PaintDemo {

  JButton jbtnMore;
  JButton jbtnSize;
  JLabel jlab;
  PaintPanel pp;

  int bsize = 1; // holds current border size
  int cidx = 0; // holds current color index.

  // Array of colors to cycle through.
  Color colors[] = {Color.RED, Color.BLUE, Color.GREEN };
```

```
boolean big; // use to toggle size of panel

Timer borderSizeT;  // timer for border size
Timer borderColorT; // timer for border color

PaintDemo() {

  // Create a new JFrame container.
  JFrame jfrm = new JFrame("Painting Demo");

  // Specify FlowLayout for the layout manager.
  jfrm.getContentPane().setLayout(new FlowLayout());

  // Give the frame an initial size.
  jfrm.setSize(240, 260);

  // Terminate the program when the user closes the application.
  jfrm.setDefaultCloseOperation(JFrame.EXIT_ON_CLOSE);

  // Create the panel that will be painted.
  pp = new PaintPanel(100, 100);

  // Make the buttons.
  jbtnMore = new JButton("Show More Data");
  jbtnSize = new JButton("Change Border Size");

  // Describe the graph.
  jlab = new JLabel("Bar Graph of Random Data");

  // Change the border size.
  ActionListener borderSize = new ActionListener() {
    public void actionPerformed(ActionEvent ae) {
      pp.changeBorder(colors[cidx], bsize);
      bsize++;
      if(bsize > 5) bsize = 1;
    }
  };

  // Change the border color.
  ActionListener borderColor = new ActionListener() {
    public void actionPerformed(ActionEvent ae) {
      pp.changeBorder(colors[cidx], bsize);
      cidx++;
      if(cidx == 3) cidx = 0;
```

```java
      }
    };

    // Create and start the timers.
    borderSizeT = new Timer(200, borderSize);
    borderColorT = new Timer(1000, borderColor);

    borderSizeT.start();
    borderColorT.start();

    // Repaint the panel when the Show More Data button
    // is clicked.
    jbtnMore.addActionListener(new ActionListener() {
      public void actionPerformed(ActionEvent ae) {
        pp.repaint();
      }
    });

    // Set the border size of the panel when the
    // Change Border Size button is clicked.
    // Changing the border size automatically
    // results in a repaint.
    jbtnSize.addActionListener(new ActionListener() {
      public void actionPerformed(ActionEvent ae) {
        if(!big) bsize = 5;
        else bsize = 1;
        pp.changeBorder(colors[cidx], bsize);
        big = !big;
      }
    });

    // Add the buttons, label, and panel to the content pane.
    jfrm.getContentPane().add(jlab);
    jfrm.getContentPane().add(pp);
    jfrm.getContentPane().add(jbtnMore);
    jfrm.getContentPane().add(jbtnSize);

    big = false;

    // Display the frame.
    jfrm.setVisible(true);
  }

  public static void main(String args[]) {
    // Create the frame on the event-dispatching thread.
```

```
      SwingUtilities.invokeLater(new Runnable() {
        public void run() {
          new PaintDemo();
        }
      });
    }
  }
```

15. **Rework the applet in Project 10-1 so that the direction of scroll reverses at periodic intervals. For example, have the text scroll left for a while, and then right for a while, and so on. The precise timing is up to you, but the answer shown in the Appendix reverses scroll direction every 20 seconds.**

Here is one solution:

```
// Answer to question 15.

import javax.swing.*;
import java.awt.*;
import java.awt.event.*;

/*
This HTML can be used to launch the applet:

<object code="ScrollText" width=240 height=100>
</object>

*/

public class ScrollText extends JApplet {

  JLabel jlab;

  String msg = " Swing makes the GUI move! ";

  ActionListener scroller;

  Timer stTimer; // This timer controls the scroll rate.
  int counter; // use to reverse the scroll.

  // This value controls when the scroll direction changes.
  int scrollLimit;

  // Initialize the applet.
  public void init() {
    counter = 0;
    scrollLimit = 100;
```

```
    try {
      SwingUtilities.invokeAndWait(new Runnable () {
        public void run() {
          guiInit();
        }
      });
    } catch(Exception exc) {
      System.out.println("Can't create because of "+ exc);
    }
  }

  // Start the timer when the applet is started.
  public void start() {
    stTimer.start();
  }

  // Stop the timer when the applet is stopped.
  public void stop() {
    stTimer.stop();
  }

  // Stop the timer when the applet is destroyed.
  public void destroy() {
    stTimer.stop();
  }

  // Initialize the timer GUI.
  private void guiInit() {

    // Create the label that will scroll the message.
    jlab = new JLabel(msg);
    jlab.setHorizontalAlignment(SwingConstants.CENTER);

    // Create the action listener for the timer.
    // This version reverses the direction of scroll
    // every 20 seconds.
    scroller = new ActionListener() {
      public void actionPerformed(ActionEvent ae) {
        if(counter < scrollLimit) {
          // Left-scroll the message one character.
          char ch = msg.charAt(0);
          msg = msg.substring(1, msg.length());
          msg += ch;
        } else {
          // Right-scroll the message one character.
          char ch = msg.charAt(msg.length()-1);
```

```
        msg = msg.substring(0, msg.length()-1);
        msg = ch + msg;
        if(counter == scrollLimit*2) counter = 0;
      }
      counter++;
      jlab.setText(msg);
    }
  };

  // Create the timer.
  stTimer = new Timer(200, scroller);

  // Add the label to the applet content pane.
  getContentPane().add(jlab);
  }
}
```

Index

CPSIA information can be obtained
at www.ICGtesting.com
Printed in the USA
FSOW04n1337010316
17414FS